PUBLICATIONS
OF THE
ARMY RECORDS SOCIETY
VOL. 2

THE ARMY
AND THE
CURRAGH INCIDENT
1914

The Army Records Society was founded in 1984 in order to publish original records describing the development, organisation, administration and activities of the British Army from early times.

Any person wishing to become a Member of the Society is requested to apply to the Hon. Secretary, c/o The National Army Museum, Royal Hospital Road, London, SW3 4HT. The annual subscription entitles the Member to receive a copy of each volume issued by the Society in that year, and to purchase back volumes at reduced prices. Current subscription details, whether for individuals living within the British Isles, for individuals living overseas, or for institutions, will be furnished on request.

The Council of the Army Records Society wish it to be clearly understood that they are not answerable for opinions or observations that may appear in the Society's publications. For these the responsibility rests entirely with the Editors of the several works.

IN MEMORY OF   20ᵗʰ to 23ʳᵈ MARCH 1914.

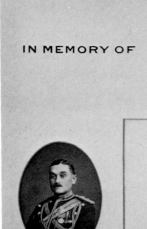

EXODUS. Chap 17
Verse Nº 11.

EXODUS. Chap 17
Verse Nº 12.

And it came to pass, when
Moses held up his hand,
that Israel prevailed:
and when he let down his
hand, Amalek prevailed.

But Moses' hands were heavy;
and they took a stone, and
put it under him, and he sat
thereon; and Aaron and Hur
stayed up his hands, the
one on the one side, and the
other on the other side; and
his hands were steady until
the going down of the sun.

Hubert Gough's letter of resignation framed with photo-
graphs of his brother Johnnie (top) Arthur Parker (left) and
Maurice MacEwen (right) and verses of *Exodus* (see
Documents 32, 106 and 201).

THE ARMY
AND THE
CURRAGH INCIDENT
1914

===

EDITED BY
IAN F. W. BECKETT

PUBLISHED BY
THE BODLEY HEAD
FOR THE
ARMY RECORDS SOCIETY
1986

British Library Cataloguing
in Publication Data

The Army and the Curragh incident.
  1. Curragh (Kildare: County) Mutiny, 1914
  2. Great Britain, *Army, Cavalry Brigade
  3rd* — History
  I. Beckett, I.F.W.   II. Army Records
Society
  355.1'334   DA960

ISBN 0-370-30738-0

© The Army Records Society 1986
Printed in Great Britain for
The Bodley Head Ltd
30 Bedford Square, London WC1B 3RP
by The Bath Press, Avon
Set in Linotron 202 Ehrhardt
by Wyvern Typesetting Ltd, Bristol
First published 1986

For Trina

The British Academy generously assisted the research for and preparation of this book with a grant from its Small Grants in the Humanities Fund.

CONTENTS

MAP

Ireland in March 1914   *page* 32

EDITORIAL
ACKNOWLEDGEMENTS

Reproduction of documents in the Royal Archives appears by gracious permission of Her Majesty the Queen. Other reproductions from Crown copyright material in the Public Record Office and other repositories appear by permission of Her Majesty's Stationery Office.

The editor also gratefully acknowledges the generosity of the following in enabling him to consult and, where requested, to reproduce archives in their possession and/or copyright: The Earl Bathurst; Lord Mottistone; Lord Sackville; Lord Esher; Lord Robertson of Oakridge; Lieutenant Colonel the Viscount Allenby; Viscount Lambton; Lady Patricia Kingsbury; Lady Pamela Humphreys; Sir Charles Fergusson, Bt, and Adam Fergusson Esq.; Sir Hector Monro, M.P.; the Rt Hon. Julian Amery, M.P.; Mrs Myrtle Dutton; Mrs Denise Boyes; Mrs Diana Pym; Mrs Jean Morris-Eyton; Miss Helen Forestier-Walker; Mrs J. Clay; Mrs D. D. Crichon; Mrs S. Silean; Mrs J. Broadribb; J. Johnston Esq.; M. A. F. Rawlinson Esq.; F. C. Wynne Esq.; William Bell Esq.; Mark Bonham Carter Esq.; Commander H. G. D. de Chair; the Executors of Vice-Admiral H. T. Baillie-Grohman; Major A. C. J. Congreve; Dr P. Howell; Lieutenant Colonel Michael Brooke; R. H. Smith Esq.; the Trustees of the Imperial War Museum; the Trustees of the Beaverbrook Foundation; the Trustees of the British Library Board; the Trustees of the Broadlands Archives; the Trustees of the Liddell Hart Centre for Military Archives, King's College; the Clerk of the Records and the House of Lords Record Office; the Trustees of the National Library of Scotland; the National Register of Archives (Scotland) and the Scottish Record Office; the Public Record Office; the National Army Museum; the Army Museums Ogilby Trust; the Bodleian Library; Nuffield College, Oxford; the Master, Fellows and Scholars of Churchill College,

Cambridge; the Warden and Fellows of New College, Oxford; Birmingham University Library; Hertfordshire County Record Office; Peter Liddle Esq. and the 1914–1918 Archive at Sunderland Polytechnic; the City of Manchester Leisure Services Committee and Manchester Central Library; the Brotherton Library, University of Leeds; *The Times* Archive; the Royal Artillery Institution; the Queen's Royal Irish Hussars; Service Historique, Vincennes; H. Beddington Esq.; and Ian Crum Hamilton Esq.

In a project of this nature, involving a variety of archives, the assistance given the editor has been considerable. The following are therefore thanked for all their help in the preparation of this volume: Field Marshal the Lord Harding of Petherton; Rt Hon. the Lord Charteris of Amisfield; Sir Robin Mackworth-Young; Sir Joseph Cheyne, Bt; General Sir James Marshall-Cornwall; Major-General James Lunt; Brigadier A. D. Myrtle; Colonel H. A. G. Brooke; Colonel J. S. Cowley; Lieutenant Colonel A. W. J. Turnbull; Lieutenant Colonel J. M. Hewson; Lieutenant Colonel D. C. R. Ward; Lieutenant Colonel H. J. Orpen-Smellie; Lieutenant Colonel A. A. Fairrie; Major T. A. Ferrier; Major A. F. W. Astle; Major A. G. B. Cobbold; Major J. H. Wylie; Major W. H. White; Professor Bryan Ranft; Professor James Joll; Dr Gerry de Groot; Dr A. P. W. Malcomson; Dr K. M. Wilson; Dr Hew Strachan; Dr R. A. Morriss; Dr Peter Anderson; Dr Duncan Anderson; Mike Garden Esq.; Ivor Malise Graham Esq.; J. C. G. Montague-Jones Esq.; John Pym Esq.; G. Fergusson Esq.; I. D. Brown Esq.; C. C. Johnston Esq.; G. H. Martin Esq.; Tony Allen Esq.; Bob Goodall Esq.; Mrs M. Stewart; Mrs W. W. Cheyne; Mrs J. G. Nutting; Miss Jane Langton; and the County Archivists of Bedfordshire, Dorset, Durham, Essex, Hampshire, Kent and Wiltshire.

Every effort has been made to trace individual copyright owners of the documents reproduced in this volume but some have proved elusive: in these cases, the editor apologises for any omissions.

Special thanks are due to Rod Suddaby, Clive Hughes and Peter Simkins of the Imperial War Museum; to my colleagues at Sandhurst, especially Ned Willmott for assistance with naval matters; and to Patricia Methven, who has represented the Army Records Society, and to Guido Waldman, who has represented The Bodley Head, during the preparation of the volume. Both Dr John Gooch, the Society's Chairman, and Dr Keith Jeffery, the Society's Secretary, have been sources of considerable practical assistance to a struggling editor. None of the foregoing are, of course, responsible in any way for any errors of interpretation on my part in the introduction or for the selection of documents.

I am particularly grateful to the British Academy for its generous grant towards research expenses and the preparation of the manuscript.

RMAS December 1985   **IFWB**

NOTE ON EDITORIAL METHODS

It has been the practice in all but a handful of the documents to reproduce them in full, with the exception of opening and closing familiarities. Where material has been omitted, this is denoted by asterisks. Grammar and spelling have not been changed although, where a particularly extraordinary phrase or word appears, this has been emphasised by the addition of [sic]. Where a common mis-spelling recurs, as in the diary of Sir Henry Wilson, only the first is indicated to draw attention to the fault. All other additions in parentheses denote alterations to or additions to the original document by its author.

The title accorded individuals at the top of each document is that borne at the time the document was written, later titles or ranks being indicated in the relevant footnotes or biographical notes. Although Brigadier-General was, strictly speaking, an appointment in 1914 and not a rank, it is treated as such rather than classing those holding it as Colonel (temporary Brigadier-General). Hubert Gough is, in fact, described as a Colonel in some documents.

The source of each document is given in full at the bottom.

The documents are arranged in three sections and sub-divided into themes. Within each section or part, documents run in strict chronological sequence.

A rigorous selection was required in order to keep the size of this volume within bounds. Nevertheless, no key document is omitted although it has been the practice to exclude documents otherwise available in existing printed sources. Thus, telegrams printed in the White Papers dealing with the Curragh Incident are not reproduced here.

For abbreviations used in source references, see page 387.

INTRODUCTION

The events at the Curragh Camp near Dublin on Friday 20 March and Saturday 21 March 1914, and the subsequent drama played out in London over the course of the next nine days, have long been regarded as particularly significant in British military history. Indeed, the basic narrative is relatively familiar to many: how Brigadier-General Hubert Gough and fellow officers of the 3rd Cavalry Brigade threatened resignation rather than be used in the apparently planned military coercion of Ulster into accepting Irish Home Rule; how Gough secured a written guarantee that the army would not be so employed from the Secretary of State for War, J. E. B. Seely; and how Seely together with the Chief of the Imperial General Staff, Field Marshal Sir John French, and the Adjutant General, Lieutenant-General Sir John Spencer Ewart, all resigned when that guarantee was repudiated by Asquith's Liberal Cabinet. Although sometimes erroneously referred to as the Curragh 'Mutiny' rather than, more appropriately, the Curragh 'Incident', it remains one of the very few occasions in modern times when the British army could be said openly to be challenging civil supremacy over the military in peacetime.[1]

As such, and for the light it throws upon British military and political affairs immediately prior to the First World War, the Curragh has continued a subject of both general and academic interest. Books specifically relating to the affair were published in 1956 and 1964, written by A. P. Ryan and Sir James Fergusson respectively. Both had the advantage of access to surviving eye witnesses, all of whom have since died, but Ryan was primarily concerned with producing a straightforward narrative and Fergusson had the subsidiary intention of rebuffing criticism of his father, Major-General Sir Charles Fergusson, whose adroit but controversial handling of the 5th Division prevented dis-

1

THE ARMY AND THE CURRAGH INCIDENT, 1914

sidence from becoming even more widespread within the Irish Command. Others have since examined the Curragh in the context of the Irish Home Rule question or in relation to the careers of some of the leading participants such as Gough and French.[2] However, no previous account has been based upon all the surviving primary sources, access to some archives being granted for the first time in the preparation of this volume.

Most historians studying the Curragh have invariably encountered its abiding mysteries. Some have speculated that even the availability of sources closed to them might not necessarily solve all the problems associated with the intricacies of Unionist claims of a Liberal 'plot' to coerce Ulster and radical counter-claims of an attempt by the army to thwart the 'will of the people'.[3] (In the context of British 1914 politics it must be recalled that the term Unionist relates not only to Ulster Loyalists but also to members of the Conservative party, who had been so described since 1886.) To some extent, those predictions have proved prescient but, by emphasising the wider impact of the Curragh affair upon the army, this selection of documents illuminates a number of aspects that have remained obscure or gone unremarked.

Thus, while reproducing the key documents relating to the alleged 'plot' to coerce Ulster, Section 1 includes others indicating the growing concern within the army that it might be drawn into a civil war by military action in Ulster. Section 2 reproduces documents which frequently modify the accepted version of events both in Ireland and London between 20 and 30 March 1914. Finally, Section 3 presents largely new evidence on the impact of the Curragh upon the army outside Ireland and the degree of support engendered for the 3rd Cavalry Brigade. Similarly, it provides some illustration of attitudes within the Royal Navy where equally strained relationships within the officer corps have been almost totally ignored. The section also makes clear the continuing implications of events on the very eve of a world war, many previous studies tending to assume that the Curragh Incident was essentially closed by Asquith's assumption of the office of Secretary of State for War on 31 March 1914.

I

Superficially, it might have been supposed that the British army was unlikely to suffer a convulsion such as that induced by the Curragh. By 1913 only 20,780 men or some 9.1 per cent of the army's rank and file were Irish, the 2,655 men enlisted in Ireland on normal engagements in 1912/13 registering only marginally higher at 9.6 per cent of all such enlistments.[4] Although a military career was highly regarded among the Anglo-Irish and Anglo-Irishmen such as the former Commander-in-Chief, Field Marshal Lord Roberts, and the Director of Military Operations in the War Office, Major-General Henry Wilson, were prominently represented in the army's highest ranks, the popular conception of an officer corps dominated by them is highly questionable. There are no readily available statistics of officers' nationalities but the overall percentage of Anglo-Irishmen may have been small. One study of the 108 Major-Generals on the active list in July 1914 has indicated that only twelve of the 89 whose origins can be positively identified were Irish and two of these were Catholics. In a nominally Irish regiment such as the 5th Royal Irish Lancers, only five out of 28 officers serving in March 1914 had identifiable Irish connections.[5] Similarly, the exemption offered to officers domiciled in Ulster during the Curragh Incident applied to only five out of the 77 'doing duty' in the 3rd Cavalry Brigade [Document 31]. Only one officer in the 14th Infantry Brigade was eligible for exemption [46]. However, it is clear that others serving in Ireland did have Irish origins including Hubert Gough himself and one subaltern of 80th Battery, RFA, whose father was serving in the Ulster Volunteer Force (UVF), but whose home lay fifteen miles beyond the recognised boundary of Ulster [53].

Ireland was not regarded as being of any great strategic significance by the army, little consideration having been given to its defence or role since the re-orientation of British strategic policy in 1905/6.[6] The avowedly constabulary role of the army in Ireland also appeared of less account. There had been serious riots in Belfast in 1907 and 1912 but, on the latter occasion, troops had been committed only reluctantly and the number of nominally Irish battalions allowed to serve in Ireland had actually been increased from four to ten out of 21 in 1908.[7] Surviving letters from officers serving in Ireland prior to the outbreak of the Curragh evince little concern at the growth of the rival sectarian para-military organisations— the UVF and the Irish Volunteers. But this only reflected the belated recognition of the extent of the problem by both the Royal Irish Constabulary and the government itself.[8] In any case, the general perception of the UVF in particular among officers was the determination of its leaders to avoid clashes with troops and its willingness to keep order.[9] Consequently, many British officers in Ireland refused to believe that trouble could arise [9, 122] and the Commander, Lieutenant-General Sir Arthur Paget, expressed his own disbelief in February 1914 at 'being asked to concentrate my men to move against the forces that are (I believe) in being in the north of Ireland'.[10] Among junior officers, political discussion was either discouraged or took second place to regimental point-to-points and other leisure activities [37, 49, 56, 58]. It is not too surprising, therefore, that senior officers, including Sir John French, were held seriously to underestimate the true depth of feeling within the army with regard to Ulster [3, 24, 121, 123, 141].

Nevertheless, disquiet existed in many quarters at the possibility of being ordered to coerce Ulster into accepting Home Rule as early as the summer of 1913 [1, 2]. Calculations of the numbers likely to resign their commissions in such a contingency were widely canvassed [3, 5, 6, 7] and never amounted to less than fifteen per cent of an officer corps of just under 13,000 regulars. This did not necessarily imply an objection to Home Rule *per se* but derived from a belief that the complexion of the resulting administration in Dublin would be unacceptable and would reward those nationalists who had done most to denigrate the army in the recent past [8, 12, 16, 43].[11] But there was also widespread sympathy for the Ulster Loyalists, extending even to those who ultimately stood by their duty in March 1914, which stemmed from the Unionist instincts of the officer corps as a whole [36, 41, 63, 193, 209]. Certainly, there was no shortage of serving officers in either army or navy prepared to communicate directly with Unionist politicians during the Curragh crisis [54, 69, 131, 135, 141, 150, 153].[12]

It must also be recognised that the anxieties and instincts of officers regarding Ulster were deliberately fostered by those who perceived that the army might prove an instrument through which Liberal policy might be forestalled, a fact not lost on government supporters in subsequent debates.[13] Much Unionist rhetoric was aimed at the army from the autumn of 1913 onwards, ranging from Sir Edward Carson's announcement of pledges received from 'some of the greatest generals in the army' to Rowland Hunt's circulation of mildly seditious literature and Andrew Bonar Law's invitation to officers to emulate the army of James II and refuse support for any 'despotic intention' of government.[14] But rather more than rhetoric was involved; the consideration given by Bonar Law between December 1913 and March 1914 to amending the Army (Annual) Act, so that the army could not be used to coerce Ulster, is well known.[15] Although the idea was abandoned on 19 March, other schemes were still under consideration. Carson and Lord Milner raised the possibility of establishing a guarantee fund to reimburse officers who resigned their commissions and lost their pensions[16] and the idea of such an indemnity was revived during the Curragh Incident [135], Sir Marcus Samuel offering £10,000 to start the fund off.[17]

Within the army, there were some officers only too willing to act in close co-operation with the Unionists, principally Roberts and his immediate coterie including Henry Wilson and Major-General Sir Henry Rawlinson [3, 5, 16]. Roberts was concerned at the fate that might befall the army [13, 16, 90, 94] but there can be little doubt that he intended to use his considerable influence to full effect. Consequently, many contemporaries believed that he was primarily responsible for generating the crisis in the army.[18] Had the attempt to amend the Army (Annual) Act proceeded, it would have been accompanied by an open letter drafted by Roberts with the assistance of Bonar Law and Carson[19] while it was also the old Field Marshal's intention publicly to declare the Home Rule bill unconstitutional if the King signed it [3, 5]. Nothing better illustrates the essential cynicism of Roberts and his circle than their attitude to the Territorial Force [13–15, 165], which was now to be pressed into the political service of those who had spent six years denigrating it in order to ensure its collapse as an obstacle to the introduction of conscription.[20] Indeed, there is something of a correlation generally between those advocating conscription and those supporting the cause of Ulster. Roberts, too, had suggested a retired Indian army officer, Lieutenant-General Sir George Richardson, to command the UVF. A number of other former British officers also served with the Loyalists including Captain W. B. Spender, whose attempt to leave the army to do so had become a *cause célèbre*.[21]

As a result of such influences, there was concern that discipline was being steadily undermined. Such views were shared by the Adjutant General, Ewart, and the King [3, 4, 6], who not only sounded out opinion within the army but also expressed his fears to Asquith.[22] Having taken a robust line with Spender, neither French nor Seely were inclined to compromise on discipline, the former threatening courts martial for any transgressions [4, 22] and the latter delivering a somewhat incoherent exhortation to the assembled commanders of the home commands on 16 December 1913 [6, 10]. It is not clear how far Seely's views were actually disseminated but they remained official policy [88].[23] For some Irish regiments, it was already too late [11].[24]

If Seely at least believed that policy on discipline was unambiguous, the same could hardly be said for the government's views on the actual employment of troops in the eventuality of Ulster resisting Home Rule by force. Irish affairs had not detained the Cabinet prior to the introduction of the first Home Rule bill on 11 April 1912[25] and, as late as November 1913, the Liberals were still hopelessly split on the possibility of making provision for Ulster's exclusion from legislation now twice rejected by the House of Lords. Asquith intimated to the King in October 1913 that force might prove necessary and the former Secretary of State for War, Lord Haldane, also favoured measures approximating to those used for the suppression of strikes in South Wales in 1910.[26] A cryptic note from Paget to French on 19 October 1913 mentioned 'partial mobilisation' as a subject for discussion in forthcoming consultations in London while, two days later, the army's acknowledged expert on aid to the civil power, Major-General Sir Nevil Macready, was offered an Irish command.[27] Macready declined but was sent to Ireland temporarily in November, ostensibly to report on the constabulary. Macready later claimed that he returned from Ireland to find that the government had decided against the use of force although, in fact, he had told Henry Wilson this before he left England [5]. In the event, the only action taken was a Royal proclamation on 1 December 1913 banning further importation of arms into Ireland.

Since the situation in Ireland did not appear noticeably worse in March 1914 than it had in November 1913, the subsequent military movements were totally unexpected [25, 26, 37]. Although some mystery still shrouds the formative period of the Curragh Incident, it would appear that the decisive factors were the Unionist rejection of David Lloyd George's exclusion proposals on 9 March 1914 and new police reports presented to Cabinet on 11 March, which estimated the UVF at 80,000 men with 17,000 weapons. Rumours of a possible raid by the UVF on arms depots in Ulster, which had originally surfaced in November 1913, bore some relation to reality in terms of UVF plans to proclaim a provisional government. However, such a move would only have taken place once the Home Rule bill reached the statute book and those reports extant indicate that the rumours were unsubstantiated. Government fears may have been sustained by a private letter to Asquith from the military correspondent of *The Times*, Charles à Court Repington, and certainly articles on the UVF Repington was preparing were sufficiently alarming for his editor to fear a reaction damaging to popular sympathy for the Unionists.[28] Neither police reports nor any other sources of information were subsequently produced by the government in its own defence and Sir John French initially discounted the rumours, only to be convinced of the need for action by their constant re-iteration [30]. If other information was available, it has not survived.

As is well known, a Cabinet sub-committee was established on 11 March 1914 under the chairmanship of the Marquis of Crewe to consider the government response. Crewe fell ill and with the Chief Secretary, Augustine Birrell, and the Attorney General, Sir John Simon, taking little part in the proceedings, the conduct of affairs devolved upon Seely and the First Lord of the Admiralty, Winston Churchill. On the advice of the sub-committee, orders were issued to Paget to take precautions for the safety of arms depots at Omagh, Armagh, Enniskillen and Carrickfergus [17]. As Paget's response was tentative [18], he was summoned for consultations in London on 18 and 19 March. The instructions given him are one of the most controversial aspects of the Curragh Incident since, at his own request,[29] they were never committed to paper.

A total of fourteen individuals are listed in the surviving documents alluding to the discussions as having taken part in the proceedings [23, 30, 57, 73, 125]. French, Seely, Ewart and Paget were present on all formal occasions with Churchill, Birrell, Crewe, Macready and the First Sea Lord, Prince Louis of Battenberg, attending the majority. Asquith and Lloyd George were present at a meeting in 10 Downing Street on 18 March and Asquith was again present at a final hurried discussion there on the late evening of 19 March. Simon, the Home Secretary, Reginald McKenna, and Seely's private secretary, George Nicholson, were each present on one occasion. The Cabinet had already approved the precautions ordered on 14 March [19] but, on the morning of 18 March, it was decided to add Dundalk to the four locations originally specified as requiring protection. This and the later addition of Newry has been regarded with suspicion[30] as they were not arms depots, were not in Loyalist areas, and were nodal centres useful for larger operations. In fact, the evidence of French and Ewart suggests that the reason was the security of artillery units at Dundalk and Newry. It was also decided to move the 1st Dorsets from the exposed Victoria Barracks in Belfast and, in the event of hostilities, to appoint a

Military Governor in Belfast and to attach three intelligence officers to Paget's command as he had no such services available [20]. At the subsequent meeting in 10 Downing Street, Asquith not only approved the immediate appointment of Macready as Military Governor with a dormant commission but also that all planned movements should be completed by early on 21 March [21]. The necessary instructions were telegraphed to Ireland in Paget's name.[31]

It was always insisted that the movements ordered, which the military advisers present all opposed,[32] were only precautionary and no participant has recorded them in any other sense, not even Ewart who was a Conservative with no reason to shield the Liberal government after his resignation. As one historian has commented, even if the worst possible construction is placed on the moves, they still amounted to relatively little.[33] However, there was obviously a belief that even limited movements might provoke reaction from the UVF or, conceivably, from the nationalists [56, 65, 125] and there can be little doubt that larger military operations were discussed. Paget's concern to wrest 'concessions' on behalf of officers domiciled in Ulster [22] suggests this, as does the appointment of the intelligence officers and Macready, whose suggested title of 'Military Governor' was opposed by Simon on the grounds that it represented the 'language of civil war'.[34] Moreover, when Macready fell ill from an undisclosed ailment on 19 March, Paget's Major-General in charge of Administration, Major-General L. B. Friend, was quickly substituted[35] on a temporary basis. Overall responsibility for large-scale operations was also decided within the War Office on 19 March, this being vested in the Director of Military Training, Major-General Sir William Robertson, after Henry Wilson successfully evaded it.[36] Paget's chief of staff, Brigadier-General G. T. Forestier-Walker, was also working on a draft plan for field operations by 22 March [45], if not before.

Similarly, Paget was explicit in terms of the reinforcements he could expect when he spoke to his immediate subordinates at his second conference in Dublin on the afternoon of 20 March, repeating the details to the officers of the 3rd Cavalry Brigade on the following day [54, 56, 62–5]. It must be said that, despite Seely's confidence [29], the sheer practical difficulties of undertaking any large-scale operations in Ulster were manifest from the beginning [24, 26–8, 45]. Thus, the fact that the Commander at Aldershot, Lieutenant-General Sir Douglas Haig, later claimed that he had never seen any plans to move the 1st Division from Aldershot [123] and the obvious bewilderment of both Friend and the Royal Irish Constabulary Commissioner in Belfast [73] may indicate that planning never went much beyond the preliminary stage. As Macready destroyed all his own personal papers and his autobiography is less than informative, it is impossible to judge what he understood his role to be, had he reached Belfast as intended.

What appears to have done most to precipitate the actual crisis at the Curragh, once the initial movements had been ordered, was the heated debate in the House of Commons on 19 March, the Home Rule Bill having been introduced for its second reading for a third time ten days earlier. Carson's dramatic departure from the House, amid rumours of his possible arrest and of the probable declaration of a provisional government once he reached Belfast, prompted a last meeting before Paget himself departed for Ireland [30]. The experience left Paget in a highly excitable condition [83] and may well have convinced him finally that he would indeed be 'leading his army to the Boyne'.

Equally affected was Churchill, whose immediate predilection to use the navy to bombard Belfast into submission was a striking precursor of a rather more costly enterprise a year later. Churchill, of course, had added to the prevailing tension with an inflammatory speech at Bradford on 14 March and it would appear that the failure of the Unionists to accept Lloyd George's exclusion proposals had persuaded the First Lord that the government must now press ahead with Home Rule.[37] It is not true, as was claimed in the House on 23 March, that Asquith did not learn of the movements of the 3rd Battle Squadron until 21 March, since the forthcoming practice off Lamlash was discussed in Cabinet on 17 March [19]. Both Ewart and Nicholson also suggest that the actual date of assembly of the squadron, if not its reinforcement with elements of the 4th Destroyer Flotilla, was discussed openly on 18 or 19 March [23, 125]. However, it is conceivable that the decision was that of Churchill alone on 19 March.[38] The very different nature of the other naval movements, all of which had specific purposes such as the transportation of troops if Ulster's Great Northern Railway Company refused to carry them north, and Asquith's cancellation of orders to the squadron on 21 March provide circumstantial evidence of this. So, too, does Churchill's reaction to the news of Carson's departure [30].

The wider naval movements, together with the lack of evidence concerning Macready, are perhaps the only fully unexplained circumstances surrounding the genesis of the Curragh crisis. The balance of evidence available does not substantiate a 'plot' to coerce Ulster. If coercion was truly intended then it was conceived in such haste that any large-scale operations would have had to be improvised. Little or no thought was given by the politicians to the long-term implications of any military occupation of Ulster. Although it may have been intended to seize public buildings in Belfast, the military movements ordered did not include any provision for disarming the UVF and it would appear that a large measure of bluff was involved. In such circumstances it is hard to fault the judgement of one historian that the entire episode arose as 'a characteristically hesitant and mismanaged expedient' of the Asquith government,[39] or at least some of its members. But, whatever the real intentions of Seely or Churchill towards Ulster when Paget left London on 19 March, that officer's incapacity to hold the responsibility of command in such a situation was to throw all into utter confusion.

II

By the time Paget arrived back in Dublin early on Friday 20 March 1914, those instructions telegraphed by him from London had already been put into effect. In the 5th Division, Sir Charles Fergusson had received the orders from Friend at 5 p.m. on 19 March.[40] Fergusson had been due to dine that evening with

Hubert Gough and the Inspector of Cavalry, Major-General E. H. H. Allenby, who was over in Ireland for the beginning of the annual training season. Fergusson's absence alerted Gough to the movements and he promptly sent a letter of enquiry to his brother, Brigadier-General J. E. Gough, who was Haig's chief of staff at Aldershot [25]. Other accounts also recorded the posting of guards with ball ammunition at barrack gates [37, 43, 55].

It is perhaps important to emphasise that, throughout the Curragh Incident, no direct orders of any kind were disobeyed by any officer or man. Thus, all the precautionary movements as well as further orders to prepare artillery units for action on the evening of 20 March [53][41] were fully complied with. Both Gough and Lieutenant Colonel Maurice MacEwen of the 16th Lancers also testified their willingness to obey direct orders when they were subsequently interviewed in London by Ewart [74, 78, 95, 124]. In view of such ready compliance to orders, notwithstanding the circumstances, Paget's error in appearing to offer a choice to his subordinates as to whether to obey orders or not on the morning of 20 March is all the more culpable.

The two main sources for the remarks of Paget at the first conference on the morning of 20 March are the accounts by Gough and Fergusson [61, 71, 96], other recollections by Friend and Brigadier-General S. P. Rolt of 14th Infantry Brigade being recorded at second hand [73, 122]. Although Gough and Fergusson, whose account precedes the former by twelve days, differ in some respects, the general impression conveyed by Paget was clearly the need to place a formal ultimatum before all officers in view of imminent active operations against Ulster. The 'ultimatum', of course, offered those officers domiciled in Ulster the option of 'disappearing' while operations were undertaken. Those unable to claim the exemption who refused to take part in operations would be dismissed without pension. Why Paget chose to act as he did is unclear. His own explanation, conveyed to London by his military secretary on 22 March [78, 125], was that he deemed it necessary to 'find out upon what General and other officers' he could rely. In subsequent versions, Paget was to lay the emphasis solely on ascertaining the views of senior officers

[57, 68] and to deny that he ever intended an ultimatum placed before junior officers [170].

Gough, no doubt incensed by Paget's attitude, telegraphed his brother [79], and proceeded to put the ultimatum first to Lieutenant Colonel Arthur Parker and the 5th Lancers, quartered in Marlborough Barracks in Dublin [70, 71]. After a further consultation with Friend, he motored to the Curragh and issued the ultimatum to the remaining officers of his brigade [49, 56, 63, 71, 74]. Fergusson immediately put down the ultimatum on paper for the benefit of artillery, engineers and other supporting units [33] while Rolt and Brigadier-General G. J. Cuthbert of 13th Infantry Brigade carried it verbally to the infantry battalions.[42] According to the memoirs of Brigadier-General Count Gleichen, the ultimatum was not put to his 15th Infantry Brigade in Ulster itself[43] but Fergusson certainly wrote to all units there. The element of the 1st Duke of Cornwall's Light Infantry moved to Ulster received such a communication from Fergusson and, more crucially, officers of the 1st Norfolks in 15th Infantry Brigade had it put to them 'about serving against Ulster' in Gleichen's presence although, admittedly, this was not until 22 March [50, 59, 66]. Most of the divisional artillery and supporting units had received the ultimatum by the evening of 20 March but, in some cases, it would appear that infantry battalions did not get full details until the following morning [36, 40, 42, 43, 54, 75].

The gravity of the decisions forced upon officers need hardly be stated, the effect being compounded by the brevity accorded some in making them [34, 43, 70].[44] Fergusson later suggested that there was safety in collective action [193] but this ignores the lack of any degree of premeditation[45] and the harshness of individuals' choices. Some assumed that dismissal could be a course followed only by those who could afford it [126, 138] and it is true that an approach was made to the Unionists to secure financial guarantees on behalf of some comtemplating resignation [135]. The reticence of Lieutenant Colonel Ian Hogg of the 4th Hussars in following Gough is also partly explained by his lack of means [74] although it must also be said that Hogg declined the domicile option to which he was entitled. However,

Hubert Gough was at pains to point out the financial difficulties facing some of his officers [72] and others in the 5th Division also consciously eschewed pensions or imminent promotion in deciding upon resignation. All keenly felt the injustice of the choice presented them [43, 47, 50, 53, 190]. Both Macready and one of his staff believed that it was quite unnecessary for Paget to have stressed the loss of pensions at all,[46] thus making it appear that officers were being forced to 'barter their honour'. More succinctly, after hearing Gough's account in London on 22 March, Ewart recorded in his diary that, 'Paget must be mad.' [78]

In the 3rd Cavalry Brigade sixty officers resigned [31]. It is not clear whether Gough was included in this total as he had written a separate letter of resignation for Friend [32], although it was never actually submitted. Paget's first telegram to London gave the figure only as 57 officers,[47] to which Gough was later added [38], and this erroneous total is that invariably quoted in many accounts. Gough also estimated that about five officers in each infantry battalion had resigned[48] but the exact figures are unknown. Nine officers initially resigned in the 2nd King's Own Yorkshire Light Infantry as did ten in the 2nd King's Own Scottish Borderers, nine or ten in the 2nd Manchesters, thirteen of the 1st Duke of Cornwall's Light Infantry and a majority in the 1st Norfolks [40, 43, 50, 66, 75].[49] Among the field artillery, seven out of fifteen officers in XV Brigade resigned, six in XXVIII Brigade, and possibly six in VIII Brigade [36, 53, 54].[50] Some, of course, did not resign [36] while many others were undecided [43]. In the 3rd Cavalry Brigade, Hogg and his second in command, Major Philip Howell, believed that there must have been a misunderstanding [49, 56] and, to play for time, induced Gough to send a letter to Paget giving the numbers willing to resign but also requesting additional information [31].

Paget's reaction to the crisis he had induced in his own command was a disastrous decision to address the 3rd Cavalry Brigade on the morning of 21 March to 'put a little heart' into his officers [38]. His rambling discourse [49, 56, 63–5, 74] did little to reassure his audience. Even Lieutenant Colonel R. W. Breeks of III Brigade, RHA, who had decided not to resign, found

Paget unconvincing and, according to Gough, Breeks argued heatedly with Paget. Howell and Hogg were prepared to accept Paget's guarantees and they managed to persuade all but six of the officers of the 4th Hussars to withdraw their resignations.[51] Those of the other regiments stood.

Gough, Hogg and Breeks all allude in their accounts to Paget's use of the King's name in his appeal for obedience to orders, a point of some importance in view of the subsequent controversy. Fergusson had received the same impression, that the King had authorised all orders issued, when Paget spoke at the second conference on Friday 20 March to explain his proposed plan of operations in greater detail [61, 62]. Upon that peg Fergusson hung his arguments while undertaking an extensive round of visits to his troops on Saturday 21 March in order to try and nullify the impact of the resignations among the cavalrymen. Fergusson was genuinely appalled by the prospect of the army breaking up and the political repercussions for country and Empire [59, 62, 193]. Although he had failed to convince Gough and did not convince all of his audiences, Fergusson's speeches held the majority of the 5th Division's officers to duty [40, 42, 43, 54, 69, 75]. But in many cases officers withdrew their resignations unwillingly and made it clear by memorial or letter that it was only the use of the King's name that had induced obedience to distasteful orders [41, 46, 51, 61, 66].

The success of Fergusson and his artillery commander, Brigadier-General J. E. W. Headlam,[52] in restoring discipline by force of personality implies that the personality of Hubert Gough was equally instrumental in influencing his officers to take a different course. All accounts of Gough's remarks to his officers on 20 March indicate that he declined to give specific advice to individuals but, of course, his views were known. One officer later concluded that Gough's parting remark, that 'as for myself, I am damned if I am going', could not have been 'more calculated to influence us to follow his lead and back him up at whatever cost'.[53] Another crucial influence among the cavalrymen was Parker of the 5th Lancers, with whom Paget had a number of unsuccessful interviews [70]. Ewart, Seely and Seely's private secretary, Nicholson, all identified Parker as being particularly intransigent once Gough and his colonels reached London and there is also a previously unremarked telegram from Paget on 21 March that suggests that Parker alone had prevented Gough and the others from withdrawing their resignations [44, 95, 125].[54] Where popular commanding officers took such stands, it was perhaps inevitable that 'crowds of waverers' [143] would follow. In this regard it can be noted that cavalry officers on detached duty invariably sent in their own resignations automatically merely on the strength of sparse telegrams from the Curragh [168].

One of Fergusson's arguments was that, if officers refused to do their duty towards Ulster, then the rank and file would be equally free to choose their own course of action in industrial disputes requiring military intervention. Gleichen referred obliquely to officers having little objection to coercing the nationalists of the south of Ireland [196] while the contrast with aid to the civil power in recent industrial troubles in England was made much of by Radicals and Labour representatives in the House of Commons and the working-class press.[55] For obvious reasons, there is far less evidence available on the attitudes of the rank and file in Ireland or elsewhere. Those accounts available [54, 55, 58, 60, 67, 76, 150] suggest that those termed the 'better educated' took the same line as their officers. The remainder had no interest in politics and would have obeyed any order given them. This was equally true of the cavalry regiments, despite the enthusiastic scenes when Gough and his colonels both left and returned to the Curragh [55, 67, 74] and the substantial proportion of Irishmen in their ranks. Some other Irish units were rather more disaffected [189].[56]

III

The first news of events at the Curragh to reach England was almost certainly Hubert Gough's telegram to his brother [79], which Johnnie Gough eventually read about 2 p.m. on Friday 20 March. After replying [80], Johnnie Gough hastened to London to seek out Henry Wilson. In the early evening he and Wilson telephoned both French and Seely [77, 81, 122] but succeeded in contacting only French in person. Neither French nor Seely's private secretary responded in any positive way since French was summoned from the theatre, where he had gone with Churchill, at about 9.30 p.m., after Nicholson had brought Seely the first of Paget's telegrams [30, 125]. Ewart arrived at 11 p.m. [78], at which time his good sense prevailed over Churchill's bombast and it was decided to order Gough, Parker and MacEwen to report to the War Office and to refuse all other resignations. Asquith was informed after the receipt of Paget's second telegram after 11.35 p.m.

Following further telegrams between Paget and the War Office concerning the state of affairs in the 4th Hussars, Hogg was summoned to London as, eventually, was Colonel F. F. Hill commanding No. 11 District in Ireland, who had also resigned.[57] These were not the extent of the messages being passed between London and Ireland since Hogg had composed a telegram to Churchill as a former officer of the 4th Hussars [39], although it did not reach the First Lord until the following morning. By that morning of 21 March, Haig, who was on leave at Littlehampton, had received a letter sent by Johnnie Gough on the previous evening [81] and Roberts had received a telegram from Hubert Gough [86]. Wilson saw Bonar Law early on the morning of 21 March and Geoffrey Robinson of *The Times* during the afternoon [77, 91]. Alerted by Johnnie Gough, Lady Lugard also contacted Bonar Law [87], but the Unionist leader had already learned something of the crisis from an anonymous telegram received on the previous evening [83]. Foolishly, he later attempted to deny the existence of the telegram.[58]

In the contacts so quickly established between the officers of the 3rd Cavalry Brigade, their military supporters in London, and Unionist politicians, there is perhaps the suggestion of something insidious. At the very least, it was intended to profit from the errors of Paget. Roberts began to pressure French after reading the first reports in the press on the morning of 21 March. There followed an unpleasant telephone conversation between the two men and interviews for Roberts with both the King and Seely [89,

90, 94], at which Roberts protested his innocence of involvement. In view of Roberts' meeting with Johnnie Gough on 22 March [98] and the warm terms in which Hubert Gough addressed Roberts' daughter as 'My dear Aileen' [72], it might appear unlikely that Hubert Gough had as little recent contact with the old Field Marshal as Roberts claimed.[59] It must also be noted that, apart from the continued contact between Gough and the Unionists through Wilson, there were other intermediaries such as Lady Lugard and a relative of the Goughs, Mrs Bagnall.[60] Yet another emissary appeared on 22 March in the form of a member of the Irish racing fraternity at the Curragh, Captain Greer [97, 134] while Johnnie Gough established contact with Austen Chamberlain.[61] The King had not learned of events until he read the press either [88, 91] but, thereafter, he not only had audiences with Asquith, Seely and French but was fully informed on the views of Gough through one of his equerries [97] and his assistant secretary, Clive Wigram. Indeed, Wigram was actually present at the London home of the Goughs on the morning of 22 March but reference to this and to another communication between Wigram and Wilson on 24 March was omitted from the published version of Wilson's diaries [77]. Similarly, the accounts of events in Ireland by Gough, Breeks and MacEwen were widely circulated as the source notes reproduced with the documents in this volume indicate only too clearly.

For the government and its military advisers, the crisis posed the immediate problem of formulating an appropriate response when accurate information was wholly lacking. From the beginning the government was outmanoeuvred by the Goughs, Hubert arriving in London with the intention of seeking a written guarantee that there would be no military coercion of Ulster [49, 74]. Henry Wilson had actually presented a draft of such an agreement to French on 21 March [77] but it is impossible to know how far this approximated to that secured by Gough two days later. On the morning of Sunday 22 March, Gough consulted with his brother, who had sent in his own resignation on the previous day [85, 92, 93, 122],[62] and with Wilson. Before he was interviewed by Ewart and Macready, Hubert Gough had also received a letter from Roberts, which the latter had left at the War Office [90] and which indicated that the government realised that Paget had blundered. Gough, MacEwen, Parker and Hogg, whose telegram to Churchill had conveyed the first real indication of the nature of Paget's mistakes, were then interviewed in turn at the War Office [74, 78, 95, 97, 124, 125]. Colonel Hill was also in the War Office that day but did not apparently have his formal interview with Ewart until 24 March. Although there was some personal animosity between Gough and Macready, the interviews were less strained than has sometimes been suggested and they only confirmed Ewart's original belief that Paget was to blame.

Evidence for the movements of the principal military participants after the interviews ended is somewhat sketchy. Wilson continued contacts with the Unionist politicians and the press; Ewart met the Army Council; MacEwen met Lieutenant Cecil Howard, who advised him of growing military support for the stand of the 3rd Cavalry Brigade; and Johnnie Gough met both Haig and Roberts [74, 77, 78, 98, 122, 136]. Hubert Gough's two accounts of the day [97, 124] are silent on his movements. Yet, from the account by Nicholson, there must have been further consultations since he recorded that 'at several moments during the Sunday the officers concerned, with the exception of Colonel Parker, were prepared to go back to their duties but they felt unable to do so so long as he stood out' [125]. More evidence is available for Asquith, Seely and French, all of whom saw the King with Asquith issuing a statement, at the King's suggestion, that there had been a 'misunderstanding'.[63]

By contrast with some of the accounts of 22 March, those for Monday 23 March are far more detailed in chronicling Hubert Gough's further interviews with Ewart, French, Paget and Seely [74, 77, 78, 122, 124, 125] and the latter's eventual agreement to provide a written guarantee. One version of the guarantee was prepared by Captain W. Childs of Macready's staff at the request of Seely from a draft by Nicholson,[64] but the final draft was that of Ewart who sent it over to the Cabinet room. Subsequently, Ewart also sent over a note drafted by Gough and his colleagues [99], who had become alarmed at the possibility of being 'trapped' by the document into coercion under the guise of maintaining law and order. Ewart's draft had been amended by Asquith in Cabinet but Seely, who returned from an audience with the King just as the Cabinet was adjourning, then added the celebrated final two 'peccant paragraphs' without doing more than glancing briefly at Gough's note. Seely had believed both that the document as it stood would not satisfy Gough and also that he had the discretion to amend it without further consultation, a view in which Lord Morley with whom he was conversing at the time apparently concurred.[65] After discussion with his colleagues, Gough requested further clarification of the final document to which French agreed, initialling his concurrence with Gough's interpretation of the document [100]. It was a significant victory for Gough [103].

Much of the credit for securing the guarantee has been given in the past to Wilson, largely on the evidence of his own testimony that he suggested the letter drafted by Gough and also prompted the request for further clarification from French. There can be little doubt of Wilson's importance in raising support for the Goughs and in keeping the Unionists fully informed [77, 101, 120, 132, 138, 144]. However, Wilson was but one of a number of individuals gathered in the War Office on 23 March to advise Hubert Gough and it should be noted that the Curragh Incident shattered the former friendship between Wilson and Johnnie Gough. From the latter's point of view, Wilson had known of the military movements in Ulster but had done little until pushed into action by the Goughs [97]. Certainly, Hubert Gough, MacEwen and Parker all gave full credit to Johnnie Gough rather than Wilson for securing the victory in London [106, 201][66] and it would appear that Johnnie Gough should rightly replace Wilson as the key figure in the negotiations.

For Ewart and French the outcome of the negotiations at first appeared entirely satisfactory in view of the widespread military support for the Goughs reported to them. Speeches made by government representatives on the night of 23 March, notably by Lord Haldane, gave every indication that all was well. Thus, on the following day Ewart felt confident in refusing Colonel Hill's request for a similar written guarantee to that given Gough on the grounds that government statements negated its necessity.[67] But the nature of Seely's initiative soon became apparent [78, 105] and Asquith publicly repudiated the guarantee on 25 March. It might be added that a number of indirect approaches were subsequently made to try and retrieve the actual document [206, 210] but Gough had immediately put it in trust for his eldest daughter.[68] Seely offered to resign as did the Army Council as a whole [108, 109, 115] but Seely's resignation was refused. French and Ewart believed that they had been placed in an impossible situation, having induced Gough and his officers to return to duty on the strength of a document they had accepted in good faith as representing Cabinet policy. They therefore pressed their own resignations on 26 March [110, 111]. Enormous pressure was exerted in order to find a compromise solution to prevent their resignations. Haldane in particular, with the assistance of Haig, laboured hard to retain them through a public statement that would satisfy all parties [112–15, 117]. At the same time others were pressing French to resign [77, 104, 116, 121] including Field Marshal Lord Grenfell; Lord Esher; Sir George Riddell; the journalist, H. A. Gwynne;[69] and French's own ADC, Major A. Fitz Watt.

Haig's role is rather more ambiguous in these crucial days. He had initially counselled Johnnie Gough to be calm [82, 84] and also advised Hubert Gough on the morning of 23 March to settle and return to the Curragh as soon as possible. Yet, Haig had also brought French the unwelcome news of the overwhelming support for the Goughs at Aldershot [82, 123] and, although advising Haldane, ended by feeling that French must resign [82, 102, 155]. Significantly, neither Johnnie Gough nor Robertson [122, 142] had any idea prior to the crisis of the course Haig would follow and his actual conduct bears every appearance of keeping a foot in both camps. Clearly, however, Haig blamed the French for placing the army in a difficult position and the crisis widened the rift between them.[70]

Ultimately, the statements drawn up by Haldane failed to

satisfy both the soldiers and Asquith [118] and another attempt to mediate through the agency of the Committee of Imperial Defence also failed. At least a new army order [197], which was to remain in force until 1944, emerged from the negotiations on 27 March but, three days later, French and Ewart's resignations were announced [119]. Seely had little choice but to resign as well and, after some speculation, Asquith himself took the office of Secretary of State for War on 31 March.[71]

IV

One of the principal reasons for French and Ewart's relief at getting Gough back to the Curragh was their strong impression that, if they had not succeeded, 'we might have a sympathetic strike and widespread resignations throughout the Army' [78]. Indeed, French remarked to Ewart on 24 March that he would have signed anything to get Gough back to Ireland and he spoke in similar terms to Riddell five days later.[72] It has been generally accepted that there was considerable support in the army for Gough but previous accounts have rarely examined its extent. There were, of course, officers who did not approve of Gough's action but they were very much in the minority.

Within the War Office, the majority were clearly ready to resign [74, 77, 132, 141, 146], including Wilson, Robertson and the third director in the Chief of the Imperial General Staff's department, Major-General F. J. Davies. It has been suggested that neither Wilson nor Robertson were committed to the support of the Goughs.[73] Wilson's diary certainly indicates that he was wavering on whether or not to resign at different stages but he would almost certainly have been pushed into resignation by the action of his colleagues and those of his staff, whom he had personally done so much to politicise during the Curragh Incident. Similarly, rather too much trust has been placed in Robertson's urbane account in his memoirs of advising officers including Colonel (later Lieutenant-General Sir) Stanley Maude, to 'go away, make their minds easy, and get on with their work, as I felt sure that in the long run any intention there might be of employing troops against Ulstermen would be abandoned'.[74] But Robertson himself had done much to ensure that result through advising on all manner of obstacles to coercion [28] and the evidence of his support for the Goughs is overwhelming [77, 141, 144]. Indeed, the letter he wrote to Johnnie Gough is unequivocal [142]. But, if many officers found no difficulty in supporting the Goughs, there were some within the War Office with doubts [144]. The evidence of Macready, Childs and also Lieutenant Colonel George MacMunn all points to considerable pressure being applied to such officers to an extent which made the atmosphere 'unpleasant'.[75]

Cowans and von Donop, who sat respectively as Quartermaster General and Master General of Ordnance on the Army Council with French and Ewart, together with most commanders of the home commands were primarily concerned with what might be termed 'damage limitation' [78, 82].[76] Nonetheless, Ewart still acknowledged when a number of senior officers met him and French at the War Office on 26 March for a previously arranged session on discipline that, 'it would not have been difficult to get up a revolution had one been of that mind.' At least two of those present—Smith-Dorrien and Rawlinson—were supporters of the Goughs [126, 127, 136] and this support in the senior ranks of the army extended to both the Inspector of Infantry, Capper [158], and the Inspector of Cavalry, Allenby. Wavell, whose own decision to stand by his duty is well known, claims in his biography of the latter that Allenby had no part in the Curragh Incident and 'with his unquestioning loyalty to superior authority, there can be no doubt what his views were'.[77] Allenby certainly had no direct role in the affair and had every intention of avoiding one, remarking to MacEwen when troop movements began on 20 March that 'this was no place for him' [74]. However, his support for the Goughs is clear [130, 141].

Support at Aldershot was overwhelming [106, 123, 141, 149, 155, 159, 163], it being claimed that only one officer in the entire command was prepared to coerce Ulster. Further notable areas of support for Hubert Gough were the Guards [125, 131, 133, 139, 152], staff at the Royal Military College at Sandhurst [145] and staff and students at the neighbouring Staff College. One officer on the Staff College course took the view that duty must prevail [143] but this was not shared by his peers and Wilson found plenty of support for the necessity of French's resignation when he met his Staff College contacts at the latter institution's point-to-point on 28 March 1914 [77]. Not unexpectedly declarations of support came from other cavalry regiments but also from Scottish regiments and units throughout Britain including the 18th Brigade at Lichfield which, like the 1st Division at Aldershot, would have been used to reinforce Paget in large-scale operations [135, 138, 140, 150, 154, 215].[78]

Had there been operations requiring such reinforcement, then it was widely rumoured that the Territorial Force might be employed to replace regulars in garrison. However, Territorials were equally unwilling to play any role in coercion [78, 134, 137, 151, 165, 167] and this was true of other reservists.[79] Support was also forthcoming from the army overseas [161, 166][80] although, again, some officers believed that duty should come first and General Sir Ian Hamilton was one senior officer prepared to stand by the government [156, 160].

Even less remarked than support for the Goughs among army units outside Ireland has been the attitude of the Royal Navy. The ships of the navy would almost certainly have become involved in larger operations both in terms of blockading or even bombarding the Irish coast and in terms of landing shore parties. In a volume devoted to the army, there is regrettably no space available to give the Royal Navy more than a passing mention but a number of documents are reproduced [128, 129, 147–9, 153, 163, 169] which indicate the widespread disinclination among naval officers to take part in the coercion of Ulster. Such disinclination extended to the most senior ranks.

Such sympathy for the actions of the 3rd Cavalry Brigade could hardly fail to have had an enormous impact throughout the services but most accounts have tended to neglect this aspect of the Curragh Incident. The subsequent allegations over the 'plot' to coerce Ulster have been exhaustively recounted elsewhere.[81] However, it is worth repeating that those concerned with exposing the Liberal government such as Milner, F. S. Oliver and L. S. Amery, derived much of their information from serving officers. Wilson, the Goughs, MacEwen and even Howell were so involved [175][82] and the number of junior officers communicating with Unionist politicians has already been noted.

Other officers were rather more concerned to present their actions during the crisis in the most favourable light, notably Paget. Paget's version of events was demanded both by the government [170] and by the King, when the issue of the use of the King's name became public. The latter began when a copy of Lieutenant Colonel Brett's letter to Rolt [41, 109], showing the use Fergusson had made of the King's name to ensure his division's loyalties, had been transmitted to Buckingham Palace. Paget tried to shift the blame to Fergusson and produced a series of statements by others who had attended his second conference on 20 March to show that Fergusson, like many others that day, must have 'misunderstood' [171, 178, 181, 182, 184, 187]. Fergusson shouldered the blame [172, 183] but the King and his secretary, Lord Stamfordham, remained unconvinced [173, 174, 180] as the correspondence dragged on into July 1914.[83] Paget evidently contemplated resignation [176, 184–6] but not immediately and, in the event, did not resign. His continued survival mystified both Hubert Gough and Ewart [212, 218, 222] and gave currency to the theories of the 'plot' since the government appeared to be shielding Paget excessively. But, once March had passed, Paget's removal would only have served to re-open the affair and this the government and the Army Council preferred not to do [186].[84]

Asquith had announced that he would answer no more questions on the Curragh Incident in the House of Commons on 29 April 1914 but this no more ended the repercussions within the army than had his assumption of the War Office, a post he continued to hold until August 1914.[85] Ireland was quiet in the immediate aftermath of the events of March [188–90, 196][86] but tensions increased again with the successful gun-running by the UVF at Larne on 24 April. The renewed prospect of involvement in aid to the civil power was not welcomed [202, 215–17]. Not least, it could pose awkward problems for those who had refused to coerce Ulster in March and whose views remained unchanged since aid to the civil power did not necessarily imply coercion [217, 220, 223, 225]. However, the head of the army was now Sir Charles Douglas, who succeeded French as Chief of the Imperial General Staff to general acclaim. Far more confidence was placed in Douglas' ability to prevent troops being involved in coercion and the new CIGS was consciously attempting to rebuild the army's relationship with its Army Council.[87] It is clear that the movement of any troops in Ireland was treated with considerable caution[88] but, in any case, enquiries made in April into the discipline of the army in Ireland and elsewhere and its willingness to be used for military operations in Ireland conclusively demonstrated that the army was still deeply disaffected [209, 213, 214].[89] The situation was no better by July [226, 227] and, in endorsing a paper drafted by Wilson,[90] the Army Council acknowledged on 4 July 1914 that the army was incapable of being employed for coercion [224]. In effect, the divisions within the army after March ruled out any attempt by the government to return to a policy of coercion. This did not necessarily imply that the army could not be used in Ireland in other circumstances and the affair at Bachelors' Walk in Dublin, in which troops of the King's Own Scottish Borderers fired on a crowd, killing three after the landing of guns at Howth, contrasted sharply with the army's actions towards Loyalists in March.[91] Nor was the disastrous impact on discipline the only result of the Curragh. The French military attaché had been remarkably perceptive in his assessment of Paget prior to the crisis [7] and, after it, he noted both the lack of unity in the army and the detrimental effect of the Curragh upon recruiting [192, 228]. His latter point was not lost on other observers, who also viewed the Curragh Incident as bad for recruiting.[92]

Part of the malaise within the army was the irretrievable damage done to personal relationships. Both Howell and Fergusson had expressed the hope in March that those who stood by their duty would not be victimised by the majority [49, 52, 191]. Unfortunately, cries of 'scab' and 'blackleg' were already being recorded by Howell on 22 March and Fergusson proclaimed himself a 'fallen idol' three days later [193]. Fergusson was much distressed by anonymous letters, which Gough also received, and angered by the claim taken up in *Blackwood's Magazine* and by some of his friends that he had intended to provoke Ulster into reacting against troops sent there [221]. Not unexpectedly, Hogg was a particular target [194, 195, 198, 205, 206, 210] as was Colonel Sir Philip Chetwode who had reluctantly accepted temporary appointment to Gough's command. In fact, Chetwode never left England but this did not save him from abuse [149, 206]. Howell was regarded with great suspicion by Hubert Gough [206], a suspicion that would doubtless have been even more pronounced if all Howell's wide range of contacts during the crisis and its aftermath had become apparent [155, 175, 204].

Much of the invective, including that aimed at Paget [206, 218, 222] and French [199–201, 206, 218, 219], emanated from Hubert Gough. It is noticeable that Gough's contemporary accounts invariably portray his opponents in unflattering terms. One is described as 'white and cheeks trembling' [71], another as 'white, shaky, twitching lips & cheeks' [97]. But Gough was not alone in vilifying French and Paget in such terms and as well as permanently blighting the relationship between Roberts and French, the March crisis also served to destroy that between Paget and Haig [107].[93] Gough, of course, was hardly popular in all quarters [212] and Wilson's reputation for intrigue was much enhanced. Yet, surprisingly few military careers were damaged by involvement. Wilson was to rise to become CIGS and, of course, to be assassinated by Irish nationalists; Gough to command an army, although he was dismissed in controversial circumstances in March 1918. Fergusson believed that he did suffer in later years although he rose to command a corps in the Great War. Paget's career most certainly was effectively ended by the Curragh and he failed to secure an active command during the war. More unjustly, Ewart languished in the Scottish Command.[94] The crisis also took its toll of French [124, 149] and, while many believed that he would soon regain his place at the head of the army, French himself did not. In July Churchill described French as appearing, for all his composure, as 'a broken man'. Interestingly, one soldier who many believed had lacked character was Rolt of 14th Infantry Brigade [122] and, during the war, Rolt broke down.[95] Many other leading protagonists were not to survive the next four years, among them Johnnie Gough, Philip Howell and Ian Hogg. Seely would never hold high political office again, although he commanded the Canadian Cavalry Corps with distinction during the Great War.

If some of the animosities forged in March 1914 were clearly to be of account during the next four years, a still greater legacy was the effect of the Curragh upon the relationship between soldiers and politicians. The great fear of Fergusson had been that the army would be dragged into the political arena over Ulster when there were far greater dangers at home and abroad which necessitated unity [193]. In particular, Fergusson and others believed that the radicals might force and win a general election on the cry of 'the people versus the army' [78, 132, 158, 193]. Not all felt that the attempt to fashion a more 'democratic' army which might follow such an election would be altogether disastrous [204] but most undoubtedly believed that the army would be best excluded from politics [82, 144, 155, 157, 209].

The desire to prevent the army becoming a 'tool' of politicians, to which even Hubert Gough subscribed,[96] did not, in reality, sit easily with the fact that the army itself had most clearly played politics. Wilson and Rawlinson had every expectation that the army would assist in bringing down the government [77, 120, 144].[97] Thus the contempt showered on to the politicians [138, 140, 154, 166, 223] was wholly cynical in the context of the army's political victory in paralysing the government's policy towards Ireland. That result boded ill for civil-military relations in the course of the next four years and, ultimately, for the future of Ireland itself. Even in the midst of greater drama, the army's action in March was not forgotten in Ulster [229].

Within the government, the events of March 1914 strengthened the hands of those opposed to the use of force and led to a resigned acceptance of the continued existence of para-military sectarian organisations. As a result of the damage done to the army, the government was neither capable of preventing any declaration of a provisional government in Belfast, nor of responding adequately to the gun running that was the sequel to its paralysis. Only compromise was possible. Although the outbreak of the First World War led to the passing of an unamended Home Rule Act in September 1914, with immediate suspension for the duration and the promise of an amending bill for the exclusion of Ulster at that time, the Curragh was the more important factor in undermining the government's original policy in Ireland.[98]

Soldiers believed that they had prevented civil war in the spring of 1914[99] but it was at the price of almost destroying the army as an institution. What then saved the army was the First World War but, as Sir George MacMunn later observed, that also had its price:

I often wonder if General Seely and Mr Churchill ever offer little candles to the memory of William Hohenzollern for restoring the officer cadre of the British Army and Navy for them, even though it died in the process.[100]

SECTION I

The Approaching Crisis

Ireland in March 1914
Showing existing troop locations, projected
reinforcements, and naval dispositions.

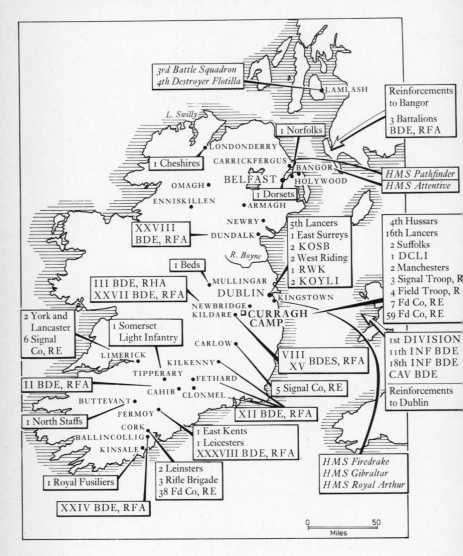

3rd Battle Squadron
4th Destroyer Flotilla

LAMLASH

Reinforcements
to Bangor

3 Battalions
BDE, RFA

1 Norfolks

L. Swilly

LONDONDERRY

CARRICKFERGUS

BANGOR

1 Cheshires

BELFAST

HOLYWOOD

HMS Pathfinder
HMS Attentive

OMAGH

ENNISKILLEN

ARMAGH

1 Dorsets

NEWRY

4th Hussars
16th Lancers
2 Suffolks
1 DCLI
2 Manchesters
3 Signal Troop, R
4 Field Troop, R
7 Fd Co, RE
59 Fd Co, RE

XXVIII
BDE, RFA

DUNDALK

5th Lancers
1 East Surreys
2 KOSB
2 West Riding
1 RWK
2 KOYLI

R. Boyne

1 Beds

III BDE, RHA
XXVII BDE, RFA

MULLINGAR

DUBLIN

NEWBRIDGE

KINGSTOWN

KILDARE

CURRAGH
CAMP

1st DIVISION
11th INF BDE
18th INF BDE
CAV BDE

2 York and
Lancaster
6 Signal
Co, RE

1 Somerset
Light Infantry

CARLOW

Reinforcements
to Dublin

LIMERICK

KILKENNY

VIII
XV

BDES, RFA

TIPPERARY

FETHARD

II BDE, RFA

CAHIR

CLONMEL

5 Signal Co, RE

BUTTEVANT

1 North Staffs

FERMOY

CORK

XII BDE, RFA

BALLINCOLLIG

KINSALE

1 East Kents
1 Leicesters
XXXVIII BDE, RFA

1 Royal Fusiliers

2 Leinsters
3 Rifle Brigade
38 Fd Co, RE

HMS Firedrake
HMS Gibraltar
HMS Royal Arthur

XXIV BDE, RFA

0   50
Miles

I

Geoffrey Robinson
to Charles à C. Repington

The Times

[Carbon]   2 July 1913

I am so much obliged to you for finding out that information for my young soldier friend. Your meeting with the Defence Committee yesterday must have been an amusing affair.[1]

I am rather concerned about the growing effect of the Government's Irish policy on the moral of the Army, and incidentally, of course, on the other public services. So far as one can foresee the Government is not sufficiently fatuous to allow the thing to come to actual fighting, but it looks as if they might come very near it. Meanwhile, I hear already of officers preparing to go and fight for Ulster, and others preparing to send in their papers and get out of the whole business, and of others arguing that it is the business of a soldier to obey constituted authority, and that this is not the hundredth case when rebellion is justified. No doubt the majority are still unmoved and trust vaguely that some sort of settlement will be reached. But I cannot help feeling that the kind of conversation which is going on in messes must be extremely prejudicial to the best interests of the Army, and I contemplate an article pointing this out.[2] What do you think about it?

The Times, Dawson/Repington Mss

33

2

Charles à C. Repington
to Geoffrey Robinson

Maryon Hall,
Hampstead.

[Holograph]   3 July 1913

I am also concerned about Ulster & the Army. I know that many officers will *wish* to resign, & that some NCO's are talking of refusing to fight against Loyalists, and, if blood be spilled, I have no doubt that there will be great indignation & that a very serious feeling will be aroused.

I have no doubt that our line ought to be to deprecate in the strongest manner any inconsiderate and hasty action on the part of officers in the Army. We can sympathise with them, share their indignation, and throw the whole onus of any trouble upon the Government. But we should, I think, in a temperate but firm manner, hold up the maintenance of discipline as the first duty of the corps of officers, and even suggest that disciplinary measures will have to be taken against any who desire to retire for the purpose of aiding Ulster in resisting the law. We *dare not* admit politics to the Army, and I think that you should make a special appeal to regimental feeling and invite senior officers to set an example & to repress at the first symptom not only any rash dispositions on the part of officers, but also any conversations & tendencies which might lead the younger hotheads astray. The firmest discipline that we have is that of the regiment, & if this goes all else goes with it. We must have no compromise with illegality on the part of the Army. It might be the end of us.

The Times, Dawson/Repington Mss

3
Notes by Brigadier-General J. E. Gough on 'Home Rule'

[Holograph]   September to December 1913

The following incidents are of interest and are perhaps worth putting on paper.

In Sept (1913). I heard from Sir W. Robertson (who had been a good deal with the King during the Army manoeuvres)[3] that he wanted to speak to me about the attitude of the Army as regards Ulster.

I saw Robertson at the War Office, he told me that Lord Stamfordham (The King's Private Secretary) wished to see an officer who could give him a sober opinion, and that he (Robertson) had suggested my name. I was asked to write to Lord S and arrange an interview. This I did with the result that I went to Buckingham Palace about the middle of October.

I was shown into Lord S's room where I found Lord S. He was very nice, offered me a chair & drew up one for himself & said he had been told that I would give him a straight and valuable opinion as to the probable attitude of the Army in the event of it being employed to coerce Ulster.

I said that this was a difficult question to answer as it depended upon how the situation presented itself at the moment, & more especially on the attitude of Ulster. If Ulster had put herself in the wrong by a popular outburst in the form of rioting or attacks on convents etc., then many officers would no doubt obey any orders that the government might issue. If, however, Ulster maintained a fairly correct attitude, & her leaders kept their men in control— then I thought many officers would refuse to serve against Ulster & a certain number would actually join the Ulster forces. At the same time, I added, much depended upon the lead given by senior officers, & my impression was that the lead would be forthcoming and I thought that perhaps as many as 40% to 60% of the Officers would refuse to serve.

Lord S said that the situation was undoubtedly critical & it was his business to try and get at the facts of the case, he did not know what the government might try to do, but he hoped & trusted that a compromise would be effected & matters not pushed to extremes. He said he found it very difficult to even talk to the King about the possible attitude of the Army as it was terrible even to think that the Army might refuse to obey orders & what the ultimate result might be.

I said I agreed but the blame could not be attached to the Army, but must be borne by the government which could issue orders so repugnant to the feelings of the Officers. The Officers & the Army were more loyal to the King & were prepared to sacrifice more for the Empire than any other body of men in the British Empire. People like myself felt strongly on the question of Ulster, and speaking for myself my reasons were three.

(1). I wanted a loyal government. Loyal to King and Empire. But the Nationalist party would not be loyal. We know what they had said & done as regards the King & late Queen—and what their attitude had always been to England's enemies & specially during the S.A. war. The idea of these disloyal men becoming our rulers was an outrage to every decent feeling I possessed.

(2). I wanted a clean government—one which would rule for the good of the country & in which the government officials would be upright & honest. I was firmly convinced that the Nationalist party would not give us a clean government, but instead we would have corruption & graft, & probably the country would be inundated with unscrupulous Irish American low class politicians.

(3). I could not tolerate the possibility of having a priest-ridden government. No matter whether the priest were Roman Catholic—Protestant—Mahomedans or Hindus. Knowing the Irish priesthood as I do I had little doubt that religious beliefs would enter into politics and administration.

I pointed out that as far as I understood history, these three questions roused human passions more than anything else, & that as far as I was concerned I was prepared to assist Ulster by *every* means in my power—always provided Ulster did not put herself out of court by committing atrocities or something outrageous. I laid stress on the fact that my whole life & ambitions had practically been limited to thoughts for my family, my country & the army & it was a bitter blow to find myself forced into the present position, but I had thought out the question and had no doubt in my own mind that I had come to the correct & honourable position. I had every reason to believe that many officers thought as I did.

I ended up by saying that I spoke freely & frankly because I thought it the right thing to do, as one of the most serious aspects of the situation was the possible belief by those in authority that no-one was prepared to do more than talk, and also I understood Lord Stamfordham wished me to speak quite frankly. I added that I realised that what I had said might affect my career but that I made no secret of my views. I however avoided saying anything in the Army which would tell against discipline, but at the same time officers in the Army were seriously uneasy & the Irish question was the subject of constant discussion. I pointed out that the objection was not that officers objected to Home Rule qua Home Rule, if there was a reasonable prospect of an Irish government being loyal, honest & not priest-ridden then Ireland might have Home Rule tomorrow for all I cared.

Lord Stamfordham thanked me and said that he hoped nothing would occur which would necessitate my services being lost to the army or the country. He added 'I do not want to flatter you but I can honestly say that it would be a serious loss.'

When I said goodbye I told Lord S that I had been asked by someone (Princess Alexander of Teck)[4] why I did not resign if I felt so strongly on the matter? My answer was that I saw no reason why I should throw up my career because an injustice *might* be done, I preferred to wait until the injustice had actually been done, but that I made no secret of my intentions. He said he understood & thought I was right.

During the manoeuvres in September 1913 I spoke quite

frankly to Sir Spencer Ewart & Sir D. Haig. The former appeared to sympathise with my views, while Sir D. Haig struck me as anxious to avoid discussing the subject and not to realise that Ulster was in earnest.

In Oct. 1913 I spoke to Prince Alexander[5] & the Princess and told them what I proposed to do. The Prince agreed & spoke bitterly of the present government. The Princess also spoke bitterly about the government but said that I ought to resign. I answered her as stated above.

On the 27th December 1913. Sir H. Rawlinson told me that Lord Roberts wished to speak to me about the Army & Ulster. This I take it was the result of Rawlinson & Henry Wilson repeating some remarks I had made to them a few days previously.[6]

I went to Englemere & Lord R. had a talk to me. I told him practically what I had told Lord Stamfordham. He said he agreed but thought it premature for him to take any immediate action. He said that he had written a letter to Bonar Law when the latter was at Sandringham & the letter had been shown to the King. In the letter Lord R had said that the Army could not be asked to coerce the King's friends against disloyal nationalists & that the Army would refuse to obey such an order or at any rate a large proportion of the Army would refuse. The result to the Empire might well be absolutely disastrous. Lord R. said that he had made up his mind as to his action, he proposed to wait until the Home Rule Bill had been passed by the House of Commons, when (if ever) this happened, he (Lord R) would write direct to the King & tell him that the Army could not be used without disaster, & to urge the King to refuse to sign the bill. Lord R. said that if things were brought to extremes, he for one would be in favour of actively assisting Ulster. He thought it would be a mistake for officers to resign when the bill passed the House of Commons, as the resignations would not be accepted & we would be no better off. If his letter to the King had no result then he was prepared to write an open letter to the papers.

I told Lord R that naturally his name and prestige would carry great weight with the Army & country, & that the Army was looking for a lead which no-one could give better than himself.

Lord R ended by saying that we ought to act together, but he trusted matters would be settled without coming to extremes.

J. E. Gough Mss

4

Field Marshal Sir John French
to Lord Stamfordham

[Holograph]

94 Lancaster Gate, W.
25 September 1913

1) I have received verbal commands from the King to place before His Majesty in writing, through you, and without reference to any other person whatsoever, my personal views as to the effect which would be produced in the Army if the Troops were called upon to oppose an Armed Resistance by Ulster to Home Rule. I was asked by His Majesty to observe the utmost secrecy in carrying out these instructions and this command has been strictly complied with.

2) I believe the spirit of discipline which permeates throughout all ranks of His Majesty's Troops to be of the highest order. They would as a body obey unflinchingly & without question the absolute commands of the King no matter what their private opinions might be.

If this spirit did not form the foundation of the whole military structure the Army would be unreliable and unfit for the purposes for which it exists.

3) Men however are only mortal and I have no hesitation in saying that the discipline of His Majesty's Troops would be subjected to a great strain if they were called upon to fire on men who are not only their Compatriots but are flying their own flag which is indeed the emblem of their aspiration.

Whether in flying that flag, and taking up this attitude the Ulster men would have public right & reason on their side is a matter of opinion, but the arguments in favour of such a view must infallibly impress themselves on the minds of a large proportion of any given body of thinking people.

4) Whilst then I think that the precept enunciated in the 2nd paragraph of this letter is absolutely vital to the existence of an efficient Army, I feel given there are many good officers & men, not possessing any logical minds, who would be led to think they were best serving their King & country either by refusing to march against the Ulster men or openly joining their ranks.

5) From this consideration I draw the conclusion that whilst the Army as a whole would obey, without hesitation, the orders of the King, its discipline would be subjected to a severe trial and there would be larger or smaller defections from its ranks, both of officers & men.

There can be no doubt that Troops required for such service would have to be very carefully chosen.

6) It is because I have strongly felt these apprehensions, that I have from the first advocated dealing with such cases of defection as have hitherto arisen in a drastic manner in order to impress upon all serving officers the necessity for abstaining from any political controversy.

RA GV K. 2553(2)/35; IWM, 75/46/8. French Mss

5
Extracts from the Diary of
Major-General H. H. Wilson

[Holograph]   4 November 1913

Sir John [French] had a long talk with me about Ulster. He is evidently nervous that we are coming to civil war, and his attitude appears to be that he will obey the King's orders. He wanted to know what I would do. I told him that I could not fire on the North at the dictation of Redmond, and this is what the whole thing means. England *qua* England is opposed to Home Rule, and England must agree to it before it is carried out. I was much struck by his seriousness. I cannot bring myself to believe that Asquith will be so mad as to employ force. It will split the Army and the colonies, as well as the country and the Empire.

9 November 1913

I went to see Bonar Law at $\frac{1}{4}$ to 10 this morning & spent $1\frac{1}{2}$ hours with him. He was quite charming to me. I told him that there was much talk in the Army, and that if we were ordered to coerce Ulster there would be wholesale defection. He fully realised this and told me Stamfordham had been to see him yesterday & had said that in his opinion 40 pc. of officers and men would leave the Army. Personally I put the pc. much *lower*, but still very serious. I then told him of Cecil's[7] idea that Carson should pledge the Ulster troops to fight for England if she was at war. I pointed out that a move like this would render the imployment [sic] of force against Ulster more impossible than ever. He was much pleased with the suggestion and at once tried to get Carson on the telephone. He was, however, away for the day. Bonar Law will see him tomorrow.

13 November 1913

This evening about 6 o'c. I went in to see Macready. He told me he was being sent over to Ireland on Sunday, ostensibly to see after the riots, etc, in Dublin, in reality to watch the North. He told me the Cabinet have settled not to try to imploy troops, as they realise at last the temper of Ulster and the Army. They are afraid of a Jameson raid on some depot. I told him there was not the least danger, and that on the contrary the North was probably going to offer her army to England if in difficulties. We discussed other points, but the really important thing is that the Govt. at last realize that they cannot imploy the Army in this work.

14 November 1913

Charlie Hunter[8] and I dined with Milner at Brooks'. Milner was emphatic in support of Ulster and said that the Unionists of England would soon have to pass from words to deeds. One of the first declarations to be made would be that, if any officer resigned, they would be reinstated when the Conservatives came into power. I was glad to hear all this.

2 December 1913

I lunched with Fred Oliver. I impressed on him the irreparable damage which the present state of affairs is doing to the Army, & the necessity of ending the disgraceful state we are in. He was fully swayed. There is no time to be lost. Already all recruits are talking in a hostile manner of being imployed agt. the north of Ireland. This questioning of orders is something quite new, if very natural in the circumstances, in our Army & is a great & pressing danger. Something must be done to end the present tension—& quickly. Oliver thinks he may be able to bring both sides together through hard talking. I hope he may.

26 December 1913

Rawly,[9] Johnnie Gough & I round the Swinley links[10] before lunch.

After lunch a short walk with the Chief.[11] I told him that we had had much talk in the morning with Johnnie Gough about Ulster, & that Johnnie had definitely made up his mind to join Ulster if the worst came.

The Chief said what he proposed to do: When the Bill had passed the Commons he was going to the King to tell him the effect on the Army, & that unless the King told him definitely that he was going to refuse to sign the bill, he (the Chief) was going to write to the papers & point out that the bill had been passed whilst the constitution was in abeyance and by the vote of the Irish who never lost an opportunity of dividing the Army & churning its waters & therefore no officer or man ought to demean himself by obeying orders to coerce Ireland. He is clear that no officer should send in his papers.

28 December 1913

We all went to 11 o'clock service. After that the Chief met an old man who was at Eton with him, Sir Charles Ryan, who told him he believed Asquith meant to imploy the Army agt Ulster.

After lunch the Chief went up to see Sir Charles & there he found Arthur Elliott who told him that Pope Hennessy[12] came to see him on Friday last [26 December] & told him that he had had 2 hours that day with Lord Morley & J. A. Spender in which he had had a most heated argument about the imployment of the Regulars agt Ulster which Hennessy said was impossible but which Morley said could & would be done & that the Army would do what it was told, & furthermore that the Cabinet could put pressure on the King to use his influence with the Army to carry out this work. This is *bad* news. I told the Chief that I thought he ought to see the King at once & warn him of what he was going to do (see 26th), but that he should first see Milner. This he will do on Tuesday next.

7 January 1914

Robertson, Joey,[13] and I had a long and serious talk about Ulster, and whether we could not do something to keep the Army out of it. We agreed to find out the feeling in Commands at the conference next week at Camberley.

12 January 1914

I am pleased with the attitude of those I have asked about Ulster & the feeling against the Government's policy.

IWM, DS/MISC/80, HHW 22, 23, Wilson diaries

6

Extracts from the Diary of
Lieutenant-General Sir John Spencer Ewart

[Holograph]   14 November 1913

Meeting of the Selection Board. Afterwards Sir Arthur Paget came to see me about Ireland. He told me that both his divisional Generals[14] thought that 25 per cent of the officers in Ireland would resign if there was any question of coercing Ulster. He himself put it at 15 per cent. He said that is was impossible to forecast what the men would do. The situation is getting very grave in Ireland and we are within sight of civil war; but I still hope and believe that some solution of the difficulty will be found. The industrial trouble in Dublin gets no better; it has now gone on for some weeks. Macready goes tomorrow to Ireland to make some private enquiries for Seely into the situation.

21 November 1913

All political interest seems now centred on the Ulster question which to my mind can only be solved peaceably by some arrangement for the separate treatment or exclusion of Ulster. The discipline of the Army is being sadly undermined by all the wild talk which is going on. Lord Wolseley[15] was quite right when he said that the coercion of Ulster would shake the discipline of the Army to its foundations.

16 December 1913

Selection Board, Afterwards Seely spoke privately to all the C in Chiefs about the state of discipline in the Army and all the loose talk which is going on in clubs and messes about the Ulster crisis.[16] A great deal of harm has already been done to the discipline of the Army and I wish the Government would find some solution of the difficulty. French and I were present and afterwards we all lunched with Seely at the Marlborough Club.

SRO, RH4/84/3, 126, Ewart Mss

7

Lieutenant Colonel de la Panouse to the French Minister of War Eugène Etienne

22 November 1913

Le Home Rule et l'armée anglaise

La question du 'Home Rule' qui va entrer prochainement dans une phase décisive, peut avoir, du point de vue militaire de graves conséquences, au cas où l'armée serait appelée à réprimer des désordres dans le Nord de l'Irlande.

L'imminence du vote de la loi a provoqué depuis quelques mois, dans l'Ulster, la formation, sous les auspices de Sir Edw. CARSON, député unioniste de Belfast l'organisation de forces insurrectionnelles, qui se disent prêtes à entrer en action . . . et chose curieuse, dans ce mouvement d'opposition au Home Rule, les non-conformistes qui votent pour les Libéraux, marchent d'accord avec les Anglicans Unionistes . . . Il est fort probable que ces hommes armés se livreront à des désordres, à des violences contre les catholiques, et que alors le Gouvernement sera obligé de rétablir l'ordre. Dans ce cas, comme la gendarmerie et la police seront vraisemblablement insuffisantes, il devra faire appel à l'Armée.

Que feront les officiers? Ceux-ci sont en très grande majorité protestants et unionistes, et ils sont de coeur avec l'opposition dans sa résistance au Home Rule. Un certain nombre d'entre eux se sont déjà préoccupés du rôle qu'ils auraient à jouer. Plusieurs ont manifesté devant leurs supérieurs hiérarchiques leur intention de démissionner dès maintenant de manière à ne pas être mis dans l'alternative ou de marcher contre leurs amis de l'Ulster, ou de refuser d'obéir à un ordre. Un Officier Général que je connais a donné à ses subordonnés le conseil de n'en rien faire, et d'attendre les événements. On estime à 15 ou 20% . . ., la proportion des officiers qui semblent résolus à donner leur démission lors qu'ils recevront l'ordre de partir pour l'Ulster.

Parmi eux figurent tous les officiers originaires de cette province qui à elle seule fournit presque tout le contingent des officiers Irlandais de l'Armée.* Des polémiques de presse ont eu lieu, sur le droit qu'a un officier de donner sa démission au moment où il reçoit un ordre. D'après les règlements militaires une démission n'est pas acceptée dans ces conditions, et je sais confidentiellement que le Secrétaire d'Etat à la Guerre ne cache pas son intention d'agir avec la dernière sévérité contre les officiers qui ne marcheraient pas et démissionneraient en masse. Le Général Sir A. PAGET, qui commande en chef en Irlande, a eu des entrevues avec M. ASQUITH et lui a rendu compte de la situation.

Sir A. PAGET est d'ailleurs tout-à-fait l'homme qui convient en ce moment pour commander l'armée en Irlande. S'il est médiocre tacticien aux manoeuvres, il est en revanche très énergique; sa grande situation sociale, les sympathies qu'il compte en haut lieu, lui assurent une grande indépendance et aussi une grande autorité. Il est probable que, dans des circonstances graves, il agirait avec autant de tact que de vigueur.

Néanmoins je suis convaincu que le Gouvt., se rendant compte des conséquences désastreuses qu'auraient pour l'armée la démission en masse d'une notable partie des chefs, hésitera à faire appel à elle. Le vote du Home Rule est fatal pour sauver le principe, mais le Cabinet évitera de l'appliquer immédiatement, et gagnera du temps . . .

. . . Il paraît certain qu'il [Asquith] ne fera intervenir la troupe Régulière qu'à la dernière extrémité. Mêler la troupe à une guerre civile et religieuse serait préparer la ruine non pas seulement de l'armée mais aussi de l'Empire Britannique.

Je n'ai jusqu' ici parlé que de l'attitude du Corps d'Officiers; celle de la troupe sera exactement la même que celle des chefs. Cela tient en grande partie au particularisme régimentaire, qui a créé dans les régiments Britanniques un esprit de corps plus puissant que partout ailleurs.

* Les familles catholiques Irlandaises n'ont pas la fortune nécessaire pour envoyer leurs fils dans l'armée.

Vincennes, Etat-Major de L'Armée de Terre, Box 7N1228, 248

8

Brigadier-General J. E. Gough
to F. S. Oliver

Blandford House,
Farnborough.
[Holograph]   1 December 1913

I have just finished 'The Alternatives to Civil War'.[17] I know you have been innundated with congratulations about it. It was a real pleasure to read & what is much rarer it should do some practical good. I was delighted to see your reference to the Army on page 56 — it is high time that people like yourelf spoke up on this question. No one can, of course, say what the Army will do — it depends upon the attitude of Ulster & how the problem presents itself at the moment. But unless Ulster does something outrageous (which is improbable), the Army will not help to coerce the loyal Unionists — at least it means the break up of the Army & goodness knows what the end of that would be.

My own point of view, which is shared by many others, is that there is nothing very terrible in Home Rule qua Home Rule. But we want a loyal Government — that is to say men at the head of the affairs who are loyal to the King and to the Empire. This we know we would not get as long as the present crowd of disloyal agitators are at the head of the Irish Home Rule party.

We want a clean Government. This we know we would not get under present conditions.

We want to be certain that religion (Roman Catholic or any other) will not enter into politics or the Government of the country. This we feel cannot be guaranteed under present conditions.

All good wishes & again best congratulations. We hope you will be able to look us up here before long.

NLS, Acc 7726/95, f 176–177, Oliver Mss

9
Colonel W. T. Furse to F. S. Oliver

1 Park View,
Cork.
2 December 1913

[Holograph]

I have just finished the 'Alternatives'.

Bravo! out & away the soberest and soundest appreciation of the situation I have seen.

It makes me thank God that you have made yourself such a position that the politicians on both sides will at least read the pamphlet and will—must—feel some uneasiness for an hour or two even if they do return to their wretched game of Pot and Kettle.

Lord! how wearisome and futile their game is!

I hate the official Unionist game almost as much as I do the Radical. As a soldier (by profession, if not by instinct) I loathe the way they are trying their best to tamper with the discipline of the Army by exploiting the traditional Unionist color—sheeplike, unthinking—of the commissioned ranks.

I agree with every word of Asquith's rebuke to Lansdowne at Leeds.

The real danger is, and has been for long, the fact that each side is acting on the assumption that the other is bluffing and that the surest way of exposing the other's bluff is to continue on his own course without any sign of flinching. At the same time neither thinks that he will really be put to the test.

Before the crisis is reached there is the danger that the desire on each side to show that we can stick it longer than the other fellow will even outweigh the wish to avoid bloodshed. This may even infect a certain number of officers.

My own belief is that though many officers talk Unionist in mess rooms and smoking rooms, there are precious few who sympathise with Ulstermen sufficiently to make them chuck their commissions and their pensions rather than obey orders to keep the peace.

That there are *some* I do not doubt for a moment.

The men, too, will do what they are told by their officers.

Even George Richardson wouldn't accept the post of C. in Chief—so I understand—until he was guaranteed his existing pension.

I trust your noble effort will bear good fruit. Bless you, anyhow, for being such a good tryer.

NLS, Acc 7726/95, f 179–182, Oliver Mss

10

Memorandum by J. E. B. Seely

[Printed with holograph additions]

War Office[18]
9 December 1913

'Position of the Army with Regard to the Situation in Ulster'

I saw Lord Stamfordham today, and told him that I should be glad if he would communicate to the King the decisions to which I had come with regard to the Army and the Ulster question.

The position was as follows:

Sir John French, as Chief of the Imperial General Staff, had constantly begged me to take drastic action against any officer or man who, by the spoken or by the written word, had suggested the possibility of disobeying an executive order; indeed, he had urged me to cashier the eccentric Captain Spender[19] in August of last year 'pour décourager les autres'. This, in my view, was the correct attitude for the principal soldier of the Army to take up, but the Secretary of State had also to bear in mind the legal position.

The law clearly lays down that a soldier is entitled to obey an order to shoot only if that order is reasonable under the circumstances. No one, from General Officer to private, is entitled to use more force than is required to maintain order and the safety of life and property. No soldier can shelter himself [from the civil law] behind an order given by a superior if that order is in fact unreasonable and outrageous.

If, therefore, officers and men in the Army were led to believe that there was a possibility that they might be called upon to take some outrageous action, for instance, to massacre a demonstration of Orangemen who were causing no danger to the lives of their neighbours, bad as was the effects on discipline in the Army, nevertheless it was true that they were in fact and in law justified in contemplating refusal to obey.

The situation was clear. Apart from the Prime Minister's public declarations making it abundantly plain that there was much common ground between the two parties, and much reason to hope for a peaceful settlement, [but] there never had been, and was not now, any intention of giving outrageous and illegal orders to the troops [deleted—to crush helpless Ulstermen by shrapnel fire]. The law would be respected and must be obeyed.

What had now to be faced was the possibility of action being required by His Majesty's troops in supporting the civil power in protecting life and property where the police were unable to hold their own. This action, in my view, was quite as likely to be wanted in England as in any part of Ireland in the immediate future; there had been attempts [deleted—by Socialists on the one hand and by unbalanced persons like Rowland Hunt on the other] to dissuade troops from obeying lawful orders given to them when supporting the civil power. This amounted to a suggestion that officers or men could pick and choose between lawful and reasonable orders, saying that in one case they would obey and not in another.

[Deleted—e.g. one man would say he would shoot an Ulsterman, but not Trade Unionist or a Socialist: another would shoot a Trade Unionist or a Socialist, but not an Ulsterman: another would shoot a Socialist, but not an Ulsterman or a Trade Unionist.]

Such a state of affairs would, of course, be impossible. The Army had been quite steady. During the past year there had not been brought to the notice of the authorities one single case of lack of discipline in this respect.

At the same time; in view of statements in the press and the public utterance of persons who ought to have known better, it was well to make the position clear.

I had arranged that the Commanders-in-Chief should attend in my room next Tuesday. I would then inform them that I would hold each of them individually responsible to see that there was no conduct in their commands subversive of discipline.

They would let it be clearly understood that any such conduct would be dealt with forthwith under the King's Regulations. If an officer should tender his resignation they would ask for the reasons, and if he indicated in his reply that he desired to choose which order he would obey I would at once submit to the King that the officer should be cashiered ['removed' substituted for cashiered].

PRO, Cab 37/117/87; Bodleian, Ms Asquith 40, f l; Nuffield College, Ms Mottistone 22, f 150–161; RA GV F. 674/13

II

W. McDowell, R. Shields and 'Ulstermen in India' to the editor of the Belfast Weekly News[20]

[Holograph Copy]

Gough Barracks,
Secunderabad.

By request of the Loyal Ulstermen of 1st Battalion, Royal Inniskilling Fusiliers we have commenced a collection in aid of the 'Ulster Defence Fund' and send as our first donation the sum of £18.6s.8d.

Though serving beyond the seas, we follow with the keenest interest the volunteer movement in Ulster, & time-expired men going home this trooping season are looking forward to taking their place in the ranks with their fellow countrymen. 'The Flag must be kept flying', & the motto of 'No Surrender' upheld. Those who will still be serving their King in India, & cannot go home for some years, sincerely hope that Ulster will win, & nothing will shake their loyalty to the Union. We are sorry we could not send a larger donation, but we hope to do better next time.

H. of Lords RO, Bonar Law Mss, 31/2/16; NAM, 7101-23-202, Roberts Mss

12

Note on a meeting between Lord Morley and Major L. H. R. Pope-Hennessy

[Holograph]   26 December 1913

In January[21] an officer met Lord Morley at luncheon & warned him what would be the result of the Government attempting to coerce Ulster. He described himself as a Roman Catholic, a Liberal & Home Ruler, but he said that he was also a soldier & he repeated his warning that the Govt. would split the Army in two—Lord Morley refused to believe this but added that in the event of the officers refusing to fight the men would. The officer, astounded at such a statement, asked him whom he considered that the men took their orders from and asked him if, in the event of very senior officers feeling it their duty to resign & go and fight for Ulster, how many soldiers would fight against them. Lord Morley was staggered for a moment but fell back on the announcement that the Government must be obeyed.

The officer came away from the luncheon with a feeling of despair that he had been talking to a man who would not face or see facts & as he said himself, as if he had been arguing with a Robespierre.

NAM, 7101-23-202, Roberts Mss; H. of Lords R.O., Bonar Law Mss, 31/2/16

13

Extracts from the Diary of L. S. Amery

[Holograph]   5 January 1914

Lunched with Henry Wilson at White's. He was very pessimistic about the whole political situation and above all anxious that the Army should not be drawn in. At the same time he was convinced that nothing would induce Asquith to listen to reason except a big stick. His view was that years of too good living, bridge etc. had made him quite incapable of any real decision, at any rate that was the impression that he received at the Defence Committee, and therefore he was certain that he would drift where Redmond and his party pushed him till the crisis came. We discussed the possibility of the Territorials doing something that would make the Government realise the situation, e.g. transferring themselves bodily to a Union Defence Force. Lord Roberts, he told me, was tremendously keen and prepared to go to any length if the situation demanded it.

17 January 1914

Unfolded Milner's views to Bobs[22] who was of course thoroughly in sympathy. He is in a great state about the effect of the whole thing on the Army and is prepared to do almost anything. The only thing really is to prevent him from using his great name except in the most effective fashion. I spent a good part of Sunday drawing up a memorandum for him starting off with the closing sentences of Bonar Law's Bristol speech which was really a veiled invitation to the Party to take up the sort of scheme we were at.

Amery Mss

14
Lord Milner to Field Marshal Lord Roberts

47 Duke Street,
London SW.
[Holograph]   6 March 1914

If you will send the £5 to me, I will pay it over, &, should you desire it, send a receipt to the donor. In that case please let me have his name.

The Covenant is going on efficiently all over the country.

There is one point which rather bothers us: a good many Territorial officers, *wanting very much to sign*, are uneasy, whether doing so would not be inconsistent with holding a commission. I think a letter from you would go far to dispel their doubts, &, in order not to let you get on to at all doubtful ground, we have consulted George Cave (H.C.M.P.),[23] about the best & most respected lawyer in the House. He has drafted the enclosed letter which with your permission I should like to give to the Press. The whole is Cave's actual words, with the exception of the phrase I have underlined, wh. of course Cave could not say about himself, though I have no hesitation in saying it of him.

If you agree, would you mind sending me a telegram to this address. It is important, if possible, to get it out quickly. I have kept a duplicate so that, the moment I have your permission, it can be given to the Press.

NAM, 7101-23-45, 129, Roberts Mss; Bodleian, Ms Milner 16, f 217

15

Draft of a letter to be published by Field Marshal Lord Roberts

7 March 1914
[Holograph Draft]   (published 9 March 1914)

The British Covenant: Earl Roberts and the Territorials

F. M. Earl Roberts has sent the following reply to a correspondent who desired his advice as to whether Territorials could properly sign the British Covenant:
Dear Sir,

In answer to your enquiry, I am advised on high authority that the British Covenant cannot possibly be held to conflict with the military duty of any officer or man of the Territorial Force. A member of that Force, when on duty, is of course subject to military law with its special and paramount obligations; but, at all other times, he retains the rights of an ordinary citizen, and in that capacity he is entitled to complete freedom of action.
Yours very faithfully,
Roberts.

Bodleian, Ms Milner 16, f 222; *Hansard* 5s, H. of C., LX, 908

16

Field Marshal Lord Roberts to H. H. Asquith

Englemere,
Ascot.
[Holograph Copy]
20 March 1914

I am unwilling to trouble you with a letter at a time of great political tension, and I certainly would not do so were it not that the matter about which I desire to write to you is one of such vital urgency as to impel me to bring it to your notice without further delay.

The statements made by yourself and your colleagues in Parliament and elsewhere show clearly that you contemplate using the forces of the Crown for the purpose of compelling the Ulster Unionists to submit to Home Rule. Having an intimate knowledge of the Army and being in close touch with British officers in all parts of the Empire, I have no hesitation in telling you that any attempt of this kind would place an intolerable strain on the discipline of the Army, and would produce within it a state of demoralisation from which it would, in my opinion, never recover.

It is certain that Civil War, or, as you call it, 'Civil Commotion', cannot be confined to Ulster, nor to Ireland nor to Great Britain. It is also certain we shall have outbreaks of violence in many of our large towns. The effect in India, where the present conditions are full of anxiety, may be incalculable, and it is at least conceivable that some European Power might take advantage of our domestic difficulties to say insulting things, or even to push inadmissible claims at a moment when we should be powerless to resist them. The officers and men of the Army are under no misapprehension as to the gravity of the situation, they are amongst the most loyal and law-abiding of any of His Majesty's subjects, but they are also intelligent men, and they realise to the full that, no matter under what legal guise the order may be given to them, they may be asked to shoot down fellow-countrymen who, like themselves, would be fighting under the Union Jack, and also, like themselves, would go to their death singing 'God Save the King'. And, please remember, as our soldiers will remember, that all this will seem to them to be done at the bidding of men who have never missed an opportunity of slandering and vilifying the Army in the grossest manner.

The officers and men of the Army are not politicians, and never concern themselves with the fate of Parties, and this very fact prevents their minds being obscured by Party cries and Party tactics, and allows them to see the true state of affairs.

So certain am I of what will happen should you make this demand upon the Army, that I entreat you to pause before taking so fatal a step.

NAM, 7101-23-202, Roberts Mss; H. of Lords RO, Bonar Law Mss, 32/2/47; RA GV F. 674/3

17
R. H. Brade to
Lieutenant-General Sir Arthur Paget

War Office
[Printed]   14 March 1914

I am commanded by the Army Council to inform you that, in consequence of reports which have been received by His Majesty's Government, that attempts may be made in various parts of Ireland by evil-disposed persons to obtain possession of arms, ammunition, and other Government stores, it is considered advisable that you should at once take special precautions for safeguarding depots and other places where arms or stores are kept, as you may think advisable.

It appears from the information received that Armagh, Omagh, Carrickfergus and Enniskillen are insufficiently guarded, being specially liable to attack. You will, therefore, please to take the necessary steps and report to this office.

Officers in command of all barracks where guns, small arms, ammunition, and other Government stores are located should be warned that they will be held responsible for all measures to ensure the safety of the stores, &c. under their custody are taken, and that at no time should barracks or buildings be left without adequate armed guards.

I am glad to add that although certain places have been specifically referred to above, the intention is that no steps should be omitted to ensure the safety of Government arms and stores in the South as well as in the North of Ireland.

White paper; Nuffield College, Ms Mottistone 22, f 197; Bodleian, Ms Asquith 40 f 5–6; PRO Cab. 37/119/44; Ibid, WO 35/209 (a)

18

Lieutenant-General Sir Arthur Paget
to R. H. Brade

Parkgate,
Dublin.

[Printed]   17 March 1914

1. In reply to War Office confidential letter dated 14 March 1914, I have the honour to inform you that in accordance with the instructions contained in that letter special precautions are now being taken to ensure the safety of Government arms and stores in this Command.

2. As regards the four places specifically mentioned, it is pointed out that:
   (a) Enniskillen is guarded by a company of the Infantry Battalion in Londonderry.
   (b) Carrickfergus is guarded by a small detachment from the Infantry battalion at Holywood, and this detachment will now be increased.
   (c) At Armagh and Omagh steps are being taken to remove reserve arms and ammunition to Dublin and Enniskillen respectively. This will take about eight days to do, and in the meantime the Commanding Officers are taking special precautions with the troops available at these depots to ensure their safety.

3. It would be preferable from the point of view of safety only to provide guards at once for Armagh and Omagh from the Infantry battalion at Mullingar, and to evacuate the recruits at these places; but in the present state of the country, I am of the opinion that any such move of troops would create intense excitement in Ulster and possibly precipitate a crisis. For these reasons I do not consider myself justified in moving troops at the present time, although I am keeping a sufficient number in readiness to move at short notice in case the situation should develop into a more dangerous state.
I would, however, point out that there is no Intelligence Service

in this Command, and that all the reliable political information is received by me at second hand, so that I am placed at a considerable disadvantage in attempting to judge the urgency of the situation and to foresee possible dangers in time to act.

White Paper; *Hansard* 5 s, H. of C. LX, 1372

19
H. H. Asquith to King George V

[Holograph Copy]

10 Downing Street.
18 March 1914

Mr. Asquith, with his humble duty to Your Majesty, has the honour to report that the Cabinet met yesterday.

It was agreed that Thursday should be given to Mr. Bonar Law for the discussion of the motion of censure, of which he has given notice.

The Committee appointed at the last meeting to consider the military situation in the North of Ireland made a preliminary report. They had come to the conclusion that the depots of arms & ammunition at Armagh, Omagh, Enniskillen, & Carrickfergus might easily be rushed, & instructions had been sent by the War Office to Sir A. Paget to have these places adequately protected by armed guards. They were also strongly of the opinion that whatever additional force might eventually be needed should be supplied not by mobilisation & the calling up of reservists, but by the movement of Troops from Great Britain.

The Cabinet after discussion approved these conclusions. The figures furnished by Colonel Seely show that there are at present about 23,000 regular troops in Ireland, of whom a little over 9,000 were quartered in the Province of Ulster.

The First Lord of the Admiralty stated that the forthcoming practice of the 1st Battle Squadron would take place at Lamlash. The Admiral Commanding in Irish waters has already taken precautions for the protection of coast guard stations. A cruiser will be stationed at or near Carrickfergus, & 2 or 3 Destroyers sent to the South of Ireland.

As a precautionary measure it was resolved that the Constabulary in the Province of Ulster, who are scattered in very small detachments over the countryside, should be placed under the authority of a single Commanding Officer at Belfast, & that arrangements should be made that, upon the necessity arising & the signal, they should forthwith concentrate at 5 or 6 important centres, to be determined after consultation with the military authorities.

Bodleian, Ms Asquith 7, f 105–106

20
Note by J. E. B. Seely

[Holograph]

War Office
18 March 1914

At a meeting held in the Secretary of State's room at the War Office, it was decided that the following precautionary measures should be carried out at once.

I) Troops should be sent to reinforce Omagh, Armagh, Enniskillen, Dundalk and Carrickfergus [Prime Minister decided 'yes' to move Friday night].

II) The troops at present in Belfast should be moved to Holywood. [Yes—leaving an adequate guard to move Friday night.]

III) A ship should be sent to Carrickfergus [Yes—also to Dundalk and Derry to move Friday night].

In the event of any overt hostile act two further steps should be taken.

I) A Military Governor of Belfast should be appointed and might possibly be given jurisdiction over the whole of Ulster.

II) Three General Staff Officers to be sent over for Intelligence purposes and possibly given some secret service money to spend.

[General Macready to be appointed Military Governor of Belfast (carrying his commission with him and announcing it when he considers best). To proceed to Holywood tomorrow night.]

Bodleian, Ms Asquith 40, f 8, 10

21
Note by J. E. B. Seely

[Holograph]

War Office
19 March 1914

At a meeting held at 10 Downing Street this afternoon it was decided that troops should be moved to reinforce Omagh, Armagh, Dundalk, Enniskillen and Carrickfergus, that the troops now in Belfast should be moved out to Holywood leaving an adequate guard (and that ships should be sent to Carrickfergus, Dundalk & Derry). The above moves to take place on Friday night.

Sir Nevil Macready to go to Belfast at once with a dormant commission to be used if & when he thinks necessary, appointing him Military Governor of Belfast.

Sir John French to select & send 3 General Staff Officers to Sir A. Paget for Intelligence purposes.

Bodleian, Ms Asquith 40, f 9

22
Note by J. E. B. Seely

[Holograph]

War Office
19 March 1914

I discussed the question of officers' resignations with CIGS, AG, and Sir A. Paget yesterday. Sir A. Paget strongly urged that in the few exceptional cases where officers have direct family connection with the disturbed area in Ulster, so that in the event of serious trouble arising their future private relations might be irretrievably compromised if they were engaged with our troops, they should be permitted to remain behind either on leave or with details. Sir John French and Sir Spencer Ewart having expressed their concurrence with this view it was decided that this course should be followed.

In all other cases Sir A. Paget wished to be able to say that any officer hesitating to comply with orders or threatening to resign should be removed. Sir John French was of opinion that such officers should be court-martialled, a view which he had urged upon me a year ago. Upon Sir Spencer Ewart pointing out the technical difficulties and delay that might be involved Sir John French agreed for the present that removal should be the course followed. Sir John French and Sir Spencer Ewart agree to this memorandum.

Bodleian, Ms Asquith 40, f 19

23

Extracts from the Diary of
Lieutenant-General Sir John Spencer Ewart

[Holograph]   17 March 1914

The Ulster Peril is coming upon us fast. In the morning Seely, Sir John French and I had a long talk in Seely's room on the situation.

18 March 1914

We had a conference at the War Office at 12 noon re Ulster crisis. There were present Colonel Seely, Sir John French, myself, Sir Nevil Macready, Earl of Crewe, Mr. Winston Churchill, Prince Louis of Battenberg, Mr. Birrell, Sir A. Paget and Mr. G. Nicholson. We decided on certain measures and movement of troops designed for the protection of barracks and depots where Arms, Ammunition and Mobilisation stores are collected. The conference was resumed at 6 p.m. in the Prime Minister's house, 10 Downing Street, where there were present: The Prime Minister, Colonel Seely, Mr. Lloyd George, Mr. Birrell, Sir A. Paget, Sir John French, self, Sir N. Macready, Mr. Winston Churchill. The whole Irish question was discussed; it was decided, inter alia, that Sir Nevil Macready was to proceed to Belfast to become, at the opportune moment, Military Governor of Belfast. Birrell undertook to put Commissioner Smith[24] and the RIC in Belfast under him. One of the battle squadrons is to proceed from Arosa Bay to Lamlash in Arran. The 'Pathfinder' and 'Attentive' (scouts) to Carrickfergus, two cruisers to Kingstown in case Northern Railway (in hands of Orangemen) should refuse to transport troops north.

19 March 1914

Conference re Ulster at War Office 6 p.m. to 8 p.m.; present Colonel Seely, Sir A. Paget, Sir John French, self, Mr. Winston Churchill & Prince Louis of Battenberg. Moves decided on: one battalion Curragh to Dundalk & Newry to protect Artillery Brigade at latter place. One company each of Bedfordshire Regiment from Mullingar to following: Carrickfergus, Omagh, Armagh, & Enniskillen to protect Arms and our Mobilisation stores. Macready was taken ill; too unwell to proceed tonight to Belfast. Maj. Gen. Friend will take his place there temporarily.

Great Ulster debate tonight in House of Commons. Carson left dramatically 'to join his own people' in Belfast. Rumours current that Government intended to arrest Ulster leader; no idea really of any such proceedings.

SRO, RH4/84/3, 126, Ewart Mss

24

Extracts from the Diary of
Major-General H. H. Wilson

[Holograph]   18 March 1914

Sir John sent for me after luncheon to talk about Ulster. He told me he had been discussing affairs all the morning at a meeting of Crewe, Seely, Winston, Birrell, Sir John, Ewart, Paget and Macready. It appears they are contemplating scattering troops all over Ulster, as though it was a Pontypool coal strike. Sir John pointed out that this was opposed to all true strategy, etc., but was told that the political situation necessitated this dispersion. He said that, as far as he could see, the Government were determined to see this thing through. He did not say when troops were to be sent. He asked whether the General Staff had done anything, and I replied that if we took it over it would fall to Robertson as Home Defence.

I then told him that in my opinion if the Government wanted to crush the North, they would have to mobilize the whole army, and that, even so, I had great doubts whether they could do it, as there would be serious work for troops in the rest of Ireland and also in the large towns of England, and that the Continent would not look on unmoved. Furthermore, there would be a large proportion of officers and men who would refuse to coerce Ulster.

He seemed surprised at all this. I told him the whole thing was a nightmare to me, and that I could not believe that the Government were so mad as to start this war. After I left him I began to think that I ought to have spoken more about his personal position as C.I.G.S. and his responsibility. I will see him tomorrow.

Later on Amery came to see me, and he is greatly impressed with the gravity of the situation. He also favours amending the Army Annual Act. Later I dined with Charlie Hunter, where were Milner, Doctor 'Jim',[25] and Carson. A long and most interesting talk. Carson says his speech tomorrow on the Vote of Censure will be his last in the House of Commons till after the Ulster question is settled. They all agree the Lords must amend the Army Annual Act.

19 March 1914

In the afternoon I had 1½ hours with Sir John, Robertson being present. I told him that I thought that the only possible way to coerce Ulster would be by mobilising the whole Army & that even then I much doubted if it could be done owing to the character & determination of the Ulstermen, the certainty of troops being required all over the north, & south and west, in the further certainty of riots in Liverpool, Manchester, Glasgow etc., then the hostility of the European Powers as well as the dangers in Egypt, India etc. Then serious disaffection in the Army, large numbers of officers & men leaving, & large p.c. of R & F refusing to rejoin.

I told Johnnie that I thought it would take 12 to 18 months to knock Ulster out; it will be the end of the Empire.

The Cabinet sure to think that they can settle the Ulster question as they would a coal strike. It is a profound mistake, & will lead to disaster. Sir John, I think, agreed with very little of what I said. He is absolutely 'snaffled' by this cursed Cabinet. I told him I thought of going to Belfast on Sunday. Incidentally, he told me that Seely had said at the Cabinet meeting yesterday that I had gone to Belfast last time on his instructions. What a liar.[26] At any rate I feel now that I have said all I can at this stage. I also told Sir John that the Cabinet must give Irish officers the option of not going over to coerce Ulster. He said he would put this & my other points before the Cabinet tomorrow.

The debate on vote of censure came off & Carson, after his speech, left the House.

Sir John had told me of some small moves of troops from Mullingar & Curragh towards the north & I tried to catch Carson when I got home at 7.30 but he had left for Belfast.

IWM, DS/MISC/80, HHW 23, Wilson Diary

25
Brigadier-General H. P. Gough to Brigadier-General J. E. Gough

Brownstown House
Curragh.
[Holograph]   19 March 1914

How goes prospects of Ulster & what is going to happen?
Things look grave.

We have been ordered to mount our sentries with Ball ammunition—to keep 10 rounds Ball per rifle in each Barrack room (same as in India)—& I have been ordered to Dublin to see the Chief (with Fergusson) tomorrow by the early train, & 'to come prepared to stay the night'.

I don't know what it means.

Small detachments are being dotted over Ulster I believe—& if Ulster takes up arms these detachments will certainly be eaten up. Such detachments, given this situation, are the worst possible policy & the poorest strategy.

As there is no question of fighting at present, I propose, as far as I can foresee my action at all, tomorrow, to quietly receive orders & carry them out. But what orders they can issue is difficult to conceive, except to dot squadrons about the country, & what good that will do, heaven only knows.

Past 11 p.m.
Just off to bed.

J. E. Gough Mss

26

Lieutenant-Colonel H. Williams to Brigadier-General G. T. Forestier-Walker[27]

Parkgate,
Dublin.

[Holograph]

19 March 1914

I think you had better come in tomorrow. I have been helping Friend & Hickie[28] all day with instructions to 5th Division for certain moves which have been ordered today & will take place tomorrow—viz.

1st Bedfords-Mullingar)—One to go north at 12 noon.
& a Bn from the Curragh)
to increase guards at Enniskillen, Omagh, Armagh, Newry & Dundalk, & a company from the Dublin garrison is to embark at Kingstown for Carrickfergus tomorrow evening.

I have sent the Bedford Regt a supply of maps—all we have in stock—& am arranging for a further supply early tomorrow for the Curragh Battalion which entrains at Newbridge at 1.30 p.m.

The orders had to be sent by officers—for which I had to arrange as de Gex[29] is away.

All the moves are to be completed by dawn on Saturday. Macready writes as if they were making arrangements to complete the Irish garrison (or is it the mobile force?) up to 20,000 men.

PRO, WO 35/209 (d)

27
Major-General L. B. Friend to
Major-General Sir Nevil Macready

Holywood,
Belfast.
[Holograph Copy]   20 March 1914

You have indeed given us plenty to do. My chief fear is that the Great Northern Railway whose Board consists of strong Ulster men may refuse to allow our troop trains over their lines tomorrow. We are endeavouring to make other arrangements by motors and by sea: but this will mean delay.

Our mobile force cannot be more than,
12 battalions
2 regiments of cavalry and
8 batteries of artillery as 1 Bttn. Infantry must stay at the Curragh and 1 Regt. of Cavalry in Dublin, the Artillery Brigades can only make up 8 batteries with 6 guns each and wagons. The 12 infantry battalions include those already in the north (i.e. 5 battalions after tomorrow) so that we shall have ready to move from Dublin and the Curragh

7 Battalions at 400 each	2,800
2 Cav. Regts. at 500	1,000
8 Batteries RFA at 120 each	960
	4,760

and if required two R.E. Field Cos.
The RFA will take several days to mobilise and concentrate as some comes from the south i.e. Cahir, Ballincollig, etc. The 5 Battalions in the North will be 1 at Londonderry, 2 at Holywood, 1 distributed between Omagh, Enniskillen and Armagh, 1 distributed between Dundalk and Newry. So that except for the latter we cannot count on them to co-operate in the field South of Belfast. These 5 Battalions are also as 400 bayonets of trained men. I hope I have made this clear and regret if I misled you

before in overestimating the mobile force. If this force is to take the field some organisation of transport will be required and this is being worked out.

Bodleian, Ms Asquith 40, f 23

28

Major-General Sir William Robertson to Field Marshal Sir John French

[Holograph]

War Office
[20 March 1914][30]

I send you these in case they may help to refresh your memory as to yesterday's talk.

'Notes on the Military Aspect'

Special difficulties of task:
a) Non-existence of arrangements of any kind for the operations (e.g. railway moves, railway protection)
b) Defection of an uncertain number of officers and men
c) Half-heartedness and distaste of practically the whole army, enhanced by good feeling which has always existed between Ulster & troops and bad feeling between Home Ruler MP's & troops engendered by S. African War episodes, etc.
d) Determination & religious convictions of Ulster
e) Practical certainty of sympathetic risings and consequent disorder in large towns in Great Britain
f) Slow mobilisation because of possible defection of senior officers and absence of many reservists
g) Awkward difficulty involved by transition from 'strike' to 'war' basis
h) Possible unfriendly attitude of Germany, and its far-reaching consequences
Is CIGS quite satisfied that the Government appreciate what the above means, and that finally to suppress Ulster may tax the

powers of our Exped: Force to the utmost limits, and be a matter of several months? Would it not be wise to put the case on paper?

Regarding steps to be taken:
a) Ulster said to have 100,000 men *now*; unmobilised we cannot muster more than 35,000 infantry at the most
b) If we send cannibalised troops into the field, it will be *very* difficult to mobilise afterwards. In fact it is usually regarded as worse than impracticable.
c) Cannot send troops into the field without *some* pretence of mobilisation, because in peace they are short of many necessary services (Has this been considered? And is it being worked out by anyone?). There is also the question of transport
d) If troops are sent to Ireland without mobilisation being ordered, defended ports will be left without infantry, and no troops will be available until about 2 days after mobilisation is ordered (e.g. If 18th Bde, 11th Bde and Scotland Bns are sent, all East Coast ports down to Dover will be without regular infantry now detailed for duty until 2 days after order to mobilise).

Regarding conduct of operations:
a) Decision needed as to whether DMO or DMT is to be responsible to CIGS. If the latter, he must be given the staff of DMO dealing with operations. *Nothing* can be done until these matters are decided. There is *much* to do.
b) If & when war arrives, CIGS should be given Government instructions, and then left to carry out the operations in accordance with recognised principles as C in C in the field.
c) To enable a plan of operations to be prepared these instructions must first be given; and the General Staff should be kept *fully* informed by AG's & QMG's branches of all that is done during 'strike' basis period.

IWM, 75/46/8, French Mss

29

J. E. B. Seely to
Field Marshal Sir John French

[Holograph]

War Office
20 March 1914

You have put to me the question of how best to meet the situation which would arise if simultaneously with serious disturbances in Ireland a menace from Germany were to arise. I think you may safely proceed on the following assumptions.

1) At the present time there is a possibility that the Ulster Volunteer Force, numbering some 100,000 men might take aggressive action which the Executive would have to meet. This would require a large mobile force of the Regular Army, with transport and Artillery on an adequate scale.

2) Apart from this possibility, the actual position is that the Army is required in support of the civil power, i.e. to safeguard Government property, to maintain law and order, and to protect the police and other Govt. Servants in the execution of their duty. This situation does *not* require a large mobile force with transport and artillery.

3) There is a possibility that Germany may take advantage of the present disturbances to attack, or threaten to attack us.

The question is, can (i) and (iii) coincide. In my considered judgement they cannot, and for the following reason.

Any serious menace of hostile attack from outside would have the result (a) that the Govt. and the Opposition would agree to postpone a settlement of their differences until the outside menace had been dealt with, (b) the Ulster Forces would cease aggressive action.

This is my individual opinion, and no other is obtainable; but it is based on an intimate knowledge of the leaders of the three parties.

If my view is accurate, the urgent problem is to find a solution for (ii) combined with (iii) together with civil disturbances on a large scale in this country.

CIGS

Will you work this problem, or series of problems out.

I should add that for practical purposes of administration so long as the present situation continues or not more than three battalions of infantry are sent from Great Britain, the matter can properly be regarded as action in support of the civil power not seriously jeopardizing our international position and thus properly dealt with through the ordinary channels. Should further reinforcements beyond the three battalions be required, the matter would become one of the General Staff under your special direction and you will act accordingly.

IWM, 75/46/8, French Mss

30

Account by H. A. Gwynne of his discussions with Field Marshal Sir John French

[Holograph]   22 April 1914

The following to the best of my recollections is the account given to me by Sir John French of the events preceding and subsequent to the late military crisis in Ireland.

Some considerable time, perhaps a fortnight, before the crisis Colonel Seely informed the Chief of the General Staff that information had been received by the Government in Ireland to the effect that while Sir E. Carson had succeeded in keeping his men well in hand, there were among the Ulster Volunteers a great number of hotheads who were not content to sit still. These had planned a great coup, nothing short of marching down to the Boyne, concentrating there and then moving on Dublin which they intended to take.

Sir John French at first pooh-poohed this information—but, when it was reiterated with many assurances that the Govt. had every reason to believe that it was quite correct, he advised that Sir A. Paget should be sent for.

It is not clear whether this advice was given prior to the first visit of Sir A. Paget early in March but I am inclined to think that this particular order was given to Paget first before March 18th on which day he arrived at the War Office. It is necessary to bear in mind that the information given by the Govt. to the War Office was repeated on several occasions before the Chief of the General Staff and the Adjutant General thought it serious enough to act on.

Sir A. Paget arrived at the War Office on the morning of Wednesday 18th March (I cannot vouch for this being the exact day but I can easily find out). Before he saw either Sir John French or the Adjutant General he was closeted with Colonel Seely alone for an hour. Sir John French put in a mild protest against this irregularity.

Then followed a more formal conference at which were present Colonel Seely, French, Paget and Ewart, the Adjutant General.

Colonel Seely repeated at this conference the information he had received regarding the march of the Ulster extremists to Dublin, and the question arose as to what steps should be taken to meet the move. The precautionary measures of strengthening the depots, which had been discussed some time ago by the War Office, were then sanctioned and the question was discussed as to what further and larger operations might be necessary. Nothing in the nature of big movements of troops was decided.

Among other questions which arose was that of Dundalk. There were stationed at Dundalk three batteries of artillery, practically undefended because the gunners only carried carbines & had no great store of small arms ammunition, & besides were not trained as infantry. Sir John French wished to withdraw the eighteen guns quietly to the Curragh but this was opposed by Seely as being provocative.

Colonel Seely then took Sir A. Paget to lunch with him, only one other person being present. The conversation turned almost entirely on the question of large operations.

That afternoon the strengthening of the depots and the other minor movements was decided upon by the W.O.

On Thursday 19th Sir A. Paget was at the War Office

discussing the final details. He also talked of the bigger operations which might become necessary and said in a wild kind of way 'I shall lead my army to the Boyne.' Whereupon French told him not to be a 'bloody fool'.

On Thursday Colonel Seely had Sir A. Paget to lunch with him. There was also present Winston Churchill and, as far as I can find out, nobody else.

It will be remembered that on Thursday afternoon Sir E. Carson left the H. of Commons for Ireland somewhat dramatically. Sir John French that same evening was dressing for dinner when he was telephoned to come at once to 10 Downing Street and he was enjoined to come by the garden entrance and not by the Downing St. door. He hastily dressed & drove down arriving about 7.30.

At 10 Downing Street he found the Prime Minister, Mr. Birrell, Colonel Seely, Winston Churchill & A. Paget.

He was informed that the Govt. believed that Sir E. Carson was gone over to Ireland to proclaim the Provisional Govt, that this might mean civil war & that it therefore behoved the govt. to take every precaution. Again the subject of the artillery at Dundalk was discussed. Sir John French was still of the opinion that it should be recalled to the Curragh but the Prime Minister overruled him & ordered a battalion to be sent to defend the batteries. At the same time, the naval preparations were mentioned. It is believed that at this meeting the P.M. countermanded the despatch of the 3rd Battle Squadron.

On Friday just before dinner or at it Sir J. French was told by Winston Churchill that if Belfast should fight, 'his fleet would have the town in ruins in twenty-four hours'.

Sir John French was at the theatre on the Friday night with Mr. & Mrs. W. Churchill when Nicholson, Seely's private secretary, came & told Sir J. French that the Secretary of State required him urgently and he accordingly rose to go. Mrs. W. sat between Sir J.F. & her husband who leaned over and asked what it was about. When told that the Secretary of State (Seely) wanted French urgently, Churchill insisted on accompanying him & remained with him & Seely for the rest of the evening.

In conclusion, it is only just to say that Sir J.F. warmly denies that there was a plot but he always adds 'unless it was devised behind my back'.

H. of Lords RO, Bonar Law Mss, 39/2/25

SECTION 2

The March Days

31

Brigadier-General H. P. Gough to Headquarters, Irish Command

[Printed]

Curragh
20 March 1914

With reference to the communication from the War Office conveyed to me verbally by the Commander-in-Chief this morning, I have the honour to report the result of my interview with the officers of my brigade.

The officers are of unanimous opinion that further information is essential before they are called upon at such short notice to take decisions so vitally affecting their whole future, and especially that a clear definition should be given of the terms 'Duty as ordered' and 'active operations' in Ulster.

If such duty consists of the maintenance of order and the preservation of property all the officers of this brigade, including myself, would be prepared to carry out that duty.

But if the duty involves the *initiation* of active military operations against Ulster, the following numbers of officers by regiments would respectfully, and under protest, prefer to be dismissed:

Brigade Staff, 2 officers.

4th Hussars, 17 out of 19 doing duty.

5th Lancers, 17 out of 20 doing duty.

16th Lancers, 16 out of 16 doing duty.

3rd Brigade, Royal Horse Artillery, 6 out of 13 doing duty, 'including R.M.'

4th Field Troop, Royal Engineers, — 1 out of 1 doing duty.

3rd Signal Troop, Royal Engineers, 1 out of 1 doing duty.

In addition, the following are domiciled in Ulster and claim protection as such:

4th Hussars, 2 officers.

5th Lancers, 1 officer.

3rd Brigade, Royal Horse Artillery, 2 officers.

White Paper; Nuffield College, Ms Mottistone 22, f 206; RA GV F. 674/18; Pragnell Mss

32

Brigadier-General H. P. Gough
to Headquarters, Irish Command

Curragh
20 March 1914

[Holograph Copy]

In accordance with the alternatives placed this morning before me and other officers by the War Office, through the medium of the Commander-in-Chief, Irish Command, of either undertaking active military operations against Ulster, or immediately resigning under pain of 'dismissal from the Service', I beg to say that my conscientious scruples absolutely preclude me from undertaking the first alternative and therefore that I hereby and under the strongest protest make a request to [resign deleted] retire from the Service.

H. P. Gough Mss; Fergusson Mss

33
Orders by Major-General Sir Charles Fergusson[1]

Parkgate
Dublin.
20 March 1914

[Typescript Copy]

C.R.A. 5th Division.
C.R.E. 5th Division.
O.C.A.S.C., Curragh.
S.M.O., Curragh.

In view of the possibility of active operations in Ulster, the War Office has authorized the following communication to Officers:

1. Officers *whose homes are actually in the province of Ulster* who wish to do so may apply for permission to be absent from duty during the period of operations, and will be allowed to 'disappear' from Ireland. Such Officers will, subsequently, be reinstated, and will suffer no loss in their career.

2. Any other Officer who from conscientious or other motives is not prepared to carry out his duty as ordered, should say so at once. Such Officers will at once be *dismissed from the Service*.

As regards (1), the words underlined are to be taken literally and strictly, and Brigadiers and O.C. Units are responsible [under penalty of Court Martial—added in margin] that only such Officers as come under that description are allowed to forward applications to 'disappear'.

As regards (2), it is hoped that very few cases will be found of Officers who elect to sever their connection with the Service.

All decision must be made at once, and applications forwarded to Headquarters 5th Division by this evening if possible.

RA GV F. 674/44(a) App A, 45; Fergusson Mss; Manchester Central Library, M 25/2/16; Bodleian, Ms Asquith 40, f 103

34
Lieutenant Colonel H. L. James to Brigadier-General S. P. Rolt, 14th Infantry Brigade[2]

2nd Manchester Regt.,
Curragh.

[Holograph Copy]   20 March 1914

The situation today is very serious. Commanding Officers have been asked to decide questions, of grave importance, very suddenly & scarcely in fairness to their Regiments: or the Army generally.

The suddenness of orders verbally issued today are scarcely possible for Army Regimental Officers to decide in a 'few minutes' on their future status in the Army.

The later-written order, taken down verbatim equally gives them 'no time' to decide.

I am sure my Regiment is most loyal & can be kept in hand to serve for all legitimate purposes but I cannot guarantee it up against ULSTER.

What is the meaning of 'Active' operations?

After most seriously & loyally considering the situation to 'His Majesty' & the Empire, I know that my officers would now prefer to resign in one body—or be dismissed, accepting the conditions, than have to throw their lot in, in civil war.

I would further add that no officer in the Battalion wishes to wreck discipline of any kind in the Bns. of the Line. Nor do they wish to leave it without leaders. They all have the honour of the Empire before them. The standing Army loyal for its legitimate use—The King who it will support.

Cannot this loyalty of His Army be recognised?

It would raise the status throughout his Kingdom & overseas Possessions. Reduce party factions in all classes. Bring together the seriousness of the times of many difficulties & make us much happier in case of emergency.

Manchester Central Library, D/3/D/1, James Mss

35

Lieutenant J. B. Gough to Major G. Gillson RHA[3] [4]

[Holograph]

'D' Battery RHA,
Newbridge
20 March 1914

I have the honour to state, in answer to the ultimatum made to the officers of the 3rd Cavalry Brigade today, that I had the option up to 5 p.m. today of either resigning my commission or joining immediately in military operations against the Protestants of Ulster. I prefer the former alternative and hereby have the honour to tender the resignation of my commission in his Majesty's forces.

Letter sold at auction in August 1984

36

Second Lieutenant W. Scott-Watson to his father[5]

[Copy]

80th Battery,
XV Brigade, RFA,
Kildare.
20 March 1914

This evening I and the other officers of our Regiment were called upon to make the most momentous decision of our lives.

We were all assembled in the Colonel's office, and he read out the following proclamation from the War Office:

In view of the possible active operations in Ulster, all officers *domiciled in Ulster* will be allowed to disappear from Ireland till the operations are over. Any officer who, from conscientious reasons, refuses to take part in these operations will send in an application by 10 a.m. tomorrow. Any officer doing so will be *dismissed the Service*. This we are all agreed is the greatest outrage that has ever been perpetrated on the Service. We have had to make this decision without any opportunity of discussing it with our people.

The words 'domiciled in Ulster' have been underlined, and under penalty of court-martial our Colonel has to state whether a man is domiciled in Ulster or not.

I had hardly time to wire for your opinion, so I have decided to carry on. Seven in my Brigade have decided to refuse, and will probably be dismissed the Service either tomorrow or very shortly.

I have decided to stay on for the following reasons:

Although, as you know, my sympathies are absolutely with Ulster, I think that at a time like this the Army must stick together. If we once start to disintegrate the Service, then goodbye to the Empire and anything else that matters.

Moreover, in case of strike duty, the men whose sympathies are fairly obviously with the strikers have to carry on and do their duty, so that now it is up to us to do the same.

I hope and pray that I have done the right thing, but anyway it is now too late for anything else, for if you don't avail yourself of this opportunity of quitting, and then later on you want to do so, it means a court martial, with a possibility of being shot.

Altogether, it is the most diabolically ingenious thing that has ever been brought in. What we especially detest is being dismissed, and not allowed to resign.

Pall Mall Gazette 24-3-1914; *Hansard*, 5 s H. of C., LX, 906

37
Second Lieutenant E. G. Miles
to his father, G. H. Miles

2nd KOSB
Royal Barracks,
Dublin.
20 March 1914

[Holograph]

Just a line to tell you that 'things are beginning to move'. You will see by the evening papers that the Bedfords have moved up North from Mullingar & also the D.C.L.I. from the Curragh. Also some of the K.O.Y.L.I. have gone up to an unknown destination from Dublin. I may add that most of the papers are exaggerating. Two warships have arrived at Kingstown. We have had orders to issue ball ammunition to the men. No one quite knows what all this means & why this 'thus-ness'. One rather amusing item is that for some time past all barrack gates have had to be kept closed by order. I dont think that we shall move North for some time to come if ever. I had a smooth crossing. This afternoon I played a game of racquets, & then went into the Club & heard some amusing comments on the Ulster Question.

There seems to me quite a panic about the North, it all seems very unnecessary. I wonder how Hugh will enjoy it. Sir A. Paget again travelled over in the same boat with me. Our point to point is next Tuesday—U.P. I think I have got a mount. Our tug-o-war team pulled over the Leinsters this afternoon thereby beating all regiments in Ireland. A splendid bit of news has just arrived. All the 16th Lancers at the Curragh and also Gen. Gough commanding Cavalry Brigade have resigned their commissions. This comes direct from a Major in the 16th Lancers.[6] The 5th Lancers are contemplating following suit. I understand that Gen. Gough said that he was going to resign & that any one else who wanted to do so would have to do it before tonight or it would be too late. I believe this is quite official. I dont think that the Government will stand much chance of arresting Carson now even if they want to. I wonder what the next move will be. At present we are all taking it as rather a joke & wondering where we shall spend the next week. I dont think that you can believe everything you see in the papers. Amongst other things all officers were this afternoon recalled off leave so it is lucky mine has just expired. Maj. Haig & Kennedy[7] are both on leave. So long now love to all. I will let you know our future address in due course.

P.S. Be discreet with any news in this letter.

Miles Mss

38
Lieutenant-General Sir Arthur Paget
to Field Marshal Sir John French

Royal Hospital,
Dublin.

[Holograph]   20 March 1914 10.45 p.m.

I much regret to have to make the following report.

The result of the interview which the GOC 5th Div & B.Gen Comg 3rd Cav Bde had with the officers in their command.

5th Div. The feeling is very bitter indeed & although the officers of the Div as a whole are prepared to do their duty, there may be trouble with the rank & file. In any case, the attitude of the troops will not be that of willing obedience.

3rd Cav Bde including the B.Gen Commanding 58 officers are prepared to accept dismissal from the Service shd they be ordered to take part in active military operations agt Ulster.

I have not had time to do more than interview the OC 5th Lancers Dublin. I very much fear without good results. I shall know more tomorrow.

This Brigade could of course be usefully employed South in maintaining law & order. But if employed in this manner it would have the worst possible effect on the other arms.

I send you this information privately, which I am sure you would wish.

I am going down to the Curragh to try & put a little heart into these officers.

IWM, 75/46/8, French Mss

39
Lieutenant Colonel I. G. Hogg
to W. S. Churchill

4th Hussars,
Curragh.
[Telegram]   21 March 1914

Today[8] all officers Cavalry Brigade required to decide whether prepared to accept liability active operations in Ulster on pain of dismissal. Enormous majority ready to accept dismissal, but later adopted proposal that authorities should be asked to define employment. Brigadier and great majority ready to undertake duties of preserving order and property, provided no initiative in offensive action against Ulster contemplated. Convinced, if tactfully handled, Brigade can be saved; but if unconditional service demanded from outset, Brigadier and practically all officers will accept dismissal. Appeal to you to ensure sensible handling.

Hansard, 5s, H. of C. LXI, 768; Pragnell Mss; Bodleian, Ms Asquith 40 f 24; PRO, Adm 1/8370/58

40
Extract from the Diary of
Lieutenant H. F. Stoneham,
2nd King's Own Yorkshire Light Infantry[9]

[Holograph]   21 March 1914

C.O. asks officers if willing to go to Ulster.
Officers not willing to be dismissed the service.

9 Officers resign. Gen. Fergusson persuades 8 of 9 to withdraw resignations.

Sunderland Polytechnic, 1914–1918 Archives, Stoneham Mss

41

Lieutenant Colonel C. A. H. Brett
to Brigadier-General S. P. Rolt

2nd Suffolks,
Gough Barracks,
Curragh.
[Typescript Copy]   21 March 1914

The result of the address given this morning by Major-General Sir Charles Fergusson to the officers and men of my Battalion is that the officers agree to do their duty in the matter of Ulster. I wish however to point out the chief reason for our decision: this reason is that Sir Charles Fergusson has given us the assurances of the G.O.C. in C. that the action of the Ministry in ordering the Army to take part in operations against Ulster has the full approval of His Majesty the King.

The King has given the order and we one and all obey him.

I would further point out in the most emphatic manner that our hearts are not in the work that we are likely to be called on to perform and that, until the fact of the King's approval had been explained to us, the officers had all decided to come under the conditions of the second paragraph in the War Office Secret Letter.[10]

All our sympathies are with the Loyalists of Ulster and I wish it to be clearly understood and *the fact brought to the notice of the highest Authorities* that it is not willingness to take action against the Loyalists but a sense of our duty to the King and the Army that has influenced us not to come under the second paragraph of the above quoted WO letter.

NAM, 7101-23-202, Roberts Mss; Fergusson Mss; RA GV F.674/38

42
Second Lieutenant R. Macleod to his father

80th Battery,
XV Brigade RFA,
Kildare.
[Holograph]
21 March 1914

We never knew the situation was serious until 7 o'clock on Friday night. We were then all had up in the Colonel's office and [he] explained the situation. I am not at liberty to say exactly what took place, but we were asked whether we should prefer to stay on and obey all orders or leave the service. Several of us, myself included, decided to leave rather than fight Ulster. We were afterwards given till today to decide. Our Divisional General and Brigadier General[11] came to see us this morning, and said they were both in favour of Ulster, but the situation was very much graver than it seemed, for if the Army split up on this question there would be a rising in India, Germany would at once declare war, and the labour situation was so serious in England that if there were no Army a state of chaos would result. He said also if we went to Ulster it would not be primarily to fight Ulster but to keep order, and he hoped that the measures being taken would prevent an outbreak. The leaders of Ulster were willing to give in, but they would have difficulty in restraining their more hot-headed followers.

In view of all these issues we have decided that it will be more important for us to remain in the service, however disagreeable it may be, than to look on while India goes and Germany does what she likes with us. We hope we have decided rightly, but it is a very difficult choice. When you have time, will you come over to Ireland some time next week, and I will be able to talk more freely, and tell you what I cannot put down on paper.

Sunderland Polytechnic 1914–1918 Archive, Macleod Mss; King's College, Liddell Hart Centre for Military Archives, Macleod Mss 1/1; RA Institution, MD 1150, Macleod Mss

43

Second Lieutenant E. G. Miles
to his father, G. H. Miles

2nd KOSB
Royal Barracks,
Dublin.

[Holograph]   21 March 1914

We have today been through, in all probability one of the most critical stages in our career. At 11 o'clock this morning the Colonel[12] called a conference of all officers and put forward the following question 'If the regiment is ordered to take action against Ulster in the interests of the Preservation of Peace etc. Are you prepared to go or do you wish to resign your commission.' I. 'If you resign your commission, you will be dismissed the service *without* a pension unless you are a resident of Ulster. II. If you are a resident of Ulster, you may resign your commission & have your pension. III. If you resign your commission you will be dismissed the service, even if there is no trouble & the Home Rule Question is settled peacably.' We were given *an hour* to make up our minds. Can you imagine a subaltern of 22–26 making up his mind in an hour as to whether he should shoot down Loyalists in Ulster or try to start a civil career without a bob? also officers who have served 15 to 20 years and are entitled to pensions, deciding whether they should forfeit them or not? Of course the whole thing is a threat on the part of the Government to discover how many officers they will have if they use the army.

We all sat for an hour and a half in the ante room discussing the situation & trying to make up our minds. We all loathed the idea of going to Ulster for the sake of a few dirty Nationalists who loathe the army and are most unloyal to anything to do with Britain & yet we wondered what on earth we should do if we left. Eventually we all, I think, with the exception of the Colonel, Senior Major & adjutant decided that we would *not* fight Ulster. About 10 fellows signed to say that they would resign their commissions tonight rather than go & I with the remainder signed a 'covenant'—'that we were prepared to do duty in aid of the civil power to maintain peace in Ireland, but that we would *not* take part in any organised military action against the Ulster Volunteers'—implying that we would resign our commissions tonight rather than go. After this we waited patiently for the reply, wondering what on earth we should do when we left. The reply came after lunch—our 'covenant' had been ignored and the question was 'whether we would fight against Ulster or not'. The Colonel made a speech saying that it was our duty to stay & fight for the sake of the discipline of the army & that we ought to follow the example of the generals who all had to do it against their will & finally said that we must decide whether—'our sense of discipline or our personal views on the subject were the stronger'. I personally considered the former and tremendous debates ensued all the afternoon. At about 4 o'clock in the afternoon the Colonel took a second and final 'division' on the matter with the following result:

2 Majors
3 Captains
4 Lieutenants
1 2nd Lieutenant
total   10 officers.

sent in their papers, resigning their commissions.

I and the others took our names off the list of resignations after this debate. I dont know yet whether they will accept these resignations.

The disgrace about the whole affair is that the Gov: want to find out how many officers they will have. So they made us decide instantaneously whether we would go or not, without stating any facts as to what we might have to do. Of course all the above lose their pensions & most of them are married men without means, so it hits them very hard. You cannot imagine a more trying or eventual [sic] day, when in a matter of an hour or so we had to decide between 'shooting down Loyalists and starting a fresh job on nothing'. Imagine anything more criminal than making us decide a matter which might affect our whole careers, without giving us time to think or get advice from anyone. Hardly a word except this question has been spoken and the feeling is intense.

The Colonel has spoken several times trying to persuade his officers to stay on & go North if necessary and this evening Sir Charles Fergusson, commanding 5th Division, came himself & issued a wonderful speech on the subject viz: 'duty & discipline'. I dont know what affect it will have and what the state of affairs will be tomorrow. Those who have resigned their commissions at present refuse to go at all costs and with very excellent reasons, to take action against Ulster. Over 100 officers at the Curragh are supposed to have resigned but I believe they will not accept their resignations. The 16th Lancers were ordered North today, but as there were only 3 officers, the order had to be cancelled.

The decision that most of us came to including myself was that—until the King does or says something to the contrary, he wants the Army to coerce Ulster & therefore the Army should do so, no matter how unpleasant it may be for them. Furthermore if the officers refuse to do this 'dirty work' by a breach of discipline, how can the men be expected to do it—and so in the interest of discipline & our allegiance to our Sovereign it was our duty to place discipline before personal views & see this most 'objectional duty' carried out, no matter how unpleasant it might be. As the generals & our commanding officer were prepared to do it, very much against their will, so we agreed to do it likewise. But, as our senior Major pointed out, if at any time things got too hot and we are ordered to do or commit some outrageous act, such as mowing down the Ulstermen for no apparent reason, then will be the time to 'put ones foot down' & in the senior major's words 'to then resign & risk court martial and chance being placed against a wall opposite a firing party'. These were, I think, his very words & God forbid that it will ever come to that. He thinks that the affair will settle down without trouble & so it is risking too much to resign one's commission today & so forfeit one's pension even if the matter be settled peacably tomorrow—for there will be no chance of getting back once you go out. Yet this is what the War Office want—viz; a definite decision *tonight*, without knowing in the least what is going to happen. It is a case of absolute blackmail— the question is what is one to do? Personally I have decided to stay & hope for the best, but as I say 10 of our fellows have 'sent in their papers' & over a hundred other officers in Dublin & the Curragh. This may all seem rather desperate & rash to you, but you cannot imagine the feeling of today & the arguments on both sides that have taken place.

So much for the question of resignations. All guards have been doubled & gates barred & men issued with ball ammunition. You will see by the two enclosed papers what is happening over here. They are not very reliable but will give you an idea of the situation. Things may be very different tomorrow.

Our point to point has been cancelled.

No more news at present. I will write tomorrow re the situation. NB. Be very discreet with the contents of this epistle.

Miles Mss

44
Lieutenant-General Sir Arthur Paget
to J. E. B. Seely

Parkgate,
Dublin.

[Telegram]   21 March 1914 11.2 p.m.

General Fergusson assured me late tonight that but for the attitude of Col. Parker, Brigadier & rest of Brigade would have withdrawn resignations.

Nuffield College, Ms Mottistone 22, f 215–216; Bodleian, Ms Asquith 40, f 41

45

Memorandum by
Brigadier-General G. T. Forestier-Walker

[Holograph 'Working Draft']   22 March 1914

'Organisation of the Field Force in Ireland'
Details of Troops to be sent to Ireland

1. In the event of it being found necessary to despatch troops to Ireland from the United Kingdom in connection with disturbances in the country, it has been decided by the War Office that the following troops shall be despatched:

(a) To Belfast Lough   3 battalions ⎫ from Scotland
     (probably to Bangor)   1 Bde RFA   ⎭
(b) to Dublin   1st Division — from Aldershot
                           11th Inf Bde — from Colchester
                           18th Inf Bde — from Lichfield,
                             etc.
                           A Cavalry Bde — uncertain

Batteries will have four guns and two gun wagons. All troops will bring three days supplies, and will be on manoeuvre scale, with tents and ball ammunition. It is not known whether transport, other than that held in peace, will accompany these troops.

2. The troops detailed in para: 1(a) will come under the orders of the Military Governor of Belfast, and will form part of the 'Northern Force' (see para:4). He will also be empowered to land parties from HM Ships, and these parties will act under his orders.

3. The troops of the 3rd Cavalry Brigade and 5th and 6th Divisions are at present (22nd March) distributed as follows:
3rd Cavalry Brigade
*4th Hussars (Curragh) — available for Field Force
*5th Lancers (Dublin) — 3 squadrons available for Field Force; 1 sqd to remain in Dublin
*16th Lancers (Curragh) — available for Field Force

†IIIrd Bde RHA (Curragh)—available for Field Force
†4th Field Troop, RE (Curragh)—available for Field Force
†3rd Signal Troop, RE (Curragh)—available for Field Force
*Will probably not be available owing to refusal and sickness
†May possibly not be available owing to refusal and sickness
5th Division
13th Infantry Brigade (less 1 co KOYLI at Carrickfergus)—
    available for Field Force
14th Infantry
2nd Bn Suffolk (Curragh)—available for Field Force
1st Bn E Surrey (Dublin)—available for Field Force
1st Bn DCLI ½ at Newry ½ at Dundalk
2nd Bn Manchester Regt (Curragh)—available for Field Force
15th Infantry Brigade
1st Bn Norfolk (Holywood) Under Belfast Military Governor
1st Bn Bedford regt—2 cos Enniskillen
                   1 co Omagh
                   1 co Armagh
1st Bn Cheshire Regt (Londonderry)
1st Bn Dorset Regt (Holywood)
Div troops as in Army List (less 1 sec 7th or 59th Fd Co RE at
    Holywood)—available for Field Force
6th Division
Bn at Kinsale to remain
Bn at Limerick—½ remain ½ Tipperary
One Bn at Cork to remain
One Bn at Fermoy to remain
One Bn Cork⎫ In case of the assembly of the Field
One Bn Tipperary⎬ Force, three of these battalions to go to
One Bn Buttevant⎭ Dublin, and one to the Curragh
One Bn Fermoy
Divisional Troops as in Army List—available for Field Force

Eventual Disposition and Organisation of whole Force
4. On the arrival of the troops from England, the organisation of
the Forces in Ireland will be as follows; subject to War Office
approval:

(a) *Northern Force*
Commander— GOC, Belfast District
Staff
Northern Bde
Commander—Brig. Gen. A. E. W. Count Gleichen
Staff—staff of 15th Inf Bde
Norfolk Regt
Dorset Regt
3 Bns from Scotland
One Bde RFA from Scotland
1 sec Field Co RE
1 sec Div Signal Co
The RIC available in the District
Landing parties from HM Ships as may be demanded
(For details of transport, etc., see note at end)
(b) *Southern Force*
Commander—The C of F
Personal Staff—as in peace
Army Headquarters
General Staff Branch
BGGS—Brig Gen Forestier-Walker
GSO2 (Op)—Major Buckle[13]
GSO1 (Op) or GSO3 (Op) (has been asked for from War Office)
GSO1 (I)—Lt Col Williams
GSO2 (I)—Maj Earle
GSO3 (I)—Capt Walcot[14]
Adjutant General and Quartermaster General's Branch
DA & QMG—Col Hickie
AA & QMG—(has been asked for from War Office)
AQMG—Col Edye[15]
APM (To be found from the Command)
Camp Commandant (To be found from the Command)
½ *Cav Div*
Commander ⎫
Staff   ⎬ To be appointed by the War Office
3rd Cav Bde and attached troops

—Cav Bde (from England) less one sqn
1st Division (as in Army List)
Div Supply Col ⎫
Div Ammn Col ⎬ to be improvised—see note
Div Field Ambulance ⎭
5th Division
Commander—Maj Gen Sir Charles Fergusson
Staff—Peace Staff supplemented by War Office
11th Inf Bde
13th Inf Bde
14th Inf Bde (less 1 DCLI)
Div Troops as in Army List
Div Supply Col ⎫
Div Ammo Col ⎬ to be improvised—see note
Field Ambulance ⎭
Army Troops
1 sqn of Cavalry Bde from England
18th Inf Bde
'B' Signal Co
Army Troops Supply Col (To be improvised—see note)
Equipment of Northern and Southern Forces
Troops arriving from Great Britain will bring three days supplies, and will be on manoeuvre scale with tents and (presumably) gun and rifle ammuniton on a scale unknown. Batteries will have 4 guns and 2 gun wagons. The troops now in Ireland, which will form part of the Northern and Southern Forces, will be equipped on the same scale.
(c) *Line of Communications*
IGC—Maj Gen Friend
Staff—Col de Gex ⎫ Supplemented as required
     Lt. Col Romer[16] ⎭ from the Command or outside
Troops. As required, from Army Troops, Southern Force
(d) *Garrisons*
    (i)   Under IGC
           Londonderry 1 Bn Cheshire
                        Regt
           Enniskillen   2 coys Beds

Armagh	1 coy Beds
Omagh	1 coy Beds
Dundalk	2 coys DCLI
Newry	2 coys DCLI

(ii) Under GOC Belfast District

Carrickfergus—   1 coy KOYLI

(iii) Under GOC, 6th Div. HQ Dublin

Staff—Peace staff of 6th Div supplemented
     as required from the Command

Dublin 3 Bns 6th Div

Curragh 1 Bn 6th Div

Limerick ½ Bn 6th Div

Tipperary ½ Bn 6th Div

Cork 1 Bn 6th Div

Kinsale 1 Bn 6th Div

Fermoy 1 Bn & 2 Batteries 6th Div

Fethard
Clonmel
Kilkenny   } RFA, RE, ASC, as in Army List
Ballincollig
Waterford

(e) *Coast Defences*
(exclusive of defended port of Belfast)
Commanders and troops as in Army List

5. Note on Supply

It is understood that the troops coming from Scotland to the neighbourhood of Belfast will be supplied from England or Scotland. It is suggested that a similar arrangement be made for the troops already at Holywood Barracks, Belfast, and at Carrickfergus.

No difficulty is anticipated in supplying the Southern Force, and the garrisons under GOC 6th Division under arrangements to be made by the Staff in Ireland.

All garrisons under IGC are already supplied with one month's provisions, and arrangements are in progress to supply certain of them with one month's groceries.

6. Note on Transport
Horses and Transport

The question of the provision of horses and transport will require consideration.

Horses and carts are none too easily obtained in Ireland for manoeuvres, when it is known that they will be required for a week or so in the neighbourhood of their homes.

It is considered that Powers for impressment of horses and transport, both horse and motor, will be necessary.

Under the most favourable circumstances, it will take some days to provide these horses and transport as no previous arrangements are possible.

Transport Drivers

6th Division can find some, but not enough to complete the requirements of the whole Army.

Strengths and requirements of troops from England

It would be well if the Irish Command could be given as soon as possible, the strengths and requirements of the 1st Division, the 11th and 18th Brigades and of the Cavalry Brigade.

The more they can bring in the way of transport the better for us and the sooner the Army will be made mobile.

It is hoped that they will bring their own supply and medical units.

PRO, WO 35/209 (d)

46

Brigadier-General S. P. Rolt to Major-General Sir Charles Fergusson

14th Infantry Brigade
Curragh
[Typescript Copy]   22 March 1914[17]

With reference to the secret communication dated Parkgate, Dublin, 20 March, 1914,[18] I have interviewed all the officers in the Brigade under my command with the result that one officer has sent in an application to be permitted to disappear on the ground that his home is in Ulster, and one other officer has intimated that he cannot conscientiously carry out his duty, if ordered to proceed on operations against Ulster.

All the remainder are prepared to do their duty.

I feel it my duty, however, as Brigade Commander, to inform you of the unanimous feeling of myself, my staff, and the officers of the Brigade under my command.

We are unanimously in sympathy with the Ulster loyalists and regard with the utmost disgust the possibility of having to lead our men against them.

We are prepared to do our duty because:

(1) We realize that we must obey the orders of our King under any circumstances.

(2) We consider it incumbent on ourselves to preserve, as far as is in our power, the British Army from disruption.

I feel it my duty to bring these points officially to your notice in order that you may know the state of the 'moral' of the troops in the event of operations.

RA GV F.674/44(a) App C; Fergusson Mss; PRO, WO 35/209 (g)

47
Captain F. A. Forster to his family[19]

1st Royal Fusiliers,
Spike Island,
Queenstown.
[22] March 1914

[Holograph]

Pretty work going on in this country—what?

You'll have read of the majority of the officers in the Cavalry Brigade sending in their papers. You may take it as absolutely true—and they were all refused as many others also were I believe.

And so no doubt you'll soon see Seely answering questions in the House, and saying that no 'papers' of officers are lying in the War Office, which will be true, as they've all been sent back. And no doubt he'll go on to say that no officer will be required to fight against his relatives in Ulster. That is partly true, as if your home is *in* Ulster, and you can prove it, you can be excused going—but all the rest of us have been told that resignations will not be accepted—and if we refuse to go where sent we'll be tried by General Court Martial—and in any case forfeit all claims to pension. At present my regt: is not under orders to go—but of course all leave is stopped— and we are all kept sort of 'standing by'.

The leave business hits me, as I was to have gone to stay with Nugent 10 days before I actually take up the job and go into it all with him—and now I'll have probably to take it over in a day, and without going round the outlying places with him.

Arthur was rather sad at going off I think—but he had a good time on the whole. I expect you saw him again on Fri: & Sat: before he went. I've not heard from him yet about his interview that he went over for.

I am busy packing up my household goods today, as I always am, once a year at least. It will be restful being able to sit down in 1 place for 3 years—if I ever get there!

If only both parties can keep their heads—we may have a Gilbertian situation of the Army & the U.V.F. fraternising, & uniting in keeping order!

IWM, P.473 (1), Forster Mss

48

Second Lieutenant R. Macleod to his parents

80th Battery
XV Brigade, RFA,
Kildare.

[Holograph]   22 March 1914

Can you tell me how many of my relatives or friends will take up arms for Ulster? Have I any relations living in Ulster? Has Father or Jock gone there? I want to know as I gave as one of my reasons for not going to Ulster that I had relations fighting on the other side. I have now been allowed to remain behind at first if we move. Will you kindly answer my questions as soon as possible, as I will probably have to state the no. of my relations on the other side, and after everything is over I may have to quote them as justification.

Everything here is confidential and I cannot say what is happening. I will let you know when it is over.

I heard yesterday that troops were only being sent over to prevent a row between the Ulstermen and the Nationalists, and to act as a kind of demonstration.

Sunderland Polytechnic, 1914–18 Archive, Macleod Mss; King's College, Liddell Hart Centre for Military Archives, Macleod Mss 1/1; RA Institution, MD 1150, Macleod Mss

49

Major P. Howell to 'Wug' [C. Wigram]

4th Hussars,
Stewart Barracks,
Curragh.

[Holograph]   22 March 1914

You have probably heard by now full details of the trouble here but some notes direct may interest you. Who exactly is responsible I know not but we are pretty well all agreed that the crisis is due not to political passion but to an absurd want of tact! 48 hours ago the Grand Military and the like were the sole topics of conversation—all are sick to death of the subject of 'Home Rule' and for weeks I've never heard it mentioned in the mess or hunting field.

Then suddenly a bolt from the blue—officers all summoned and told that they must within two hours undertake to fight against Ulster to the end, or resign, and that resignation meant dismissal. 5th and 16th Lancers resigned in a body at once. Hogg and I realised that there must be some fatuous mistake and persuaded our officers to wait for further information. We suspected Goughie's hotheadedness at first but it soon was evident that he was not to blame for the other generals all confirmed his views. However, we persuaded Gough to hold up the resignations and then drafted a letter[20] to which after hours of discussion the whole brigade eventually agreed, and quiet was more or less restored.

Then next morning (Saturday) down came 'A.P.' himself and in about half an hour, with, no doubt, the best intentions in the world, succeeded in wholly upsetting the apple cart again. How much he said on his own and how much by instruction I do not know but the general impression left upon those who kept calm was this, that there'll be no Army left in Ireland unless we can get at its head someone who will talk both sense and tact. It's no use exciting men with pictures of all sorts of hypothetical dangers and difficulties which have not yet arisen and then trying to 'dum-kao'[21] them into undertaking to perform duties they dislike. And it's no good saying several different things at once or things which are not quite clear.

5th and 16th Lancers and most of the gunner resignations all went on again, but again we have kept back the 4th Hussars: and persuaded them to adhere to the original letter of which I send you the draft (no reply yet). We maintain that A.P. and Mr. Birrell have both given their guarantee: the others want something further and in writing, so Gough and the three C.O.s have gone over to try to get it. The real and worst difficulty of all is to stop recrimination. Cries of 'scab' and 'black leg' *almost* began yesterday and were only stopped by good humour and ridicule. They could easily start again and spread, especially if idiots at home are going to sneer at the 4th Hussars and wire heroics to the others.

The net result of this business is a very nasty situation which is by no means ended. Any real or fancied ill treatment of Goughie would mean the break up of the brigade, for instance. For we all love him and would stand by him. But if the authorities at home will smooth him down, send him back and then *leave us to ourselves* all might go well again.

I think that had this affair not arisen it is just possible that the troops might have drifted into active operations against the Ulstermen: but that is out of the question now. If we do anything at all it must be clearly for 'law and order' and nothing else. I suppose that I'm about as moderate and impartial as anyone here, for in principle I'm a Home Ruler and am not swept away by Ulster heroics. Resignation seems to me uncalled for, unpatriotic and unwise: more likely to provoke civil war than stop it—or at any rate limit it once started. I'm prepared to stick it out against the stampede, though we who do so don't find it pleasant—semi-insulting messages and telegrams are already pouring in! *But* loyalty of this sort does not mean readiness to coerce—to attempt anything more than law and order; nor ability to put up with threats and pressure—and if the W.O. try any more 'dumkaoin' we go.

Those are the views of the Moderates: those of the extremists you can well imagine for yourself.

On the whole the greatest danger seems to me leaving the conduct of a very delicate situation in the hands of a pompous old ass—whom no one respects. I don't know how they can get rid of him now or who they can put in his place but go he certainly ought to. Sir Charles Fergusson is first rate and has worked wonders with his division. He knows how to deal with human nature which A.P. most obviously does not. I write all this on the chance of its helping affairs—and you must take the opinions expressed for what they are worth, and honest.

RA GV F.674/17

50
Extracts from the Diary of
Major E. P. Strickland, 1st Norfolks

[Holograph]   22 March 1914

Arrd. Holywood about 9. Found Gleichen in my room—I have to take Oakes.[22] Friend also here, in Col's. House. Ballard[23] saw all officers at 9.45 & put it to us about serving against Ulster. All Cavalry Bde (3rd) practically have resigned—a lot of ours will, JBO,[24] HRD,[25] and self, said we might do it under protest, but I don't think I could go the whole hog. Went down & saw Mrs. C. didn't stay long as Mrs. B.B.[26] arrived—There is hellish excitement, but I fancy it worse in London than here.

23 March 1914

In all local papers what happened here yesterday. Ballard very concerned about it. Took Mrs. C up to see football, officers v Dorsets. Won 1–0. Then band in Tea Room. We are by way of being confined to barracks.

25 March 1914

Gleichen & Macready spoke to all officers in Ante Room at 9. G read letter from Fergusson, asking us to obey the King, etc. M said a lot about Govt never meaning to coerce Ulster, not very convincing, & gets us no forwarder.

30 March 1914

Spoke to Genrl: Macready about me writing to CO Manchester,[27] & arranging to see him, etc. He says it's quite safe for me to do it.

IWM, P.362, Strickland Mss

51

Lieutenant Colonel H. L. James
to Brigadier-General S. P. Rolt

2nd Manchester Regiment,
Curragh.

[Holograph Copy]   23 March 1914

My Battalion after the address given on Sat: 21 March 1914 by Major General Sir Charles Fergusson, The G.O.C. Commanding the 5th Division (& presumably under orders from the C. in C. in Ireland), decided to remain loyal under *protest*, provided an order was given *personally, in writing from His Majesty 'the King'* that we should only be required for protection duty on stores etc. & to keep general order, but for *no 'active' operation* in ULSTER or elsewhere under the present crisis.

Has this order been received. No communication has been received.

Manchester Central Library, D/3/D/1, James Mss

52

Major-General Sir Charles Fergusson
to Lieutenant Colonel H. L. James

Curragh

[Holograph]   23 March 1914

Forgive me for keeping this paper[28] of yours so long—I have taken no action on it, as the feelings it expresses have already been represented to the highest quarters.

The whole thing has been terribly & sadly mismanaged, & it is heartbreaking. But nothing will induce me to believe that wrong can be right, and I say that a soldier must stick to the first principles of duty & discipline; Whatever other people may think or do, his duty is plain.

I don't say a word against anyone who sees the matter in a

different light. I respect their convictions as I expect them to respect mine.

Manchester Central Library, D/3/D/1, James Mss

53
Second Lieutenant R. Macleod to his father

80th Battery
XV Brigade, RFA,
Kildare.
23 March 1914

[Holograph]

You may be interested to hear about everything that has happened but it must be strictly confidential.

On Friday afternoon I returned from playing golf at the Curragh about 6.40. As soon as I arrived in barracks my Major (Major Birley)[29] told me that I should have to decide that night whether I would obey orders to march and take part in operations in Ulster. If not, I would have to resign. At 7 we were called to the Colonel's office and we had a document read to us, which it was said was sent from the Army Council and sanctioned by the King. This said:

(i) Officers whose homes were in Ulster would be allowed to 'disappear' provided they took no active part in the operations.

(ii) Any officer who for conscientious or other reasons objected to service in Ulster would be instantly dismissed the service.

(iii) All other officers would have to obey implicitly all orders issued them.

It further stated that it was hoped that there would be very few officers who would elect to be dismissed.

There was no doubt in the minds of all present that active operations in the field were contemplated.

When the question was put to us 7 out of 15 officers, myself included, elected to be dismissed. Some others might have gone but could not afford to go as dismissal would entail loss of pension and all other privileges. We were given till 8 next morning (Saturday) to reconsider our decisions. We discussed the matter till late that night but I did not alter my views.

It was pointed out next morning that if many officers went the Army would split up, and the effect of this would be:
(i) A rising of the native population of India and the massacre of the white inhabitants.
(ii) A probable attack on us by Germany.
(iii) A rising of the socialists and syndicalists in England.

He [Fergusson] further pointed out that at first the measures were only undertaken for the purpose of law and order. We were then given till a little later to decide.

General Headlam—our brigadier general & General Fergusson our divisional general came & discussed the matter with us, & finally we all decided to stay on for the time being.

All officers and men had to stay in barracks and officers on leave were recalled on Saturday.

On Saturday night we got an order to mobilise 3 guns and wagons of each battery, and we had everything completed by 2 a.m. ready to move off at half an hour's notice.

As only 3 officers in each battery were being taken I applied for leave to stay behind, the officers going not holding such strong views on the subject as myself. I gave as my reason that I would probably have relatives fighting on the other side. This request was granted for the time being.

All Sunday we stayed in barracks expecting an order to move. Church parade was cancelled. However, no order came, and this morning the situation was obviously easier as officers were allowed to leave barracks provided they did not go far and left their address behind. We are still ready to move off at short notice.

Several officers who elected to be dismissed under Clause 2 of the 'Ultimatum' had their requests refused. Hewson[30] a subaltern in our battery was refused permission to disappear because his home was 15 miles outside Ulster. His father is an officer in the Ulster Volunteer Force.

Have I any relatives likely to fight for Ulster? I said that probably you would, if necessary, as you had signed the Covenant.

If I had been ordered to Ulster, I would have helped to keep law & order. I will order rooms for you at the Station Hotel from Thursday onwards. Let me know when to expect you.

Please remember me to all at 4 P.G.

Sunderland Polytechnic, 1914–1918 Archive, Macleod Mss; King's College, Liddell Hart Centre for Military Archives, Macleod Mss 1/1; Royal Artillery Institution. MD 1150

54
Captain J. V. Ramsden
to his family[31]

XXVII Brigade, R F A,
Newbridge.
[Holograph Copy]   24 March 1914

Your wire came just now. The strain of these last days has been too awful. The King's name has been forsworn—and everyone except Gough and Sir Charles Fergusson have lied.

On Friday at 6.30 p.m. I got a wire ordering me to rejoin at once. I got to my office on Saturday at 9 a.m. after a beastly journey. There my Colonel,[32] in tears, gave me a circular letter.

'In view of the possibility of active operations in Ulster, 1. officers whose families are domiciled in Ulster may apply for permission to "disappear". They will not suffer by such action and at the termination of operations they will be restored to their position. 2. officers who from conscience or other reasons are not prepared to do their duty will be instantly dismissed. 3. Brigadiers and Lt. Colonels will under penalty of trial by court martial see that no officer takes advantage of clause 1 who should come under clause 2. (I am not absolutely certain of the wording of this clause).'

Appended was a nominal roll of officers of the Brigade with a column headed 'Are you prepared to do your duty in Ulster'. (In some units this was 'Are you prepared to do your duty to the utmost extent of modern war').

I wrote 'No' thereby accepting instant dismissal.

Immediately after we were informed that Sir Charles Fergusson—commands the Division—would see all the officers of the Brigade in the Mess. He came at 11.30 a.m. and we all (ten) expected to be asked for our swords. He spoke to us like a *man*. He hated the whole business. He apologised for the raw and uncouth wording of the letter which he had taken down from Sir A. Paget's instructions. He told us that the only chance of averting bloodshed was to be undivided and appealed to our most sacred traditions. He further assured us that Sir A. Paget had given his positive assurance that all the movements (Fleet, 3 Battle Squadrons plus 3 *Divisions from England* plus from Ireland) were under His Majesty's direct and personal sanction, but that Sir A. Paget had not been able to get this *in writing*. Every officer and man here now knows that someone (? A.P. himself) lied as His Majesty has assured General Gough that he knew nothing about any movements at all. He then had all the men (of every unit) in turn formed up and assured them that it was the King's order and asked them to be loyal to the King.

We were all so upset that all but one of us would have followed him. I need not tell you that Sir Charles himself is one of the finest and most straight men I have ever met. Poor man, how he must suffer at the way he has been lied to and deceived. Nothing further happened except that we were ordered to get ready to move at once—again verbally.

On Sunday I saw Lloyd George's speech saying they would push the Bill through '*at all hazards*'. This meant nothing less than butchery and completely opened our eyes. Sir C. Fergusson had assured us on Sir A. Paget's authority that no firing was to take place if possible. I went to my Colonel and carefully and clearly repeated my refusal in unmistakeable terms and asked him to tell our Brigadier General RA so that there might be no misunderstanding.

I am glad to say he did so—so in our Brigade there are definite refusals—2 Majors, 2 Captains, 2 subalterns—the remainder did not I think seriously understand what was asked of them, so suddenly did the whole thing take place.

On Friday evening when this Memorandum was presented to the Cav Brigade all officers with exceptions—accepted dismissal—i.e. something over 50. On Saturday morning the Press asked Sir A. Paget if there had been a large number of resignations. He replied that there was no truth in the rumour (technically correct, since all refusals had been *dismissed*). Meanwhile where am I? Asquith says we have never been deposed—the Memorandum said we were to be *instantly* dismissed, but I am still doing my daily work, though it seriously upset the calm and routine of my office and gave my Colonel severe colic pains!

Now General Gough has come back and I hear from his Brigade that French threatened to have him shot (!)—that the King has approved of his action and denied all knowledge of what was passing. It seems that Churchill, Seely and French arranged his coup for Friday after Parliament rose so that nothing could be done to ventilate this iniquitous business till Monday. A. Paget (who is universally considered a liar) now seems to have given nothing but *verbal* instructions—why? Every officer here knows that a huge force was to be thrown into Ulster—again? Why? According to Sir C. Fergusson to show the Ulstermen that resistance would obviously be useless, but since the Divisions would have been at *peace* strength as they did not dare call up the reserves, not more than about 50,000 men (if 3000 were to be sent from England) and battleships could have been sent. The Artillery would have been represented by only one fifth of their proper numbers—again a silly 'try on'.

At present everyone is furious. They say the Cavalry Club is going to expel Churchill and Seely ought to be kicked out of White's, and both of them ought to be tried for High Treason.

The men are equally furious. I feel *perfectly sure* they would not have fired on the Ulstermen, in fact whole Battalions have said it. It is not the officers but the men who will not be made into butchers by Churchill and his tyrannous crowd.

H. of Lords RO, Bonar Law Mss, 32/1/57

55

Private C. Smith to his brother, W. H. Smith and sister-in-law, Mrs A. Smith[33] [34]

16th Lancers
Curragh Camp.
[24 March 1914]

[Holograph]

Thanks very much for letter received this morning (Tuesday), and at present trying to scribble some news. I have plenty to do as you may guess. As re the papers lately there has been some truth and some untruth. Well Harry last Thursday all the guards on the Curragh were doubled and served out with ball ammunition, as if for active service. Also extra guards put on at different points, also the roads guarded by armed men. On Friday my regiment was ordered to the North of Ireland destination unknown. Officers of my regiment many distinguished men amongst them, The Colonel, Lord Holmpatrick,[35] and all others held a conference and decided not to go to Ulster to fight such loyal men, as they are, and were in Africa. They informed all officers on the Curragh, at finish all decided to send in their papers. Of course then the big heads in Command had to follow suit, and at finish practically useless without officers, of course for the time being. Then Saturday all C.O.'s had to visit the War Office.

We gave our Colonel a good send off, every man in the Regiment was there to cheer him. Then the news came, that he was coming back Tuesday morning. One Squadron (C) was sent to escort him in from Kildare, they were in Review Order, which looked lovely. The Regimental Coach was drawn by 4 horses of the Maxim Gun Section, drivers also in Review Order. All men in Barracks waited to cheer him in and my word it was a reception. Then the Colonel and General Gough stepped out of the Coach and gave a speech thanking men of all ranks for backing them up in their fight with the War Office, which was a bloodless fight, and saved many lives. In Monday's Sketch there are photos of the [illegible].

In Tuesdays also photos of the 16th in Review Order, The

Crack Cavalry Regiment who refused to invade Ulster. Mr. Charlton a P.O. photographer, is a Sketch correspondent and has photos of everything that has been worth taking. If you want any photos of any regiments on the Curragh send to Mr. Charlton, Postmaster, Hare Pk P.O., Curragh. Everything now is rather quiet, we still have armed men on guard with ammunition.

Dear Harry, I don't think there is any more I can tell you at present. If anything striking occurs, I will at once let you know. Do you agree with our officers move, as re marching on Ulster, as I do not. Of course if we had orders from our officers to go there and fight I would not trouble in the least. It would be a change to do something exciting, in fact I would love to go on Active Service. No doubt you think I am a very bad writer by this letter, well I am doing it in drill time 1–1.2 time, as I am rather busy with parades. Last Tuesday we had a funeral, a young soldier was on night guard over the horses and whilst walking through the stables a horse kicked out and caught him on the right temple, am sorry to say that he died a quarter of an hour later. I was bearer, one of six. His name was Pte. Mercer. On Wednesday I was Field Officers Orderly in Review Order. Plenty of work getting ready. As regards writing every day, I do not think it necessary, unless I have something special to tell you, in such cases I will write. I must thank you for the presents enclosed, as they came in handy at the time. Pleased to know that Alma liked the Shamrock. I would have written to you then but I did not have time. Please give my best wishes to Alma and I trust all is well at present. I am in my prime.

Must now close as I have plenty to do.

Smith Mss

56

Notes by Lieutenant Colonel I. G. Hogg on the events of 20–23 March 1914

4th Hussars,
Curragh Camp.
25 March 1914
(with later additions)

[Typescript Copy]

1. In March 1914 4th Hussars formed part of 3rd Cavalry Brigade, of which 5th Lancers were at Dublin, 16th Lancers and 4th Hussars at the Curragh and III Brigade Horse Artillery at Newbridge. Br. General H. de le P. Gough, C.B. Commanded the Brigade with Major Kearsley[36] 5th Dragoon Guards as Brigade Major.

2. On March 20th 1914 Gen. Gough returned from Dublin whither he had been called to see Gen. Sir A. Paget, commanding the Forces in Ireland. He called all officers of the Brigade (except 5th Lancers in Dublin) to meet him in 16th Lancers Mess at 3.30 p.m. The subject of the conference was not stated.

3. General Gough told us that he had been instructed by the Commander in Chief to put the following proposition before us:

In view of the possibility of active Military operations taking place in Ulster immediately, officers must decide whether they are prepared to obey all orders or not. In the latter case officers domiciled in Ulster would be allowed to 'disappear' and would be reinstated without prejudice to their careers at a subsequent date. All other officers must resign and would be dismissed the service with loss of pensions. An answer must be given by 6 p.m.

The General told us he had been called on to decide and had accepted dismissal as the proposal was contrary to his whole upbringing, religion and feelings, and that he would leave each officer to decide for himself and could not offer any help or advice in the circumstances.

We all understood that the inquisition was ordered by the War Office.

I asked my officers to reassemble in our own Mess and left.

4. The question came as a bombshell to us, as I had discouraged all discussion of the Ulster question in the Mess and nobody had, therefore, thought out his position.

We all resented being called upon to decide such a question at a few hours notice under threats and therefore decided to accept dismissal, two officers claiming the protection of the domicile clause.

5. Major Howell, Captain Stokes (adjt.)[37] and myself then went to the Brigade office where we found the Brigadier, Brigade Major, Colonel Breeks RHA, and one or two others. On Major Howell's suggestion it was resolved to endeavour to gain time and to make our position clear on paper. The letter marked A.[38] was accordingly drawn up, signed by the Brigadier and sent to Dublin.

6. After dinner I wrote a telegram to Mr. Churchill, an old brother officer, and 1st Lord of the Admiralty, Marked B,[39] and, after reading it to Major Howell and a few of my senior officers and by telephone to the Brigadier, I sent it off at 8 a.m. next morning Saturday 21st.

This ended Friday 20th March.

7. On Saturday March 21st General Sir A. Paget came down and called all officers of the brigade to meet him at 11 a.m. (except 5th Lancers).

Sir A. Paget spoke for about $\frac{1}{2}$ hour without any notes, the gist of what he said as it remains in my mind is as follows:

(a) He was appalled at our action and the disgrace to the Army.

(b) He had no orders from the War Office to carry out an inquisition but merely wished to put certain possibilities before us and to know our probable course of action.

(c) Certain 'precautionary movements' of infantry had been made to guard certain stores in Ulster and some guns at Dundalk. These moves were made as much out of fear of action by 'Hibernians'[40] as by the Ulster Volunteers.

As a matter of fact they had all been accomplished without disorder and the troops had been received with ovation by the Ulster Volunteers.

At the same time he had to be ready for disturbances and to support them if, as he had thought possible, any movements of troops had caused a blaze in Ulster. These supporting movements would have involved some 20,000 troops including 10,000 from England and a portion of the Navy.

(d) A large camp had been prepared on the Boyne.

(e) He had no intention of carrying out coercion measures against Ulster. Had it been necessary to move large bodies of troops into Ulster he would have marched at their head himself, and if they met the Ulster Volunteers he would ride forward and talk to the Ulster leaders. If the Ulster leaders chose to fire he would not ask his troops to return their fire but after the first burst would go forward himself to parley. He only wanted Cavalry to act as Scouts so as to prevent his bumping unexpectedly into the Volunteers and losing control over the situation. As a matter of fact a Cavalry Regiment would be sent South to protect the Protestants there against possible action by Hibernians.

(f) All the moves had been intended to prevent bloodshed, not to provoke it.

(g) Did we not trust him as C-in-C to make good his word that there should be no bloodshed. If not he would resign.

(h) He himself would not obey orders from Politicians, if he did not know they had the sanction of the King.

(i) General Gough and the Colonels were to go to London that night.

This address naturally made different impressions on different minds. To mine, discarding the wild and minatory phrases, it seemed to give the assurance that had been asked for in Gen. Gough's letter of the previous evening, and to mean that now that the precautionary movements for the protection of guns and stores had been successfully carried out, no further action was necessary or contemplated unless the Volunteers or Hibernians took the initiative.

8. After Sir A. Paget had gone, the remainder of the day was spent in discussions as to whether Sir A. Paget's speech could be interpreted as a valid assurance or not. In the end Gen. Gough, Lt. Colonels Parker and MacEwen decided to adhere to their resignations and go to London. I told Sir C. Fergusson that I would accept Sir A. Paget's speech as an assurance but felt that I must press for leave to accompany the other senior officers to London as if the War Office repudiated my interpretation of Sir A. Paget's speech or took vindictive measures against the other senior officers, I, and I felt sure my officers, would wish to stand by their resignations.

9. I then went back to officers, told them my decision and asked for theirs. The paper marked C.[41] explains itself.

10. I crossed to London with Gen. Gough, and Lt. Cols. MacEwen and Parker. We were ordered to report ourselves to the Adj. General at the War Office at 10 a.m. on Sunday 22nd March.

11. Before proceeding to the War Office I went to the admiralty and saw Mr. Churchill. He told me that my telegram was the first intimation that the Government had received of any alternatives having been put before us. That from the telegraphic report of the incident from Sir A. Paget it had appeared to the Government to be a concerted refusal to obey any orders which might be given to us to proceed to Ulster engineered by our brigadier. He admitted that my statement put an entirely new complexion on the incident and that his assistance would be at our disposal. He also gave me his personal assurance that no coercive measures had been contemplated unless Ulster assumed the initiative.

12. At the War Office we were seen separately by the Adjutant General, Sir J. S. Ewart, with whom was General Sir N. Macready, Director of Personal Services, my evidence was as follows:

That I was prepared to obey all lawful orders given by duly instituted authority for the preservation of law, order and property. That I could conceive a situation amounting to Civil War in which case, should it arise, I thought every officer must decide his own course of action, and that the present situation would not have arisen but for the inquisition of 20th.

I further said I had withdrawn my resignation on Sir A. Paget's appeal but should resign if vindictive measures were taken against officers for a situation not, in my opinion, of their creation.

We were ordered to attend again on Monday 23rd.

13. On Monday 23rd Br. General Gough was taken to see Field Marshal Sir John French and then Colonel Seely, Secretary of State for War. At 12 noon Lt. Cols. MacEwen, Parker and myself were taken to Sir John French's room and left with Gen. Gough for 15 minutes at the expiration of which Sir John said he would return and ask for a decision.

Gen. Gough told us that he had been told, the Army Council would recognise that a mistake and honest misunderstanding had arisen, that they would consider the situation as being put back to Thursday 19th, that they were glad to know he did not refuse to obey orders for the maintenance of law and order and that, though Government reserved the right to use all the troops in any part of the King's Dominions for that purpose, they did not intend to use them for the coercion of Ulster. Gen. Gough said he had asked for this in writing as verbal messages had already given rise to misunderstandings and was to call at 4 p.m. to receive a written memorandum. We all agreed to return to duty and Gen. Gough told Sir John French our decision on his return to the room. The written document is marked D^{42} and annexed.

This ended the crisis so far as 3rd Cavalry Brigade was concerned.

> (Sgd.) I. Hogg
> Lt. Colonel
> Commanding 4th Hussars.

Captain Stokes

25 March 1914

Do you agree that this memorandum written for the historical records of the regiment is a correct statement of facts so far as the incidents at the Curragh on 20th and 21st March are concerned.

(Sgd.) I.H.

2

I agree that the facts are correct—though Sir A. Paget's speech gave one great misgivings.

(Sgd.) A. V. W. Stokes.
Captain.
Adjutant 4th Hussars.

3

28 April 1914

I wish to make it quite clear that the interpretation of Sir A. Paget's speech was mine and that those officers who followed my lead did so out of a sense of loyalty to me as C.O. and not in every case because they agreed with my interpretation.

I have added some notes by other officers of the brigade given to me by the Brigadier so that the different interpretations can be seen.

(Sgd.) I.H.

28 April 1914

My dear General,

If you have a moment to spare after dinner would you look through attached and see if you think it is a fair account of the action of this unit for our records.

If it strikes you as incorrect or too ex parte will you put a query?

It is written for posterity.

Yours
(Sgd.) Ian Hogg

— — — — — — — —

I think this is a very fair, correct statement.

Was interested to hear that Winston C. thought I had 'engineered' the trouble!

That was caused by the d-d rot that French, Paget, and other W.O. officers have been talking about me for years!

They did not *know* me in reality *at all*—what b-y fools they are—as well as b-y liars (luckily!)

(Sgd.) H.G.

Pragnell Mss

57
Lieutenant-General Sir Arthur Paget
to King George V

Parkgate,
Dublin.

[Typescript]   25 March 1914

With reference to the audience granted me on the 23rd instant by Your Majesty, and the debate in the House of Commons on the same day, a report of which I have just received, I think it my duty to place before your Majesty a short statement of the circumstances that led up to this debate; circumstances which culminated in a garbled account being given to Your Majesty of what I said to my senior officers last Friday.

Some weeks ago I reported verbally to the Secretary of State for War and to the Prime Minister that, in view of the political unrest in the country, certain of my Depôts containing Arms and Ammunition were practically unguarded, and might easily be raided, and were, in any case, a source of temptation.

On the 15th March I received a letter from the War Office, directing me to take immediate steps to safeguard Depôts and other places where stores were kept.

I at once initiated steps to remove Reserve Arms and Ammunition from the more isolated spots, and, in a letter forwarded to the

War Office on 17th instant, I pointed out that, from the point of view of safety, it would be advisable to provide special guards at certain points. I expressed, however, my opinion that such movements of troops would cause intense excitement in Ulster, and might possibly precipitate a crisis; and that therefore I did not consider myself justified in moving troops at that juncture.

On the 18th March, in obedience to a telegraphic summons, I interviewed the Secretary of State for War, and reported to him verbally in the sense of the above letter, I received orders from him to despatch at once the guards which I had recommended for safety reasons, and I sent cipher instructions from England to carry out the moves, for which orders had been previously drafted before I left Dublin. These moves were to be completed by the early morning of the 21st March.

I received no other orders from the War Office, except to return and take whatever action I thought right to maintain law and order, in the event of any of my troops, then on the move by road and rail, meeting with opposition.

Holding, as I did, the opinion that the movement of troops which had been ordered might precipitate a crisis, I considered it necessary to summon an immediate conference of senior officers, since I was not certain that all my Brigadiers were of my own opinion that duty came before any other consideration. Had any of my senior officers refused to obey or act in the circumstances which, in my opinion, might arise at very short notice, the results would have been even more serious than the present position. I knew that all troops were loyal to their Sovereign, but I had doubts as to their loyalty to His Advisers.

This Conference, which was attended by the General Officer Commanding 5th Division, and the Brigadier-Generals of the Cavalry Brigade, and the 13th and 14th Infantry Brigades,[43] was held at 10 a.m. on the morning of the 20th instant.

I informed the officers that I had received orders to carry out certain movements of troops, and that the Secretary of State for War had assured me that these movements were only in support of law and order. I told the officers, however, that though these movements were in themselves undoubtedly in support of law and order, I was of opinion that they would cause great excitement, and that possibly there might be opposition. In the latter case I must be prepared to move at once to the support of my troops, and that a situation might then rapidly evolve which might set Ireland ablaze by Saturday, and would lead to something more serious than quelling of local disturbances.

I then informed the officers that, in view of the possibility of active operations in Ulster, the War Office had authorized me to make the following communication to officers:

Officers whose homes were actually in the province of Ulster might, if they wished to do so, apply for permission to be absent from duty during the period of operations, and would be allowed to disappear from Ireland. Such officers would be subsequently reinstated and would suffer no loss in their career.

I added that any officer who, from conscientious or other motives, was not prepared to carry out his duty should say so, and, in answer to a question, I said 'such officers will at once be dismissed from the Service'. I expressed the hope that very few cases would be found of officers who elected thus to sever their connection with the Service.

As regards the exemption offered to officers whose homes were in Ulster, the limitation was to be interpreted strictly and literally. I explained to the assembled officers that it would be necessary to hold a Conference in the afternoon, in order to explain possible developments and my plans, and that no officer could be allowed to attend this Conference who did not mean to carry out the orders given to him. Consequently, any officer present who had doubts as to his conduct must decide before 2 p.m. I then asked if any officer present wished to make any remark.

Brigadier-General Gough then explained his own position, and stated that he could not claim exemption as a resident of Ulster, but that, on account of birth and upbringing, and many friendships, he did not see how he could bear Arms against the Ulster loyalists, and that, if he did take up Arms against them, he could never face his friends again.

I informed General Gough that no exemption could be made

in his case, that he must consider his position seriously, and that I hoped I should see him at the second Conference.

The Conference then broke up, and General Gough did not attend the second Conference in the afternoon.

On hearing late that day that a number of officers of the 3rd Cavalry Brigade intended to resign, I went down on the following morning to the Curragh and, to save the reputation of these three Regiments and the credit of the Forces in Ireland, I made certain concessions of which I have already informed Your Majesty verbally,[44] which I did not think that they could possibly refuse. I cannot hold myself justified in making these concessions, but had General Gough and his Officers trusted me and withdrawn their resignations, the critical situation with regard to the Army, as disclosed by the debate in the House of Commons last Monday, would never have taken place.

IWM, 75/46/8, French Mss; RA GV F.674/35; BL, Add Mss 51250, Paget Mss

58
Second Lieutenant E. G. Miles to his sister Mildred Miles

2nd KOSB,
Royal Barracks,
Dublin.
[Holograph]   25 March 1914

Many thanks for your letters & please thank Father for his. I am using this paper as I have a good deal of news. As regards the present state of affairs things seem brighter. I expect that Seely's resignation will introduce some new change, John Dunville, M.F.H. told us yesterday at the point-to-point that in a private letter from Carson the latter told him that the resignation of officers was the very worst thing possible for the cause of Ulster. What his arguments are I don't know, but that is a thing which most people have not realised. As regards the Labour cry about the aristocratic & plutocratic army & what will happen in the next Labour trouble, I think the whole thing is nothing more than a party cry. These Labourites & Socialists seem to imagine that the entire feeling was amongst officers only, but I know for a fact that it was not. Amongst the sergeants & other better educated N.C.O.'s the feeling was the same as that of the officers & I feel sure that if they had promoted the N.C.O.'s to officers that they would also have declined to go North in the same way that their officers did. As regards the men, the type of man we get has no feeling beyond his pocket & his stomach, the reasons being that he is uneducated & unintelligent. Consequently on such an occasion as this he has no conscience & treats the whole affair in the most light hearted way as being rather a joke. If the private soldier had a conscience as some of the better ones do, such as cavalry & engineers, I feel quite sure that under these circumstances he would detest to go north to Ulster, as much as the officers, only he would do it if he was told to owing to the discipline & the fact that he could not get out of it. Therefore I think that John Ward & others are absolutely wrong in their cry about officers versus Government etc. & what will happen in the next Labour troubles because on this occasion the men, at any rate the intelligent ones & the N.C.O.'s are with the officers in their opinion and the other unintelligent ones having no conscience and as I say no feeling beyond their pocket & their stomach do not understand the crisis & so treat it light heartedly. I am by no means abusing the gentlemen who think of nothing beyond their pocket & stomachs in fact people say, from experience, that this is the very best man you can have in war, in fact far better than some of the educated & intelligent men who think they know too much. The former is the fellow who is going to help you through in war, whereas the latter will probably fail you at the most critical moment, this is the opinion of some of our officers who have had a wide experience. Again to argue with John Ward, I have known Labourites distributing seditious and Socialite tracts to our men during the last strikes & on every occasion the tracts received a very poor reception & if the donor of such made an appearance in barracks he was in all probability hastily removed by the men at their own accord. So Mr. Ward is not quite right in his opinion of what Tommy Atkins thinks on the subject of Socialism & Labourism. I remember an occasion at Holywood during the strikes[45] when a seditious socialist came to the barrack gates & proceed to issue tracts & use grave threat to the sentry (a recruit of under 4 months service) the Soc: told the sentry that if any of our men came out to keep order in the strikes the mob 'would break their sculls & roll them in the mud &c' to which the young recruit replied 'its not we men what want to fight you, its our officers what make us' & with this [sic] words he pushed the very revered socialist back through the gate by the shortest route & advised him to go elsewhere with his tracts. What this young fellow of only 4 months service meant, was that although he was not too keen himself to fight his 'brothers', his officers had told him he had got to keep order & so he was going to do it & was having no nonsense with the 'tractor'. On one instance at Aldershot the men put a Soc: into a horse trough when he started delivering similar tracts in the barracks.

Now as regards the officers, you will see that Gen. Gough has returned & so also the officers, who by the way never really went out, as they only signified their intentions of resigning, hence the Government's prompt denial that 100 officers had resigned. The general feeling seems to be that those officers who signified their intention of resigning should do so, even if the affair is now settled. It seems rather hard but there are arguments on both sides. On the one side of course financial loss & loss of position in army & on the other they say, that it would prove that it was not done as a political or party move but as a matter of conscience, & being a matter of conscience still they should, feeling it impossible to hold a commission, resign. For example, if an English Officer married a German wife—he should resign his commission—because in his conscience he knows that he is not prepared under all circumstances to do what he is told by the King, e.g. go to war with Germany, which would of course be impossible if the wife was a patriotic German—& so feeling that he would be unable to do so, he should resign before he is asked to, namely as soon as he marries. This is the argument that many put forward, it seems rather hard & drastic but there is something in it after all. Several of our officers who stated that they flatly refused to go to Ulster, if called upon to do so, feel still bound by their conscience, in spite of the enormous loss that it would mean, & mark you this loss is far greater than the average man imagines, it is not only financially (as when honour & conscience are touched finance is not considered) but loss of employment & even greater loss of comradeship with the other officers. I think that the last mentioned is perhaps the greatest of the three. So now you see what the Government have done for their army & the 'nice' position that they have put their officers in. I wonder how much the general public realise about this. I am not speaking about myself as I am only young but I know exactly what our older officers think & one of them (an Irishman) told me that the matter had haunted him for some time past. We have had long and continuous debates on the subject ever since I returned & I have listened to them all with the deepest interest. The Colonel[46] gave his views on the subject the other evening & the reason why he did not 'resign' with the other officers, but I will not give them to you here. I sincerely hope that our officers will not go, for nothing would be more detestable than to feel that you had gained anything (as regards promotion) by the resignation of one's brother officers under such exceptional circumstances. One would almost feel it one's duty to go too, but then there is the other side, apart from finance. So I hope that affairs will turn out well & that no one will have to go. I know that one of our majors has written a letter asking if he resigns now, the '*crisis*' being over, having a conscience as I previously stated, if he will get his pension. Money is detestable, but after serving 15 to 20 years, with war service, & having a wife and family one has to think twice before forfeiting a pension of £300 or so a year. It would be a good thing if there was a little more 'conscience' in politics today & a little less thirst for money. I am glad that Seely has done the right thing at last, if rumours are true, as it was the only honourable course open to him. There is one other point that I dont quite understand, the politicians? (John Ward & Co) talk about 'the officers refusing to fight against their own class'—surely there are far more of the men's class than the officer's class in the Ulster army & so why should not the men object just as much as the officers in this case, & a good many of them do. I heard from a colonel that Lord Bobs & the King have been in consultation a great deal & that on one occasion Bobs handed over his field-marshal's baton, but I take it that it was promptly returned.

Now that I have expended a great deal of ink on 'letting off steam' we will start the news. Our point to point was cancelled on Monday night, however, Tuesday morning brought brighter prospects so at the last moment we decided to hold it. I was unfortunately Orderly Officer so I had to run round & get some one to answer for me, as everyone wanted to go & see the race, it was rather a difficult task, eventually I got the Quartermaster to do it. So we all hurried out to the Course about 24 miles out. Ours was the second race so we were none too soon. I had rather a shock when I 'weighed' in, I had on a shirt & a very thick Alpaca pink racing coat, a racing cap, also a pair of breeches, a light hunting saddle & I turned the scale at 14 stone, the weight being 12.7, so I rode considerably overweight. Nine of us started. The course was 4 miles long and as we missed the 1st 3 jumps as the course was about 4½ m wide. Then we had about 30 obstacles to get over most of them fairly big some very big. We started in a bunch, at about the 10th jump a fairly large bank Rifler did not jump quite large enough so we both rolled over in the mud, he seemed to catch the bank with his chest. I caught him at once & got on again. I still had I think 3 behind me. I think that fall gave the old horse rather a knock because he seemed to get tired rather soon. At about the 15th fence Hartley[47] came up & joined me and we road [sic] on together. The old horse grew tireder & tireder, especially as the going was heavy & I myself was getting fearfully done, as I was not in training, at the 24th jump a large bank and ditch on the far side (Leighs horse had fallen here & was still in the ditch, about 8 ft. deep, & Leigh was waiting on the bank being unable to get him out) I jumped just to the left of Leighs horse, but Rifler pecked & I being very done lost a stirrup which dropped off, meanwhile Hartley had gained on me at this jump, old Rifler was now fearfully done so I took him on at a slower pace wondering at every jump if he would get over all right, which he did and eventually we finished the course both absolutely 'done'. Kennedy was down at the last jump, his horse having fallen for the second time was lying on the ground 'winded' he was leading when he fell. Joynson[48] won the race on Cup-o-Wisdom, the horse that won last year, the Colonels horse Whistling Rufus (ridden by Hammond) was second, also 2nd last year & Hartley was third. Cobden 5th[49] Dering 6th[50] (these two overtook me when my horse was so done at the end) Myself 7th Pennyman 8th[51] & Kennedy & Leigh[52] did not finish. It was a great race. I was so done that I was riding entirely by balance over the last fences or rather banks & ditches. It is rather a beastly sensation riding a tired horse over those ditches because I always felt that he would jump short and break his back. They had one or two large ones at the end. Every horse was done & almost everyone fell. The course was excellent but rather too long (4 miles) & rather too big for our horses which were not absolutely in training. On the whole it was a topping day—and I think we put up a very good race. We got more fellows round the course than in either of the Hunt Races. Poor old Rifler had to carry an extra 1 st 7lbs but he jumped beautifully only was dead beat at the end. I am terribly stiff today—Today I lunched with Mrs. Doig (tell Violet as she knows her very well & she enquires after them both). Tell Mrs. Cherry that 'the' Miss Hammond was there at lunch and is staying over here till next Friday week.

Tell her (Mrs. Cherry) that 'when interviewed by a press representative he (me) declined to give an opinion until a later date'—By the way you gaily sent on the photo of Ben, in spite of my instructions, so I enclose it now—Please give it to Mrs. Cherry & remind her that she said she would like one, some time, on the night that she dined with us (the *only* occasion) about a month ago. Good news 4 subalterns being promoted Captain— According to the new Reg[ns.] the Signalling Officer only exist in time of peace to train the men, so on Mobilisation or Manoeuvres I am going back to my old billet of Transport Officer. Many thanks for the pyjamas. Please thank Nell for her letter just received—I have got plenty of work to do just at present. I am playing a good deal of racquets—I am beginning to know the Morning Post by heart since the last few days. I have had no time to read 'bar—bit—bat &c' I am glad to hear that the hens have increased their capacity. How is Bertie? The Barrack gates are still bolted & there are still 6 ammunition carts (full) outside the guard room. Tonight we (the Mess) received anonymously several copies of the poster we had in our hall of 'John Redmond & the Highlander'. The words 'Have you forgotten' at the top were crossed out & replaced by 'We know you have not forgotten' and the postmark was Belfast. I dont know who sent them & I am afraid they had to go straight into the fire as no party literature of such a type is allowed in the Mess, especially not under the existing circumstances—we try to avoid the political aspect as much as possible—

Have you got the pony and cart yet or are you waiting until after the Ulster crisis? I dont think I can write any more as it is now 12 oc midnight and this is the 12th sheet. I had a letter from Granny and answered it in due course. Tell her any of this news that may interest her as I cannot write another long letter. So long now— Love to the family and the detachment over the road.

Miles Mss

59

Major-General Sir Charles Fergusson to Major-General L. B. Friend

Ballyfair,
Curragh.
[Typescript]   25 March 1914

During the last few days I have refrained from sending to you any written reports regarding the attitude and feelings of the Officers and men of the Division under my Command, for two reasons:

(1) It was sufficient for the purposes of the moment that the Commander of the Forces should know that all ranks were

prepared to carry out any orders he was pleased to give. Of this he was aware, from my verbal reports made to him from time to time.

(2) I did not wish to add to the difficulties and worries of the moment by sending in a report which, however carefully worded, might possibly create a needlessly alarmist sensation.

Now however the situation is, at least temporarily, less strained, it is right that you should be informed of what has passed, and of the present condition of affairs.

On Friday evening, March 20th, after Brigadiers and O.C. Units had interviewed their officers, I reported that the situation as regards notices of resignations of Officers was on the whole satisfactory.

Next morning however, Saturday 21st, I was told by Brigadiers that, owing to the action of the 3rd Cavalry Brigade having become generally known, there was a great change in the demeanour of both Officers and men at the Curragh, Newbridge and Kildare. It was reported to me that a very large number of Officers had decided to follow the lead of the Cavalry Brigade, and that the situation was very strained.

On this, I paraded each unit Infantry and Artillery in turn, and addressed first the Officers and then the men.

In the afternoon I went to Dublin and saw all doubtful Officers of the 13th Infantry Brigade and the 1st Bn East Surrey Regiment which is also quartered there.

I also wrote at length to the troops of the Division on detachment at Newry, Dundalk, and in the Belfast area.

By Saturday evening I was able again to report to Headquarters that all the troops of the Division so far as those within reach were concerned, could be relied on; and that the resignations of Officers would be limited to a few individual cases.

This estimate of the situation has been confirmed by subsequent enquiries, and by reports from O.C. Units. I have not yet heard officially from Units of the 15th Infantry Brigade, which is not now under my command; but I understand that they have taken the same views as the rest of the Division.

During these days various movements of troops were ordered, and were carried out expeditiously and cheerfully; noticeably in the case of a section of the 59th Company R.E. which marched from Barracks within one hour and a half of the receipt of the order from Headquarters.

I wish however to report officially, for the information of the Commander of the Forces, that the attitude of Officers in the Division is correctly set forward in the attached letter from the Brigadier-General Commanding 14th Infantry Brigade.[53] That letter accurately represents the feeling of all ranks in the Division, and I wish to associate myself and the Officers of my Staff with the expressions contained in it.

I recognise that such an expression of opinion would, under ordinary circumstances, be hardly consistent with discipline. But I respectfully submit that in the present extraordinary crisis it is a matter of duty to state clearly the conditions which exist and which have to be faced. And I further venture to hope that the proofs of loyalty and discipline which the Officers and men under my Command have given in the recent crisis, under considerable stress and temptation, may be held to excuse this representation of their feelings.

RA GV F.674/44(a) App B; Fergusson Mss; PRO, WO 35/209 (g)

60

Captain F. A. Forster to his family

1st Royal Fusiliers,
Spike Island,
Queenstown.
[25] March 1914

[Holograph]

Thanks for yours.

I can't tell you anymore than you see in the papers now— except that from inside one felt absolutely certain that movements on a big scale were intended against Ulster at the end of last week.

One's own views are, as stated in Parliament by some cove at the time of the American colonies war—When a soldier's country is fighting he has no call to question the right or wrong of its course, but when it comes to civil war he can & should obey his own feelings.

What the Radicals will slur over, unless the Opposition bring it out today, is that officers did not refuse to go to Ulster. They were given the opportunity by the Govt: of not going, and accepted it at whatever cost.

You ask about men. Unless they've been quartered up there, they don't think much about it—but now that the example has been set I don't think they'd fight the U.V.F. and I'm certain they'd follow the example of their officers.

Its all very unfortunate & *terribly* bad for discipline. But if it has saved civil war I suppose we must hold it cheap at the price.

Hope your horse meeting was successful. A friend of mine sold a bad hunter to a sausageman the other day and got a better price for it as meat than he would have as a hunter! But it was not 'broken down' or 'worn out'. The man told him horses weigh so much more than beef & are better value in that way!

I've applied for my leave again from 1st. I hope I may get it as things have quietened.

The Senate of Manch: Univ:[ersity] want me to dine!

IWM. P. 473 (2), Forster Mss

61

Major-General Sir Charles Fergusson
to Lord Stamfordham

Ballyfair,
Curragh.

[Typescript]   27 March 1914

I am sorry that your letter dated yesterday[54] reached me too late for a reply to be sent by this evening's post.

I have of course seen Colonel Brett's letter already. It was given to me on Saturday last by his Brigadier, and handed by me to Sir Arthur Paget the same evening.

As regards the secret letter to which he refers, I can only explain by going into the matter in some details:

On Friday 20th March Sir Arthur Paget at a conference of senior officers under his Command, gave certain instructions as to the situation and the possible developments that might take place.

He said that he had obtained from the Secretary of State for War the concession that officers who actually had their homes in Ulster would not be required to take part in operations in that province. They might 'disappear', without any ultimate adverse effect on their career or position.

He went on to say that other officers must understand that, if they were not prepared to do their duty, they must say so. Their resignations could not be accepted, and they would be dismissed the Service forthwith. He mentioned that the Secretary of State for War hoped there would be very few of such officers. We were told to put the above before our officers at once, and that immediate decision was imperative.

We were all under the impression, from the manner of the communication and from the references made to the Secretary of State, that this was given us on War Office authority. And in putting down on paper the terms of the communication to be made to officers in furtherance of these instructions, I used the words 'The War Office has authorised the following communication to be made to officers'.[55]

That was my understanding and interpretation of the verbal communication made to me by Sir Arthur Paget. Brigadier General Rolt, Commanding the 14th Infantry Brigade, to which Colonel Brett's Battalion belongs, in communicating with the Officers under his command used almost identically the same words.

Colonel Brett apparently assumed, not unnaturally, that the communication was in the form of an extract from a War Office letter, whereas it was merely a memorandum embodying the verbal instructions of the GOC in Chief who, as I and others understood him, conveyed it to us with the authority of the War Office.

The answer therefore to your question is that there was no War Office secret letter. What Colonel Brett refers to is the memorandum conveyed to him (either written or by dictation) from his Brigadier, which stated that it was by authority of the War Office that certain questions were put; and which he erroneously supposed to have been an extract from a War Office letter.

I hope this is clear. I am enclosing a copy of the memorandum which I issued to certain officers under my command, which is practically identical with what was put to Colonel Brett, and which explains the misconception.

As regards the other more serious point: Sir Arthur Paget at a subsequent conference in the afternoon of the same day went into details of what might conceivably take place.

I asked him if I might take it that the orders were sanctioned by His Majesty. He replied in the affirmative.

When interviewing Officers next morning, when the situation was very critical (I mean, as to whether the Officers and men would obey orders or not), I was repeatedly asked the same question, and I replied that I had myself asked the GOC in Chief, and he had replied Yes.

I fully admit that throughout that day in appealing to Officers and men to remain loyal to their duty I said that as the King's soldiers we had no option but to loyally carry out the orders we received without question.

I do not wish to shelter behind the GOC in Chief. In any case, the orders having come to me through my superiors in the ordinary course I should have held that technically they were from His Majesty, and respected them as such. And I would under the extraordinary circumstances prevailing, even without the assurance of the GOC in C above referred to, have felt justified in using the same argument to Officers and men.

I reported to Sir Arthur Paget the same evening that I had quoted his assurance, and as already stated handed him Colonel

Brett's letter in which reference is made to that asurance. I have since on more than one occasion referred to the matter in conversation with him.

Until the receipt of your letter tonight, I had not the slightest conception that I had unwittingly deceived the Officers and men under my command. And I would add that my action throughout has been taken under the firm impression that I was carrying out both technically *and in reality* the orders of His Majesty. Nothing short of that consideration together with my sense of duty to the Army would have induced me to have withheld my resignation, whatever the consequences.

RA. GV. F. 674/44; Fergusson Mss

62

Account by Major-General Sir James Fergusson[56]

[Typescript Copy with holograph additions]

Curragh
27 March 1914

FRIDAY MARCH 20TH

The Commander of the Forces held a Conference at Headquarters in Dublin at 10 a.m.

At this were present the following Officers:

H.Q. Staff	Major-General Friend
	Brigadier-General Forestier-Walker
5th Divn.	Major-General Sir C. Fergusson
	Brigadier-General Rolt
	Brigadier-General Cuthbert
3/Cavy. Bde.	Brigadier-General Gough
Comdr. 11 Dist.	Colonel Hill

The Commanding-in-Chief's personal Staff Officers did not attend.

The Commander of the Forces began by saying that what he had to say might appear theatrical. But the situation was very serious. Certain measures were to be taken, and it was conceivable that trouble would result. The whole place would be in a blaze, he thought, tomorrow. Precautionary measures had already been taken, and he detailed those which had already taken place. There were war ships at Belfast Lough, at Kingstown, and at Lamlash. Other troops would in the event of disturbance have to be moved. I think he added (at this Conference) that in the event of such disturbance, such an enormous force would be displayed that Ulster would be convinced of the impossibility of resistance. I am not clear whether it was on this occasion, or in the afternoon, that he explained that the Government buildings in Belfast were to be occupied at daybreak next morning, and explained the reason. This was, that the Government were determined that no aggressive act on their part should start the conflict. If anyone started the fighting it should be the Ulstermen. Should they anticipate the Government by occupying these buildings the Government would be forced to turn them out, and bloodshed would result. By occupying these buildings now, the onus of any aggressive act would fall on the Ulstermen. He reiterated over and over again that there was to be no aggression on the part of the troops; he would expect them to accept punishment without returning the fire, in the hopes that an opportunity would offer for parley, and the Government terms accepted.

Sir Arthur Paget then said that he had been in close consultation at the War Office until a late hour the previous evening. He said that the promise that had been made him some time ago, to the effect that opportunity would be given in good time to Officers who wished to resign to do so, could not be kept, as the situation had arisen suddenly. He had after much persuasion been able only to secure from the War Minister certain concessions. He had first succeeded in persuading Sir John French, had told him that he could make no impression on the Minister for War, and subsequently at the last moment by Sir John's help had obtained the following concessions from Colonel Seely.

First. Officers actually domiciled in Ulster would be exempted from taking part in any operations that might take place. They would be permitted to 'disappear', (that being the exact phrase used by the War Office), and when all was over would be allowed to resume their places without their career or position being affected. [Added note: This Sir Arthur states was not his meaning. He only meant to point out that Officers who refused to obey orders must stand the natural consequences—He did not mean to ask their intentions]

Secondly. Officers who stated they were unwilling to serve might tender their resignations, but these could not be accepted. And Officers doing so would be forthwith dismissed from the Service.

(In the afternoon, I think, Sir Arthur added that they would probably be tried by Court Martial, or, if not, dismissed without that formality.)

The phrase 'domiciled in Ulster' was to be strictly interpreted as those who actually had their homes within that province. They must certify this on paper, and must give their word of honour to take no part in any operations on the side of Ulster. Brigadiers were to be held responsible, under penalty of Court Martial, that they had verified so far as possible the genuineness of such applications.

Sir Arthur referred to the difficulty of obtaining these concessions, and said that the war Minister had, with regard to the latter class, said 'I hope there will be very few of these'.

[This point is of some importance, in view of the subsequent alleged misunderstanding as to these being War Office instructions. I am certain that the remark was quoted in such a connection that it was understood by me, at any rate, to refer to the latter class, because at the time it passed through my mind that this was a very sanguine view to take. And it explains why all those present apparently got the impression that the whole communication to be made to officers was based on War Office instructions.]

Sir Arthur then said that if any one of us present was not prepared to take his part he must come to a decision, and in that case he must not attend the second conference to be held that afternoon, as none but those who were prepared to do their duty could be admitted to further councils. Brigadiers were to go at once and put the alternatives before the officers. Decisions must be prompt, and the numbers who were not prepared to do their duty notified without delay, if possible by that evening. Turning to General Gough, he said that a squadron of Cavalry from Dublin was to be held in readiness to march northwards next morning if required.

He then said 'Has anyone any remarks to make'? The only one who spoke, after a pause, was General Gough, who pointed out that although his home was not actually in Ulster, he was intimately associated with that part of Ireland. Sir Arthur Paget replied that the domicile condition was absolutely to be strictly interpreted, and that he (General Gough) could not be held to come under that clause.

The officers present then withdrew. Sir Arthur's last remark was 'Tell your Officers to trust me, and I will guarantee that there shall be no bloodshed'.

My Brigadiers went off to their Commands to interview their Officers. I drew up a memorandum for the Unit Commanders of my Division who had not been present at the Conference, embodying the terms that were to be put to them and their Officers, and despatched by A.D.C.[57] by train to the Curragh with orders to issue it to them. On arrival there he met General Rolt, who had returned by motor car and the latter saw a copy of my memorandum and issued it to his Battalion Commanders. [Added Note: This is wrong—He had already communicated with them. But he satisfied himself that his communication was practically identical with mine][58]

At about 2 p.m. the second Conference was held at the Royal Hospital. There were present, besides the Commander of the Forces the following Officers.

6th Divn.	Major-General Pulteney
	Brigadier-General Doran
	Brigadier-General Ingouville Williams[59]
5th Divn.	Major-General Sir C. Fergusson
H.Q.S.	Major-General Friend
	Brigadier-General Forestier Walker
	Colonel De Gex

General Friend reported that General Gough had expressed

his inability to attend, and the Commander-in-Chief expressed his great regret at the decision.

The Commander of the Forces said that he believed we had all read his speech at the Corinthian Club,[60] which gave his views. Were officers prepared to accept them?

Those present notified that they were prepared to do so, General Doran stating his repugnance to the situation.

Sir Arthur then went into details already given at the first Conference. He and the Staff Officers present supplemented them by further explanations, giving in detail the force that was to be used in Ireland.

I understood that should there be any disturbance in the north, the 5th Division supplemented by the 11th Brigade from Colchester would move probably to the line of the Boyne. It would be reinforced by the 1st Division from Aldershot. The 6th Division less necessary garrisons from the South which were subsequently worked out by Generals Pulteney and Friend, would move to Dublin reinforced by 18th Infantry Brigade from England. The 3 Infantry Battalions from Scotland and some Artillery would land in the North, and I understood would garrison certain points forming a ring round Belfast i.e. LARNE. [Added Note: Omitted by copyist—see MS draft: Ballymena—some point west of Belfast—Lisburn—] HOLYWOOD. BANGOR which latter was to be the Naval base. A Naval Brigade was to be landed at Bangor.

It was explained at length that there was to be no act of aggression. That a big demonstration would, it was hoped meet the case. No firing on any consideration until Sir Arthur personally authorised it, and that order would not be given until (as explained in the morning) all other means had failed. Meanwhile, strict orders were to be given to all detachments that on no account must there be any conflict with the opposing side. If a party of troops out of Barracks were molested or their progress impeded, they were to withdraw to Barracks.

At 2.45 p.m. the 6th Division Brigadiers left to return to their Commands and shortly afterwards the Conference broke up. I returned to the Curragh by the 4.15 train.

The impression left on my mind by the events of the day were genuinely that the measures to be taken were primarily precautionary. The occupation of the Government Buildings in Belfast did not seem to be in any way intended as a provocative measure; the reason explained to us seemed perfectly natural and reasonable. It was conceivable however that some of the Ulster adherents might get out of hand and attack the police, and thus initiate an outbreak which would entail the adoption of the preliminary measures already decided on, and further movement of troops in support. The reasons given by Sir Arthur Paget for the reinforcements from England as a demonstration also seemed comprehensible. It never occurred to me from anything that was said that any provocative act was contemplated, or that there would be any further movement at all unless disturbances ensued on the occupation of the Government Buildings. [Added note: I recognised however that circumstances might lead to a grave situation, involving active operations. Hence the wording of my memorandum to Officers]

Sir Arthur Paget said more than once: 'They wanted to use the soldiers as a bait, (i.e., in occupying the Government Buildings in Belfast), but I would not have that, and told them it was a matter for the Civil Power, not for soldiers'.

This expression however conveyed nothing to me beyond that the occupation of the Buildings was considered a necessity, and yet might possibly lead to disturbance; and hence the necessity of being prepared for all eventualities.

During the conversations (I do not remember where) I said to Sir Arthur Paget that presumably the order was from the King. He replied 'Do you think for a moment that I would accept it unless I knew it had the sanction of the King? Of course it is his order.' He was so emphatic that I had no hesitation afterwards in repeating this, when I considered it necessary, to Officers and men. And I reported that evening (Friday) that I had done so.

He further said that it was reported by the Secret Service that great internal trouble was brewing in London, Liverpool and other large towns, and that there was great anxiety on this score. I understood him to say that the Labour party was determined to make a big effort to advance their policy by taking advantage of the crisis. Anyhow the impression left on my mind was that an internal convulsion of the country was a probability of the near future.

I do not think that there is anything further to note with reference to these conferences except that Officers were to be recalled from leave, and that troops might be called on to move at short notice.

On reaching the Curragh about 5.45 p.m. I met all Staff Officers, Brigadiers and O.C.R. and A.C.C. I asked their decisions, and they all intimated their detestation of the use of troops against Ulster, their resentment at the way in which their decisions had been demanded at short notice, and finally their decision (under protest so to speak) to do their duty as ordered.

I then explained the situation to them in confidence, and asked as to the decisions of officers serving under them. They stated that with a few exceptions, their officers had expressed their intention to do their duty, but made unanimously the same representations as are given above.

About this time I became aware of the decision of the 3rd Cavalry Brigade, and undertook to forward General Goughs letter to Headquarters notifying this decision, by my A.D.C. who left for Dublin at 8 p.m. bearing also my report to the Commander of the Forces that, so far as I had received reports, the Division as a whole had returned satisfactory answers.

Later in the evening, feeling uneasy as to the effect of the action of the 3rd Cavalry Brigade, I arranged to address officers and men of different units of the Division quartered at the Curragh early next morning.

Saturday 21st March

On reaching my office about 9 a.m. I met Brigadier General Rolt and Headlam, Commanding 14th Infantry Brigade and Artillery. They told me that the situation was very serious. The example of the 3rd Cavalry Brigade had become known, and many Officers, in some units practically all, were prepared to resign. At 9.30 I saw the 2/Suffolk Regiment in the Gymnasium. First I saw the officers privately. Their attitude was very strained, in some cases almost truculent. After speaking to them I addressed the battalion as a whole. Half an hour later I saw the officers and men of the 2 Manchester Regiment in the same way. They were more amenable in their manner than the first named battalion, but obviously the feeling was very strong.

I then motored to Kildare and afterwards to Newbridge, addressing officers and men of the Artillery in the same way. Here the atmosphere was rather different, in the sense that there seemed less resentment, though many senior officers were obviously torn in two as to what it was their duty to do. Some of the scenes were very painful. Before leaving both these places, however, I was assured of their support in the line I advocated. At Newbridge the example of the R.H.A. had obviously had its effect in upsetting the situation.

I did not use exactly the same arguments to all units, though generally my remarks were similar. In some cases it seemed necessary to say more than in others; in some cases questions were put showing the special difficulties which presented themselves to the minds of officers.

I told them that the first duty of soldiers was to obey the orders of their King and of constituted authority. I said this order was the King's, and must have been issued with his sanction. That, for me, was enough.

I pointed out the responsibility of influencing those under us. Personal considerations must give way to the duties of our respective position as commanders of troops. I would be no party to anything that tended to weaken discipline. Logically, we officers could not refuse to obey the present orders and yet expect our men to obey orders when they, on strike duty for instance, were placed in difficulties similar to those now confronting us.

I spoke of the far reaching consequences of a disruption of the Army. That the country without a disciplined and united Army would be at the mercy of the mob. I alluded to the probability of even bigger questions arising if the Army broke up, that the Monarchy, Society and the Empire itself might be shattered.

Finally I assured all that no aggressive measures of any kind were contemplated or would be tolerated; and in cases where further assurances on the point seemed necessary, I quoted the statements of the Commander of the Forces to that effect.

I admit that I used the King's name freely; it was the most effective argument with those who were most stubborn. Loyalty to the King was in fact the determining factor in inducing many officers to withhold their resignations.

Some party newspapers assert that I made it clear that Ulster was to be provoked into taking the first steps of aggression. This of course is twisting what I did say into another meaning. I considered it necessary to explain the situation fully to prove my assertion that the Army would take no aggressive action, in cases where that seemed to be the main difficulty in Officers' minds. I am sure they understood me perfectly, but for party purposes in their letters to relations, the statement is made to read in a different light.

No doubt, in ordinary circumstances, I was indiscreet beyond expression. But the situation was absolutely critical. Had I not taken a strong line, and used every conceivable argument to convince officers and men of what I was told, and what I believed, to be the 'innocent' intentions of my superiors, the Division would have gone the same way as the Cavalry Brigade and Horse Artillery. It would practically have been in a state of mutiny.

I considered it essential to face the situation, and to say and do anything to save it. I said nothing that had not been said to me by the Commander of the Forces, and that was not absolutely honest; but it is obvious that much that I told them was given to me confidentially, and should not under ordinary circumstances have become public.

I am of course prepared to take the fullest responsibility for my action. If it is blamed, I can only point to the fact that as a result, the Division remained loyal; and that its discipline is absolutely intact, strengthened rather than weakened by what has passed.

There is little more to relate:

The Commander of the Forces interviewed the Officers of the Cavalry Brigade about noon, and left it to me to receive their decisions, and if these were adverse, to issue certain orders to their senior officers. I tried hard to influence General Gough and his Commanding Officers but without success.

In the afternoon I went to Dublin and interviewed the Officers of the 1st East Surrey Regiment and all officers of the 13th Infantry Brigade who were 'doubtful'. This interview was also successful.

I reported the situation to the Commander of the Forces at the Royal Hospital about 7.30 p.m. and returned to the Curragh.

During the next few days, I received answers from Commanders of detached troops of the Division, to whom as already stated I had written, giving satisfactory assurances of the present attitude of their officers.

The actual state of feeling of officers and men of the Division has been fully reported by me to the Commander of the Forces in a letter dated 26th March, of which a copy is attached.[61]

It only remains to add that the loyalty and support given me by my Staff, my Brigadier Commanding Artillery, Infantry Brigades, and Officers Commanding Units was beyond all praise. They worked hard and never spared themselves. Their influence had a most marked effect in allying excitement and helping all to keep their heads.

RA GV F.674/44(a); Fergusson Mss; Bodleian, Ms Asquith 40 f 104–106, BL, Add Mss 51250, Paget Mss (Partial); PRO WO35/209 (g)

63
Account of events on Friday, 20 March and Saturday, 21 March by Lieutenant Colonel R. W. Breeks, RHA

Newbridge
28 March 1914

[Typescript]

Friday March, 20th, 1914.
Order received from G.O.C., 3rd Cavalry Brigade 'All Officers to attend at 16th Lancers Mess at 3.30 p.m.'

Brigadier General Gough then made us a perfectly calm brief statement to the effect that the G.O.C. in C., Ireland, had called him and other Generals to a Conference and had informed them:

That immediate active operations against Ulster were imminent.

That he, General Gough, had been ordered to decide at once, himself, and to obtain a decision that night in time to forward to Head Quarters, from each officer in his command on the following ultimatum:

i. Officers whose actual home was in Ulster were to be permitted to be absent from duty during the operations in Ulster and could disappear.

ii. All other officers had to decide if they would carry out their duties and obey all orders even if operations were to be carried out to the extreme limits of war against Ulster. But if their consciences did not allow them to do the above, they were to send in their resignations and would be dismissed the service.

General Gough then told us that, being an Irishman, his mind was made up and he had resigned his commission. He told us that in this crisis he declined to give advice to anyone. We must each and all decide ourselves as our consciences dictated. He then dismissed us to our own quarters to decide. We, the R.H.A., were to telephone numbers up to the Cavalry Bde. Office, under the two headings, to catch the 5.30 post, if possible. I told my Officers to meet me in the Mess in an hour's time and stayed behind with General Gough to see if there was any further information to be obtained. We learnt that the same ultimatum had been presented by General Fergusson to the 5th. Division. I met my officers in the Mess and told them that my views were as follows:

(a) That the Army was being used as a pawn in a party game.

(b) That therefore, in my opinion, the Irish Officers' duty was clear, viz., that no option was left them except to take advantage of the Ulster clause or resign.

(c) That the case of other officers was different—the call on their feelings, conscience and religion were not so definite and that they must weigh very carefully their duty to their King, their men, and their oath, against their very strong feelings on the subject of the projected operations, which as far as I could see, were a party move & totally unwarranted by the circumstances at that time in Ulster on the plea of law and order. That I could not honestly in the exceptional circumstances of the case put any pressure on them, except that they were to weigh very carefully and honestly both sides; As far as I was concerned I was of opinion that my feelings toward the political situation were not of so deep a nature, as to override my feelings towards my duty to the Army. That also two wrongs did not make a right and that I did not think that I ought to break with the long tradition of non-political action which the Army held because the other side had chosen to use the Army as a party weapon. But that I was certainly of opinion that a contrary decision on their part was fully justified.

The decision came to, telephoned to Head Quarters, Cavalry Brigade, was as follows:

Officers domiciled in Ulster   2
Officers resigning commissions   6
Officers staying on in the Army   5

This information with numbers from each Cavalry Regt. was forwarded to Head Quarters, Irish Command, with covering letter as appears in the published reports of correspondence in white paper C.D. 7318, signed by General Gough March 20th.

The next morning, Saturday 21st., I took up to the Cavalry Brigade Office the resignations of the Officers.

I received an order that the G.O.C., in Ireland, wished to address all officers of the Cavalry Brigade at 11 a.m. The gist of Sir A. Paget's statement was as follows:

He earnestly desired us to reconsider our decisions. These resignations would not be accepted and that officers who declined to go to Ulster would be tried by G.C.M. That though operations were about to be initiated against Ulster we were to trust to him that they would be of a purely defensive nature. That in proof of this he called our attention to the moves that had already taken place which were merely necessary strengthening of exposed garrisons in view of the danger of their being rushed by either party. That he had even given orders to one battalion that if they met any form of resistance they were to go back to barracks. That he was about to mass or was making arrangements to mass at least 20,000 men on the Boyne. That Camps were being prepared for these men, but that he was determined to forbid these men whom he was leading, to shoot even if shot at, and when face to face with the Ulster Army, he would advance with his Brigadiers, call a halt and parley. He also stated that he could do without cavalry and was willing to give a guarantee to the Cavalry Brigade that they, except for scouting purposes, would not be used offensively, merely on the lines of communications. Sir A. Paget was most emphatic that any disobedience of these orders was disobeying the King. The officers were then dismissed and General Gough and myself, Col. Hogg and Col. MacEwen left with the C-in-C. He repeated some of his arguments and elucidated some points.

I must confess that Sir A. Paget's speech was absolutely unconvincing and inconclusive. That his idea of a sort of pantomimic battle revolted most of us.

I then went out and consulted with the G.O.C., Cavalry Brigade and O.C.'s Regiments, telling my officers to meet me later in our Mess.

Then some differences of opinion arose. Some R.H.A. Officers and the O.C., 4th Hussars and some of his officers hoped that in spite of the unconvincing nature of Sir A. Paget's speech, all officers might be able to take his statements as to the strictly defensive nature of the operations at their full value, but others thought it was impossible for him to give such a guarantee. General Gough and the OC.s then went to see General Fergusson who had been deputed to receive the decisions. We saw a copy of what we understood to be the War Office instructions in which no mention was made of a choice of action being given to any officers except those domiciled in Ulster. General Fergusson again put the case against resignation before us fairly strongly, but insisted that a definite decision had to be given at once to the choice put before us by all officers.

He said that he had received from Sir A. Paget his word that every movement projected and made had been expressly sanctioned by the King and that he thought this statement was the deciding point. But he had to acknowledge that the massing of 20,000 men on the borders of Ulster was certainly moral coercion to say the least. We agreed to go out and consult our officers again. General Gough and the officers of the 16th. and 5th Lancers could not see their way to alter their decision. Col. Hogg and some officers of the 4th Hussars were undecided as to the validity of Sir A. Paget's guarantee. General Gough and the other officers commanding went over to the War Office being superseded in their commands (except Col. Hogg) and handing over to the next senior. I saw my officers and explained the situation up to date. My officers were of opinion (with the exception of those domiciled in Ulster) that they were prepared to withdraw their resignations on General Sir A. Paget's guarantee, if General Gough was satisfied with it, which he was not. Also, they were quite prepared, as were all the Cavalry, to withdraw their resignations, if the War Office endorsed the covering letter mentioned above in the sense of giving a guarantee that the operations were of the purely legal nature of preserving law and order and property and not to initiate civil war in Ulster. We decided to wait in hopes that General Gough would be able to arrange matters at the War Office.

I deeply regret to say that now the matters are a good deal worse. We all, even myself and the officers who thought with me, think that the King's name has been used to deceive us.

NAM, 7101-23-202, Roberts Mss; Ibid, 8001-6-5, MacEwen Mss; Pragnell Mss; J. E. Gough Mss; H. of Lords RO, Bonar Law Mss, 39/2/20; Birmingham University Library, Austen Chamberlain Mss, AC 14/3/6; PRO, WO 35/60/2; RA GV F. 674/83; BL, Keyes Mss, 3/17

64

Notes by Brigadier-General H. P. Gough of interview between Sir A. Paget and officers 3rd Cavalry Brigade (less 5th Lancers) at the Curragh Camp, on Saturday 21st March, 1914

[Typescript]

29 March 1914
(with later additions)

Present: Sir A. Paget and A.D.C. (Lieut. Mackintosh),[62] all officers 3rd Cavalry Brigade in barracks (about 35), including self, Major Kearsley, Col. Breeks, Col. MacEwen, Col. Hogg, Major Gillson, Major Campbell,[63] Major Howell, etc.,

At 11 a.m. Sir A. Paget entered the room and sat at the only table, asking us to sit down, which we did as best we could on available accommodation.

Sir A. Paget commenced by saying that he was our friend and asked us to trust him as our General and our Chief and he would see that we were not placed in any positions which we might object to. He said he did not know why so many officers had resigned because he had no intention of making war on Ulster and to prove it he would take us into his confidence and divulge some of his 'plans'. Only moves had been ordered that were necessary to protect 'stores' etc., and even these moves were precautions mainly directed against the 'Hibernians'. The 'depot' at Enniskillen was dangerously exposed to Hibernians; 'his' guns in Dundalk—a low-lying town surrounded by hills 'peopled by Hibernians'—were very exposed and every soldier would know that guns must have the protection of other arms.

He had moved some troops by sea (he now thought it was a mistake)—merely to avoid their marching through the streets of Belfast—Why should we think military operations were intended against Ulster when everywhere his troops had been received with ovation in Ulster? To such an extent was he prepared to go to avoid fighting that he had given orders that if a Battalion met with opposition in its march it was to turn round and go back to barracks. And if fighting took place against Ulster Forces he would order all his men to lie down and not return the fire and then 'he and his Generals' would advance alone through the firing line and parley with the men of Ulster.

As far as the Cavalry were concerned they would not be required to take any serious part in any fighting—not more than one Regiment would anyhow be employed—he would send one Regiment South to maintain order there. A Squadron or two might be employed on the lines of communication.

Of course he would have to employ some scouts for 'of course he did not want to march along and bump unexpectedly into a large force of the enemy' (Note—but no war was contemplated). These scouts need not fire a shot, they would only bring him information, 'just as they do at manoeuvres'. Even if a squadron should be on his flank in an engagement 'of course, if it cleared his flank for him he would be very pleased' but if it took no active part he would be content.

He then went on to say that it was necessary of course 'to hold the line of the Boyne' while 25,000 troops were being brought over from England (Note—he said there was to be no war previously). He said he had expected that only 'a few religious fanatics' would accept dismissal.

He said that if officers liked to 'indulge in the luxury of sentiment' they must pay for it, like other things. He said that no resignations would be accepted. He said that senior officers would be tried by C.M. He said that we must clearly understand that this was the direct order of 'the Sovereign' and asked us 'if we thought he would obey the orders of these dirty swine of politicians'.

Then, as no move took place, he said we must decide again and let General Fergusson know, and if there was no change, that I and the C.Os would 'hand over command', cross to London that night and report to the War Office next morning.

Some of these statements were made in the presence only of myself, Major Kearsley, Col. Breeks, MacEwen and Hogg.

Col. Breeks had some heated words with Sir A. Paget, but I have forgotten exactly what they were; they were mainly expressing the resentment felt at the grave decision demanded from Officers, apparently for no cause, in a very short time and with 'practically a pistol at one's head'.

I remarked that I did not see how resignations could be refused, as they had been demanded from officers at the Chief's own order. Also that though sentiment might be a luxury men had died for it. Sir A. Paget also remarked that I need expect 'no mercy' from Sir J. French and I replied that I did not ask any mercy.

Sir A. Paget then left.

Officers considered his speech. The majority seemed to think it unsatisfactory, both from the point of view of assurances offered that no organized attack was intended on Ulster, and also from the puerile and dishonest suggestions and subterfuges put forward.

31 March 1914

Sir A. Paget said that all his 'moves' had gone off well—that his troops were being welcomed everywhere but he must confess there was one move being made by the Government to which he did not agree, but which might upset everything.

Initld. R.H.K.

After reading over my version and agreeing that all in it was a true statement.

(Initd.) H.P.G.

17 April 1914

Later on that day (21.3.14) during a conversation I had with Sir Charles Fergusson, he told me the outline of the plan against Ulster viz., that the Army and Navy were to blockade Ulster, and that the police were to seize important public buildings in Belfast.

H.P.G.

NAM, 7101-23-202, Roberts Mss; Ibid, 8001-6-6, MacEwen Mss; Pragnell Mss; H. of Lords RO, Bonar Law Mss, 39/2/20; Birmingham University Library, Austen Chamberlain Mss, AC 14/3/8; PRO, WO 35/60/2; RA GV F.674/83; BL, Keyes Mss, 3/17

65

Account of Lieutenant-General Sir Arthur Paget's remarks on Saturday 21 March by Lieutenant Colonel M. L. MacEwen, 16th Lancers

[Typescript]   31 March 1914

Sir A. Paget stated that:

1. Though active operations were intended by the Government against Ulster, he had no intention of carrying them out.
2. That in case of a collision with the Ulster Army, he would reverse the ordinary procedure and go forward in front of the firing line with his staff. After the first burst of firing he would hoist the white flag and confer with the Ulster Volunteer leaders and then go home.
3. That he would have a force of 20,000 to 25,000 men on the River Boyne almost at once.
4. That the Navy were going to co-operate.
5. That he did not want the cavalry at all except perhaps one regiment.
6. That he would suppress a bogus disturbance in the South and send the cavalry there to get them out of the way if we would withdraw our resignations.
7. That the Cavalry need not fight but could run away or hoist the white flag if it came to the pinch.
8. That he might want some scouting done by the cavalry; but their only job would be to bring back information so as to prevent his being surprised; they need not fight.
9. In the event of a big battle the Cavalry would be placed out of the way on the flank and need not take part—though if he (Sir A. Paget) were getting the worst of it—it would be up to the cavalry to help him.
10. That by the action of the officers in resigning disgrace was being brought on famous Regiments.
11. That it was not a soldier's job to indulge in sickly sentimentality.

12. That he had anticipated only a few resignations on the part of religious fanatics.

13. That General Gough and the Colonels if they persisted would be tried by G.C. Martial.

14. That the other resignations would not be accepted.

15. That it was now too late to exercise the option given us.

16. That he would march infantry to the cavalry lines and disarm the regiments concerned.

17. That he would never have agreed to these active operations if he did not know it was the King's wish.

18. That the Ulstermen would be forced to fire the first shot.

19. That we were to trust him absolutely and he would see us through. That if we did not trust him absolutely, he would resign at once.

20. That if his infantry during the advance met a body of Ulster Vol. Force blocking their way that they would be ordered to turn about and return to barracks or camp.

21. That he (Sir A. Paget) had for some months been trying to get the W.O. to give officers who did not want to serve against Ulster the opportunity of avoiding that duty.

22. That all he had got from them was that officers with domicile in Ulster could disappear till the conclusion of hostilities and then would be re-instated without loss or damage.

23. If officers refused to go now there were worse things than dismissal as they would find out.

24. That his action in sending troops to Dundalk was aimed at the Hibernians, who were drilling in considerable numbers in the neighbourhood. That he feared they would raid the guns at that place.

25. That his troops had been received most enthusiastically everywhere, much to his surprise.

26. That there was not an inch between the two parties in Parliament, so near were we to a settlement of the whole question.

27. That it was not worth while sacrificing our careers when the whole thing might be over the next day.

28. That Ulster seemed quiet, but the Government had made

one dangerous move, which he was not at liberty to disclose, but which might cause an immediate rising in Ulster.

29. Sir A. Paget put this question to General Gough during this conference, but at once withdrew it as unfair;

'What would you have done if I had ordered your Brigade to Ulster yesterday?'

30. Sir A. Paget distinctly stated, that up to the last moment before leaving England he had been trying to get Sir John French to excuse from active operations against Ulster those Officers who had conscientious objections.

NAM, 7101-23-202, Roberts Mss; Ibid, 8001-6-7, MacEwen Mss; Pragnell Mss; H. of Lords RO, Bonar Law Mss, 39/2/20; Birmingham University Library, Austen Chamberlain Mss, AC 14/3/7; Brooke Mss; Churchill College, WMYS 2/5, Wemyss Mss; PRO, WO 35/60/2; RA, GV, F.674/83; BL, Keyes Mss, 3/17

66

Memorandum by J. Gretton, M.P.

66 Ennismore Gardens,
London SW
31 March 1914

[Holograph]

I have seen a letter written last week by a subaltern officer in the Cornwall Light Infantry at Newry.[64] He stated that the battalion was moved hurriedly north; one half of the battalion was sent to Newry; there were thirteen officers. After arrival there, the Colonel[65] summoned the officers, told them that trouble was expected in Ulster and they would probably be required for active operations. He asked them if they were willing to act; if not, they must send in their resignations, and they would be dismissed the Service with disgrace; that they had half an hour to decide. The officers said they were unwilling, and the Colonel urged them to agree, making an especial point that the operations, if undertaken, had the sanction of the King. The officers then consulted: they felt that as the King's name had been used, a strong appeal had been made to their loyalty to the throne that their men were in the 'affected area', and they ought not to abandon them in such a situation: that only half of the battalion was there, and they had no means of knowing what their brother officers might do. The thirteen officers, therefore, drew up a memorandum[66] in which they stated that they strongly objected to taking part in active operations in Ulster, and that they agreed to go only for the two first reasons stated above, laying emphasis on the fact that they responded to the appeal made to their loyalty to the King.

Subsequently, a five page letter[67] arrived at Newry from General Sir Charles Fergusson, which, the subaltern officer who wrote, says, repeated at length the statements made by the Colonel of the battalion to his officers. This letter was read and shown to them.

RA GV F.674/56

67
The wife of an NCO to her parents[68]

Cavalry Brigade,
Curragh Camp.
March 1914

[Copy]

Well dear Ma & Dad, things have been very serious here this last week, and we are still under guard with fixed bayonets all over the camp and at our quarters, every married man has ammunition and rifle in quarters, and no one allowed out of camp. Of course there are many miles of camp on the Curragh, we can get plenty of walks but no one is allowed to enter Camp. What do you think of all our Cavalry officers resigning, that is George's fighting brigade. . . . It was one of the finest things that they could have done. They new [sic] the men could not do it, so they done it themselves, although the men's hearts were the same way if they dare, but all our men say they would have been shott [sic] first than take arms against Ulster, but I don't think things are quite settled yet. . . . But of course we must stick it, it is all in our army career. . . . General Gough had a lovly [sic] reception when he came over from England, all the Cavalry turned out in review order and escourted [sic] him home in his carriage as if he were a King. I cannot describe what it has been like here this last week, everything and everybody up to war strength and ready to move off in five minutes notice, but still we are all smiling with it all.

H. of Lords RO, Bonar Law Mss, 32/2/13; *Bristol Times and Mirror*, 4 April 1914

68
Statement of
Lieutenant-General Sir Arthur Paget

Parkgate,
Dublin.

[Holograph]   1 April 1914

After receiving the instructions of the Secretary of State for War, on the 19th March, I returned at once to Dublin and summoned a conference to meet at 10 a.m. on the 20th March. This conference was attended by the General Officers Commanding 5th Division, 13th and 14th Infantry Brigades, 3rd Cavalry Brigade, and by two of my own Staff officers, viz., the Major-General in charge of Administration, and the Brigadier-General, General Staff. The Officer Commanding No. 11 District was also present.

I explained to these officers that I had received orders to carry out certain moves of a precautionary nature. The Government believed that the precautionary nature of these moves would be understood, and that they would be carried out without resistance. I said that I personally did not share that opinion, and that I thought that the moves would create intense excitement, and that the country,—and if not the country, then the Press— would be ablaze on the following day. I said that the moves might possibly lead to opposition, and might even eventuate, and in the near future, in the taking of active operations against organized bodies of Ulster Volunteer Force under their responsible leaders.

No notes were taken at the Conference, and I cannot quote the exact words used, but such was the general impression which I wished to convey, and which as a fact I did convey to the six officers whom I subsequently questioned.

I stated that I had been in close consultation with the War Office on the previous evening and had endeavoured to obtain concessions for those officers who might feel deeply on the subject. The most that I had been able to obtain from Colonel Seely, and that only at a late hour, and by the help of Sir John French, was the following:

Officers actually domiciled in Ulster would be exempted from taking part in any operation that might take place. They would be permitted to 'disappear' (that being the exact phrase used by the War Office), and when all was over would be allowed to resume their places without their career or position being affected.

In answer to a question put to me I said that other officers who were not prepared from conscientious or other reasons, to carry out their duty, would be dismissed from the Service at once. I said that Colonel Seely had expressed the hope that there would be very few cases of officers claiming exemption.

I said that, as regards the Ulster domicile exemption, I should hold Brigadiers personally responsible that no officer should be exempted unless he fulfilled strictly the conditions laid down, and, in answer to one officer who pointed out the difficulty of ascertaining the facts, I said that very great care would have to be exercised, as an officer granting an exemption to an officer not properly qualified to receive it would render himself liable to trial by Court-Martial.

I said that a second conference would be held at 2 p.m. on that afternoon, at which I would discuss the details of moves which it might be necessary to make, in case of resistance to the precautionary moves which were then in process of being carried out.

It was, in my opinion, necessary that I should know before that conference was held, whether the senior officers present were of my way of thinking, viz, that duty came before all other considerations. I therefore said that I could not allow any officer to attend the second conference who did not feel that he could obey the orders given him in the eventuality which I had sketched. Any such officer would be expected to absent himself from the second conference, and I should know what he meant.

It is, therefore, quite correct that I did insist on knowing the intentions of these seven officers before the eventuality actually arose.

I had no intention, however, of ascertaining the intentions of subordinate officers. My intention was that the senior officers present should simply inform those officers subordinate to themselves of the exemption granted, and of the penalty of refusal to obey orders in the case of officers not affected by the exemption clause. I wished particularly to make it clear to officers that they could not simply resign their commissions and retire from the Service, in possession of pensions and without penalty. Three of the officers present understood me completely, but the remaining four officers understood me to mean that any officer who was not prepared, from conscientious or other motives, to carry out his duty was to say so, and would then be dismissed from the Service.

I do not understand now how the misconception arose in all cases, but Brigadier-General Forestier-Walker (one of the officers who shared the misapprehension) informs me that, not seeing why Colonel Seely should hope that there would be very few cases of officers claiming exemption owing to a domicile in Ulster, he jumped erroneously to the conclusion that I had made a slip in quoting Colonel Seely's remark and that the latter had really meant that he hoped that there would be very few cases of officers who would be dismissed from the Army rather than do their duty.

It is easy to see that from this it would be a natural step to infer that something in the nature of an alternative was to be put to officers.

Be that as it may, certain officers did leave the conference under a wrong impression, and, as a consequence, the majority of officers of the 5th Division were informed that, if they could not claim exemption, and were not prepared, from conscientious or other motives, to do their duty, they were to say so at once, and would be dismissed from the Service.

The officers of the 3rd Cavalry Brigade were informed in the same sense, but with this variation, that I understand they were told that those who were not prepared, from conscientious or other motives, to do their duty, might resign their commissions, but would be dismissed from the Service.

I regret extremely that this misapprehension arose, and I alone am responsible for it.

White Paper; Bodleian, Ms Asquith 40, f 109–115; PRO. WO 35/209, (e)

69

Second Lieutenant R. Macleod
to his father

80th Battery
XV Brigade, RFA,
Kildare.
[Holograph]   4 April 1914

The 8th Brigade here (4.5 Howitzers) received just the same orders as ourselves and were ready to move at half an hour's notice. Captain Barber-Starkey[69] told Hunt about it. The denial is perfectly untrue.

*   *   *

On March 21st General Headlam addressed all the Artillery Officers at Kildare in the Mess. He said that he hoped no one would apply to be dismissed. He said that soldiers had sometimes to shoot down strikers with whom they sympathised, and it would be a bad example if we did not do so when ordered. General Fergusson, who was just coming, would explain the situation.

General Fergusson commanding 5th Division also addressed us and told us that he was a Conservative and all his sympathies were with the Ulster people. But he was going to see the thing through, and he hoped we would all do the same. He had seen Gen. Sir A. Paget the day before and had it from him that the notice we had on Friday came from the Army Council. General Fergusson said the 'ultimatum' was an insult to any officer, but he did not know who was responsible. Four divisions[70] were to be sent to Ulster. We were to stand as much punishment as possible without replying. All strategic points had already been seized. If the Army split up on this question, it would be the end of the Empire.

Sunderland Polytechnic, 1914–1918 Archive, Macleod Mss; King's College, Liddell Hart Centre for Military Archives, Macleod Mss 1/1; Royal Artillery Institution, MD 1150

70

Account by Major J. B. Jardine[71]

[Holograph]

5th Lancers
7 April 1914

On the morning of Friday, March 20, 1914, Sir Arthur Paget, C in C, Ireland met by appointment all his Generals and laid before them an ultimatum, which they, in turn, were to lay before their officers. Officers were given the following alternatives of action, viz:

1. They were to say that they were prepared to take part in active operations in Ulster.
2. If they were not prepared to do so, they were to send in their resignations, when they would be dismissed the Service, forfeiting their pensions.
3. Officers domiciled in Ulster, on a written statement from them to that effect, would be put on halfpay temporarily, but would not lose their pensions.

Our Brigadier, General Gough, left the meeting and came direct to our barracks, where he laid the ultimatum at once before the Colonel[72] and officers, giving them two hours in which to decide. All except two decided to be dismissed. Meanwhile General Gough proceeded to the Curragh and laid the ultimatum before the rest of the officers of his brigade, with the result that all the officers of the 16th Lancers, most of the Royal Horse Artillery, and six of the 4th Hussars did the same. Sir Arthur Paget, after getting the news of the resignations of the 5th Lancers, came himself to our barracks that afternoon to try and persuade the Colonel and his officers to reconsider their decisions.

Amongst other appeals to the Colonel was one that he should go to Ulster and then 'chuck it' when the fighting began when he and others who did the same would have to stand a court martial. The Colonel's answer was: 'But that would be deserting our men!' Sir Arthur Paget also told him that Ulster would be in a blaze on Saturday.

Again, on Saturday morning, the C in C summoned the Colonel to him, and attempted to persuade him; of course, on each occasion the Colonel repeated the C in C's remarks to his assembled officers—thrice in all, but their decisions remained unchanged.

Sir Charles Fergusson, at the Curragh, was especially successful in that many infantry officers withdrew their resignations. He appealed to their loyalty to the King.

As regards the officers who had chosen the alternative of dismissal, the authorities went back on their words and refused their resignations in the course of the morning. At about 11 o'clock on Saturday morning, the Colonel, as he had been ordered, reported to Headquarters finally that the decision of his officers was unchanged. He then received orders to hand over the Regiment to his second in command, and leave for the War Office by the night mail.

From midday of Friday 20th till midday of Tuesday 24th all barrack gates were closed, and double sentries, with ball ammunition, were put on them. One squadron was 'standing to' with orders to be ready to start for the North.

RA GV F.674/1

71
Further notes on the events of
Friday 20 March 1914 by
Brigadier-General H. P. Gough[73]

7 April 1914
(with later additions)

[Typescript]

At the interview at 10 a.m.—Generals Fergusson, Rolt, Cuthbert, self, Friend, and Walker, also Colonel Hill, present.

Sir A. Paget said that I need expect 'no mercy' from my old friend in the War Office, meaning, I suppose Sir John French. (This was said somewhere about the middle of the discourse).[74] He said that 'he did not expect any bloodshed, we were too strong'. He said '*the Fleet*' was in Belfast Harbour, and some ships also in Dublin Bay. I asked 'if the act of clemency, as I might call it, extended to officers domiciled in Ulster, would not it be extended to other officers resident in Ireland, whose feelings and sentiments might be equally involved in this question'? Sir A. Paget replied—No, that the clause about officers in Ulster was the last and only concession that would be granted.

He said that though he did not expect bloodshed he was not a prophet and officers must understand that once they embarked on this course and went with him he would expect them to go to the 'bitter end'. I cannot remember if he said this in the course of his statement or as a result of a question, but he distinctly used words to this effect.

He said that at his meeting at 2 p.m. (when I gathered General Pulteney and the General Officers, 6th Division, would be present) that he would divulge his 'plans' and that if any officers were not prepared to carry out everything that he then ordered, they were not to attend. As I left the room he addressed a remark to me personally, why I cannot think, 'you need not expect any help from the other side'.

Directly I left the room Fergusson said, 'come along and let us talk over this'—Rolt came with us. Fergusson was very agitated, white and cheeks trembling. As soon as we got outside he began arguing 'that the Army must hold together, that we must not break up the Army, etc.,' Rolt seemed very averse to going against Ulster. I did not argue, I listened.

Fergusson went away saying that he had decided to go. I said I would not go. Rolt received orders from Fergusson to go down to the Curragh and to put the alternatives to the officers of his Brigade.

I went down to Kingsbridge in the motor with Rolt and wired from there to my brother telling him of the alternatives and my decisions. I then went up to the 5th Lancers Mess, found Col. Parker there, called him out and told him. He threw himself on his sofa (we were in his study) and said 'It is monstrous—monstrous, I won't go—I won't go'. We went back to the 5th Lancers Mess and told all the Officers we could collect (about 13) of the alternatives. I said these were big crises but every man must decide for himself according to his conscience. I then left their barracks.

I went straight back to Head Quarters and in to see General Friend. I told him of my decision. He was very nice and seemed very sorry. He asked me 'if I could not look on it as he did, merely to maintain law and order'. I said—No, if it was law and order now it might develop into civil war at any moment and then it would be much worse and dishonourable to leave Sir A. Paget, and therefore, it was better and more honourable to do it at once.

He then asked me if I would see Sir A. Paget. I said I would rather not, it could not alter my decision and would only be painful to us both, but I asked him to convey to Sir A. Paget that my decision was not caused by any feelings towards himself and that I thought he had done his best for us in the matter of terms at the War Office.

I then asked Friend what he wanted me to do, and said that I looked upon myself as dismissed the service and expected to see myself in the Gazette as such on Tuesday. Friend said that I had better carry on as usual for the present and send him a letter that evening asking 'to retire'. But he said he would speak to Sir A. Paget first and wire me (which he did at 4.30 p.m.).

I then asked him what action he required of me as regards the

Units in my Brigade? Friend said I was to see the Officers and find out the numbers of those who were prepared to accept dismissal and that the results were to be wired to him that evening.

I told him that I had seen the 5th Lancers already, & though I know nothing definite and no figures, I thought at least 20 would not go and would rather be dismissed.

He seemed surprised and upset and begged me to let him know results soon as 'if there were many resignations it might make the Government alter their policy'. I then left.

[Added 16/4/14 . . . Friend also said 'I have not got a very pleasant job either; I have to go up to Belfast tonight as military governor'.]

I caught the 2 p.m. train and arrived at the 16th Lancers at 3.30 p.m. and met the assembled officers there. I gave them the alternatives, refused to answer any questions and left. I returned to my office with my Brigade Major. I was followed by several of the senior officers. We talked over the matter, On Major Howell's suggestion we decided to try and gain time and therefore drew up the letter (which afterwards appeared in the white paper)[75] asking for information. We never got any reply to this. We went round to see Generals Fergusson and Rolt with the object of getting them to send in a similar letter and so gain time, but as far as I remember, got nothing definite from either of them.

NAM, 7101-23-202, Roberts Mss; Ibid, 8001-6-4, MacEwen Mss; Pragnell Mss; J. E. Gough Mss; Brooke Mss; RA GVF.674/83; BL, Keyes Mss, 3/17

72
Brigadier-General H. P. Gough to Lady Aileen Roberts

[Holograph]

Brownstown House,
Curragh.
10 April 1914

Very sorry for the delay in answering you, but I had to go round and make sure of some facts first, before answering.

(1) As regards the letter your father wrote to me and left with Seely at the W.O.

Yes. I did get it. It was handed to me by the Hall Porter, I think, at the main entrance of the W.O. when I first arrived there on Sunday—22 March.[76]

(2) As regards what Fergusson said to various officers of his Division. He seems to have said something to this effect—(it is impossible now to get the *exact* words) 'That the troops will be expected to take a good deal of punishment before they return any fire.' The impression he made on his hearers seems to have been, not so much that he wished to irritate Ulster into striking the first blow, as to persuade officers to go on this job, unwilling as they were, by making out that their attitude was to be purely defensive and no offensive was asked of them. This was exactly the same argument as Paget made use of, in addressing us on Saturday. Both of them enlarged also on their intention of 'parleying' with the men of Ulster before any offensive or firing was to be permitted by the troops, but neither of them seemed to realise that everybody else had been 'parleying' for some years! Nevertheless, they both tried to impress us with confidence in the results of these 'parleys'. In fact, they both produced every futile argument to persuade us and all other officers to go—just to go—we need not do anything when we went, but for Heaven's sake go. That was the general line of their appeal!

As regards your third query—the average income of officers in this Brigade, which included gunners and sappers—I think you might take it at £300, for young unmarried officers.

But a married officer, like Colonel Parker, who is a poor man, though he may have £600 a year of his own—had to consider his wife and family. Parker has a girl just out, and a boy at the University, so he had to face many difficulties by resigning.

Col. Hill, who resigned, is a poor man, married, and was within three months of earning a pension of £500 a year.

We are all wondering here, how Paget can stay on, and look any of us in the face again.

The enclosures—being accounts from various sources of the incidents of Friday and Saturday[77]—will interest you, and help you to realise why our feelings towards Paget are what they are.

NAM, 7101-23-202, Roberts Mss; NLS, Acc 7726/147, Oliver Mss

73

Memorandum by C. Wigram of a conversation with Major-General L. B. Friend

Brookville House,
Raheny,
Dublin.

[Holograph]   14 April 1914

On March 19 A.P. attended a Cabinet meeting, at which the P.M., L-George, McKenna, Winston, Seely, Birrell were present, and probably some others. A.P. afterwards said that McKenna, Winston, & Seely talked a lot about military tactics, and that L-George talked a lot of nonsense, to which A.P. paid no attention.

General F's opinion was that the Cabinet were under the impression that the Ulster Provisional Government was going to be set up in a day or two. (A.P. said that both Seely and Birrell had announced that reliable information to this effect had been received). The Government meant to forestall them. General F. thinks that at this Cabinet meeting measures were discussed for strengthening the depots etc, and for occupying with troops the chief government offices (like Postal and custom house etc.) in Belfast. A.P. probably demurred against such employment of his troops in Belfast, and consequently it was decided to send Macready direct from the W.O. as Military Governor of Belfast. After this Cabinet meeting A.P. conferred with Seely and French, and returned to Ireland that night (19 March).

On the 20th A.P. interviewed his officers and unfolded his plan of campaign. General F. says that A.P. has never shown him any letter from Seely, and was under the impression that A.P. had only oral instructions from the Cabinet, and Seely.

Macready fell sick on the 20th and General F. was sent as Military Governor to Belfast that night. It was at first proposed that he should be sent up in a gun boat and to sneak into Belfast in plain clothes. His instructions from A.P. were very sketchey, and he did not know what he was meant to do, except that all the troops, the two ships in the Lough, and police in the Belfast District were under his orders, and the area of Belfast District was laid down. He thought that as Macready was being sent direct from the W.O. some line of action had been decided upon, and was under the impression that the Police had received orders what to do, and that he was to support the Police. For this purpose the troops in Belfast had been moved out to Holywood.

On arrival in Belfast he (General F) sent for the Commissioner of Police, and asked him what his orders were, and if his police were concentrated and were going to occupy the Post Office, Custom House and other Government offices. The Commissioner stared and said his police were at their ordinary duties and knew nothing about taking any special action.

General F issued some routine orders as Commandant of the Belfast District, describing the area; and nominated Gleichen as O.C. military forces, Capt. Robinson[78] of one of the ships re. naval forces, and the Commissioner of Police as O.C. police; and announcing his headquarters—He then sat tight. These orders do not appear to have fallen into the hands of the Unionists, as they are very strong evidence of the intention to establish a kind of Martial Law in the District. General F. said his force consisted of about 1000 soldiers, 100 sailors armed with rifles 20 with cutlasses, and the police. He thought about 23,000 Ulstermen could be mobilised in a short time, and he did not at all like the situation in which he had been placed and was very glad to get back to Dublin.

General F's opinion is that the Government originally intended to occupy the public offices in Belfast on the 20th with troops, but on A.P. demurring decided to send Macready up as a Military Governor either with orders to employ troops for this service or to employ police first. Macready fell sick, and by some glorious and fortunate muddle Friend received no definite orders, and being a cautious man did not precipitate a crisis.

I might add that N.C.[79] was never asked by Birrell as to any move on the part of Ulster to set up a Provisional Govt, nor did he give him any information to this effect.

N.C. was never consulted, and was rather surprised to be ordered by Birrell to place his police in Belfast under the Commissioner of Police under the orders of Macready.

General F. says that all A.P.'s staff are very fond of A.P. and feel very much for him, as he has been let in by these politicians.

A.P. always stands by his staff whatever errors they may commit, and is always ready to take the blame on his own shoulders. When he received oral instructions from the Cabinet & Seely, he evidently expected similar treatment. General F. admits that A.P.'s remarks to the 3rd Cavr. Brigade on the 21st at Curragh when he went down to persuade these officers to withdraw their resignations were very indiscreet. General F. says A.P. went down alone with an A.D.C., and must have lost his head.

RA GV F.674/77

74
Account of the events 19–23 March 1914
by Lieutenant Colonel M. L. MacEwen,
16th Lancers

[Pencil holograph]

No date
[April 1914]

Returned from shooting trip in India to the Curragh on the afternoon of [March] 19th. Travelled by Stranraer-Larne & curiously enough was in same carriage with Capt. Craig—Carsons right hand man in Ulster. Did not have any talk with him much as I should have liked to.

[March] 20th Allenby was inspecting A. Sqn. (Neave) at Sqn. training. Heard on getting to parade that Gough had been summoned to meet Paget in Dublin, also all other generals. Allenby in good form but would express no opinion about Ulster. On return from parade learnt that the D.C.L.Is had been sent north by train during the forenoon. Allenby refused to stay for lunch & said this was no place for him.

During lunch got telephone message from Gough to say he wished to meet all officers of the Bde in our mess at 3 p.m. Things seemed to be moving & everything pointed to trouble in Ulster.

I had sounded various military officials on my way through London & was met by the invariable answer to all questions 'You have taken the shilling & must carry out any orders you may be given'.

Went to the bronze medal jumping at 2 p.m. & Nash won comfortably on McTaggert's[80] horse. The Genl. was a few minutes late at our Mess & on coming in, without any preliminary talk gave us the ultimatum that has been quoted in the papers & in Parliament. He told us he personally had resigned—refused to answer questions & left the room. Before he left I said I felt sure I could give the answers for all the 16th. Hogg, 4th Hussars, exclaimed 'I cannot resign I am a poor man'. The faces of all the officers in the room were a study—no bombshell could have had as much effect.

The G.O.C. left orders for the decisions of all officers to reach the Bde Office by 5 p.m. All officers of other Regts. left the mess at once & when the officers of the Regt. were left alone with me, I told them I had personally strong feelings on this subject & did not wish to influence other officers. They must act each according to conscience & must clearly understand that no one would be thought the worse of for taking a different point of view from me.

I then wrote my resignation & left the mess. The adjutant informed me ten minutes later that all officers present had resigned & I instructed him to wire all officers away from the Regt. stating ultimatum & asking decision.

Every officer on the list of the Regt., absent or seconded answered this wire by resigning. Lt. Penrose[81] Signal Troop (attached), also resigned.

I went to Bde office & met all senior officers of the Bde & a document[82] given in 'white paper' was drawn up to gain time & try to find out exactly what was meant. This document was suggested by Howell but Kearsley also was trying to put the brake on Gough. Gough talked of going to Belfast at once.

I went to talk to James Comding. Manchesters in the evening & found the ultimatum had not been put so plainly to them & they had decided to go to Ulster.

Saturday 21st, Parade cancelled [ordered Sergts. Mess meeting for 12 noon to explain situation; but all] Officers of Bde were later ordered to meet Paget at Div. H.Q. at that hour.

I have already given a list of statements[83] made by Sir A.P. at this conference & if I had not resigned before I should certainly have done so after it.

I informed the Brigade Major before we left the room that I saw no reason for altering my decision. On leaving the Conference I met Sir C. Fergusson who tried to persuade me to take the other view & said he would give anything to be able to do so.

In half an hours time Sir C.F. called the G.O.C. & colonels to his room to get our decision as Sir A. Paget had gone back to Dublin. Hogg, 4th H, had withdrawn his resignation after Paget's conference. Breeks, R.H.A., had all the time been willing to go to Ulster. [Parker (5 L) had remained firm in Dublin]. Gough & I would not change our decision—Sir C.F. made the most stirring appeal to us to save the army & the country etc. etc., & handled the matter as only a man of the highest principles could do & in absolute contrast to Sir A.P.

He persuaded us to go away & reconsider the matter again.

I went back to the mess but found practically all the officers out so decided to stick to our line of action. Went back to Div. H.Q. & found Gough of same opinion. Breeks willing to go against Ulster—Hogg was in a very excited state crying & speechless but decided to withdraw his resignation.

Gough was then given Sir A.P.'s orders which were to hand over command of the Bde to the next Senior available (in this case Breeks) & go at once to London and report at the W.O. Sunday morning at 10 a.m.

I got similar orders namely to hand over Command to Leny[84] & go to London. Hogg then asked Breeks if he would give him leave of absence to go to London & see how matters stood.

Had only an hour to catch the train at Kildare. All the Regt. turned out to see me off & the Sgts. took the horses out of the brougham & pulled it for a considerable distance with drag ropes. There was great enthusiasm & excitement. All officers then came on to Station. Feeling was very strong of absolute determination not to be fooled or cajoled by politicians or senior officers at the W.O.

I did not personally see the remotest chance of coming back again to the Regt. & made arrangements to go on to Scotland from London.

Met Parker on the mail boat & Gough, he & I had a talk over the probable course of next days interview at the W.O. We decided not to tolerate any wigging or telling off of any kind & on the other hand not to listen to persuasion unless the idea of coercing Ulster were given up.

Arrived at Euston Sunday, March 22, early morning to find a crowd of reporters awaiting us on the platform. Left Gough to deal with them which he did summarily. After changing clothes at home, went to breakfast at the Senior to meet Genl. Babington,[85] who had wired to say he was coming up to help. Found he had delayed a day so went on to W.O. & met there Gough & his brother & Parker. We all went upstairs & Gough was shown at once into the A.Gs room & remained there a considerable time. When he came out I was called in & found Sir S. Ewart & Sir N. Macready there. The former on shaking hands said 'This is a most serious business'. I agreed.

He then read out several questions & Sir N. Macready wrote my answers which I read over & discussed before finally passing. The A.G. first called for an account of what happened at the 16 Lcs. Mess on Friday afternoon, Mar. 20th. Next asked a formal question as to whether I considered myself justified in questioning any orders I received & using my own judgement as to whether I obeyed or not. I answered 'No—Had I received orders I should have obeyed them. I received no orders of any kind.'

Sir N. Macready here remarked to the A.G. 'I knew MacEwen would, I have had him working for me on strike duty'. He then suggested to Sir S. Ewart that we should drop the official interview & have a talk as friends.

We went over most of what had happened [& I said that it seemed a hard bargain to place our commissions & pensions against the coercion of Ulster, but we had all jumped at it, & had the bargain been much harder we should still have jumped at it].

I kept off the subject of Sir A.P's Saturday interview with us, except to say that we considered his proposals out of the question & not honourable. Sir S.E. asked the feeling of the N.C.Os & men & I told him how they had turned out to give me a send off.

Sir N.M. asked me pointedly supposing everything were washed out & I went back to the Regt. could it be employed in holding posts or on lines of communication in case of operations in Ulster.

I replied 'No. I am certain it could not. The feeling of all ranks has now been declared strongly & any action such as you suggest would be considered an act of coercion against Ulster.'

The interview then ended, & I was told to stay within call of a telephone number which I gave to the A.G. Parker was then interviewed & after that we talked matters over & all were pleased that tact had been used with us instead of bullying as we had anticipated.

Cecil Howard came over to see me in the afternoon & told me the W.O. were all coming out if the Govt. persisted in their plan of operations. I gathered today from Gough's brother[86] that Aldershot were likely to do the same.

In the afternoon got a letter from the A.G. ordering me to be at the W.O. at 11 a.m. tomorrow Monday, March 23rd.

Monday morning went early to the Senior to see Genl. Babington & tell him everything as I had only wired him so far. He had delayed coming for 24 hours as the papers said Sir J. French had gone over to Ireland to interview us.

Genl. Babington had been busy already in the interests of the Regt. & had asked permission to be present at all interviews at the W.O. where the Regt. was concerned. His sympathy & advice were invaluable.

We walked down to the W.O. & met Gough & his brother & Parker.

We learnt for certain the action of Aldershot & the W.O. Staff—all solid with the Curragh, & that the attitude of the authorities towards us was in consequence likely to be more friendly. Gough bore the brunt of this mornings work an interview with Sir J. French & then one with Seely [at which Sir A.P. was present]. He gained the point that we should have a guarantee in writing that the troops would not be employed in coercing Ulster. He had to impress on Sir J.F. that none of the officers who had resigned had the slightest desire to be reinstated unless this condition was fulfilled.

About 12.30 p.m. Gough, Parker & I were called in to Sir J.F's room (A.G. also present) & in a few words the C.I.G.S. stated that there had been a misunderstanding[,] that we should have a guarantee in writing that the troops would not be employed against Ulster & that we were to be reinstated. The guarantee was to be ready at 4 p.m. [when we were to call for it]. He was quite friendly & asked after the 16 Q.L. as we left.

On reconsidering matters, as we were much afraid of being trapped by ambiguous terms in the document & politicians evasions. We thought it better to have it quite clear as to our not being employed to coerce Ulster under plea of maintaining law & order should the Home Rule Bill become law, so a letter was drawn up (see white paper)[87] to make this clear & sent in at the W.O. about 1 p.m.

Lunched at Club with Genl. Babington—wired to Regt. that prospects were good.

Returned with Genrl. B. to W.O. at 4 p.m. & we were given the 'Guarantee'.

We got the advice of Genrl. H. Wilson & wrote out explanatory footnote as to how we understood it.

Went in to Sir J.F.'s room about 4.30 p.m. (G., P. & self.) A.G. present.

Gough showed Sir J.F. the footnote & he said 'yes I read it that way' & after a few minutes thought 'Then perhaps you would like me to sign it.' Gough said 'perhaps it would be better' & he initialled it. He told Gough he might communicate the contents to his Command. Gough then thanked him for helping us all through & we left, with orders to rejoin our Regts. by the first boat.

The usual reporters met us at Euston at 8.30 p.m. & asked if we had a guarantee. Gough said—yes—a satisfactory one? Yes. completely.

We arrived at Kildare Station about 7 a.m. (24th March) found all the officers of the Regt. waiting on the platform & the greatest relief was expressed. The Regt. had asked to be allowed to form a guard of honour & escort in full dress to receive us on the Curragh & we had a great welcome home from all ranks. As Paterson, the Presbyterian Minister, said a few hours later 'the whole crisis had been guided to a satisfactory conclusion by the hand of God'. And all must agree.

NAM, 8001-6-3, MacEwen Mss

75

Account by Second Lieutenant W. H. Brooke, 2nd King's Own Yorkshire Light Infantry, of the events of 20–21 March 1914[88]

[Typescript]   [No date]

Then came the Ulster Crisis, when I, amongst others, was dismissed from the Army in disgrace for six hours. Shortly before this, Jack Noel[89] and Doody Wynne[90] and myself, three second Lieutenants had been discussing the political situation in Ulster, about the British Government of the day trying to force home rule on the Ulstermen who wished to remain loyal to the English Crown. We realised that the Army might be called on to do this dirty work and we wondered whether we ought to resign our commissions now or leave it till the last minute, and perhaps let down our Colonel,[91] to whom we were very devoted. I suggested that, before taking such a drastic step in our lives, that we ought to discuss the matter with an older officer than ourselves; so I was deputed to talk the matter over with Reggy Bond[92] who was then second in command in the Regiment.

The next day I was engaged to compete in a military jumping competition at the Curragh with my horse 'Gladeye'. Off we started next morning by train and I read the papers on the way and soon realised that we were on the verge of civil war in Ireland. Though I was left in for the final of the jumping to take place in the afternoon, I was so worried about this that I left the Curragh and caught the next train back to Dublin. To make matters worse, when I got back, I found that Jack Noel and Doody Wynne had left barracks with their companies under sealed orders as to their final destination. I guessed that they were for Belfast and felt that I had let them down by not going to see Reggy Bond that morning instead of going off to the Curragh.

I, therefore, at once rushed off to his house, where his wife told me that he was out, but that she was expecting him back any moment, and asked me if I would wait. When he came in and I told him what I had come for, he told me that he had just come back from a secret mission to Belfast, that there was going to be the devil of a row, as everyone was armed up there and were drilling and training as hard as they could. He then gave me extraordinarily good advice for he said 'Go to bed tonight, sleep on it and whatever you feel is the right thing to do when you first wake up in the morning, do it.' I did, and I was quite convinced that I should at once resign my commission.

Early that morning, the Colonel's car was waiting outside the Orderly Room; so Reggy Bond walked in and asked the Colonel where he was off to. He replied, handing him a memorandum, 'I have just received this and am going to the Divisional Commander to tell him that I am perfectly certain that my officers will obey whatever orders they are given.' To which Reggy Bond replied 'Well! I think you ought to see them about it first; Brooke came to see me last night and I gather there are others who feel the same way as he does.'

After breakfast all officers were assembled in front of the Colonel who told us that the Government wished to know what was the feeling of the officers in the Army in the event of being sent to Ulster. 'For my part', he said, 'I am quite certain that it is the duty of all officers to obey whatever orders they are given, and I propose to go to the Divisional Commander and tell him that I am quite certain that my officers will obey whatever orders they are given; but before leaving I would like to know that no officer feels otherwise. I therefore give you till 12 o'clock to talk it over and make up your minds, when anyone not prepared to go to Ulster is to come and say so.'

As soon as everyone had left the room, I went back and said 'I am very sorry sir, but I am afraid I must resign my commission.' He answered 'I am sorry you feel that way, hadn't you better think it over?' I told him I had and left the room.

At about ten minutes to twelve he sent for me again. On the way in I saw Penny,[93] another second Lieutenant waiting to go in, who told me that he felt the same as I did. The Colonel then said to me, calling me by my nickname, 'Do you quite realise it is not a question of resigning your commission, you will be dismissed in disgrace from the service. The message from the Government read, that any officer who is not prepared to obey all orders in the event of being sent to Ulster, is to say so, and he will be dismissed in disgrace from the service.' I replied that 'I would rather be publicly hanged than assist this Government to break up His Majesty's Kingdom.' The Colonel's only comment was 'I am sorry, in that case you are perfectly right', and I could see he was terribly upset.

When I left the room and got outside, I found practically every officer in the regiment waiting to come in and say that they were not prepared to obey all orders in the event of being sent to Ulster. This was the feeling towards the Government's ultimatum throughout the army in Ireland. The junior Officers saved England from a civil war.

The next thing that happened was, the Brigadier[94] called all the mutinous officers together. He knew no more than we did, but appealed to us to reconsider our decision, saying that he had served in the army many more years than we had, and that he was quite convinced that the first duty of an officer and soldier was to obey, and he ended up by saying that if any officer would like to talk the matter over privately with him, that he would be only too pleased to do so. I felt that now I was no longer in the army, I could tell him what I thought of him, so I stood up and said that I would like to talk to him. We then both retired to a corner of the room and I said to him 'I cannot understand how you can consider yourself a loyal soldier to the King, when you are willing to help this Government to break up His Majesty's Kingdom. There is bound to be a civil war; do you imagine for one instant that this damn Government will take the blame for it?—not they, they will throw it all on to the shoulders of the King.' All he could answer was, 'No you are wrong, I am sure you are wrong.' I went out of the room a happy man; he left the room I am quite sure a very unhappy man.

In the meantime I gather that His Majesty had got to hear of the critical situation and was extremely angry that his army should have been used for political purposes. He had orders sent out to all Commanders in Ireland that his officers were to be told the whole truth, that the Army was not to be used to coerce Ulster and they were to be asked to come back.

At any rate at about 6 p.m., the Divisional Commander arrived on the scene and addressed the mutineers in the same room as that in which the Brigadier had seen us a few hours before; but the Divisional Commander had got his orders and knew the whole situation by now. He told us that the Government had thought the Ulstermen were wavering about accepting home rule, and that by the display of a little force, that they would accept it (how remarkably stupid a British Government can sometimes be); but before taking action, they wished to know what were the feelings of the Army in Ireland on the subject, and had therefore sent out this ultimatum to the officers. That he was now here to tell us that the Army would not be used to coerce Ulster, and that all officers were to be asked to come back. This being the situation now, combined with the threat of war by our neighbours over the seas (Germany), he felt quite sure that we would all return to our duties. We were all greatly relieved.

*   *   *

One more little undercurrent of the Ulster Crisis was, when Jack Noel and Doody Wynne, as I mentioned previously, were sent off with their companies under sealed orders as to their final destination, they were sent up to Belfast in one of His Majesty's destroyers.

They had dinner on board, and a guest at dinner was a German Officer. At that time nobody was taking very seriously possible war with Germany, and naturally the chief topic of conversation at dinner was the Ulster crisis. I haven't got the slightest doubt that this German Naval Officer at once got through to his government that England was on the brink of a civil war, which may have given Germany the final fillip to declare war.

Brooke Mss

76

Account by Bandsman F. C. Wynne
1st East Surrey Regt[95]

[Typescript]   [Circa 1960]

About March 1914 there were rumours of being sent to Ulster to put down any insurrection by the Ulstermen. This led to all sorts of rumours and we heard, on very sound authority, that the Cavalry officers at the Curragh would hand in their papers if they were ordered to Ulster.

There was no suggestion that any of our officers or of any of the regiments in Dublin were taking this line. As for the men, they were so in the dark that there was no variation in their duties or any talk or worry about going to Ulster.

One afternoon one of the duty sergeants told us that he had been speaking to a lady in Dublin. She said 'Will they be sending you to Ulster?' He replied that he did not know. She then said 'Do you think they will make you shoot anyone there?' He replied that he didn't think so. Finally she said 'I think it will be terrible if it happens. Will you shoot at them if you are told to?' 'Madam', he replied, 'whatever my orders are, I will have to carry them out.'

We were much impressed by this conversation. The question of actual bloodshed never occurred to us. No one thought it would really happen. The British soldier in those days was incredibly out of touch with public affairs and appallingly ignorant of political matters. No one, to my knowledge, except the officers perhaps, had any thought of looking at orders through political glasses and there was never any question of disobeying orders in the minds of the rank and file. Of that I am convinced. And that was the end of the Curragh Incident as far as we were concerned because it all blew over as worse things loomed over the horizon.

IWM, FCW, Memoirs of F. C. Wynne, p. 38

77
Extracts from the Diary of
Major-General H. H. Wilson

[Holograph]   20 March 1914

No further moves till 6 oc when Cecil telephoned for me to
come home to see Johnnie Gough.

Johnnie had had a wire from Hubert saying that he had been
ordered either to undertake operation against Ulster or dismissed
the service, & given 2 hours in which to make up his mind. He, of
course, took the dismissal. I can't help thinking that Paget has
made a d— fool of himself. I telephoned Johnnie French who
knows nothing about it & talked windy platitudes till I was nearly
sick. After much difficulty I persuaded Johnnie not to send in his
papers till tomorrow while we must find out if this is all true . . .

21 March 1914

Hubert Gough and some 50 officers of the Curragh Camp
have resigned because, as far as I can make out, they were asked
to operate against Ulster. I was at Bonar Law's at 9.30 a.m. and
told him how serious everything was, and how on my present
information I thought it would be imperative to back Hubert, I
had several interviews during the day with Sir John. Robertson
backed me like a man. Joey was away. I told Sir John there was still
time to stop the breakaway of the officers if he made Asquith take
instant action, but it must be done at once or the General Staff
would break away next. Sir John not yet 'seized' with the gravity of
the situation. After much coming and going of Sir John to Seely,
the latter asked what the army would agree to, and I was asked to
put it in writing.

This I did in the form of a promise on the part of the
Government not to imploy the army to coerce Ulster to accept the

Home Rule Bill, and the reinstatement of Hubert and all his officers. Sir John took this paper to Seely, and I gathered that it was not agreeable to Asquith and his crowd.

I still kept impressing upon Sir John the appalling gravity of the situation but I cannot get him to realize, & he talks like a child. At 7 oc I went to Seely. He opened the talk by thanking me for the way I have behaved during a trying two years, because he knew my sympathies were with Ulster, and so forth, and he consequently wished to thank me as S. of S. I replied that no thanks were required as I had only done what I considered right. We then had $\frac{3}{4}$ hour about the present crisis. I told him the same story as I had told French—no officers on the General Staff at the War Office, the regiments depleted of officers, a hostile Europe, our friends leaving us because we have failed them and our enemies realizing that we had lost our army.

Seely, owing chiefly to the most marvellous vanity & partly owing to appalling ignorance remained untouched. At $\frac{1}{4}$ to 8 Bonar Law came to see me at No. 36 and we talked over the events of the day. I am more than ever determined to resign, but I cannot think of a really good way of doing it.

22 March 1914

Came back at 12 oc. Went to Sloane Square to see Hubert and Johnnie Gough. I joined them & Clive Wigram talking things over. I got from Hubert a written account of what happened on Friday last. Arthur Paget put to the Brigadiers (Hubert and Cuthbert) the alternative for them and their officers of undertaking 'active operations against Ulster' or 'dismissal with loss of pension'. Officers belonging to Ulster would 'disappear' and be reinstated after the operations were over in their proper seniority. On this Hubert and 56 out of 60 Curragh officers elected for dismissal.

All this is a perfect God-send for me, because I can now write and say that I understand these alternatives were put before these officers, and, if and when they are put before me, I will give the same answer. Therefore I am in the same boat as Hubert and demand same treatment. Great coming and going here all day of a number of fellows all wanting to know what they are to do. I explained new situation. Motored out to Bonar Law, but missed him, he however came round here to see me, and wanted me to go and dine at Landsowne House to meet Balfour and Austen.[96] I thought wiser not. I gave Bonar Law my copy of Hubert's report of what A.P. said, and told him he might use it. Geoffrey Robinson came to see me & report that Asquith sent for him & he (R) read over the columns for The Times tomorrow. It is, of course, quite valueless.

At 10 oc Simon & Amery came in to report. So passed an eventful day, but my own mind is quite easy as to what I shall do & how I shall do it. A great number of persons in all day & their confidence in me & friendship is very pleasant.

23 March 1914

I went to B.L. at 9.10 a.m. Told him that I was going to claim equal treatment with Hubert & that I felt confident the whole G.S. would follow me; told him Hubert had been in to breakfast & we had determined on our plan of campaign which was that any proposals made must be made in writing & must state that he would not be called on to imploy his troops to coerce Ulster to accept the planned H.R. Bill.

Went to W.O. 10.30. Hubert saw AG at 11 oc & after long & somewhat hostile interview with Seely he came to see me at 12.20. The S of S had agreed to put in writing that the Govt. would only ask troops to assist the Civil Power in keeping law & order. Hubert said he thought that was reasonable, but I objected absolutely because when the H.R. Bill was passed the coercion of Ulster would at once come under this head, so after much talk we drafted a letter[97] & gave it to Spencer Ewart asking the question whether in the case of the H.R. Bill passing we are liable to coerce Ulster in the name of law & order. As a result of this letter we got at 5.15 p.m. a draft which seemed reasonable, but the last para. was, to me, unintelligible as it spoke of not using troops to suppress 'political opposition'. On this we wrote a short note to say that the final para: was not altogether understood but that we read it as meaning that troops would not be used to coerce Ulster to accept the present H.R. Bill & might he so inform his officers, Hubert took this[98] in to Sir John who promptly wrote underneath that he also read the para: in that sense, so this was enough & Hubert caught the night mail, MacEwen & Parker being with him. They were also present at interview when Sir John wrote his note. So was A.G.

24 March 1914

I saw Robertson & Joey & told them I was anxious to tell Sir John that the Govt was sure to round on Sir John for having allowed Hubert (& me!) to read a definite promise into the final para: of their paper. Robertson went in to Sir John to try to tell him this, but only got his head snapped off, which amused me. However, he found out that Sir John has not yet told Seely of the little addition he made to the letter to Hubert last night. This is stupid. Bonar Law rang me up in the morning and we discussed the day's work. I told him how Hubert went back, and on what guarantees. He also told me he was putting up Arthur Lee[99] to ask Seely some questions this afternoon. Arthur Lee also rang me up and talked about the situation, which I explained. No further developments during the morning.

After lunch Ollivant[100] came to see me and told me an amazing story. He said as a fact (and I believe him) that Winston had drafted orders to the 3rd Battle Squadron and 2 Flotillas to go to Lamlash under Lewis Bayley, and from there to make a regular Jameson raid on some Ulster stronghold. This was frustrated by our action in the army. He told me he considered Winston was both bad and *mad*. I at once gave this information to Robertson to send to Clive Wigram for the King & this was done.

After this, Gwynne, the editor of the *Morning Post*, came to see me, and he told me that one of the Cabinet had been to see him and tell him he knew nothing of all this work with the army, was very much annoyed, and thought that Sir John ought to be 'outed' for giving such misleading information. Later on I saw Sir John. I told him that I thought he would be kicked out by the Government when they found out what he had written for Hubert, and that in that case the army would go solid with him.

Spent an hour before dinner with Sir Arthur[101] at the F.O. before dinner. I told him all our story & also about Winston's Lamlash plan.

After dinner Baird (p. sec. to Bonar Law) came to see me & told me B.L. wanted to see me after breakfast tomorrow. He said they had been unable to get any answers out of Asquith or Seely & that later in the Debate John Ward said that the Country was tired of being governed by the King & the Army & that this had received a flurry of cheers from the whole Radical side. We are moving fast & we may perhaps be going to bring conclusions between the King & the Army and the Extremists. I rather doubt it.

25 March 1914

Baird came up at 11 p.m. from B.L. to ask if I could guarantee the army standing fast. I can of course. I wired Hubert at midnight to stand like a rock. This is vital. Any false move now on our part would be fatal. So long as we hold the paper we got on Monday, we can afford to sit tight.

26 March 1914

Talk with Bonar Law and Milner after breakfast. It seems to me Johnny French must resign, but the rest of us must stand fast unless the Government take action against Hubert. Wired him again to keep absolutely quiet. Sir John sent for us three Directors at 1 o'c. and told us he had resigned, but that Seely would not accept. Directly after, all C.s in C. and Divisional Commanders came into the C.I.G.S.'s room and told him the army was unanimous in its determination not to fight Ulster. This is superb. At 3 o'c Sir John sent for me to talk things over. He told me the Cabinet are all opposed to his going and were trying to find some way out of it. I told him that he and Ewart must stick to their resignations, unless they were put in a position to justify their remaining on in the eyes of officers. While we were talking Ewart came in, and I repeated all I had said with emphasis, and made Ewart read Grey's speech of last night. While this was going on, and I was gaining ground, Haldane sent for Sir John. On Sir John's return he sent for me again and told me that Haldane had said that he had consulted the Prime Minister and that they had agreed on Sir John's writing to Hubert and telling him privately that the pronouncement made by Haldane last Monday held the field & was the Govt.'s opinion. He said, 'No orders were issued, no orders are likely to be issued, and no orders will be issued, for the coercion of Ulster.'

27 March 1914

Sir John was 2½ hours with Cabinet before lunch and 1 hour after lunch. He stood firm on Haldane's speech of last Monday. Asquith was to have made a statement at 11 o'clock last night, then 12 o'clock today, and in the end got up at 5 o'clock and said nothing except to read ridiculous Army Order which has been brought out. Sir John was charming to me and thanked me, etc. He showed me the letter on which he stood, drawn up by Haldane in his own house and signed by Haldane and Sir John. After some platitudes it said that Sir John took his stand on Haldane's speech of last Monday, and that Asquith should make this clear.

28 March 1914

I saw this morning the text of Asquith's statement last night. There is absolutely nothing in it which in the faintest degree changes the situation. Sir John sent for me and told me how he stood. He told me of the two Cabinet meetings at which he was present yesterday, and of how he remained firm in his determination to adhere to Haldane's speech of last Monday. His resignation (and, of course, Ewart's) remain temporarily in abeyance. He asked me my advice as to whether he should resign or not, and told me that Jack Cowans and Von Donop had both been to him begging him not to go. I told him in my opinion that he ought to go, and I pointed out that the Army Council were completely out of touch with the army, and that we could not afford to be stupid again and must, therefore, make sure of what the army was saying. I told him that before he came to a final decision one way or another I should like to consult the officers of the Staff College, a place which represented the opinion of the whole army. To this he agreed and I drove down to Arborfield, where they were having their point-to-point. I consulted the following: Sir

Charles Knowles (a great friend of Ewarts), Robb, Percival (5th), Archie Montgomery, Hugo Montgomery, Kiggell, Anderson, Cory, Harper, Gillman, Stopford, Sillem, Vic Couper.[102] These again consulted with their friends and then reported. The result was perfectly unanimous opinion that he must resign. Got back at 8 o.c. Telephoned to Sir John but he was out, will telephone in morning. It seems to me his course is quite clear. He must go & set us an example of what a gentleman should do.

29 March 1914

I telephoned to Sir John at 9 a.m. and told him the result of my mission to the S.C. yesterday & I arranged to go & see him at 5 o.c. Charlie [Hunter] came in at 11 o.c. to say that Milner had said to him yesterday: 'They talk a lot about Gough, but the man who saved the Empire is Henry Wilson.' This of course, is much too flattering. I lunched at Bonar Law's house, only Carson there. We talked about the situation in all its bearings. Carson told me of Macready's state visit to him, and of his return visit, of the visits of all officers of the *Pathfinder* to him,[103] and of the petty officers, of the friendship between the Navy and the Ulster boys, and of the signalling practice that goes on between the two, and of how excellent the Ulster men are.

We discussed the question of Sir John's resignation & they agreed with me that this would beat the Cabinet as it would carry with it the loss of Seely, Morley & Haldane.

At 5 o'clock I went up to Sir John at 94 Lancaster Gate. I was much upset to find he was still havering. He had been for hours with Haldane who had produced another letter to square the circle again.[104] I read this letter carefully several times. It is from Sir John to Asquith. It sets out that Sir John had conceived that, by giving Hubert the assurance, he was only carrying out the instructions of the Government, that the idea of any soldiers dictating to the Government was just as distasteful to him and to every soldier as to the Cabinet, and that they never have done so. Hubert simply wanted to have the situation clearly defined. Then followed a paragraph to which I took grave exception, and which Sir John cut out in consequence—it said that Asquith's statement on Friday last had satisfied Sir John and, he thought, all others. This would never do. Finally it wound up by saying that he believed it was the Government intention not to coerce public opinion in Ulster, nor to initiate any movement which would result in active operations there, and that the whole incident might be considered as closed. So no action would be taken against Hubert and the letter which he held.

The idea then is that Asquith should read this letter out to the House of Commons tomorrow, and that then Sir John and Ewart should withdraw their resignations. Provided this is done and the obnoxious paragraph is cut out, I should be inclined to agree. Sir John, of course was still quite fluid. He showed me a letter from Mrs Asquith to him beginning with 'Dearest Sir John' & 'imploring him for the sake of the Army & for the sake of Henry' to withdraw his resignation! There is no doubt that the Govt. would be on its last legs if Sir John goes, hence the frantic endeavours to retain him.

I hand the whole movement once more for Sir John but he is not able to grasp and to hold the situation for any length of time. We then drove down together to St. James Palace where I left him at Stamfordhams. Gwynne is to see Sir John at 7 p.m. At 9 p.m. I rang up Gwynne and he told me Sir John was resigning. He said that he saw Sir John and saw the letter, and even with the obnoxious paragraph cut out, he objected in toto & on this Sir John told him he might announce that he had resigned. This is splendid. Rang up B.L. & told him & added that it was now his business to drive the wedge deep into the Cabinet by causing the down fall of Seely, Morley & Haldane. A good day's work.

IWM, DS/MISC/80, HHW 23, Wilson Diary

78

Extracts from the Diary of
Lieutenant-General Sir John Spencer Ewart

[Holograph]   20 March 1914

I went after breakfast to see Macready who is too unwell to think of starting for Belfast until the night of Sunday 22nd; I then went on to the War Office and had conference at 11 a.m. with Seely and French. Paget crossed over to Ireland to resume command last night.

There will be great head lines tomorrow in the newspapers re our precautionary moves of troops in Ulster; these however are not provocative in any way. They are merely designed to protect barracks, arms and ammunition. I still hope that some way will be found out of the present impasse, but things look sultry. Despite what Lord Wolseley and Roberts have said I believe that the Army may be relied on to do its duty, as long as there is no question of *actively* coercing Ulster into accepting Home Rule. We must take all precautionary measures to protect our depots and arms and ammunition, and to protect life and property if need be; nothing more.

The foregoing lines written a day ago are hardly a correct prophecy for at 11 p.m. I was sent for to Colonel Seely's house where I found Seely, French, Winston and Lloyd George who had received a telegram from Paget saying that the 5th & 16th Lancers' officers preferred dismissal. Also Brig. General Gough and Colonel Hill commanding 11th District preferred dismissal rather than employment in Ulster; he feared that the same state of affairs prevailed in the 4th Hussars. We wired instructions and that Gough and the three Colonels were to be sent over at once to report to me; they would be relieved of their commands and we would send other officers to replace them. Meanwhile resignations of other officers were to be refused. Winston talked very big about bringing the officers over in a battleship to be tried by court martial. I however urged that we should wait to hear what the Senior Officers concerned had to say. I felt at great loss to understand why the trouble had occurred in the 3rd Cavalry Brigade, as we had ordered no officer or man at all to move of the Cavalry Brigade in connection with our precautionary measures. From Seely's house 24 Old Queen Street we walked over to see the Prime Minister at 10 Downing Street. I did not get home until 2 a.m.

21 March 1914

I saw French and Sir Philip Chetwode and we arranged that latter officer should cross over to Ireland to take Hubert Gough's place in command of the 3rd Cavalry Brigade at the Curragh. Later on, however, we suspended his orders as reports arrived of rather extraordinary action towards the Cavalry officers by Paget. We had several conferences during the day and I saw Seely, French & Winston.

22 March 1914

My 53rd birthday. At 10 a.m. Brig. General Gough, Colonel MacEwen, 16th Lancers; Colonel Hogg, 4th Hussars; and Colonel Parker, 5th Lancers reported to me and successively I heard what they had to say. Macready being present and taking notes. Paget must be mad. In an absolutely uncalled for way he put a pistol to the heads of the officers of the 3rd Cavalry Brigade and gave them the alternative of serving against Ulster or sending in their resignations (which meant dismissal) by 5 p.m. All the officers spoke most nicely and said that had the brigade received orders to move, even to Belfast, they would have gone like one man, but given the alternative by Paget they were obliged to say they would not fight against Ulster. Paget ought never to have put such a dilemma to them, and no one was more surprised than I was that he should have done so.[105]

At 11.30 a.m. I went to an Army Council meeting at Seely's house, where I found French, Cowans, Seely, & von Donop. I told them the story and said I thought that the officers were not to blame considering the position Paget put them into. Seely was all for removing Gough whatever was done to the three colonels, but all the Military Members feared that if drastic action was taken we might have sympathetic action at Aldershot and throughout the Army.

23 March 1914

We went at 10 a.m. to the War Office where first French and then Seely saw Gough, and we asked him if he was prepared to go back and command his brigade. He said he was but that it would be very difficult indeed for him to get control of the officers and men again unless he was given some assurance in writing that they would not be employed to coerce Ulster into acceptance of the Home Rule Bill. Seely said he would see what could be done as he thought it was desirable that something should be put in writing. Gough disclaimed all idea of refusing to obey orders for the protection of life and property. Seely said he must go over to the Cabinet and would I draft such an assurance as Gough had asked for consideration of the Cabinet. I drafted it and a little later sent it over to the Cabinet. I got a message from the Cabinet asking me to send it over to the Cabinet and later on as Hubert Gough was going to lunch he handed me a letter[106] which was very material to the question then under consideration by Ministers. I sent his note to me over at once to the Cabinet and was led to believe the note had reached its destination. Eventually, about 2 p.m. I think, the memorandum which I had drafted came back from the Cabinet. My original document had been corrected in the handwriting of the Prime Minister, but two very important paras had been added in the handwriting of Seely which practically pledged the Cabinet not to apply coercion to Ulster. Seely sent me a message that he would sign this document if possible, but that, if he was in the House, I and French were to sign it on behalf of the Army Council. French and I had no doubt whatever that the memorandum quite accurately represented the considered opinion of the Cabinet. I pointed out to French that it would be impossible for us to sign the two concluding paras. which really pledged H.M.'s Government unless the paper was also signed by a Cabinet Minister. I said to French 'This may become an historical document and we must be very careful what we do.' He agreed, and at 4 p.m. we went to the House of Commons determined to get Seely's signature. Unfortunately he was in the House and we could not personally see him, but Nicholson his private secretary got Seely's signature for us. We then returned to the War Office and about 5 p.m. we saw Colonel Gough and the three Colonels, ordered them to return that night, and handed Gough the document. He asked for a quarter of an hour to consider it and then returned saying that he was quite satisfied but put on paper a supplementary question asking French if he understood that the concluding para meant that under no circumstances would his brigade be called on to coerce Ulster. French wrote on the paper 'that is how I read it' but neither French nor Gough asked my opinion.

I asked if all four officers understood that they had verbal orders from me as AG to return that night to the Curragh and Dublin respectively and they said they did. We then got Chetwode on the telephone and told him that he would not be required now to relieve Gough at the Curragh.

In the evening various important speeches were delivered in the House of Lords and House of Commons, the most important announcement being by the Lord Chancellor (Haldane) that 'No orders had been issued and no orders were likely to be issued for the coercion of Ulster.' Lord Morley was more discreet, but the speeches generally seemed to confirm the document which we had handed to Gough.

24 March 1914

At 11 a.m., with von Donop, MGO, I saw Colonel Hill, Commanding 11th District, who had been placed by Paget in the same dilemma as Gough, had similarly tendered his resignation, and had been ordered to report to me. I told him much what I said to Gough and told him that he could resume command. He asked if he could have the same paper guarantee that Gough had received and I told him that this request was 'subversive of discipline'. Gough, I said, had received the paper before any authorative statement had been made in Parliament, but now that the Lord Chancellor had spoken so decisively in the House of Lords there was no excuse for making such a request. As Seely had suggested to me before the interview, I read him what Lord Haldane had said and added 'Surely you have some trust in Sir John French and me.' He said 'I will take your advice, Sir, and go back.' I afterwards saw Seely, Winston & the Military Members.

In the afternoon I was sent for to the House and saw the Prime Minister, the Chancellor of the Exchequer, and Mr. Churchill in Mr. Bonham Carter's[107] room. They asked me to produce all papers in my possession relating to recent occurrences and I produced the letter handed to me by Gough about 1 p.m. which I sent over to the Cabinet and they remarked that they had never seen it till that moment. I said 'Well I sent it over to the Cabinet in a Cabinet box and it came back to me from Colonel Seely.' They then examined the original of my draft for the Gough document and the added paragraphs. The Prime Minister said 'The corrections in pencil to the first three paras are in my handwriting but who added the last two paras?' I said 'Is it not Lord Morley's writing?' for I had heard something from Seely that Morley had drafted some addition to my original memo. Winston, however, said 'No, that is Seely's writing' and I then saw it was, though it was larger than usual. The only other document they carefully scrutinised was a statement made to me last Sunday by Major Kincaid-Smith, Paget's M.S., who had said that Paget had been compelled to act as he did because he felt that the precautionary moves he was making might lead to further action and that he felt 'it necessary to find out upon what General and other officers' they could rely.[108] The Ministers were discussing what papers it was desirable to lay on the table of the House, and attributed importance to this statement. Later a wire was sent to Paget to ask if he accepted and corroborated his M.S.'s statement which he did.

I left the room perfectly staggered for it now appeared that Seely must have added off his own bat to a Cabinet document which I and French had signed believing it to be a Cabinet decision and on the strength of which officers had been induced to return to duty.

Nothing but necessity would ever really have induced us to give Gough any assurance on paper, but we felt that, unless the

Cavalry officers could be induced that afternoon to return to duty, we might have a sympathetic strike and widespread resignations throughout the Army.

Bethune warned us that the Territorials were ready to resign in large numbers; Haig said there would be a sympathetic move in Aldershot; half the officers in the War Office could not be trusted. What we did we did to prevent something worse happening, though it was all a bad blow to discipline. French said 'I would have signed anything yesterday to get those fellows back to duty'—and he was right. We might have had something like a general mutiny.

25 March 1914

Seely saw the Army Council, we learnt what had happened and that he would that night in the House tender his resignation. He then went to the Cabinet. After he had gone we got Nicholson, his private secretary, to write over to him to Downing Street to say that if he resigned we wished to resign with him.[109] Later on he told me that though he should announce his resignation the Prime Minister did not intend to accept it—which seemed rather like a sacrificial goat and no knife.

In the evening Seely made a long speech in the House; he took the whole blame for what had occurred and said he had unwittingly deceived his political colleagues and placed his military colleagues in a difficult position.

26 March 1914

French and I saw Seely at 10.30 a.m. and tendered our resignations. We felt that we were in an utterly false position; we had in good faith used this precious Cabinet document to induce officers to return to their duty and to allay excitement in the Army and now we found it repudiated in both Houses and Seely made the (temporary and political) scapegoat. This sort of work may do for politicians but it wont do for soldiers. Seely saw the Prime Minister and we were told that our resignations would not be accepted pending a Cabinet meeting and some statement in the House. There were a great many rumours of our resignations in the evening papers and wild excitement in London.

In the morning French and I saw the following generals at the War Office—Smith-Dorrien, Mackinnon, Haig, Grierson, Plumer, Lloyd, Rawlinson, Lomax, Murray & Snow.[110] This meeting was rather unfortunate. It was ordered four days ago and was designed to give French an opportunity of speaking on the discipline of the Army. But we did not cancel it and coming as it did just when there were rumours in London of the resignation of French and myself, it looked as if we might be contemplating some coup d'etat. There was a considerable crowd all day outside the War Office with many press men and photographers. The generals all spoke most freely, said we had the Army at our back, and promised that even if our resignations were accepted, they would stay at their posts and try to keep everyone quiet. But it would not have been difficult to get up a revolution had one been of that mind, I fancy.

27 March 1914

Poor me who shuns publicity of all kinds!! I found myself a sort of 'Boulanger'[111] with my portrait in every paper in the kingdom. How I loathe this and where is the door of escape from an impossible situation.

I met French at 10.30 a.m. and he then went over to a Cabinet meeting to which I was called a little later. We were present at the meeting of a number of Ministers and were given a draft of a Government 'face saving' statement to be made that night by the P.M. We asked for time to consider it as we were soldiers and not ready speakers and were told to return at 3 p.m., for another Cabinet meeting. I lunched with Seely at his house meeting his father, a nice old man, and his children and at 3 p.m. went back to Downing Street where we saw the P.M., Sir E. Grey, Lord Haldane, & Lloyd George. We could come to no agreement as to a statement which would meet the Government position and at the same time help us soldiers out of the difficulty. Everybody was very friendly but we could not compromise and eventually we said that the P.M. would make his own statement and we would reserve the question of the withdrawal of our resignations until later.

At 5 p.m. the Prime Minister made his statement.

At 5.45 we (French and I) saw the Lord Chancellor and he gave us a copy of it.

28 March 1914

I saw French, Cowans, & von Donop at the War Office at 10.45 a.m. and we decided to do nothing definite until Monday. Cowans wisely points out that if we press our resignations these good people, in desperation, may go to the country on the cry the people v the Army and get back with a thumping majority. Politics don't influence my personal conduct the least, but I don't want to be the instrument of injury to the Army. I shall do nothing today at any rate. I don't think Asquith's statement last night of the new Army Order[112] helps us very much.

29 March 1914

I and French went to Colonel Seely's House at 11 a.m. and then on to the Lord Chancellors at 12 noon. Here we stayed till 3 p.m. trying to concoct some letter to be written by Sir John French to the P.M. and read in the House, with the object of enabling French and me to withdraw our resignations without loss of honour and influence with the Army. I did my level best to reach some compromise and Lord Haldane coined many subtle phrases. At the end Sir John French seemed to think that the draft letter[113] might be the basis of compromise but said he must think it over for the night. I had not very much hope of it.

30 March 1914

I met Sir John French at 10.30 a.m. at the War Office. He said he had seen Lord Esher and others and that Lord Haldane's draft letter had too much of the lawyer about it and would never satisfy the Army or justify us. He said he was quite determined to stand by his resignation and I was more than thankful that he arrived at that decision. We at once saw Cowans and von Donop who agreed. At 12 noon we went to Downing Street and saw the Prime Minister, the Lord Chancellor, Sir E. Grey and Colonel Seely. The Prime Minister said he saw it was useless to try to shake our purpose. They all spoke most kindly. Seely said he must also now again resign, though Sir J. French tried to dissuade him. It was arranged that the resignations of all three of us should be announced that evening in the House. The Prime Minister said he had decided to become S of S for War himself which seems a wise move. There was a great debate in the evening in the House.

At 6 p.m. Seely, French and I went to Buckingham Palace and were successively given audience by His Majesty. I talked with him for about 20 minutes and discussed all the sad chapter of accidents through which we have come. He said he thought that French and I were adopting the only possible course in adhering to our resignations and that it was the best thing in the interests of the Army. As I took leave His Majesty said 'You shall not be long left out of it, if I can help it.' He said that Paget had made a nice mess of it, as he has.

SRO, RH4/84/3, 126, Ewart Mss

79
Brigadier-General H. P. Gough to
Brigadier-General J. E. Gough[114]

[Telegram]

Curragh.
20 March 1914

Have been offered dismissal service or undertake operations against Ulster. Two hours to decide. First means ruin of army as others will follow. This only consideration that counts. Am taking first contingency. Do you think if am right reply paid parkgate.

J. E. Gough Mss

80

Brigadier-General J. E. Gough to
Brigadier-General H. P. Gough

Farnborough
20 March 1914
[Telegram]   3.40 p.m.

I will not serve against Ulster and if you are dismissed my resignation goes in at once. Wire what happens to you.

H. P. Gough Mss; J. E. Gough Mss

81

Brigadier-General J. E. Gough to
Lieutenant-General Sir Douglas Haig[115]

Blandford House,
Farnborough
[Holograph]   20 March 1914

This afternoon I received a telegram from Hubert, 'Have been offered dismissal service or undertake operations against Ulster' and ending up with 'Have accepted the first contingency'.

You know my views which mean everything to me. I wired back to Hubert 'I will not fight against Ulster if you are dismissed. My resignation goes in at once'.

I told Gen. Lomax that I was going to London to see if it was true that Hubert was to be dismissed & if a fact to resign my commission.

So far I have only been in telephonic communication with Sir J. French & Seely's private secretary & I gather that there *may* have been a mistake. So I will go to the War Office tomorrow morning & find out for certain and then act according to my conscience.

It is only right that I should keep you informed of what I have done & I will let you know the result of my War Office visit.

NLS, Ms 3155/91(h). Haig Mss

82

Extracts from the Diary of
Lieutenant-General Sir Douglas Haig

[Holograph]   21 March 1914

Bad day. We play [golf] after lunch. I wire Gen. Gough to be calm! and arrange to return Aldershot next day.

22 March 1914

Played 2 rounds of golf. Doris[116] & I left by motor at 5.20 & reached Govt House [Aldershot] at 7.15 p.m. Found most of the servants had been away. Mrs. Morris the cook still away!

23 March 1914

Went by 9.18 a.m. with Genl. Gough to London. Saw Hubert G. at Sloane Square. Went to Ho of Lords at 11.40. Saw Lord Haldane. Gave him Gen. Gough's account of orders given by Paget. Walked to Downing Street with Lord H—went to War Office. Saw Col. Seely's Pw Sec, the AG & Sir J. French—Gen. Robb & 2 Goughs lunched with me at Marlboro. Saw Lord Haldane at 3.45 at Ho of Lords—returned by 5 p.m.

25 March 1914

Rode as usual. At 12 o'c I held meeting of GOC's of Divs & Brigades, about 14 present. Pointed out danger of Disruption in Army to Empire and begged them to induce regt officers to give up dabbling in politics. We were all united to do anything required short of coercing our fellow citizens who have done no wrong. Seely resigned but PM declines it.

26 March 1914

Doris & I went to London by 10.18 train. I attend meeting at 12 at War Office of C in Cs and 4 Divl Generals. French & Ewart explain what orders they gave, etc. They tell us they had resigned because Govt repudiated promises given not to use Army to coerce Ulster. See Ld Haldane after lunch. He did not know of resignations. We walk to House to see Prime Minister. See Gen. French in Ld Haldane's room & walk to War Office with him to draft letter.

27 March 1914

Go to London by 12 train. Cabinet sits from 10.30 onwards—
at 4.20 breaks up but PM not sure what to say to House. He
makes statement at 5 p.m. re French's resignation—still
uncertain as to situation. I return by 6 p.m.

NLS, Ms 3155/2(m), Haig Mss

83

Extract from an incomplete account of events by Lord Milner

[Holograph]   20 March 1914

While the thing is still fresh in my memory, I want to put on
record my own personal experiences of what will surely be
regarded in the future as one of the strangest incidents of recent
history—I mean the revolt of the Army (for it was revolt) brought
about by the action of the Government in undertaking or contemplating the military occupation of Ulster. As it happens I was in a
position to be in closer touch with those events than most persons
could be who were not themselves members of the Government
or the official class. What I shall put down here will be merely the
facts without any comments or inferences.

At a meeting of the Union Defence League on the morning of
March 20th, Walter Long handed me a slip of paper on which
were written certain words which it was stated Sir Arthur Paget
had been overheard to use on departing from Euston the previous
night. They were to the following effect—'25,000 men and naval
assistance,—it is all horrible but it may prevent more bloodshed
in the end'. At this time, the morning of Friday the 20th, I was
greatly puzzled by this report and could not make head or tail of it,
but in view of subsequent events it has naturally remained
impressed upon my memory.

On the evening of Friday, March 20th, I dined at Mrs.
Bischoffesheim's, the party was a small one, consisting of Lady
Londonderry, Bonar Law, F. E. Smith, Sir Matthew Wilson,

recently returned to Parliament for Bethnal Green, Sir Ernest Cassell, and a young man whom I did not know.[117] There was possibly one other person present, but I think not.

I was the last to arrive, and it struck me at once on coming into the room that something unusual had happened. After I had shaken hands, Bonar Law, who was standing by the fireplace, beckoned to me and said, 'You will want to see this' and handed me a telegram which he had just received. The telegram was dated Curragh, 5 something p.m. and was to the following effect: 'General and all officers Cavalry Brigade resigned'. The telegram was unsigned and we were all of us somewhat in doubt whether it might not be a hoax, or if not a hoax at any rate an exaggeration. There was practically no conversation on any other subject during the whole evening, and while the discussion was carried on in a superficially calm tone we were no doubt all more or less excited.

After dinner several members of the party tried by telephone in various directions to discover whether there was any more news either confirming or not confirming the rumours. These efforts resulted in nothing very positive but on the whole it became more evident as the evening wore on that something pretty serious had happened.

I left about 11 and went straight home, having made up my mind that it was no use trying to find out anything certain that night, and that we should know more in the morning.

Bodleian, Ms Milner 157, f 78–86

84
Lieutenant-General Sir Douglas Haig to Brigadier-General J. E. Gough[118]

[Telegram]

Littlehampton
21 March 1914

Hope you will not act precipitately. I feel equally strongly on subject as you. There is no question of Army fighting against

Protestants or against Catholics. Our duty is to keep the peace between them.

NLS, Ms 3155/91 (h), Haig Mss; J. E. Gough Mss

85

Brigadier-General J. E. Gough to Lieutenant-General Sir William Franklyn[119]

48 Sloane Square
Chelsea
[Holograph Copy]   21 March 1914

In view of the military movements which have been ordered against Ulster, and the action of the GOC-in-C in Ireland in giving officers two hours to decide between dismissal from the service or an undertaking to act against Ulster, I have the honour to hand in the resignation of my commission as an officer in HM's Army.

J. E. Gough Mss

86

Brigadier-General H. P. Gough to Field Marshal Lord Roberts

Curragh Camp
[Telegram]   9.15 a.m. 21 March 1914

Yesterday all officers in Ireland offered by War Office alternative of instant dismissal or undertaking active operations against Ulster. I accepted instant dismissal. Practically all officers Cavalry Brigade done same, and total about 100 officers Dublin and Curragh. What is (the) situation in England? What action do you advise?

NAM, 7101-23-202, Roberts Mss

87

Lady Lugard to Andrew Bonar Law

[Holograph]   21 March 1914

Is it of any interest to you to know that General Hubert Gough who until today commanded the Cavalry Brigade at the Curragh was sent for by instruction from Gen. Paget and required to choose between marching on Ulster and resigning his commission. He was given two hours in which to make his decision and he of course decided to resign his commission.

You will know whether it is in accordance with Army Regulations that this course should have been followed.

Practically all the officers of the Cavalry Brigade which he commanded have resigned their commissions in protest. These have not yet been accepted. But Gen. Hubert Gough and his two Colonels have been summoned to London by the W.O. and Col. Chitwood [Chetwode] has I understand been appointed in Gen. Gough's place. Gen. Hubert's brother Gen. John Gough who held the post of Chief of the Staff at Aldershot has today resigned his commission.

I may mention confidentially that I have received my information from Gen. John Gough whom I have seen this afternoon and you may take it as strictly accurate.

Possibly you know it already but it occurs to me that you may have to deal with the matter on Monday in the House and may wish to verify further details between this & then. I should hardly venture to write but for having met you at Lady Wantage's[120] on Monday.

H. of Lords RO, Bonar Law Mss 32/1/38

88

Note by J. E. B. Seely

War Office
21 March 1914

[Holograph]

I saw the King this morning at 11 o'clock. He expressed surprise & annoyance that he had not been informed beforehand of the events which had led up to the resignations of the officers of the 3rd Cavalry Brigade. I stated in reply that with regard to the general policy to be pursued about the resignations of officers in connection with the Ulster question, I had communicated to Lord Stamfordham for submission to HM the policy which was to be pursued towards the end of last year (Dec. 9th).[121] That I had told the GOC's and that I had understood that the policy had HM's approval. I said I would send him a copy of the memorandum prepared at that time.

With regard to the actual movement of troops I understood that the Prime Minister had told HM on Tuesday last at 11 o'clock of the movements which had been approved by the Cabinet. HM told me that he had no recollection of this having been mentioned at all, adding that there had been so much to discuss that it had been perhaps omitted accidentally at his interview with the Prime Minister.

I then read to HM the telegrams sent & received last night between Sir A. Paget & myself with reference to the resignations of the officers of the 3rd Cavalry Brigade.

HM asked whether the question had not been put to these officers in an unfair manner. I said that we had no official information on this but from an unofficial telegram from OC 4th Hussars[122] it would appear that Col. Gough was suddenly placed in a dilemma with which it was unfair to confront him. On the other hand it might be that this was only Col. Gough's view and I could on no account prejudge the case against Sir A. Paget who had had a most difficult task to perform and had done it very well.

HM asked what were the proposals as to the 4 officers now on their way from Ireland, i.e. the Brigadier and the CO's, 3rd

Cavalry Brigade. I said we must ascertain from them at their interview with the A G tomorrow their version of the circumstances.

If, as I anticipated, they stated that what I call an unfair dilemma was put to them and that had they been asked if they would obey orders in support of the civil power they would have agreed, I would suspend action until I had heard from Sir A. Paget with reference to their statements.

If on the other hand any of the officers had taken the other line & had stated that they claimed deliberately to choose which order they would obey in supporting the civil power, I would recommend to HM that he should be tried by court martial or removed as was considered advisable by the Army Council. I presumed that this course would receive HM's approval. HM said he would accept the advice of the Army Council.

Bodleian, Ms Asquith 40, f 32–34

89

Note by Field Marshal Sir John French of a telephone conversation with Field Marshal Lord Roberts

[Holograph]   21 March 1914

LORD ROBERTS. I am speaking from Ascot. What do you think of this terrible state of affairs?

SIR J. FRENCH. It is very difficult to speak about such matters on the telephone.

LORD ROBERTS. I hope you are not going to associate yourself with this band of (certain epithets were used which I could hardly catch). If you do you will cover yourself with infamy.

SIR J. FRENCH. I must do my duty as a soldier like everyone else and put up with whatever consequences may ensue.

LORD ROBERTS. Goodbye.

RA GV F.674/15; IWM, 75/46/8, French Mss

90
Note by J. E. B. Seely

War Office
21 March 1914

[Holograph]

Lord Roberts came to see me today at the War Office. He said that HM had told him he understood that he (Lord R) had sent an insulting telephone message to Sir John French, insulting both to Ministers & to Sir John French.

Lord R said he had told HM that this was contrary to the facts. He felt very strongly on the Home Rule question but he never had and never would say a disrespectful word of the Prime Minister or his colleagues, especially those responsible for the Army & the Navy or of the Chief of the Staff. If any such impression had been conveyed by the telephone message, which was from Ascot to London & consequently hard to hear, he regretted it & hoped I would accept his assurances that no such statement had been intended.

He said HM had also told him that I had said that he (Lord R) was responsible for most of the trouble with officers in the Army.

HM had suggested his coming to see me and report what he had said to HM; that the only communication he had had with officers on this subject had been to tell them on no account to resign their commission on hypothetical grounds. He had had no communication with Colonel Gough & had he been appealed to by him he would have given him the same advice.

I thanked Lord R for his explanation on both points.

He then said he wished to appeal on behalf of Colonel Gough who had telegraphed to him[123] & from whom he now gathered that he (Col. G) had been confronted with the dilemma of agreeing to take part in aggressive action against Ulster to compel her by force of arms to accept the Home Rule Bill or resigning his commission in 2 hours.

I said that if the dilemma had been put as stated, which I could not, of course, admit, it was contrary to the intention of myself and the Army Council. I did not wish to take advantage of his refusal, insubordinate though it was, and thus ruin his future career.

Lord R asked if he could write a letter to Col. Gough to meet him on arrival to explain what I had said in order, as Lord R put it, that Colonel Gough might realise that there was some hope for him if he could satisfy the AG that he would have replied to a question more properly put in a proper & subordinate manner. Lord R read the opening sentences of his letter in the above sense.

I know nothing of its further contents except that Lord R asked if he might ask Colonel Gough to come & see him and I replied that if Colonel Gough was in a position to do so I could not object.

He re-iterated his disclaimer of having intended to say or having said anything discourteous of W. Churchill, myself or Sir John French.

Bodleian, Ms Asquith 40, f 35–37

91

Extracts from Diary of Geoffrey Robinson

[Holograph]   21 March 1914

A day of tremendous excitement & strain in London. All ideas of a 'weekend' (I ought to have gone to Englemere) were abandoned very early & I spent the greater part of the morning at the Travellers Club, since my own house became intolerable with telephone calls. There I did some writing & talking, going out from time to time to see Ld Milner & others & eventually learning what was going on from HHW, who got to his house from the W.O. for a short respite between 2 & 3. He told roughly what had happened in Dublin the day before—Paget's meeting with his brigadiers & colonels, the option to undertake aggressive operations against Ulster or be dismissed, Gough's answer & unanimous support by the Cavalry Brigade. W was obviously in a state of great nervous tension & I fancy that he & most of his colleagues had been preparing their own memorandum to the effect that they must all be held liable to any action taken against Gough. He was going back to his office & thence to Wilfred Ashley[124] at Stanmore for the night.

I went down to the office then & dictated the facts of the situation, which by this time however were getting into the evening papers, did some other telephoning, correspondence, interviewing & arrangements, & finally adjourned at 5 to Buckingham Palace to see Ld. Stamfordham. Him I found in an almost hysterical condition—he'd never thought to live to see such a catastrophe, violent letters & telegrams were pouring in, the King had known nothing whatever of the trouble till he read it in the Times. What did people really expect him to do? had I fresh news, etc? I told him I came not to bring news, but to call for 'information & guidance', that in my humble judgement there was no reason yet for drastic intervention by HM, & that in any case I was at hand if he wanted to communicate with me. French was expected at the Palace as I left. Asquith, Seely & others had already been. I walked on to the Maxses,[125] where I ought to have been playing tennis, got home about 7, & ended an agitating day with a tête-a-tête dinner with Lady Londonderry!

Bodleian, Ms Dawson 64, f 23–27

92
Brigadier-General J. E. Gough to Lieutenant-General Sir William Franklyn

48 Sloane Square
Chelsea
22 March 1914

[Holograph Copy]

You very kindly said that you would hold over my resignation until you heard from me. A kindly action which I much appreciate.

I wish you would destroy the original paper[126], and I enclose another which I wish to take its place and to be dealt with by the Army Council.

These are hard times but I feel no doubt but that I am right.

J. E. Gough Mss

93
Brigadier-General J. E. Gough to Lieutenant-General Sir William Franklyn[127]

[Holograph]
48 Sloane Square
22 March 1914

In view of the action of the GOC-in-C in Ireland in giving officers a few hours to decide whether they would undertake operations against Ulster or be dismissed the service, I wish to place on record that I am in agreement with those officers who decided to accept dismissal. Further I think it is only right for me to make it clear that any action taken against these officers should equally apply to myself.

Nuffield College, Ms Mottistone 22, f 217-219; J. E. Gough Mss; Churchill College, DRBK 3/7 de Robeck Mss

94
Field Marshal Lord Roberts to Field Marshal Sir John French

[Holograph]
Englemere,
Ascot.
22 March 1914

I was astonished, when with the King yesterday, to learn from His Majesty that the Secretary of State had told him I had, when speaking to you through the telephone[128] called the Ministers

'Swine and robbers'. Of course, you know I never made use of such expressions or anything like them.

My sole object in ringing you up yesterday was—after reading in the papers that Hubert Gough and 100 other officers had resigned their commissions on account of being asked whether 'they were prepared to undertake military service in Ulster or be dismissed from the service, their pensions being forfeited'—to warn you that, whatever obloquy the Government would draw on themselves by such action must be shared by you, and to express my hope that, under no circumstances, would troops be employed to coerce Ulster to accept the present Home Rule Bill, as I felt how seriously it would affect the Army. It was for this same reason I called upon you at the War Office last Thursday and, finding you were engaged, wrote to you a note from the House of Lords asking you to have a quiet talk with me about the Army, and, if you would, to dine and sleep at Englemere the following day. On all these occasions my desire was to help an old friend and comrade who, I felt, was placed in a very difficult position.

It would be a grave misfortune if you and I were unable to work together during this very serious crisis. [129]

NAM, 7101-23-202, Roberts Mss; IWM. 75/46/8, French Mss

95

Notes by Lieutenant-General Sir John Spencer Ewart on the interviews in the War Office

[Holograph]   22 March 1914

Notes by the Adjutant General on his interview with Brig. General Gough, Lieut. Cols. MacEwen, Parker and Hogg. Sir Nevil Macready was also present. (Sunday March 22 1914).

I must preface these remarks by saying that when Brig. Gen. Gough came into the room he said that if any use was to be made of any notes taken at the interview he ought to be furnished with a copy of them.

I told him and the Commandg Officers that I was taking notes for my own guidance as it was necessary to be so very clear as to what their answers were to certain questions I intended to put to them.

They were given no copies of the notes and I probably gave them the impression that no public use would be made of their answers, J S E 24.3.14. The questions which the S of S instructed me to put to them were as follows:[130]

(1) What was the question put to you by the G O C?

(2) Did you understand him to mean that you were to decide at once whether in the event arising of a general offensive movement by the Army for the coercion of the Protestant Counties of Ulster you would take part in that movement if ordered to do so, and that he would recommend your immediate dismissal unless you gave him the assurance he sought?

(3) Am I to understand that apart from this hypothetical question you claim to choose which, if any, lawful order you should obey when called out in aid of the civil power for the protection of life and public and private property?

Brigadier Gen. Gough stated that at 6.30 p.m. on Thursday he got orders to attend at headquarters. He arrived there at ten a.m. on Friday. There were present Sir Arthur Paget, General Fergusson, Colonel Hill the Chief Staff Officer and Generals Rolt and Cuthbert. Sir Arthur Paget said, in effect, active operations were to be begun against Ulster—the place might be in a blaze by Saturday—had been in close communication with the War Office and had the following instructions from the War Office and CIGS to convey to officers.

Officers domiciled in Ulster would be allowed to disappear and be reinstated without detriment at end of operations, but must give word of honour that they would not fight for Ulster. Officers who were not prepared to take part in active operations from conscientious or other scruples must send in resignations at once and be dismissed the Army. It was to be fully understood by Officers Commanding and Brigadier Generals that any officers who avoided service on an incorrect plea of domicile in Ulster would be tried by court martial—resignations were to be sent in by that evening—Brigadier Generals directed to go and give their information to their commands and report by that evening. This answers questions (1) and (2).

Question (3). He first had to make up his own mind and did ask Sir A. Paget for a clearer explanation of domiciled in Ulster and whether it applied to those domiciled in the South. Sir A. Paget said no. Gough saw 5th Lancers in their ante-room and gave statements as above but answered no questions and gave no advice. Every officer was to decide for himself. He saw all three regiments. After seeing the 5th Lancers he saw General Friend and told him that he could not undertake to fight against Ulster.

In answer to question (3) General Gough said 'No, I quite agree that apart from any question of civil war, no soldier would have the right of choosing to hesitate to obey any order given him in support of the civil power. I felt very keenly being placed in a position with no warning with a pistol at my head, to make my mind up in the most serious moment of my life with no chance of consulting anybody.' General Gough referred back to General Friend whether resignations were to be submitted at once and understood from him that they were to be submitted forthwith.

Col. MacEwan, 16th Lancers said. Question (1) and (2) 'The question was put to us in the form of an alternative. In view of active operations against Ulster, officers must be prepared to go to the furthest extreme in their actions or resign by 5 p.m. (it was then 3 p.m.) which resignations would involve dismissal and loss of pension—the only exception being officers domiciled in Ulster. I understood civil war would commence next morning—and the urgency of Sir A. Paget's message was due to this.'

Question (3) 'If I had been ordered to Ulster with my regiment we should have carried out any order in spite of conscience and personal feeling, but being given an alternative it altered the whole situation—the officers were given the offer and accepted it—no premeditation and consultations among them but I told officers to act solely according to their own conscience—given the option we thought we were being given a bargain but a hard one.'

Col. Parker, 5th Lancers. Questions (1) and (2): 'We were asked if we would act against Ulster or resign our commissions and be dismissed the service without delay. This occurred about 11 a.m. on Friday. Then I asked General Gough how long we had to make up our minds. General Gough said he would wire. About 1 p.m. I got a wire from General Gough to send in their resignations forthwith. I called the officers and told them it was the parting of the ways, whether they would see the thing through or take the consequences. I went away for an hour and then the Adjutant gave me the resignations. All resigned except two—I went into the ante room and the officers who were there asked me what I should do. I said that my mind had long been made up and my resignation would go in with theirs. I then went to see General Friend to tell him the state of the regiment. Sir A. Paget came up in the evening—he said "I see you have taken the alternative of resigning and I think you are making a mistake—you are not being asked to coerce Ulster but the moves that I am making are merely to keep order and guard stores"—he said "Would you object to keeping order". I said "No, but I will not move against Ulster." Sir A. Paget then said—"Why not go on with your regiment and keep law and order and then if it came to a question of coercing Ulster why not then resign? You might be court martialled and shot but you should not mind that—you would be no worse then than you are now".'

Question (3) 'I would not take part in anything that would lead to the coercion of Ulster. For instance, if my Regiment was on the border of Ulster and the police, while executing warrants of arrest, were fired on and I was told to support them, I should hold that it would be against my principles to do so of course under the present circumstances. I should not hold it my duty to protect Government property in Ulster.'

Col. Hogg. 4th Hussars. (Question 1, 2) 'The whole thing never ought to have arisen. It was suddenly broken to us.'

Question (3) 'Short of civil war I am prepared to lead my Regiment. I could claim the domiciled clause but would not. The regt all but 6 said they would obey my orders. The six required time. The thing has been made so difficult—all the regiments would have moved at once had an order been received and no alternative given!'

Bodleian, Ms Asquith 40, f 69–72

96
Statement given by Brigadier-General H. P. Gough to Lieutenant-General Sir John Spencer Ewart

[Typescript]   22 March 1914

Interview in Dublin

Sir A. Paget said that active operations were to be begun against Ulster and that the whole country would be in a blaze by Saturday. That he had been in close communication with the War Office and he had the following instructions from the War Office and the Chief of the Imperial Staff to convey to the officers.

Officers domiciled in Ulster will be allowed to disappear and would be re-instated in their positions without detriment to their careers at the end of operations in Ireland; but they must give their word of honour that they would not fight for Ulster.

Officers who were not prepared to undertake active operations against Ulster from conscientious or other scruples were to send in their resignations at once and would be dismissed the Army. It was to be fully understood that the officer commanding and Brigadiers or any officers who avoided service on an incorrect plea of a domicile in Ulster would be tried by Court Martial. Resignations were to be sent in that evening.

All the Brigadiers were directed to go down and deliver their message to the Units of their Brigade and to collect and forward the results.

NAM, 7101-23-202, Roberts Mss; Ibid, 8001-6-4, MacEwen Mss; RA GV F.674/20; Ibid, F. 674/83; BL; Keyes Mss, 3/17

97
Brigadier-General H. P. Gough to
Mrs Nora Gough

[Holograph]

48 Sloane Square
6.25 p.m. Sunday
[22 March 1914]

Sent you off a wire about an hour ago giving you a brief summary of day's proceedings, which I hope, my precious sweet little Queen, was some comfort to you. It has been a busy & most interesting day! On such questions of extreme gravity to me & nations, it seems almost wrong to say so, but I have positively enjoyed it! I am afraid they have raised the lust of battle & certainly hardened one's temper, & made it *most uncompromising*.

Mac & Parker are simply *splendid*, calm, indifferently cool, & absolutely uncompromising. Hogg is white, shaky, twitching lips & cheeks, full of talk & explanations, & trying to run with the Hare & hunt with the Hounds!

J arrived at 9 & accompanied me to the WO where he heard of what had taken place & the 'terms' offered us by AP—he said our case was *unshakeable*. At the WO we were shown in, *individually*, to AG—Sir Spencer Ewart—& a General Macready. My manner was haughty, uncompromising & stiff, *to a degree*! They were most suave. I was merely asked for a statement of facts, & then each of the others went in & made the same statement. The result I think was simply damning to AP.

I have seen here—Clive Wigram, Greer,[131] Henry Wilson. Letters from Tom Bridges—who is sending in his papers tomorrow—Johnnie—Henry Wilson (*entirely* under pressure from J!!) & many others send in what amounts to practically resignation tomorrow! Greer has put all facts before Bonar Law, & Johnnie before Austen Chamberlain, & a vote of censure is I believe to be moved in the Commons tomorrow night. The King has had all details from (1) Clive Wigram. (2) Frank Dugdale who has shown King Godfrey's (& Gibbon's) letter.[132]

The Government all in the greatest difficulty, & the WO

authorities, with that rogue & buck-stick Sir John French at their head, are in a most damnable dilemma. Rumour says Sir A.P. will be ruined & recalled!! Altogether, there is a hell of a storm brewing & in full blast, all over your poor husband & the 2 firm men, who stood by him in the moment of stress, & refused to sell their honour or right, for which guidance & support, we may indeed humbly thank God. Truly it seems, as if He was going to bring us out triumphant from a hopelessly critical situation, with all the odds against us.

Mother & Annie Style here. Lily dining. Annie & I teaed with her & brought her back.

No more now. Fondest love. God bless & guide you & us both. PS. Don't mention names of people supporting us, etc.

H. P. Gough Mss

98
Field Marshal Lord Roberts to Major-General H. H. Wilson

Englemere,
Ascot.

[Holograph]   23 March 1914

Johnny Gough was here yesterday. He showed me the state-ment drawn up by Hubert after his interview with Paget. After haranguing the officers, he asked them whether they were prepared to undertake operations against Ulster or be 'dismissed the Service'.

As you will hear his Brigade command has been filled up. This before he had been heard at the War Office! I think the man who has taken his place[133] ought to be ashamed of himself.

When I had my interview with Seely, he told me that Paget had put the ultimatum to Gough and the Cavalry Colonels in a way that was never intended. That there was no idea of the Cavalry Brigade or any troops going to Ulster, that precautionary measures only were being taken, and that the Cavalry were to go to Limerick. If this is true, Paget must be mad because he spoke about the way in which he would use the troops on his advance towards Ulster—'he would keep the Cavalry in the [illegible] position'. As I told Seely moving troops at all was a most provocative measure, and if Paget had not put the ultimatum correctly, Gough could not be punished by losing his command.

Lansdowne, Balfour, Bonar Law and A. Chamberlain dined together last night. Austen C asked me what I thought of the ultimatum.[134] I said I thought it was 'monstrous and insulting'. We must all stick to Gough now. The more officers resign the worse will be the plight of the Government. Keep me informed of what goes on.

IWM, 73/1/18, Wilson Mss

99
Brigadier-General H. P. Gough to
Lieutenant-General Sir John Spencer Ewart

[Holograph]

War Office
23 March 1914

On thinking over the points raised by the Secretary of State this morning, the question has arisen in my mind, and it will undoubtedly be one of the first questions asked me by my officers, when I see them, viz:

In the event of the present Home Rule Bill becoming law, can we be called upon to enforce it on Ulster under the expression of maintaining law and order?

This point should be made quite clear in your draft letter, otherwise there will be renewed misconceptions.

White Paper; Monro of Williamwood Mss

100

Memorandum given to
Brigadier-General H. P. Gough

[Copy Typescript with
Holograph additions]   23 March 1914

You are authorized by the Army Council to inform the officers of the 3rd Cavalry Brigade that the Army Council are satisfied that the incident which has arisen in regard to their resignations has been due to a misunderstanding.

It is the duty of all soldiers to obey lawful commands given to them through the proper channel by the Army Council, either for the protection of public property and the support of the civil power in the event of disturbances, or for the protection of the lives and property of the inhabitants.

This is the only point it was intended to be put to the officers in the questions of the General Officer Commanding, and the Army Council have been glad to learn from you that there never has been and never will be in the Brigade any question of disobeying such lawful orders.

His Majesty's Government must retain their right to use all the forces of the Crown in Ireland, or elsewhere, to maintain law and order and to support the civil power in the ordinary execution of its duty.

But they have no intention whatever of taking advantage of this right to crush political opposition to the policy or principles of the Home Rule Bill.

(Initialled) J.S.

War Office.   J.F.
March 23rd 1914.   J.S.E.

We understand the reading of the last paragraph to be that the troops under our command will not be called upon to enforce the present Home Rule Bill on Ulster, and that we can so assure our officers.

(Sgd.) H. P. Gough

This is how I read it.

(Initd.) J.F.

23/3/1914.

C.I.G.S.

White Paper; NAM, 8001-6-8, MacEwan Mss; J. E. Gough Mss; Monro of Williamwood Mss; Nuffield College, Ms Mottistone 22, f 230–232; IWM, 75/46/4 French Mss; Pragnell Mss; BL, Keyes Mss, 3/17

101

L. S. Amery to Andrew Bonar Law

Eaton Square, SW1.

[Holograph]

23 March 1914

Before leaving this afternoon Gough received a written assurance to the effect that the troops under his command were 'not to be used to coerce Ulster to accept the present Home Rule Bill'. He is going to read this out to his officers on parade tomorrow morning.

Seely first offered him verbal assurances which he refused to accept, then several varieties of written assurances which tried to evade the point & it was not till after five o'clock that French took down to Seely at the House the draft Gough was prepared to accept, & Seely signed it.

I had all this from Henry Wilson just now, & we tried to get through to you but could get no reply on the telephone.

H. of Lords RO, Bonar Law Mss, 32/1/46

102

Lord Haldane to
Lieutenant-General Sir Douglas Haig

28 Queen Anne Gate
Westminster
[Holograph]   23 March 1914

It is, I think, all right & I need not come to you at 1.

If you wish to see me I will manage 3.45 at my room at the House of Lords, & you can count on finding me there.

Seely has seen Gough & Paget & has come to a satisfactory arrangement on the lines you & I talked over.

The Govt has not the least intention of beginning active operations against Ulster, & Paget agrees that Gough might have misunderstood him.

Anyhow Gough remains in his position. He was spoken of at the Cabinet today with high appreciation of his qualities.

NLS, Ms 3155/91 (h), Haig Mss

103

Note by H. A. Gwynne on a conversation
with Brigadier-General H. P. Gough
at Euston Station

[Holograph]   23 March 1914

Brig-Gnl. Gough said: 'I have got the assurance I asked for; they are in my pocket and I am taking them back to my brigade. I dictated the terms, and wrote them with my own hand. The document was signed by Gnl. French. I have the assurance that my brigade will not be used for political purposes to force Home Rule on Ulster.'

I heard him congratulate Col. MacEwen and chaff him on carrying his sword (without a cover). He said 'you are taking it back with honour'.

At the door of the sleeping saloon Viscount Crichton,[135] Col. Parker & Col. MacEwen had a conversation and were evidently pleased at result of the negotiations at the War Office.

IWM, Gwynne Mss

104

H. A. Gwynne to
Field Marshal Sir John French

Morning Post,
346 Strand, WC.
23 March 1914

[Holograph]

I have given very deep thought to our conversation of this afternoon and I venture to put before you one or two points which have occurred to me that I think may be worthy of your consideration.

There is one outstanding point in the whole matter and it is round this point that the whole difficulty centres. *It is that the Army will not consent to be used to coerce the Ulster people to submit to Home Rule.*

Any settlement which does not recognise that absolute fact is no settlement at all but only a postponement of the difficulty. If Colonel Seely tries to arrange the matter in a way which will allow the politicians to argue hereafter that there is nothing in the settlement which might prevent the Army being used in Ulster, *once the Home Rule Bill has become law*, then we shall have a similar state of things to that which occurred on Friday but it will spread throughout the whole Army.

My object in writing this to you is to urge you to settle the thing *now* once for all. Let us freely acknowledge that the Secretary of State and many officers of high standing and experience have up to Friday totally misunderstood the temper of the Army. That excuse holds good no longer. Everybody knows now that the whole Army is absolutely determined not to be the instrument to coerce Ulster.

In such a case, why shut our eyes to the obvious fact? Your duty seems to me to be quite clear. It is to acknowledge that very many officers of high standing have in the past few months misunderstood the state of the Army; that they understand it now and lay it down to the politicians as an absolute incontrovertible fact that the Army will not allow itself to coerce Ulster. It is therefore your clear duty to put this forward and declare to the politicians that no settlement or agreement or statement will do the slightest good unless the Government say in plain language that they have no intention of allowing the Army to coerce Ulster. If they say that, the Army is saved: if they say anything less officers of the Army will resign en masse and the finest force in the world will be ruined.

Excuse my venturing to put all this before you. You know I am more of a soldier than a politician and that my whole object is to safeguard the Army which is in terrible danger.

Today you have the power to insist on these terms, tomorrow it may be too late. If the difficulty is put off it will recur with added force and immense danger to the Army.

Brotherton Library, Glenesk-Bathurst Mss; Bodleian, Ms Gwynne 19; IWM, 73/1/18, Wilson Mss; Ibid, 75/46/8, French Mss

105

H. H. Asquith to King George V

10 Downing Street
24 March 1914

[Holograph Copy]

Mr. Asquith, with his humble duty, thinks it right to acquaint Your Majesty at once with acts which have only come fully to light today.

The letter to be addressed by the Army Council to Genl. Gough was carefully considered and settled by the Cabinet yesterday; and it was not until the debate in the House was over that Mr. Asquith was shown a copy of the letter actually delivered,[136] which contained a paragraph—added on his own authority by Colonel Seely—of which the Cabinet had never approved, and which they would almost certainly have disapproved.

This is the paragraph which is described in today's press as a 'written assurance' that troops will in no case be used for the 'coercion' of Ulster.

Further, Mr. Asquith & his colleagues did not learn until this afternoon that General Gough had yesterday morning in a letter addressed to the Adjutant General demanded such an assurance.

It is impossible for the Cabinet to condone the course which has been taken, and it will be their duty to give a full explanation in the House of Commons tomorrow.

In the view of the Cabinet, it was wrong to demand from the officers any assurance as to what their conduct might be in a contingency which might never arise, and it is at least equally wrong for an officer to demand any such assurance from the Government.

Their position in the matter was clearly & publicly stated in both Houses yesterday, and the Officers were entitled to nothing more.

RA GV K. 2553(4)/44

106

Brigadier-General H. P. Gough to Brigadier-General J. E. Gough

[Holograph]

Brownstown House
Curragh.
24 March 1914

This is the first letter in the real sense of the word, that I have had time to write since my brief epistle to you last Thursday night, and it is going to be again to you.

No words of mine can ever tell you what your support has meant to me during this four days struggle.

What you did in arousing the spirit of the Army was immense, but it was very little in comparison to your own stout heart & resolute spirit beside me in those somewhat critical moments. When my heart began to fail & my resolution to waver, as it did under the strain sometimes, you held me up & I can never be grateful enough to you for doing so. You did for me what Aaron & Hur did for Moses during the battle against the Amalekites!![137] All I can pray is that if, & when, you are in a crisis, that you will find me as prompt & as resolute in your support as you were in mine. I have one great regret, viz that old Father[138] was not there to see us in the struggle & to take our hands in the victory. Do you remember the old man lying, dying, & sending for us after dinner to say his last farewells, & how when we came into the room, he said with that extraordinarily gallant smile of his—'Two very smart young men'?—I would have given anything to hear him say to us on Monday evening—'Two very gallant & honest young men'!

I want you to send me your best & last photo. I am collecting Parker's & Mac's, & I am going to place the 3 photos round my resignation, in a frame, & put underneath those 2 verses out of Exodus 17 (11.12)—with the dates! It will be quite an artistic memento of a great battle.

I will later on send you the file of all the telegrams I received, as soon as Mac & Parker here have read them. It is interesting to see how many & who rallied to the Flag!

One was from the 2 Batt Worcesters—'who drank your health last night'[139]—I liked that awfully. I don't know a single fellow in it. But as they are quartered at Aldershot, you might in one of your rides, look them up & tell them how awfully nice I thought it was of them, & that I will answer as soon as I am able to find the time.

I have been thinking again over your dinner with Seely[140] & I am inclined to withdraw the advice I gave to you, to go to it. My resentment & Contempt for him, for Paget, & for French, rises more & more, & is not abating *at all*. There is no question of maintaining or supporting military authority in dealing with a d—d civilian, & his manner was so insolent & the miserable subservience of these Field Marshals & full Generals so marked, that

I am inclined to think it best policy to treat him with the utmost contumely. But think it over. It may be now too late. All well here. Shall have to smooth the path for all those who did *not* stand by us over here. I don't think it would do to humiliate them, poor devils, more than is possible, & if we make them feel they are still comrades, we have given them an example which will raise & strengthen all their hearts & courage on any future occasion. Love to D.[141]

J. E. Gough Mss

107

Field Marshal Lord Roberts to Major-General H. H. Wilson

Englemere,
Ascot.
[Holograph]
24 March 1914

I don't think I can write or ever speak again to French.[142] He must have known and agreed to the wicked plans of Government to quietly assemble troops in Ireland, and then proceed against Ulster as if it were inhabited by a rebellious enemy instead of our own kith and kin, whose sole desire is to be the loyal subjects of the Crown, and who would be fighting under the Union Jack. French has shown himself to be a poor creature, as I have always suspected him to be. He may have had a spark of more courage yesterday afternoon, but not till after it was perfectly clear that the Government was beaten, and would have to accept an ignominious defeat.

You never saw how uneasy Morley and Haldane looked when they were being turned inside out by the Opposition Lords. I rejoiced at the castigation they got.

When speaking to me thru' the telephone on Saturday morning, when I was begging French to stick to the Army, he replied that he 'intended to go through with the business', the business being to try Gough & Co by courtmartial!

And then it was base of him to run off to Asquith and Seely and tell them I had called them 'Swine and traitors'.[143] I don't remember saying these words, certainly not swine—but whether I said it was not for French to repeat the words.

IWM, 73/1/18, Wilson Mss

108

G. C. N. Nicholson to J. E. B. Seely

[Holograph]

War Office
25 March 1914

If any question of your resignation arises, the Military Members (all four) feel that it is of the *greatest importance* that you should give them an opportunity of seeing you before any decision is made. Note: This means that they will probably go with you & feel that if they do so, many will follow them & the general result to the Army would be disastrous.[144]

Nuffield College, Ms Mottistone 22, f 233–234

109

Note by Lord Stamfordham

[Holograph]

Buckingham Palace
25 March 1914

I saw the Prime Minister in order to draw his attention to a letter of 21st inst addressed by Col. Brett,[145] 2nd Suffolk Regt to his Brigade Commander stating that his Battn agreed to do their duty in the matter of Ulster & that their chief reason for doing so was the assurance given by their Divisional General that Sir A. Paget's orders from the Government had the full approval of the King. I told Mr. Asquith that the King wished to know what the orders were and he replied that Sir A. Paget received no orders.

I then discussed the King's situation and the letter which I had written to him on that subject an hour or so before. He quite agreed that the insinuations & attacks against the King from both sides of politics were most unfair & he promised to say something in the House on the subject that afternoon. He further added that only last week he had declared to the King that His Majesty's action throughout these past months had been in every way thoroughly constitutional.

He spoke openly of the disastrous mess into which the military question had got through 'human stupidity' & told me of Col. Seely's resignation which, however, had not been accepted.

RA GV K. 2553 (4)/47

110
Note by J. E. B. Seely

[Holograph]

War Office
26 March 1914

Sir John French & Sir Spencer Ewart came to see me this morning & stated that they wished to tender their resignations to me, because statements in a document to which their initials had been appended had been repudiated. I refused to accept their resignations on the ground that the only statements which had been repudiated were statements of the intention of HMG of which they could have no knowledge unless communicated to them by me. They saw this point but said that this further difficulty remained, which seemed to them insuperable. The officers had gone back to the Curragh on the faith of the document and would consider that Sir J. French and Sir S. Ewart had broken faith with them.

I said that if Lord Haldane's statement in the House of Lords on Monday had been handed to these officers instead of my own statement the officers would certainly have gone back even more readily than they did.

Sir J. French & Sir S. Ewart agreed that this was certainly the case and that if Lord Haldane's statement were accepted and mine rejected their honour would be saved. They agreed to accept my refusal of their resignations pending further developments.

Bodleian, Ms Asquith 40, f 80–82

III

H. A. Gwynne to A. Bonar Law

Morning Post
346 Strand, WC
26 March 1914

[Holograph]

This is what has happened up to 1 p.m. today.

This morning French and Ewart as co signatories, with Seely, of the Gough document, tendered their resignations because their action had been repudiated by the Govt. *They made no sort of conditions whatever* merely resigning because the cheque they had drawn had been dishonoured.

Seely refused to accept it then made the following proposition. If the Prime Minister would in the House reiterate the speech of Haldane's on Monday that the Govt were not at present or in the future intending to use the Army in Ulster, would the two officers reconsider their resignation? French refused any promise. But Seely went off to the Prime Minister with the suggestion.

Personally I cannot think that Asquith will make the statement. And in that case the two officers will go. But the Army will stand firm and there will be no more resignations. All the Commanders of Divisions[146]—big army officers attended at the W O today— were urged by French to take no action, since his resignation was really on a question which affected his personal honour, and nothing to do with Army politics. When I left French he was to see Winston but I think he will remain firm.

I think that if Seely was asked whether it is true that Sir John

French & Sir Spencer Ewart had tendered their resignations, he would have to admit this truth.

French insists that his resignation is made *without condition*. It is merely a matter of personal honour. If any attempt is made to indicate that he has in any way put a pistol at the head of the Govt, it is a lie.

H. of Lords RO, Bonar Law Mss, 32/1/63

112

Lord Haldane to his mother, Mary Elizabeth Haldane

[Holograph]

28 Queen Anne Gate
Westminster.
27 March 1914

Thank you for your valued letter & for the text.

I'm doing all I can with the Generals. I saw the Prime Minister towards midnight, & am to see Sir John French in a quarter of an hour, & then meet the Cabinet. If I could handle this situation alone or were back at the War Office for 48 hours I am sure I could settle matters but it is now very difficult.

NLS, Ms 5991, f 111, Haldane Mss

113

Statement by Field Marshal Sir John French and Lieutenant-General Sir John Spencer Ewart

[Holograph Draft]   27 March 1914

Sir John French and Sir Spencer Ewart have tendered their resignations and the Prime Minister has requested them to withdraw them.

They are anxious to do this if they can consistently with the duties of their position.

They hold most strongly that there can be no question of conditions being made by officers as to obeying orders, and agree that a definite Army order should be issued to that effect.

What they desire is that the Prime Minister should make a statement in the House of Commons saying that, in taking the action they did in signing the document which was handed to Brigadier General Gough, Sir John French and Sir Spencer Ewart believed themselves to be acting in accordance with the views and instructions of the Cabinet and to be transmitting these views to the officers concerned. [And did not conceive themselves to be making conditions with them—deleted.] Those views they understood to be the views which were subsequently stated by Ministers in both Houses on the same day.

They desire the Prime Minister further to say that they are in complete agreement with these declarations so far as they effect the employment of the Army.

Monro of Williamwood Mss; IWM, 75/46/8, French Mss

114

Lord Haldane to his mother,
Mary Elizabeth Haldane

28 Queen Anne Gate,
Westminster.
28 March 1914

[Holograph]

From 9.45 yesterday when Sir John French came to me by desire of the Prime Minister I have been labouring for peace.

I am in hope that it will now result. The devotion of the soldiers to their old Chief was touching. I think they felt their honour was safe in my hands & I did all I could to guard it. We had two Cabinets & I had interviews throughout the day with the two parties to the dispute.

The PM & I remained calm & Sir Edward Grey was a great help. PS. We shall know the outcome tomorrow.

NLS, Ms 5991, f 112–113, Haldane Mss

115
H. H. Asquith to King George V

[Holograph Copy]

10 Downing Street.
28 March 1914

Mr. Asquith with his humble duty to Your Majesty, has the honour to report that the meeting of the Cabinet, which began on Wednesday, was continued and concluded yesterday.

The topic which first engaged attention was the communication to General Gough of a document & of assurances never authorised by the Cabinet, in the circumstances which Mr. Asquith had the honour to lay before Your Majesty in his letter of last Tuesday.

Colonel Seely admitted his mistake and offered his resignation; which—for the moment at any rate—Mr. Asquith with the concurrence of his colleagues declined to submit to Your Majesty for acceptance.

At the adjourned meeting of the Cabinet yesterday the further developments of the situation, due to the debate in Parliament on Wednesday evening, & to the tendered resignations of Sir J. French & Sir J. S. Ewart, were fully considered. The officers just named were in attendance, and were from time to time seen & consulted by members of the Cabinet. In the end, after much consideration, the new Army Order[147] was drafted, which has since been seen & approved by Your Majesty, and the terms of the statement made later in the afternoon in the House of Commons by Mr. Asquith.

Bodleian, Ms Asquith 7, f 109

116
Major-General F. J. Davies to
Lieutenant-General Sir Douglas Haig

War Office
29 March 1914

[Holograph]

Sir John does not feel satisfied with Asquith's statement.

On the representation of Lord Grenfell,[148] who is a wise old bird, he has decided to sleep over it and take no action till Monday.

He says the only thing he cares about is what the Army thinks. In my opinion it is not what the Army *thinks* but what is *best* for the Army.

It is quite possible that the issue may turn out to be a much greater one than what the Army thinks, it may develop into an appeal to the nation on the question of Army v H of Commons, involving the Army in a stand up fight with the radical party, which can ultimately have only one issue.

On the other hand, of course, if any suitable officer could be got to take Sir John's place and could do so with a clear conscience, things might settle down for the present.

It is a time when Sir John wants cool heads round him and I think it would be a very good thing if you came up early on Monday, as it is quite likely you may be of great use. PS. Of course you have heard nothing from me.

NLS, Ms 3155/91 (h), Haig Mss

117

Draft Statement prepared for Field Marshal
Sir John French by Lord Haldane

[Draft Holograph]

29 March 1914

I have read what you said on Friday afternoon in the House of Commons. I may say that any notion of an officer bargaining about his orders is as repugnant to me as it is to you and I may add that General Gough expressed the same view to me at the interview with him on Monday. I understood General Gough only to ask for a document, as something which he might have in his hand to enable him to allay dangerous misapprehensions and excitement in his brigade. I handed it to him in the belief that it represented the considered opinion of His Majesty's Government. In doing so I conceived that I was simply explaining what I took to be, and to have been throughout, the intention of the Government not to use the army for the purpose of coercing opinion in Ulster or undertaking active operations there. What you said on Friday I have carefully considered and I think that the imputation which you conveyed to the House of Commons is substantially just what I meant to convey to General Gough, not in a process of bargaining, but as an explanation of what I feared he and the public generally might have misinterpreted. It is a real pleasure to me to be able to convey to you that what you have said satisfies my own sense of what I owe to the Army and to myself and I believe that it will satisfy others [for I should say that] nothing could be more important in the best interests of the army than the creation of an impression that the word of a member of the Army Council or indeed of any officer could be lightly set aside after it had served its immediate purpose. It was this consideration alone that prompted me and the Adjutant-General to tender our resignations and we wish to remove any impression in the mind either of the public or of the army that we have been actuated by any desire to embarrass His Majesty's Government.

I have the Adjutant-General's agreement in what I write and he concurs with me in adding on behalf of both of us that if we have not misinterpreted you, you may regard our resignations as withdrawn.

I take it that in the light of what you have made quite clear to the public mind, you will think that the wisest course in the interests of everybody is to treat the incident as closed and to take no further step with reference to the document of 23rd March, the *meaning* and origin of which are now quite plain.[149]

NLS, Ms 5910 f 186–7, Haldane Mss; IWM, 75/46/8 French Mss

118

H. H. Asquith to Lord Haldane

Sutton Courtney
29 March 1914

[Holograph]

I have carefully read the draft letter.[150] I need not say, with the utmost disposition to make any terms with French that are compatible with our Parliamentary position.

But I am satisfied we could not possibly survive any recognition, express or implied, of the Gough treaty, and it is equally clear that French will not remain except upon that footing.

I fear this is an impasse from which there is no escape: much as it is to be deplored. You have done your best to find an accommodating formula, and I gather from Bonham Carter that you cannot do more.

I see no way out of the imbroglio, but for Seely to go also and I propose myself (for a time) to take his place. Churchill, who is here, is entirely of the same opinion. I shall be up in the morning between 11 & 12 and shall hope to see you.

NLS, Ms 5910 f 180–1, Haldane Mss

119

Circular announcing the resignation of Field Marshal Sir John French and Lieutenant-General Sir John Spencer Ewart

War Office
30 March 1914

[Printed]

The Adjutant General and I have resigned our appointments and our resignations have been accepted by the Government. The issue was a purely personal one absolutely unconnected with any political consideration whatever. We should not have taken the step if we had not been quite confident that all officers, non-commissioned officers and men would continue to carry out their duties in the same loyal and whole hearted manner which has ever characterised the Army.

I feel confident therefore that I may rely upon you to maintain discipline at the same high standard as heretofore and to allay and remove by your own influence any feeling which may exist in regard to what has recently occurred.

IWM, 75/46/8, French Mss, NLS, Ms 3155/91 (h), Haig Mss

120
Major-General H. H. Wilson to Field-Marshal Lord Roberts

36 Eaton Place,
Belgravia.
[Holograph]   31 March 1914

I tried to get on to you on Sunday night to tell you that Sir John & Ewart were resigning, but I could not get through.

When I come down on Sat; I will tell you all the story which is both too long & too complicated to explain in a letter. Sir John will no doubt 'disappear' as Field Marshal & Ewart will presumably get Scotland now that Wolfe Murray has gone to succeed Hart in S. Africa.[151]

Sir John's successor is not yet fixed but I expect it will be Douglas & I have not heard any good info about who succeeds Ewart.

The pressure on Sir John to remain was very great but in the end he behaved *well*; but I will tell you the *whole* story on Saturday.

I liked, immensely, your speech last night, and I hope we shall see Morley's resignation today. Then perhaps poor fat Haldane & after that, perhaps the Cabinet.

NAM, 7101-23-88-22, Roberts Mss

121
Memorandum by H. A. Gwynne

[Holograph]   2 April 1914

On Monday March 23 I met Sir J.F. at the Bath Club and he asked me to go down to the War Office and see him as he was very much bothered over the question of Gough and the state of the Army generally in regard to Ulster. I made an appointment for 3 o'clock, which I kept, and I discussed the situation in all its bearings. Sir J.F. was very much surprised at the outburst of feeling and said that there had been blundering, and he was quite taken aback at the idea which I put before him, that it was something more than ordinary precautions of which he spoke, which aroused the feeling of the Army in Ireland. He seemed quite surprised by the extent of the naval preparations, and he told me was astounded to hear a statement by Mr. Winston Churchill on the Friday before, in which the First Lord of the Admiralty said that if there were going to be any opposition to the movement of the troops, he would pour enough shot and shell into Belfast to reduce it to ruins in 24 hours.

This statement made a great impression on Sir J.F. and he could not understand from the information which he possessed how there could be any possibility of such a disaster. He was frankly puzzled by it. At the time I saw him (3 o'clock in the afternoon,) he was not at all decided how he should meet General Gough's demands, and I wrote him a letter which I think may have had some effect.[152] I saw him again later in the day and he then told me what had happened. He also informed me that General Gough had asked him in writing, as one soldier might ask another, whether he might interpret the last two paragraphs of the communication which he had received, to mean that the Army would not be used to coerce Ulster. Sir J.F. added to the paper over his initials, 'This is how I read it.' That same evening, Sir J.F. dined with Mr. Winston Churchill at the Admiralty and there were present Seely and Lloyd George, and J.F. told me that he informed them all of what had taken place on the Monday, although, of course, Seely and the others presumably knew about it beforehand, and they all said that it was quite right and they would stand by him. Tuesday was comparatively speaking quiet, but I saw J.F. and I told him that there was sure to be a row about the whole affair and he had better be prepared to get all his papers in good order. On Wednesday I saw Sir J.F. both in the morning and in the afternoon, and by this time of course there was a great deal of excitement among the back benches of the Government, aroused mostly by Mr. John Ward's speech, and I told J.F. what I thought then was coming; that the Government would find themselves obliged by the intensity of the feeling of their back benches to go back on the contract which they had made with Gough. This in our morning interview he refused to believe, but in the afternoon when I saw him, he informed me that he had seen the Prime Minister and it looked as though his promise would be repudiated. I then informed Sir J.F. that, of course, if this took place, he would obviously have to resign.

This curiously enough came as quite a surprise to him, and he went into the next room to the Adjutant-General and told him of the new view of the case. I put forward all the arguments I could in favour of his resignation, and on Wednesday night I kept him up to the mark. I saw him again on Thursday morning, before he saw Colonel Seely, and he then informed me that he was sending in his resignation, which he did about 11 o'clock in the day. Immediately there was a tremendous fuss in Government circles. Winston Churchill saw him, Colonel Seely, and the Prime Minister saw him also. But he put it to them that he could not in honour withdraw his resignation. The Prime Minister by dint of much persuasion got him to withdraw his resignation temporarily, and immediately all sorts of suggestions were made that would allow him to remain on. He remained firm, however, all that day. Late in the evening Haldane and the Prime Minister made a most astounding proposition. It was to this effect, that Sir J.F. should write a private and confidential letter to General Gough pointing out the difficulties of the Government and also that in spite of any action the Government might take in Parliament, his, J.F.'s letter to Gough, would hold good, and to add that this private and confidential letter was written with the knowledge of Lord Haldane, Colonel Seely and the Prime Minister.

I pointed out to General F that if I were not advising him as a friend, as a politician there was nothing better I could wish than that such a letter as that should be sent, only incidentally it would ruin him for all time. He saw this and persisted in his resignation. On Friday Lord Haldane again saw him and made another proposition which was that his, Lord Haldane's statement in the House of Lords on the Monday preceding to the effect that the Army on no account would be used against Ulster, stood as the policy of the Government, and suggested a statement for the Prime Minister to make in the House of Commons somewhat to this effect: That Sir J.F. withdrew his resignation on the understanding that the statement of Lord Haldane in the House of Lords still stood as the policy of the Government. Sir J.F. was inclined to accept this, but I pointed out that in view of what the Prime Minister had said on Wednesday, it was quite impossible and that it was really only playing with the question to suggest such a thing as that. Sir J.F. was then sent for by the Government and they were all insistent on his remaining in, and they pointed out to him what a terrible thing it would be for him personally, for the Army, and for the nation; but he took his stand on the question of his personal honour and the result was that he promised to wait before persisting in his resignation until he had read the statement which the Prime Minister promised to make in the House of Commons at 5 o'clock.

This statement was made and I saw Sir J.F. that same evening and pointed out to him that it would want a whole army of lawyers to make it consistent with his promise to General Gough, and he saw quite readily that such was the case, and notified Colonel Seely on the Saturday morning that his resignation must stand. This, however, did not satisfy the Government and fresh attempts were made on Saturday and Sunday by Colonel Seely, who put it to Sir J.F. that if he, J.F. went, he [Seely] would have to go too, and particularly on Sunday morning by Lord Haldane, who again brought forward the last suggestion of a letter that Sir J.F. should write to the Prime Minister to be read out in the House of

Commons. This letter[153] was a rigmarole of legal phrases which really meant nothing and finally on Sunday night, I put it to Sir J.F. that this document was of no use and that the best thing he could do was to authorise me practically to announce his resignation which I did in the 'M.P.'[154] on Monday last the 30th March.

But even that was not the end of Sir J.F.'s trouble, for again on Monday morning an onslaught was made on him by several of the Ministers, Lord Haldane included; and again Sir J.F. was summoned to a Cabinet meeting. He stood firm, however, and they then reluctantly decided that there was nothing to do but to accept his resignation. The Prime Minister at the end of the meeting took him to his private room and said to him: 'I think it only right to tell you, Sir John, that I think you have done the right thing. In fact there was no other course open to you.' The rest of the story, of course, is public.

Brotherton Library, Glenesk-Bathurst Mss

122

Brigadier-General J. E. Gough to F. S. Oliver

Brownstown House
Curragh.
8 April 1914

[Holograph]

Here are some facts:

Thursday, March 19th. Orders received at the Curragh for ½ Bn. (Cornwall Light Inf.) to be sent to Dundalk, and ½ Bn. (Cornwalls) to be sent to Newry. This understood to be with the object of guarding the Stores, artillery & government buildings. The move was to take place on Friday (20th), &, although there was a certain amount of uneasiness as to the real object of these moves still no one imagined that there was a real crisis at hand—

(One Company also was sent from Dublin to Carrickfergus by the 'Panther'—I think—and also a detachment was sent from

Mullingar to Enniskillen—These moves I am not *absolutely* sure of, although practically so=you ought to verify this)

On Thursday night—about 7 p.m.—Hubert & Fergusson (Commanding 5th Division) received an order from Sir A. Paget ordering Divisional & Brigade Commanders to go up to Dublin to interview Sir A.P. the next morning (Friday)—No one realised what the interview was to be about, & a certain amount of uneasiness was around. Hubert wrote to me that night saying he wondered what was going to happen, & adding that if it meant moving troops up to Ulster for 'law & order' he proposed to carry out the orders without protest.

On Friday 20th Sir A.P. held his famous interview at 10 a.m. at the Headquarters Office in Dublin—There were present: Sir A.P., Maj. Gen. Friend (the Maj.-Gen. in charge of administration Irish Command), Brig. Gen. Forestier-Walker (Sir A.P.'s Chief General Staff Officer), Maj.-Gen. Fergusson (Commanding 5th Division), Brig. Gen. Rolt (Commanding 14th Brigade), Brig.-Gen. Cuthbert (Commanding 13th Brigade), Brig.-Gen. H. Gough (Commanding 3rd Cavalry Brigade) and Colonel F. Hill (Commanding the 11th District—i.e. the Depôts in the North of Ireland). I enclose a statement of this interview—marked A.[155]

As soon as the interview was over Hubert wired me a summary of what had happened. He then went to the 5th Lancers (who were quartered in Dublin) & told them what Sir A.P. had said, and the choice offered to Officers. Hubert did not at that time take the names of the Officers 5th Lancers who accepted dismissal, but it was obvious that the bulk of the Officers were not prepared to undertake operations against Ulster. Hubert then went back to H.Q. & saw Friend & told him that he (H) had made his choice & accepted dismissal, & requested instructions as to what he was to do & to whom he (H) was to [give] command of the Cav Bde. Friend said that H was to go back to the Curragh & put Sir A.P.'s question to the remainder of the Cav. Bde. (i.e. 16th L., 4th Hussars & R.H.A.) & that the result was to be sent up at once for A.P.'s information.

Rolt also returned to the Curragh. Fergusson remained up in Dublin for a further interview with A.P. at which A.P. is *believed* to have explained his 'plans'. This interview took place about 2 p.m., but I do not know what passed nor who were present besides Fergusson. Hubert was to have been present but as he had decided to accept dismissal his presence was not desired. Fergusson, however, told H that the Army & Navy were to blockade Ulster, while the police were to take some drastic steps, & H. understood this to mean that the police would seize some public buildings in Belfast (probably the H.Q. of the Ulster Provisional Govt)—

On arriving at the Curragh, H collected all his Officers & gave them Sir A.P.'s message (For an outside account of this interview see statement B). It is no exaggeration to say that the Officers were utterly staggered at the choice offered them—far from having made up their minds they almost all had considered the possibility of 'operations against Ulster' as unthinkable & not worth considering. When the Officers had made up their minds they informed H & he then wrote out his letter to HQ giving the numbers of the Officers who (1) claimed protection under the Ulster domicile clause (2) preferred dismissal & (3) accepted the alternative of 'operations against Ulster'—(A copy of this letter was published in the white paper presented to Parliament).

Rolt, in the meantime, assembled the Officers of his Bde. & the artillery of the 5th Divn. & explained the situation to them. He (R) & the bulk of the Officers in his Bde made up their minds to accept dismissal & to tell Fergusson their decision as soon as F arrived at the Curragh (where he was expected by the evening).

As soon as F arrived he interviewed his Officers & asked Rolt as the senior Officer present, for his decision. R said he accepted dismissal. F then said that it was only right that he himself shd. say what he was going to do. He, accordingly, said that he thought it his duty to go against Ulster, he gave his reasons & made strong appeals to Officers; amongst his arguments being the importance of the Army holding together & what he considered most important of all, the assurance Sir A.P. had given him that the King knew all about it & all soldiers shd. obey the King. Rolt was shaken by this argument about the King & Said he wd. go to Ulster. (I have seen Rolt & this is his own account, he told me that he really was quite uncertain in his own mind what he wd. do when he got to Ulster if fighting actually took place. In other words he was hoping for the best & did not know his own mind & had not sufficient strength of character to stand the test he was being put to: he had not thought out the problem before hand as he, in common with most Officers, had thought there never was even a possibility of the Army being asked to coerce Ulster—so much for the Army plot).

I have mentioned previously that the Cornwall Lt. Inf. were given orders on Thursday to go to Dundalk & Newry on the Friday. When Rolt returned from Dublin he found the Cornwalls actually getting into the train, & he (R) had not time to explain matters to the Cornwalls & consequently he had to let the Batn. go to Dundalk & Newry; all he cd. do was to get hold of the Colonel of the Cornwalls & ask him to stay behind until the situation had been explained—This just shows that there was no question of the Army refusing to go to Ulster to maintain law & order & it makes it difficult for Sir A.P. to explain why it was thought necessary to ask Officers to choose between dismissal & operations against Ulster. The Govt. talk glibly about the necessity of guarding stores etc. in Ulster, but there was no difficulty about it all as far as the Army (or Ulster either) was concerned, as you can see from the way in wh. the Cornwalls were quietly carrying out their orders.

On Sat (21st) A.P. came down to the Curragh to interview the 3rd Cav. Bde. I enclose three statements giving an account of their interview (i.e. the pp. marked B.C. & D).[156] You must understand that these 3 accounts are by different Officers & are drawn up quite independently & without collaboration.

Sir A.P. left for Dublin as soon as he had finished talking to the 3rd Cav. Bde. and General Fergusson was told to receive the final decision of the Officers of the 3rd Cav. Brigade. About 5 p.m. on Saturday afternoon Hubert told Fergusson that neither he nor most of his officers could alter their previous decision, & that they could not accept Sir A.P.'s guarantee. Hubert was then told to hand over command to the next Senior Officer, & that he & two of his Cavalry Colonels were to cross over to England & report themselves to the War Office at 10 a.m. next day (i.e. Sunday 22nd). The Colonel of the 4th Hussars, Hogg, had withdrawn his resignation after hearing Sir A.P.'s statement. Hubert crossed over & I met him in London at 9 a.m. We discussed matters & we then went to the War Office. Perhaps I should explain my own share in the proceedings up to this date.

I received a telegram from Hubert on Friday telling me that he had accepted dismissal. I immediately went up to London prepared to go to Ulster—as naturally I imagined that something very serious had happened in Ulster & was under the impression that Civil War had actually commenced. I saw H.W. at his house & we got on the telephone with Seely & John French & I fancy this was the first they knew of the debâcle in Ireland (this was about 7.30 p.m.) On the Saturday I went to the War Office & asked to see the Military Secretary, who at first said he would not see me as it was a political matter! I asked him to reconsider this & eventually saw him & ended by handing in my resignation. The Military Sec. agreed to hold over my resignation until I knew more from Hubert. The news by this time, Saturday midday was fairly well known to everyone in the War Office, & the fighting spirit of the Officers was gradually becoming aroused!

Well, to return to Hubert. We went to the War Office at 10 a.m. (Sunday). Hubert saw Spencer Ewart (the Adjutant General) as did the three Colonels. Hubert handed in the written account of Sir A.P.'s interview in Dublin (i.e. the papers marked A). The Adjutant General explained he was only obtaining information to lay before Sir J. French & the S. of State. The upshot of the matter was that Hubert & Co. were ordered to report to the War Office next day (Monday 23rd) at 10.30.

I returned to Aldershot on the Sunday afternoon & had my first interview with Sir Douglas Haig. I had at that time no idea what his attitude would be (so much for the Army plot!) Sir D.H. rose to the occasion & said that he for one would not shoot down the Northern Protestants, but that the Army's job was limited to keeping 'law & order'. He, Sir D.H., ended by saying he would go up with me on Monday morning & would use his influence with the War Office & also explain the attitude of the Army & Aldershot in particular.

Monday (23rd). Sir D. Haig went up with me to London. We saw Hubert & then Hubert, self, Parker (Colonel 5th Lancers), & McEwen (Colonel 16th Lancers) met at the War Office. We arranged the plan of campaign, but our main consideration was this—We would *not* fight against Ulster, & if there were going to be operations against Ulster then we *wanted* to be dismissed as we would then be free agents to take whichever side we liked in the Civil War. We did not trust the Govt; we felt we were dealing with unscrupulous lawyers, whose word was not worth a brass far-thing. We felt uneasy that these above mentioned lawyers would try to entrap us with words, & that above all they would try & force the Army into a false position under the plea of maintaining law & order.

I dont think I need go into the long story of the Monday incidents. You have probably got them from H.W. and other sources.

The main point to bear in mind is that Hubert & his two Colonels were dismissed men, at least that was their view. And the fact that Chetwode had been ordered to the Curragh to take over Hubert's Brigade, shows that the War Office was at first also under this impression. This being the case Hubert said he could not agree with Sir J. French & Seely that the incidents in Ireland would be completely wiped out. It was impossible to imagine that the situation could be brought back to what it was before Paget's ultimatum on Friday. Seely & French were anxious to persuade Hubert to put a sponge across the slate & to forget all about the incident. Hubert's argument was that he could not go back & then perhaps have the whole business on his shoulders again in a few weeks or days. He would, he said, only return if he was assured that this would not be the case. If this assurance could not be given then he would prefer to be dismissed & in any case he could not return to take up his command again. Seely at once said 'of course this was all right; there was no intention of coercing Ulster with the Army'. Hubert said he must have this in writing as it would never do to have more misunderstandings. Eventually Seely & Co. agreed to this & it was settled that a War Office letter would be drafted to this effect & that Hubert & his Colonels would then go back to Ireland. When H. came out from this interview we considered the whole affair and decided that we must have no more mistakes, and therefore Hubert wrote a letter[157] asking a *question*—i.e. what answer he was to give to his Officers if they asked him their position in the event of the present Home Rule Bill passing & how they would stand as regards enforcing the Bill under the expression 'law & order'. This was deliberately put in the form of a question, & the Govt. were free to answer as they thought best.

This is a long letter & I only hope it will give you the information you want.

P.S. *Please note*—All through the proceedings there was no mention made of offering the men any choice of dismissal or operations against Ulster. I should think this would annoy the Labour Party, & it proves that the Govt. were lying when they said the same terms were to be offered to the men as to the Officers.

J. E. Gough Mss

123
Memorandum by Lord Stanfordham

[Holograph]

Buckingham Palace
13 April 1914

Sir Douglas Haig told the King[158] that last Dec: Col. Seely summoned all the General Officers Commanding to the W.O. and addressed them as to the possible employment of troops under their command in Ireland, explained that this would only be in the assistance of the civil power in the maintenance of law & order & to protect public property but under *no circumstances would they be used to coerce Ulster.*

Since that date he has received no orders whatever with regard to Ireland or for the movement of a single man from his command to that country. He has given no orders for questions to be asked to any officers or men and has never mentioned the King's name in connection with affairs in Ireland.

On Monday 23rd March, in consequence of what had occurred at the Curragh he came to London to inform the W.O. authorities that if any punishment were meted out to General Gough all the officers of the Aldershot Command wd resign. He did not see Col. Seely who was too busy to receive him but he did see Sir J. French who seemd much surprised at this information—he also visited Lord Haldane & gave him the same warning. He is certain that every officer & man ordered to Ireland now would obey orders but *under no circumstances* would they coerce Ulster.

Sir J. French was out of touch with the Army & did not know the strong general feeling which existed against being employed against the Ulsterman.

He is aware that the King's name was made use of at the Curragh and elsewhere to induce the officers not to refuse to take action against Ulster.

RA GV F.674/75

124

Account by Brigadier-General H. P. Gough of events and interviews Sunday and Monday (22nd and 23rd March, 1914)

[Typescript]   16 April 1914

Arrived London by Irish mail and went to my mother's flat, 48 Sloane Square.

Johnnie arrived at 9 a.m. He told me that as far as he could gather, the line the W.O. meant to take up was that there was a complete misunderstanding, that the alternatives put before us by Paget should never have been put, and that we were to be reinstated.

At 9.45 a.m.—arrived at the W.O. meeting Col. MacEwen in the street and finding Parker sitting in the hall by the fire. All cheery, quite firm as to attitude, and quite indifferent as to whether we returned to our positions and the Army, or not; we were certainly not prepared to do so if we were liable to be exposed to again to such a situation as had been forced upon us by Paget, nor under any conditions were we prepared to undertake war on Ulster.

At about 10.15 a.m. shown into A.G.'s waiting room. I was put in a separate room to Colonels MacEwen and Parker. Shortly after I was shown into A.G.'s room. I found Sir Spencer Ewart (A.G.) and another.

My manner expressed my feelings, I was very stiff. I was determined that under no circumstances would I submit to any form of lecture or 'wigging'. I was fully conscious of having committed no offence and equally conscious that a most cruel and hard position had been forced upon me and other officers by the War Office and Paget, which filled me and the other officers with resentment.

General Ewart came forward very nicely and introduced me to General Macready. General Macready in his position as Director of Personal Services had been responsible for gross mis-statements and injustice to me; (Adam's case)[159] his presence therefore filled me with further resentment. General Ewart asked me to sit down and said this was a very grave business. I replied very sharply 'I am fully aware of that'. General Ewart said that he merely wanted to get from me the facts of what had occurred. General Macready began taking pencil notes. I immediately demanded that I should be given a copy of everything that was written down. I never got this copy as I did not think that anything very material had been said of which I had not already got a copy.

I then gave the evidence, copy of which is attached.[160] The letter written asking for information on Friday evening (20th instant) was shown by me to the A.G. now for the first time. It never seems to have got beyond Sir A. Paget's office.

General Ewart then asked me if I thought an officer had any right to question when he should go, or should not go, in support of the Civil Power to maintain law and order. I said 'none whatever' and I added that if Sir A. Paget had ordered my Brigade to Belfast we should have gone without demur, although I could not think why we should be wanted there.

The interview then closed and I was ordered to remain in London within hail of the telephone. Colonels MacEwen and Parker then went in and gave their evidence.

While we were in the War Office we met Colonel Hill who had been giving his evidence. This was the first intimation we had received that Colonel Hill had also resigned on Friday evening; He told me that he also had stated that on Friday Sir A. Paget had told us that 'he expected that the country would be in a blaze by Saturday'.

Later on in the afternoon. I received orders to attend War Office at 11 a.m. next day.

Monday 10 a.m. Sir Douglas Haig and Johnnie arrived from Aldershot.

After telling Sir Douglas Haig all I could of the situation we entered the War Office, and there again met Colonels MacEwan and Parker. We decided not to accept re-instatement unless we received an assurance in writing that we would not again be called on to undertake operations against Ulster.

At 11.15 I was shown (alone) into Sir John French's room and found Sir Spencer Ewart there with him. Sir John was very suave in his manner—I, very stiff. Sir J. French made me sit down. Ewart sat opposite me. Sir J. French stood, or walked about by the fireplace.

Sir J. French began by saying that he was my old friend and chief and wished me to trust him and to believe what he said. He then went on to say that there had been a great misunderstanding. I at once said 'there has been *no* misunderstanding on *my* part, Sir'. Sir J. French continued—as there had been misunderstanding we were all to return to our commands as if nothing had happened. I said that 'I am quite willing to do that, but such a grave crisis has arisen that neither I nor the other officers can return unless we receive a definite assurance that we should not be asked again to enforce on Ulster the present Home Rule Bill.'

Sir J. French then at once said that he could assure me that no such thing was intended and that the Prime Minister had given a similar assurance in the House.

I said 'The situation is so grave and there have been such serious misunderstandings that I must ask for the assurance in writing', Sir J. French appealed to me that his word should be good enough. I said of course his word might be good enough for me but I had to deal with the others, namely my officers, and that a verbal statement of what Sir John said would not be sufficient.

Sir John said 'Let us wipe everything off the slate and go back to Thursday evening'. I said it was impossible to do that as such grave events had taken place and such deep feelings had been aroused that it was not possible to ignore them and that if he and the Government were ready to give those assurances verbally what was the objection to giving them in writing.

Sir John then took 'the Times' and showed me some paragraphs in that purporting to be a statement by the Prime Minister that no active operations against Ulster were intended. He here also stamped and swore at Ewart because he could not find some announcement which he had directed to be put into the Press.

I maintained my point that I must have a definite assurance in writing. Sir John said it was impossible, the Government would not give it. I said I was very sorry but I could not return without it.

Sir John threw himself into a chair—a long and painful silence then ensued. I kept my eyes on the toe of my boot. At last Sir J. French said, addressing Ewart, 'Well, we can't do anything more for him, you will bear me out, Ewart, that I have done my best for him. He will never know how much I have done for him'. Ewart assented. I said nothing. Sir J. French said 'Very well, there is nothing for it but to take him before the Secretary of State'. We all three then left the room and went down the passage to the Secretary of State's room. On the way Sir J. French took me by the arm and said 'For God's sake Gough go back and don't make any more difficulties, you don't know how serious all this is, if you don't go back all the War Office will resign. I have done my best for you, if they had attempted to penalise you I would have resigned myself.' I said I was awfully grateful to him for all he had done for me and quite realised it. We then entered the Secretary of State's room.

We there found Colonel Seely (Secretary of State) and Sir A. Paget.

Colonel Seely's manner expressed extreme hauteur. He was most stiff to Sir John French and Ewart, and honoured me with a glare.

He very haughtily pointed to various chairs and directed us to be seated in those he named. I was very struck with the submissive attitude of Sir J. French, of Sir A. Paget and of Sir Spencer Ewart.

We were seated as follows:

Colonel Seely at the head of the table.

On his right—first Sir J. French, then myself.

On his left—first Sir A. Paget, then Sir S. Ewart.

As soon as we were seated Col. Seely, in a very truculent manner, turned his eyes on me and attempted to brow-beat me and to stare me out of countenance. I was not going to allow this and he eventually dropped his eyes. His manner then altered. From excessive truculence he went to that of superior wisdom.

He commenced a long discourse, explaining to me the relation of the military to the Civil Power, that in order to maintain law and order the Civil Power was justified in using the force necessary, but no more, etc., etc. I know all this very well, as it was taken almost verbatim from the Manual of Military Law. I listened with attention however in order to discern, if possible, what point he was endeavouring to make, and to be on my guard in case he attempted to place me in a disadvantageous position.

He then wandered on to explain that the action taken in Ireland had merely been aimed at the security of stores, etc., from 'hot-heads' on both sides.

He assured me that he had every reason to fear, on excellent information, that grave disorders might break out at any moment in the west and the south.

He then said that the questions that had been put to us by Sir A.

Paget arose out of a misunderstanding, enlarged on the illegality of putting hypothetical questions to soldiers, and said we were to return to our commands.

I then said that of course I would be glad to return but that neither I nor the two colonels concerned felt that we could again run the risk of finding ourselves in the very grave situation that had been forced upon us and therefore we must have an assurance that we would not be asked to enforce the present Home Rule Bill on Ulster.

To this Colonel Seely replied that the Prime Minister had made a statement 'that it was not, and never had been the intention of the Government' to coerce Ulster, that he had explained to me that all the moves ordered had been entirely precautionary and that the assurance given me by the Army Council as assembled at the moment should surely be amply sufficient for me.

I replied that such might be the case in ordinary circumstances but that the situation was so serious and such grave misunderstandings had arisen, that I must ask for this 'assurance' in writing.

Colonel Seely said this was impossible. No Government would allow itself to be dictated to, etc. I said I was very sorry, I could not go back unless I got a satisfactory assurance 'in writing'.

The situation now seemed very difficult and the outcome seemed doubtful when Sir J. French said, (in a very respectful manner) that 'perhaps General Gough had not made it quite clear that he felt that he would not be able to re-assure his officers or regain their confidence unless he could show them the authority of the Army Council, and that he felt his own verbal assurance would not be sufficient, now that feeling had been so greatly aroused'.

Colonel Seely seemed to think that this put my request in a new light, so I hastened to emphasise this view. He turned to Sir Arthur Paget and said 'Oh, I see, I think that is only a reasonable request'. Sir A. Paget assented.

Colonel Seely then said the A.G would draw up a draft

containing the assurances I asked for and that I and the two colonels would then return and take up again our commands 'with the full concurrence of the C-in-C, in Ireland'. (This latter remark being made with considerable pomposity).

The interview then broke up. It had lasted about half an hour with Colonel Seely and another half an hour previously with Sir J. French.

I then went to the waiting room and met my brother, Colonels MacEwen and Parker. I told them of the interview and of the final result. We talked it over and then the point struck us that we might again find ourselves in the same difficult situation or even in a worse, in case of the Home Rule Bill being placed on the Statute Book. We then wrote the note to the A.G. asking for elucidation on this point and which letter appeared in the white paper.[161]

It was now about 1.30 p.m. We left.

We returned to the War Office at 4 p.m. to get the letter from the Army Council.

We were told that Sir J. French was away at the House getting the letter signed.

At about 4.30 p.m. he returned and I was at once sent for. I found General Ewart and Sir J. French both in the room. They were standing by the writing table.

Sir J. French at once handed me the letter. I asked his leave to read it which he granted. I read the letter very hurriedly. It seemed to cover us from the recurrence of our late difficult situation, but as I felt the gravity of the whole matter, I asked if I might be accorded 15 minutes to consider it, with Colonel Parker and MacEwen.

Sir J. French seemed somewhat upset at this request, he said that time was important, that the King was waiting to know if all had been settled, and he added that he hoped we would be satisfied with this, that he could not possibly 'go any further' with us.

I said I thought the paper would be sufficient to protect us but again repeated that these matters were now so grave and serious that I could not give any opinion on any point without some little time to consider it.

I then left the room and rejoined my brother, Colonels Parker and MacEwan, and General Wilson.

We immediately considered the letter carefully. It appeared to us that the phrase 'crush political opposition' in the last paragraph was ambiguous and might mean anything. As we were determined that we would not allow ourselves to be exposed again nor permit our officers and men to be exposed to the contingency of waging civil war on Ulster, and that rather than do so we would prefer to leave the Army immediately, and as it was important to have our attitude clearly defined, we wrote out what we took to be the meaning of the last para.

I then asked Colonels MacEwen and Parker to return with me to Sir J. French, so that, firstly, in having our reading of the last para clearly stated and by retaining that statement in writing and secondly that the witness of Colonels MacEwan and Parker could always be produced, proving that the said statement had been made, the question of our having misunderstood the meaning of the paragraph would never be raised.

On entering the room I said to Sir J. French that we were satisfied with the letter and with the demands that could be made on us in future merely to obey lawful commands in support of law and order, but that as the last para in the said letter was somewhat ambiguous we would like to state our reading of it, and as the situation was very serious, we had, so that there could be no misunderstanding our words, written out our reading of the last para and with his permission I would read it.

I then did so.

Sir J. French said 'That seems all right' and then on second thoughts he said 'Let me have a look at that paper'. I gave it to him—he walked up and down once or twice reading it and then without further remark, sat down at the table and wrote under my signature 'That is how I read it.—J.F.'

We then said good-bye to him and Sir S. Ewart, thanking Sir J. French very much for all he had done for us and for all his help in the most difficult circumstances.

We then stayed talking to General Babington and a few friends in the W.O. and eventually parted to pack up and return to Ireland by that night's mail.

My brother and I took a taxi and went to my mother's flat in Sloane Square, where we had tea.

NAM, 7101-23-202, Roberts Mss; Ibid, 8001-6-9, MacEwen Mss; J. E. Gough Mss; RA GV F.674/83

125

Accounts by G. C. N. Nicholson of the events of 18 to 26 March 1914[162]

[Holograph]   [No date]

This is not intended to be more than a bald, but *complete*, statement of the incidents which took place between March 20/26th 1914. Orders were issued by War Office letter March 14 to Sir A. Paget commanding the Forces in Ireland, on March 14th, to [be ready to] move such numbers of troops as he thought necessary to protect, in case of civil disturbance the depots at Omagh, Armagh, Eniskillen & Carrickfergus. [The troops in Victoria Barracks Belfast to be moved out to Holywood as it was feared they might be surrounded & their liberty of movement restricted if left in Belfast].

The general situation was reviewed with great care during the succeeding days by a Cabinet Committee consisting of Mr. Birrell, Mr. Churchill, Colonel Seely, Lord Crewe & Sir John Simon. The result of their deliberations was communicated to the Cabinet on Wednesday March 18th and a decision was made to tell Sir A. Paget to proceed forthwith to carry out the moves indicated in the W.O. letter of March 14th. Sir A. Paget was summoned to London & on the 19th several conferences were held with him. He saw Sir John French at 11.15 & he & Sir John French came to Col. Seely's room in the course of the morning & subsequently Mr. Churchill, Mr. Birrell, Prince Louis of Battenberg, Sir John Simon, Lord Crewe & Sir Spencer Ewart all conferred together. It was fully recognised that the situation might develop, directly the precautionary moves were made and Sir A. Paget informed the conference of the number of troops he would like to have at his disposal in the event of grave disorder breaking out when these moves had been made. He was told that he had full authority to take charge of the situation and to take such steps as he considered necessary. He was also told that his requirements as to additional troops would be met and further that the 3rd Battle Squadron would be sent to Lamlash earlier than had been intended in order to be available if required. One or two scouts would be sent over at once to help with the moving of troops and the Firedrake would be off Kingstown for Sir A. Paget's own use and also to provide wireless communication with London in case other methods were interrupted.

To the best of my belief the general feeling was that the precautionary movements of troops might cause the eruption of the already smouldering volcano, that the eruption was equally likely to be caused by Nationalists as by Orangemen and that if the impression could be conveyed to the opposing sides that the Government had not the smallest intention of allowing anything like Civil War to break out, much unnecessary bloodshed might be avoided.

Sir A. Paget returned to Dublin, arriving there on the morning of March 20th. It appears that in the course of the morning he summoned a conference of his Brigadiers & Divisional Commanders and told them of the precautionary moves, indicated the possible results and said that he would hold a further conference later and that those officers who felt they would be unable to fight against Ulster should not attend the second conference (Sir A. Paget said subsequently that he felt that the time had come for him to ascertain upon what officers he could rely). Certain officers left this conference in the belief that a most cruel & unfair dilemma had been put to them: that they had in effect been asked to agree to fight against Ulster or accept immediate dismissal. This misunderstanding was apparently the cause of all the subsequent trouble. It cannot be too strongly laid down that the

Government did not then nor had they ever intended to coerce Ulster by force of arms. On the other hand Sir A. Paget cannot be wholly blamed as in a most difficult position he acted in the main with extraordinary skill & tact. None of his officers had ever faced the possible future with any feelings of cordiality and it was unquestionably due to Sir A. Paget's own personal efforts that the majority of them were perfectly disciplined & in fact all the precautionary moves were carried out in toto & without question.

The next part of the story took place in London. Colonel Seely, returning home at about 8 o'clock [on Friday March 20th] from a visit to the aero show asked his private secretary[163] who was with him to go and find out at the War Office if any news had been received from Ireland. The private secretary found at the War Office the first of Sir A. Paget's telegrams (printed in the White Paper). Colonel Seely considered the situation and at about 9.30 summoned Mr. Churchill & Sir John French, who were at the theatre, and Sir Spencer Ewart, and the whole situation was discussed and the telegram (also in the White Paper) was drafted and shown to the Prime Minister who approved it. Before it was sent the second telegram from Sir A. Paget was received and the further telegrams which passed were read out in the House by Mr. McKenna some days afterwards.

On March 21st nothing much transpired except that Sir A. Paget sent two other bald telegrams, in reply to a request for further information, in which he stated that the reason why the officers had taken up this attitude was because of a firm determination not to fight against Ulster. It should perhaps be pointed out that at about this time there were many rumours flying about to the effect that many further resignations were imminent.

It is fairly certain that if the situation had developed any further at this moment at least 19 officers of such Guards battalions as were in London would have resigned and it is quite certain that a large majority of those officers who were serving in the War Office would have resigned at once and they told Sir John French of their intentions. It did certainly seem clear that there was a grave danger of many resignations at once and if such a landslide occurred it was impossible to see where it would end. What actually happened was that the Army wanted to see what would happen to General Gough.

Sir Arthur Paget sent his Military Secretary to London on the night of Saturday March 21st and General Gough and Colonels Parker, MacEwan and Hogg came over at the same time. Major Kincaid-Smith (Sir A.P.'s MS) saw the Adjutant-General and Colonel Seely's private secretary at 10.30 a.m. on Sunday morning (March 22nd) and gave them Sir A. Paget's account of what had happened. (This was read out to the House a few days later). The Adjutant-General then saw General Gough and his officers and heard their side of the story. At this point it became clear that there had been a misunderstanding but it seemed probable that Sir A. Paget had unwittingly put his statement in such a way that there was good reason for the misunderstanding. Sir A. Paget was sent a telegram asking him to be at the War Office at 10.30 on Monday morning (March 23).

At several moments during the Sunday the officers concerned with the exception of Colonel Parker were prepared to go back to their duties but they felt unable to do so so long as he stood out. It should be pointed out that though no orders to move had yet been given to the Cavalry Brigade, it was known that if & when such orders were firm, Colonel Parker & his regiment was to go South to protect Orangemen from Nationalists. This makes Colonel Parker's attitude difficult to understand but he appears to have been stupid & pig-headed.

In the morning on March 23rd Sir A. Paget saw Sir John French & subsequently both came to Colonel Seely's room at eleven. Colonel Seely had asked for an audience of the King and this had been fixed for one o'clock. There was a Cabinet at 12. At 11.30 General Gough and the Adjutant-General also went into Colonel Seely's room and a few minutes before 12 when they had all left the room Colonel Seely told his private secretary that the whole thing had been cleared up and that General Gough & his officers were returning to Ireland.

At about 12.30 Sir John French & Sir Spencer Ewart came to the private secretary's room and produced a document they [said they] had drafted on Colonel Seely's instructions and they wanted to see him about it as soon as possible. They were told that there was no chance before 3 o'clock. Colonel Seely left the Cabinet at one to go to Buckingham Palace. At 1.35 (about) Mr. Churchill rang up the private secretary at the War Office & said the Cabinet wished to see at once the document which had been prepared. The private secretary took it over himself at once & returned at once to the War Office. As he went into his room the Adjutant-General handed him General Gough's letter (printed in the White Paper)[164] and said it was clear that Colonel Seely & the Cabinet should see it.

It was sent over at once to 10 Downing St in a taxi & simultaneously a telephone message was sent to the private secretary there saying that it was coming & that it was vital that Colonel Seely should see it at once. The box was taken into the Cabinet room where Colonel Seely was with Lord Morley discussing what the latter should say in the House of Lords that afternoon. Colonel Seely looked over the document which Sir John French & Sir Spencer Ewart had drafted and which had been amended by the Cabinet. It should be remembered that this document was the direct result of the conversation which Colonel Seely had had with General Gough in the morning and he therefore looked upon it as his own paper. It is true that he glanced at General Gough's letter but paid little attention to it. Colonel Seely added the two paragraphs at the end of the document, discussed the wording of them with Lord Morley and returned to the War Office and handed the amended document[165] to the Adjutant-General to be typed.

While it became clear subsequently that Colonel Seely was guilty of an error of judgement in adding these two paragraphs it should be remembered that he more than anyone realised the extremely critical state of affairs in the Army and the possibility of wholesale resignations if General Gough did not return to Ireland and further that he had some reason to believe that he had a more or less free hand to deal with the situation. This sentence might suggest that Colonel Seely was bargaining with General Gough but this is clearly not the case as no one in the Cabinet ever dissented from the sense of the two paragraphs and in fact they were a few days later embodied in an Army Order drafted by the Cabinet as a whole.

Nuffield College, Ms Mottistone 22A, f 3–15

SECTION 3
Consequences

126

Major-General Sir Henry Rawlinson
to Major-General H. H. Wilson

Cholderton House,
Cholderton,
Salisbury.

[Holograph]   19 March 1914

Did you see the enclosed in the Daily Mail of yesterday? My
boys[1] are becoming perturbed and are asking if they will be given
time to send in their papers before being sent to fight Ulster. A
large percentage *will not* go *to Ulster*. The question is being much
discussed especially amongst senior officers and what you will
find will be that all those who can afford to leave will leave, and
that those who can't afford it will go with very bad grace.

IWM, 73/1/18, Wilson Mss

127

Major-General Sir Henry Rawlinson
to Major-General H. H. Wilson

Cholderton House,
Cholderton,
Salisbury.

[Holograph]   20 March 1914

Last nights debate shows matters in their true light and they
seem to me to be very serious indeed—What is going to happen
no one can say for certain but out of the babble of voices two

things are clear (1) The Govt. do not want to come to terms here and now (2) They mean to use troops against Ulster. It makes me think a bit. Very much will depend on the attitude of the King as I have always said. If you ordered a Batt. from Tidworth to Belfast tomorrow you would find that a proportion of the officers, varying in different Batts, would send in their papers and ask for leave pending retirement. If you ordered that Batt. to go, after there had been riots in Belfast, the proportion of officers who would wish to resign would be larger. If you refuse their resignations all Ulstermen and quite a few others will at once desert and join the Ulster Volunteeers. Does Johnny F and the other members realise this? because we are getting very near it and feeling even amongst the younger officers is beginning to run high. They say they joined the army to fight the King's enemies and not the King's friends. I am writing to the little man to ask if I can run over and see him for a couple of nights on Tuesday next. I will be in London Tuesday and will look you up at the office but things may easily develop before then! I don't like it and see no loophole through which a peaceable settlement can be arrived at though Bonar Law's offer last night of a referendum was quite a good start for it puts the Govt. in a worse hole than ever. So long as Ulster keeps quiet and does not make a mistake there is always hope but it grows fainter every day.

Heavy snow here all the morning but it has melted and the glass has turned. I wish the Political glass would do the same.

IWM, 73/1/18, Wilson Mss

128

Extract from the Diary of
Rear-Admiral Sir Dudley de Chair

[Holograph]   20 March 1914

20 March 14. Matters looking black today; have resolved if Govt. try to use Navy to coerce Ulster, will resign.

Conference with 2nd Sea Lord[2] expressed my opinion that sea officers looked to Board of Admiralty to see they were not put into a false position. First Lord will not discuss this serious matter with me. 3rd B.S. ordered home from Arosa Bay to Lamlash & Adm. in comd. ordered to Admy.

21 March 1914

Troops in Ireland ordered to march into Ulster. First Lord wants to use the Navy to transport troops. If they land a Naval Brigade I resign & so I hope will the Board of Admty. [Later addition: Leveson & I arranging to stop this mad move & eventually were successful].

IWM, DEC/1/6, de Chair Mss

129

Sir Francis Hopwood to
Lord Stamfordham

[Holograph]

Admiralty
21 March 1914

This is a very confidential note & I am sure that the King will not know anything officially of its contents until he hears its substance otherwise than from me. It should be secret as regards Prince Louis as well as members of the Government.

I find that Churchill is pressing forward secret Naval arrangements against Ulster with great vigour & that a squadron is to go at once to Lamlash under Lewis Bayly, destroyers are to be sent to the Ulster coast & also several small cruisers to blockade. They are to have precise instructions as to action. L. Bayly has been sent for to come here tomorrow & he is to be invited to say whether he & his officers will do their duty & so forth! If he has any doubt about it we shall have the proceedings of yesterday as regards the Army over again. The Naval Lords tell me, however, that in their opinion the Naval officers will not follow the line of the cavalry officers.

Churchill wanted to send a ship last night to fetch over the 100

Cavalry officers to England but was restrained! principally because he was told no ship could be found.

Don't you think that the proper course is for you to obtain the King's authority to write to Churchill & say that H.M. is gravely dissatisfied with what has been done as regards the Army without consulting him & that he relies on Churchill not to follow the same course as regards the Navy. This could be elaborated into suitable language, would disclose nothing & should find a reply. Churchill will be in town tomorrow—he has cancelled his weekend visit I gather.

Jellicoe is very restive & anxious. He will probably field a quarrel with the First Lord on some side issue & resign.

Back Monday—but a telegram to Post Office, Margate, will fetch me sooner if wanted. I am motoring down to Chatham & then on there but no Hotel decided upon.

RA GV F.674/4

130

Major-General E. H. H. Allenby to Brigadier-General H. P. Gough[3]

London
21 March 1914

[Typescript Copy]

I was awfully distressed by the news of your resignation and that of your officers. The country cannot afford to lose your services; and I do not believe that it was intended that the question should be put in the form in which it was forced upon you. I hope, therefore, that the steps taken may not be irrevocable.

Please thank Mrs. Gough for her kindness to me. I cannot tell you how I admired her splendid courage and self control. Any other woman would have broken down; but she kept her calm, and thought for everyone.

H. P. Gough Mss

131
Extract from the
Reconstructed Diary of L. S. Amery

[Typescript][4]   21 March 1914

Mrs. Arnold-Forster[5] and others to dinner. This was the evening when three Brigade Majors from the Guards at Aldershot came to ask my advice as to whether they should not resign their commissions and join the Ulster Volunteers. I strongly advised them not to do anything precipitate, and then took them round to see F. E. Smith whose advice was to the same effect. One was Ulick Alexander,[6] both the others I think were killed in the first war.

Amery Mss

132
Extracts from the Diary of
Captain L. A. E. Price-Davies[7]

[Holograph]   21 March 1914

Great excitement in papers today. Reported resignation of Hubert Gough & other officers at Curragh & in Dublin & moves of troops.

23 March 1914

Details regarding the resignations. The govt. I think tried a bit of bluff but failed. This should shake them in their determination to use the Army against Ulster. George Cory writes to say he will resign if the Govt. push us & we decide to return to town tomorrow.

24 March 1914

Go up by 9.47 to town. George Cory to lunch who tells us about the crisis. Go to see Henry [Wilson] after lunch. War

Office still rather excited about it but General Staff held together and backed Hubert Gough for all they were worth & won.

25 March 1914

Fear that the harm to the army over the crisis is great but the government are entirely to blame.

26 March 1914

We decided to go away though just before starting Henry tells us Sir John French & Ewart have resigned.

29 March 1914

There seems to be nothing new in the situation. Sir J. French & Ewart have not given their final decision about resigning. I think the best is for them to resign & for the matter to end there. The Army has shown that it will not fight against Ulster & the fact that the Government have repudiated the guarantee matters little to us, except to those who gave it — Sir John & Ewart. The less said now the better but I am afraid it will be made a bitter party cry at the next election & that the Radicals will be again returned to Power.

31 March 1914

What a surprise yesterday when it was given out that Asquith is to be the War Minister. I walked to & from the WO with Henry today. He seemed in good spirits but thinks we have not heard the end of this business yet — Sir John French & Sir J. S. Ewart resigned yesterday. I wonder who will succeed them.

1 April 1914

I walk home with Henry. Sir Charles Douglas is to be CIGS. I am glad, as we might have had Nicholson or Ian Hamilton. Things are extraordinarily quiet now.

Army Museums Ogilby Trust, Price-Davies Mss

133
Mrs Nora Gough to
Brigadier-General H. P. Gough

Brownstown House,
Curragh.
[Holograph]   22 March 1914

I hardly know how I bear myself waiting for and longing for your news. A wire came from one 'Frank Butler' and 'Raymond' Yorkshire Regt.[8] congratulating you and the Brigade: have told them. Everyone this end of your followers working Heaven and Earth for you. Mr. Palmer and French lunched with me and are like two tigers and now say Col. Breeks says he will do what you say! and this means all the R.H.A. The 5th Lancers telephone that Household Cav. and Foot Guards will resign if made to fight. I hope and pray this is true. Mrs. Greer has been a perfect trump! (curious how fate changes). Well, my darling, I prayed so hard for you at 10 a.m. and please God our prayers are answered. I went to Church found Headlams in our seat, hang them. I felt so thankful that I stayed to fight your cause, I sang at the tip top of my voice, other women on verge of tears. (So was I if truth be known!!)

Mrs. Gillson, Freda and heaps in Church. I was rather wicked after as Lady Alice [Fergusson] asked me what news I had and I said 'Oh, none. Nothing to speak of, only the Household Cav. and Foot Guards were resigning if asked to fight.' She nearly fell flat, and said 'I don't believe it' so I said 'Oh, no, I don't suppose for a minute it's true!!' Then the 16th showed me a letter from Cecil Howard saying 'if war is pressed and Army Headquarters cease to exist who should he send his papers to?' I suppose this must be true or surely he wouldn't write it. Darling, my darling, God be with you—tell me all you can.

Everyone swarms round me expecting news.

H. P. Gough Mss

134
Lord Derby to A. Bonar Law

[Holograph]

Knowsley
22 March 1914

I hope you did not mind my referring Captain Greer to you. I
don't know whether you will have seen him but I can tell you
about him and why he wanted to see you. He is a very popular man
racing. He is the head of the Irish Turf and he is the senior
steward of the English Turf this year. He has a big horse breeding
establishment at Curragh and probably knows the officers of the
Curragh better than anybody else. He was in the Black Watch
himself. He telephoned me this morning to say he had come over
as I understood on their behalf to lay their case before you and if
possible before Lord Lansdowne. If he did not see you let me tell
you what their case is.

It appears Sir Arthur Paget, General Officer Commanding,
went to the Curragh where a great number of officers had
resigned their commissions and told each individually that he had
orders from the War Office that any man who persists in
resigning under the circumstances was not to be allowed to have
his resignation accepted in the ordinary way but to be dismissed
the Service, forfeiting of course all right to pension. Now as you
know I was opposed to any alteration of the Army Act as I felt that
once you began tampering with it, it would form a most dangerous
precedent and that if the men were actually ordered to fight the
Ulstermen they must do so, but it never struck me that they would
not be allowed the alternative of resigning their commission and
resigning it before actual fighting commenced and if the Government takes such action I think it is the most monstrous thing that
has ever been done and one that will ruin the Army for now and
for all times as you may be perfectly certain that the vast majority
of officers throughout the United Kingdom and indeed in foreign
possessions will out of sympathy do the same thing. My brother
Arthur[9] has been telegraphed for to come up to London tomorrow as I suppose you will have a Debate on the subject, but there
is one feature of it which may not have occurred to you and that is

270

the effect it will have, not only on officers of the regular army, but on officers in the Territorial Force. I do not think I am exaggerating if I say that the result will probably be that 80% of Territorial Officers will resign their commissions out of sympathy and a vast number of men will equally take their discharge. Once such a step is taken in the Territorial Army its fate is absolutely sealed.

I must remain here this week as the King is coming to me for 4 days though I think of course it is likely he will not be able to fulfil his engagements. Otherwise I would have come to see you to ask you a question which concerns myself. If war breaks out in Ulster there is not the least doubt that from Liverpool we can send them much support, and in trained men too, and I should do all that I possibly could to organise these men before they go. Under the circumstances do you think I ought to at once resign my Chairmanship of the Territorial Association?[10] I do not want to do anything rash or anything that might provoke hostile criticism from our own people and should be very grateful to you therefore if you would tell me what you wish me to do.

There is another point that I daresay has occurred to you and that is that the whole of these military and naval designs for crushing Ulster are ordered by Churchill and Seely. Two men who got their first admission to Parliament as strong Unionists but who allowed themselves to be bought by office.

The position is so serious that I really do not see what way there is out of it but I sincerely hope that Asquith may even at the last moment accept your Referendum proposal.

H. of Lords RO, Bonar Law Mss, 32/1/43

135
Note by J. L. Baird to
A. Bonar Law

[Holograph]   22 March 1914

Harry Lawson[11] telephoned this morning that 2 officers of Duke of Cornwall's Light Infantry had been to see him & were most anxious for a declaration to be made to the effect that they would not suffer permanently if they followed example of their rich brother officers in cavalry regts. in refusing to serve against Ulstermen. To do so without some such declaration means starvation for many of them & for their families.

In the 2 Battalions of Cornwall L.I. there is only 1 officer who is willing to fight against Ulster.

The idea among soldiers is that Aldershot Command will only get 4 hours notice.

Harry Lawson is personally strongly in favour of a declaration being made.

H. of Lords RO, Bonar Law Mss, 32/1/47

136
Major-General Sir Henry Rawlinson to Major-General H. H. Wilson

Englemere,
Ascot.
22 March 1914

[Holograph]

I came over here for the weekend just to see how the little man was. He is of course very much worried and shows it, Ladyship is likewise much upset and has not appeared. I was with the little man when he telephoned to you last night. Johnny Gough turned up to tea with a copy of what Arthur Paget had said to Hubert and with his own resignation which he has sent in. He went off to see Douglas H at 5.30. Brodrick came over to see the Chief at lunch & Monro Fergusson is here.[12]

I do not at all like the look of things. If the govt. continue to ride the high horse and repeat to the rest of the Army the ultimatum which they presented to Hubert, there will be a large number of more resignations as I told you in my letter of Friday. I could not accept the terms of it myself under existing conditions. Johnny said they were going to do this and Hereward[13] who was here to lunch says that it will be the same thing at Aldershot. There will of course be very important discussions in the House tomorrow when the Govt. will have to declare their policy in regard to the Army but if they think they are going to intimidate the officers by trying Hubert G by courtmartial they will find that they will only antagonise them further. I shall see Smith D[14] in the morning but I know his views which are entirely on our side. I never thought the Govt. would push matters as far as this. They must be mad. I wish someone would begin shooting in India tomorrow!! I fear that to hope for any strong line from the King is doomed to disappointment.

IWM, 73/1/18, Wilson Mss

137
Mrs Lily Bethune to
Mrs Nora Gough[15]

[Typescript Copy]

London
22 March 1914

We are thinking so much of you all, and I am glad the Regiment and General Gough are where they are. It is splendid of them and all the others. It is all a terrible business. Cecil Howard told us the end of it all on Friday night. Much sympathy with you all. Edward can do nothing, they dare not order Territorials to go, so his office is quiet and peaceful otherwise the War Office is in a turmoil. It must come right in the end after an Election which surely must be soon now. Not much of the truth gets into the newspapers so we know very little. I don't think Redmond & Co will dare show their faces in the streets without police to guard them just now.

My love and sympathy to all the 16th and yourselves.

H. P. Gough Mss

138
Major G. T. Bridges to
Brigadier-General J. E. Gough

The Grove,
Stanmore.
22 March 1914

[Holograph]

I have heard from Hubert that you have sent in your papers, (more power to you) & write to congratulate you on your attitude. My papers were going in today as soon as I heard confirmation of the position. I have just got back from Brussels[16] & am not 'oriente'. Now H.W. telephones this evening to stand fast till tomorrow morning when he is going to have a pow wow. This I will but no longer as every moment is of value & one should hang together & the Cavalry should take the lead in this—not only because they shd. be more ready to take risks but it is not a question of bread & butter to them & they can afford to be scapegoats if necessary.

My attitude in the question up to now has been that I wd do as I was told until ordered to take a part in coercion by force of arms & then I would resign.

The question has changed since Saturday, however, & I feel that one must stand by one's pals & all hang together. It is perfectly damnable for the Army however it goes & brings the axe to the root of discipline. An accursed set of scoundrels that should have run us into such a mess. If you are in London tomorrow I would like to see you. Will you send a message for me to the Cavalry Club.

J. E. Gough Mss

139

'Titwillow' [Lieutenant Colonel the Hon. C. J. Sackville-West] to Major-General H. H. Wilson

23 Upper Berkeley Street,
Portman Square.

[Holograph]

23 March 1914

I gather that Franky Lloyd is as you put it a Politician. Billy Lambton who was at dinner last night told me that the Colonels of the Guards Regiments had been informed that no resignations were to be sent in. Obviously the authorities are afraid of the example being set to the rest of the Army as it is common knowledge that the Guards won't fight against Ulster.

Its a d—d bad business, these politicians are ruining the Army—we should reap the fruits for the moment but if you sow thistles only thistles come up whatever may be the excuse for the sowing. Needless to say I am of course ready to stick by my comrades now.

IWM, 73/1/18, Wilson Mss

140

Brigadier-General W. N. Congreve to Brigadier-General H. P. Gough

18th Infantry Brigade,
Stafford.

[Typescript Copy]

23 March 1914

News travels slowly here and I have only just got my paper telling of how you have been making history. I write a line to tell you how much I sympathise with you and how rightly I think you have acted. I had long ago made up my mind to do the same—but it is dreadful that we should be driven to such action by this d—d

Government and men like Paget who I feel convinced has been bought body and soul.

Good luck to you—I am sure you will be no loser for your action in this.

H. P. Gough Mss

141

T. Riversdale Walrond to Lord Milner[17]

13 Gerald Road,
Chester Square.
23 March 1914

[Holograph]

I expect you know but still I am writing in case you don't to say—The Inspector of Cavalry, General Allenby, came to see me yesterday afternoon—just back from Ireland.

The 3 Cavalry Regiments at the Curragh are solid in refusing to go to shoot Ulster men. The men were up with the officers. The Inspector of Cavalry will stand by them.

We had some of the Directing Staff of the WO here last night and they will not work *either in the WO* or out of it against Ulster. The 3 Directing Generals are with them. Wilson, Robertson and Davies—all have told Seely that their position is the same as that of the Goughs. Seely blustered at first and said he would 'cashier the lot' but I believe he is frightened now.

Gen. French won't believe the bulk of the General Staff and told Seely some time ago that he would have no difficulty with the Army and they decided (I *believe* with the knowledge and approval of the King) to send 25,000 men against Ulster. Arthur Paget stood up with French and Seely—but instead of sending the troops quickly and *pretending they were to keep order* gave away the whole sham by sending for all the Cavalry Officers of his brigade and giving them the choice *before they started* of shooting down Ulstermen or being *dismissed* without pension (& they of course became warned).

Thank God for a fool. The Horse Artillery were solid with the Cavalry.

I *hear* so were Gren. Guards & Scotts [sic]—but am not absolutely certain.

The Irish Guards have a Radical Col.[18] & we don't know about them.

The soldiers are loathe and distrust the Unionists as a party (and so do I) so they won't give any more information [than] they can help—but I think you ought all to work on together, and I said I should tell you. Can I see you today any time for a short time—as there are several things you can help us to work up to get every ounce of value out of everything.

These men are willing to sacrifice money and careers & everything and it is important I think that not *one* should be sacrificed.

French & Seely if they have to climb down but want to sacrifice the 2 Goughs who were the first to revolt. [sic] You can imagine their spite against them. Gen. Henry Wilson is splendid, brave as a lion and what is even better in dealing with these people cunning as a fox. I am going to take this to 47 on the chance of seeing you. Some of the Gen. Staff are coming in at 1.30 to be fed and to tell me *exactly* how the Army Council have taken their resignations. The Aldershot troops are I believe going to call for a guarantee.

Bodleian, Ms Milner 41 f. 61–65

142

Major-General Sir William Robertson to Brigadier-General J. E. Gough

[Holograph]

6 Mansion Place, SW.
23 March 1914

I hope the result of the last few anxious days will be quite satisfactory, and that the Govt. now realise what they are up against. You may rely upon the General Staff at Horse Guards continuing to do all they can, and as the air has now been beautifully cleared are no longer finding it uneasy to mince words. I wish you could have heard Balfour in the House this afternoon & what was said about the Goughs & the Army. He made a really big speech, & tore the other people to pieces. Your wife must have had a very anxious time. Give her our kindest regards. It was excellent news to me that Haig was solid. I half feared he might take another view. It has made the position so much cosier. I think you should now take a break for a day or two, & let us see what will happen. One thing is now quite clear—the army is not for the job. Dont answer this.

J. E. Gough Mss

143
Captain H. C. Jackson to his mother

Staff College,
Camberley.
[Holograph]   23 March 1914

Thank you very much for your loving sympathy. I had a wire from General Kiggell this morning saying that he was writing.[19] I shall get his letter first post tomorrow.

The two Goughs are the two most brilliant soldiers in the Service—one is forty-two, the other fifty-three—one of them has the VC, both of them have deserved it many times. Their father had the VC, their grandfather was the Lord Gough of the Punjab wars, so you must realise what their feelings are at leaving the service. But they are Irishmen, and have always openly said that they would not go.

They are two of the most popular men in the Army, and crowds of waverers will follow them.

Don't think that I don't feel as they do about it, but where we differ is that I can see *no* justification in allowing one's private sentiments to stand in the way of what I consider is my duty as a soldier.

Sir Arthur Paget, who is commanding in Ireland, has a son here, but he has no news.

I will wire you tomorrow if Kiggell gives me leave, and I shall start at once, if he undertakes to fix it up with the War Office. As far as I know, none of my Regiment have resigned.

What I referred to was that 200 men of the Dorsets laid down their rifles and refused to go. This has since been contradicted.[20]

There is a fellow here in one of the Cavalry regiments at the Curragh,[21] all of whose officers have sent in their resignations. He is in a bit of a fix.

If they really did not foresee this, it shows how terribly out of touch with the Army the War Office authorities are.

For the moment all eyes are centred on the War Office, but what is Asquith going to do?

With much love to Dolly.

Fergusson Mss

144
Captain A. P. Wavell to his father
Major-General A. G. Wavell

[Holograph]

London
23 March 1914

For your eye only, I write the history of what has happened in the army, as far as I know it, in the last few days. Of course as always happens on these occasions there are a good many wild stories flying about and a good deal which is still obscure.

The point which hasn't been cleared up yet is exactly what the Government meant to do and exactly what instructions were given to Paget, but there seems little doubt they had decided on a policy of immediate coercion or it is inconceivable that even an ass like Paget could have said what he did. Anyway the thing began by Paget sending for Gough and asking him, according to Gough's own account, if he was prepared to undertake immediate active offensive operations against Ulster. Any officer who was domiciled in Ulster would not be called on to serve, but any C.O. giving such indulgence to an officer not bona fide domiciled in Ulster would be court-martialled and any officer not prepared to serve against Ulster was to send in his name by a certain time (a few hours) and would be dismissed the army without claim to pension. Gough at once handed in his resignation, went down to the Curragh, briefly put before the officers of the brigade the choice they had to make, whereupon they resigned en masse. Paget then motored down to the Curragh, called a meeting of the officers and said that Gough had misunderstood him, that there was no intention of using the troops against Ulster—they were only asked to keep law and order. The colonel of the 4th Hussars (a very sound level-headed fellow who was at the Staff College with me) followed by his officers withdrew their resignations on that understanding. The others refused to. They were then all ordered over to London (Gough and the C.O.s of the regiments) and on Saturday were interviewed individually by Seely and French. I believe the question put to them was 'were they prepared to keep law and order in Ulster'. Gough said 'yes' but proceeded to qualify it with all the things he would not do. The result was that Gough, the officers of the 5th and the 16th persisted in their resignations, the 4th were still prepared to withdraw theirs. They were then given till this morning to think it over. Meantime all sorts of conferences and audiences were going on all Sunday and all today.

When I went to the War office this morning, a large number of officers apparently had their resignations in their pockets. Apparently what happened today was that the three General Staff directors went to French and said that they would resign and that there would be wholesale resignations in the Army, unless Gough and the officers of the 3rd Cavalry Bde. were reinstated and a written pledge given by the Government that the Army would not be used to coerce Ulster. The Government, amazing as it appears to me, gave way. I imagine Sir John French and other members of the Army Council threatened to resign. Anyway at 5 o'clock this evening Wilson had all his directorate in and informed us that

Gough and his officers were going back to Ireland with a signed pledge that the Army should not be used against Ulster. He did not read the actual pledge but what he did read us was a statement signed by Gough with regard to the interpretation of the final paragraph of the guarantee, which it seems was obscure. Gough's statement was: 'I understand the meaning of the last paragraph to be that the Army will not be used under any circumstances to enforce *the present Home Rule Bill on Ulster.*' This was counter-signed by Seely authorising him so to interpret it to his officers on parade.

Well, there you are. The attitude of the majority of officers is that the Army by the action of these officers has saved the situation, won a great victory, etc. I cannot agree. I think they have won a political battle to the ruin or great danger of the Army and the country. For it is a political victory; how can you call it other when the Army refuses to enforce the *present* Home Rule Bill? It seems to me deplorable that those words should be used. And Wilson made no secret of his opinion. He actually said: 'The Army have done what the Opposition failed to do' and 'will probably cause the fall of the present Government.' What right have the Army to be on the side of the Opposition, what have they to do with causing the fall of Governments?

No, to my mind, this has been fought on the wrong issue. The issue on which I too, I think, would have acted as the officers concerned did was the action of the Government in holding a pistol at the officer's head and trying to coerce him by threats at his pocket, saying 'You must do this or be *dismissed the Army* losing your livelihood and your pension.' It is inconceivable to me how an English Government could have done such a thing. But they should have refused to answer the question, especially on a mere verbal statement, and should have insisted on having a definite offer in writing and time to consider. It is a thousand pities that the protagonists were a fool like Paget and a hothead like Gough.

Of course the Government will now try to make a scapegoat of Paget. Their attitude in the House this afternoon was that there was no intention to coerce Ulster, that Paget made unauthorised statements and that the officers resigned under a misunderstanding. Lawyers and liars all.

And the attitude of Sir John French and the Army Council amazes me. Here we have a body of men at the head of the Army who acquiesce in an order like that being framed, fail to see what the effect on the officers will be, and yet submit to *pressure from their subordinates* to get the decision rescinded.

We are only at the beginning of this thing. The truth must come out and then ...! We have to realise that we have a Government which has not even the courage of its convictions, an army which takes sides in politics, and leaders of that army who do not lead but yield to pressure from their subordinates.

How is the country going to take that state of affairs? And how are you to preserve discipline after this, how are you to use your Army to keep law and order against strikers when once the officers have successfully resisted an attempt to use them to enforce a law which they do not approve?

One lacks perspective at present of course. But I see only disaster from what has happened. We seem to have lost our balance and hard-headedness; this Ulster business should have been settled a year ago, only that it was a good weapon in the political game.

Better destroy this letter, which is written for *you alone*. Perhaps things may turn out better than I expect.

Wavell Mss

145
Captain C. N. French to
Brigadier-General H. P. Gough[22]

[Typescript Copy]

R.M.C. Sandhurst.
24 March 1914

Will you accept my congratulations and thanks for what you have done for the Army. As far as one can tell from the papers you have saved the situation for us. The feelings of practically everyone here are entirely with you and the great majority were prepared to follow you and the 3rd Cav. Brigade if need be. However, I hope you have shaken this infernal Government so badly that they will give up the idea of coercion.

It is difficult to write the loathing and contempt one has for the WO if they misled the government about the real feelings of the army. I cannot believe that they were so completely out of touch as to have misled honestly.

H. P. Gough Mss

146
Major W. Gillman to
Brigadier-General H. P. Gough

17 Hill Street,
Berkeley Square, W.
[Typescript Copy] 24 March 1914

My best congratulations. News filters slowly into these water tight compartments of MO, but we were all going out on Saturday morning when we first heard the true state of affairs, and only remained till Monday at Henry Wilson's request.

Thank God A.P. ran up against you to start with and not some drivelling time-server who would have plunged us in Civil War to save his skin.

I hear that only 1 officer in the Aldershot Command would have obeyed the ultimatum, and he did it owing to an innate spirit of opposition to everything suggested by his brother officers, rather than from a pro-government feeling.

What a science political lying is![23]

H. P. Gough Mss

147
Captain F. M. Leake to
Rear-Admiral J. M. de Robeck

H.M.S. Pathfinder,
Carrickfergus.
24 March 1914

[Holograph]

It seems to me only fair to you as my Admiral to let you know that I have no intention of going against Ulster should the occasion arise.

During my stay here I have done my best to ascertain the situation on shore & find that everything possible is being done to keep things quiet, but undoubtedly in spite of this there exists an opinion on the part of responsible people that an outbreak might be precipitated by irresponsible people.

Churchill College, DRBK 3/7, de Robeck Mss

148
Katherine Keyes to
Brigadier-General H. P. Gough[24]

[Typescript Copy]   25 March 1914

A thousand congratulations on your splendid triumph, it really is magnificent to have defeated such curs. I was at Farnborough so heard all about it and Roger who feels as keen as anyone motored there on Sunday and heard all Johnnie had to tell in the evening. A batch of the most senior sailors here going to resign.

I saw your mother yesterday, she is a proud woman and please tell your wife how I congratulate her. She must have had an anxious time but it was worth it.

H. P. Gough Mss

149
Captain R. G. A. W. Stapleton-Cotton to Rear-Admiral R. E. Wemyss[25]

Flag Captain's Office,
Portsmouth.
[Holograph]   25 March 1914

Very many thanks for your letter & cheque. Weather here has been too vile for trade—gales, rain & snow all the month. Olive has been staying at Cap Martin with her people as she had a bad go of bronchitis, which shook up her lungs but I hope when she returns on Friday to find she is quite right.

Home Rule now appears to be dead but it is due to a policy which cannot bring any good to the country. Military rule cannot prosper & it seems to me to be a fatal day for the Army & in a lesser degree for the Navy. The Rads & Labour Party will go to the country with the cry that the army is the tool of the Unionist & aristocratic party & not loyal to the nation & interfering with politics. Gough is a brilliant soldier but a hotheaded Irishman— there is no doubt he let his feelings run away with him. Paget was 'a Paget' when addressing them & said many foolish things which put all backs up & hardened the waverers to follow Gough. Gough's brother, who is Chief of the Staff at Aldershot, completed it.

There is little doubt that Seely, [Lloyd] George & Churchill manoeuvred behind Asquith's back with a view to force Ulster. Paget *was* ordered to deliver an ultimatum & further *was* ordered to send 3 Cavalry Brigade, horse artillery, engineer Bridging train, complete hospital equipment & siege guns to occupy a strategic position on the Irish side of the River Boyne ready to advance into Ulster. He made a most bombastic speech full of threats & finished up by saying 'By Saturday England will be in flames'. There is no doubt he was doing as Seely & Churchill told him as he was with them for 4 hours in London the day before. My brother-in-law[26] who was sent for gave me most of my information. He was telephoned for at midnight Thursday

[Friday] & went straight up to see French. F took him in to Seely & Seely said 'I want you to go over to Ireland at once to take command of the 3rd Cavalry Brigade & try to reorganise them.' Chetwode asked him why & S told him G had resigned & that all the Brigade had handed in their papers in consequence of what Paget had said to them. He stated that G had been grossly insubordinate & that under no circumstances would he be allowed to go back. C then asked to be allowed to wait until G & the Colonels had come over & seen Seely as he pointed out it was no use going over if there were no officers & further that no officer was likely to be influenced by him if they had followed such a popular man as G. Further C told S that S had put him in a very nasty position as he would be looked upon by all his brother officers as a scab but whatever happened he thought it his duty as a soldier to do as he was ordered & not to meddle in politics. Saturday Seely saw G & the Colonels & it was whilst waiting at the War Office to know the result of the meeting that C learnt that the whole of the General Staff were going to hand in their papers—he went at once to French & saw him in his room & said 'Sir John, are you certain of your own General Staff?' French replied 'Up to an hour ago I was, but my God now I can't answer for them.' C then told him the truth. F then showed him a wire from Haig at Aldershot saying he would not answer for a single regiment at Aldershot. F then went into S with C & said 'We must take back everything. I dare not order a single regiment to be moved.' S was livid & accused F of going back on his word to which F replied that he had no idea there was such feeling & that the whole General Staff had resigned. Things changed from that moment. G was given a written document signed by F & S stating they wd not be used to coerce Ulster.

F & C then retired to F's room where F broke down & said 'Great God C, the army has signed its death warrant.'

S was most insulting the whole time & C was anything but polite to him at times. They all say if anyone but Paget had been at Dublin at the time, this would never have happened—he was pompous, Pagity!! & tactless. G was very hot headed & very Irish but they say a straighter man never stepped.

It's all a bad business.

There is little Navy news. Callaghan & George Warrender, I am told, both told Churchill that they would apply to be relieved if they were ordered to Ulster. Bayly said he would go & I am told his squadron was actually under orders to go there. Thank God it never came to the point. There are now two camps in the army both very bitter against each other.

The Neptune goes as Fleet Flagship in Medit in January. Pelly goes as C. of S & Vivian as Flag Captain with Jackson.[27] Moore will eventually fly his flag in Inflexible — a pleasant station mate!!!

C in C here will I think remain on till end of the year but one never knows for certain what he will do. There are rumours now that WC will stand for Portsmouth at next General Election & that Sir H.M. will oppose him! but I doubt it there is any truth.

Sorry to send you so many sheets. I had no idea this was the 4th.

Do you think you will relieve Troubridge end of year? I hope for your sake you do as you will be tired of the shore by then. Please remember me to Mrs. Wemyss.

Churchill College, WMYS, 2/5, Wemyss Mss

150

Major G. S. Tweedie to
A. Bonar Law[28]

2nd Royal Scots,
Crownhill Barracks,
S. Devon.
25 March 1914

[Holograph]

In connection with the very serious crisis which has arisen in the Army, both the Ministerial Party & their Supporting Press have laid great emphasis on the fact that the unwillingness to serve against Ulster has been confined to the officers or as they prefer to express it to the 'aristocratic ranks' of the Army.

They have openly insinuated that the Rank & File of the Army are ready, if not eager, to take the field against Ulster. It seems unfair both to the Army & to the country generally that such a misrepresentation should pass unchallenged, & I have accordingly taken the liberty of writing to you on this matter.

Doubtless you have ample knowledge of the truth, but in case this is not so I can inform that in my own regiment, 2/The Royal Scots, the whole of the Sergeants and Lance Sergeants, with the exception of three, are heart & soul with Ulster. These men have formed their opinions entirely without argument, persuasion or suggestion from their officers, who do not discuss such matters as loyalty or obedience with their subordinates, & this means that they possess intelligence, conscience & a sense of right & wrong equally with their superiors.

I feel equally certain that the same feeling pervades the other ranks from Corporals to Privates.

We officers feel bitterly the position in which the Army has been placed & keenly resent these abominable taunts as to our 'aristocratic & class leanings' & I can assure you that the great majority of officers & men resent from the bottom of their souls this vile attempt of the Government to use it as an instrument to their Party ends.

I may further add that 7 out of 10 of our officers would not take the field against Ulster.

I must ask you to keep the name of my Regiment & my own strictly confidential, but shall be delighted if the facts I have disclosed as to attitude of the *democratic* & numerically vastly superior portion of the Army are of any service to you in the House to refute these grossly untrue statements of Labour members & others totally ignorant of the opinions & feelings in the Army.

H. of Lords RO, Bonar Law Mss, 32/1/62

151

Lord Esher to the
Editor of The Times

2 Tilney Street,
London.
25 March 1914

[Printed]

In order to prevent further honest misunderstanding in the future, and to remove from the mind of Mr. Ramsey Macdonald and others the impression that the feeling actuating General Gough are peculiar to the 'aristocratic' branches of the Army, or the result of tampering with officers by Tory agents, I think it right to make the following statement, as President of the County of London Association, responsible with others for raising and maintaining the Territorial Force in London, a branch of the Army, democratic in composition, and quite out of touch with the influences to which Mr. Ramsay Macdonald and the Chancellor of the Exchequer have quite erroneously—in my opinion—referred.

There are in the County of London today 21,000 Territorial troops. It is widely believed, I know not with what truth, that a movement of troops from Aldershot to Ireland was contemplated, involving the calling up of Reserves, and that the place of soldiers at Aldershot was to have been taken up by embodied Territorials.

From information in my possession I am convinced that when the first detachment from Aldershot is sent to Ireland we shall be faced with the resignation in London of 50 per cent—and this is a low estimate—of the officers and men of the London Territorial Force.

Furthermore, the London County Association is composed of 150 members, and of these 65 per cent will, I am confident, also resign their functions.

The ground in both cases is this, that neither directly nor indirectly will these people (most of them coming under the definition of democrats) consent to be used by the Executive of the day for what they believe to be a political purpose and with a political purpose and with a political object.

Churchill College, ESHR 4/5, Esher Mss

152

Colonel the Hon. W. Lambton to Brigadier-General H. P. Gough

Guards Club
26 March 1914

[Typescript Copy]

Just a line to congratulate you or your stand and what I hope is a successful issue of it, though from what Asquith said last night it looks as if he meant to repudiate the whole thing, and then where are we. I always knew the Army feeling was pretty strong against being employed to coerce Ulster, but Saturday was rather a revelation and showed that it is much more general than anyone expected and that your example would have been largely followed. I don't envy you people quartered in Ireland under present conditions as it must be very anxious work.

H. P. Gough Mss

153

Engineer Lieutenant F. Ranken to A. Bonar Law[29]

HMS Lurcher,
4th Destroyer
Flotilla.
26 March 1914

[Holograph]

I feel justified—& I trust you will agree with me—in giving you a statement of facts in connection with the Naval & Military movements against Ulster. The particular matter I deal with has,

I fancy, not previously come to your notice but it may, at any rate, help to build up the case you have so much at heart. At the outset I beg to explain to you that the 'Firedrake' is not my ship (see Navy List) but due to my brother officer being on leave I was implicated in her movements.

At 6.30 p.m. on the 19th inst. til instructions were received by the Captain 'D' (of the Flotilla) ordering the 'Guard' destroyer to raise steam for full speed with all despatch—this I proceeded to do & we left at 10.30 p.m. for Kingstown—a fact which was only known to the Commander[30] of the vessel & to myself (by the former's courtesy in telling me, for family reasons). Before leaving I informed the Commander that I had signed the Brit. Covenant & that I should be no party to any aggressive move against Ulster if that were the intention in sending us to Kingstown! I expressed my intention, if necessary, to resign & was warned that I should on these circumstances arising be placed under arrest.

We made a record run to Kingstown & late on Friday night after the Commander had seen Sir Arthur Paget & had been officially informed by him that the 'Firedrake' was appropriated for his personal use in order to, if necessary, convey himself & staff to Belfast or elsewhere in Ulster I expressed a desire to be relieved of my temporary duties in the ship & my brother officer was wired for a.m. on Sat. 21st & joined the ship on Sunday 22nd.

The matter as far as I, personally, was concerned was thus closed but had Sir Arthur Paget joined for passage during my regime only one course was open to me—to decline to be a party to propelling the ship.

That it was considered necessary by the War Office, or by the GOC in Ireland, to fall back on one of HM ships as the only sure means of conveying himself & staff into what they termed & considered a belligerent country is self evident proof of the depths to which the orders went during the period of tension.

The 'Firedrake' is still at Kingstown—her CO & I are, & always have been, the best of friends & while I understand that he was prepared to execute any orders given him by a superior officer & thus to treat me strictly officially the facts I have written I ask you to treat as simply links in the chain of the evidence you may desire to collect on the Ulster question.

This case of the 'Firedrake' is so narrowed down to a few officers that, while personally I should rather have welcomed dismissal than otherwise, I feel emboldened to ask you to let it appear as if your information had been purely of your own finding. 'Firedrake's' movements are quite apart from those subsequently made by a batch of ships of this Flotilla—this force left a.m. Sat. but was recalled when off Rame Head.

H. of Lords R O, Bonar Law Mss, 32/1/67

154
Colonel A. L. Caldwell to
J. Ramsay Macdonald[31]

Dover
26 March 1914

[Holograph]

I gather from your speech in Parliament on Wednesday night, that you are unable to get any information from officers.

Perhaps the following may be of interest. All the officers of the various garrisons, are in complete daily touch with one another by wire and letters.

The information given out is surprisingly accurate and early.

Thus a Major gave out at the Dover Club (supposed to be non political) on Friday afternoon last, details of the Curragh Cavalry Brigade resignations, five hours before receipt of the War Office (as detailed in the White Paper). The percentages of officers who will decline to serve at Portsmouth was given out today.

At the Dover Club, every afternoon, serving officers and those on the retired list, congregate and vie with one another in loudly criticising those in command, who are supposed to be willing to carry out the orders of the Army Council and Executive Government. Never before have I heard officers in public, so vilify those in authority and applaud those they think will not comply with orders: the clear instructions contained in the King's Regulations, forbidding public criticism of those in authority [is] being disregarded: a definite policy of open discussion is the plan. Why is Gough praised as being such a fine soldier? He and all his mounted Troops were captured in open country, during the late war. Genl. Lyttelton,[32] who reported on the capture, strongly condemned Gough for the disaster. I suppose G's influence saved him then, as now. Cherrie Emmett,[33] the Boer Commander, after the war was over, told me the trap set was of the simplest, and Gough went straight in with all his men.

Whom the Gods wish to destroy they first send mad. Clearly the present order of army officers is doomed: Gough's Cavalry leading the way.

I will be glad to give you any proper information you may desire.

PRO 30/69/1423, Macdonald Mss; *Hansard* 5 s, H. of C. LXI 1609 (Partial)

155
Lieutenant-General Sir Douglas Haig
to Major P. Howell

Government House,
Farnborough.
[Holograph]   27 March 1914

Am just starting for London but must send you a line in reply to yours of y'day.

We are I believe all united in this command as regards the following: that we will go to Ulster or anywhere & do anything required of us, short of coercing our fellow citizens in Ulster or elsewhere to submit to an Irish Parliament against their wishes.

At a meeting I had with my GOC Divisions and Brigades [4 days ago][34] I pointed out the terrible results of disintegration in the Army—our status as a Gt Power is imperilled to put it briefly—and I begged them to induce all regimental & other officers to keep aloof from politics. I urged this y'day [also] at the War Office. All agreed *the Army must have nothing to do with politics*.

I don't agree that the Army has ever left its proper position in the state. Some politicians have tried to put us in a false position for their party purposes but I trust they have failed [You at the Curragh should have put yourselves in the hands of the Army Council & left it at that!]

We [all] must trust the Army Council now, to carry out what I know to be the real intention of the Cabinet, namely not to use the Army in any way which can be interpreted as bring[ing] coercion upon the Ulsterman. The A.C. will also do their utmost to get the Army taken out of the Political arena. I feel that it is intolerable that the Army sh'd be made a political tool by each party in turn!

Don't do anything about the Education question yet.[35] I have moved in the matter & will tell you later. In gt haste.

King's College, Liddell Hart Centre for Military Archives, IV/C/2/52, Howell Mss

156

Lieutenant G. W. Nightingale to his mother[36]

1st Royal Munster Fusiliers,
Rangoon.

[Holograph]   27 March 1914

I only wrote my last letter to you the day before yesterday, but I am just off again into the jungle, so I must post at once, or I will be missing the mail again. I have very little news I'm afraid. The heat is getting rather trying, & I am glad to get out of Rangoon. Thanks very much for your last letter which I got yesterday. I had quite forgotten that the Strongmans were at Bombay. It will be nice being near them. I am glad you are better, but I hope you will have got rid of your bad throat by now. Nothing exciting has happened here. There seems to be great excitement at home over Home

Rule. I see in tonight's paper that Sir John French & Genl. Ewart have also resigned. I think it was a bit stiff all those fellows sending in their papers in the Curragh. The Hutchinsons have gone off to Ootacamund till October. Everybody has left Rangoon who can get away. The Worcesters hockey team are down here at present to play in the tournament, & 3 of them are staying in the mess. We have been 2 years & 4 days in Burma now! Its gone very quickly. I go out tomorrow at 9.30 but where I will be tomorrow evening I don't know. I hope to get back on Wednesday to shoot in a revolver competition we have with the 79th Infantry. No time for more now. Lots of Love.

PRO 30/71/2

157

Notes by Major N. Malcolm on the address given by Major A. C. Grant-Duff to the Officers of 1st Battalion, The Black Watch at Aldershot

[Holograph]   [27 March 1914]

In view of the events of the last week and of the prejudice and misrepresentation to which they have given rise it is desirable that a clear statement of these events and of the duty of soldiers in these matters should be made.

The greatest misfortune which can befall an Army is to be involved in politics. Like the Crown, to whom our allegiance is due, we have nothing to do with politics. Through no fault of its own, so far as we can judge, this disaster has befallen us and the army has been dragged, at any rate for the moment, into the mire of party politics.

In accordance, apparently, with instructions from His Majesty's Ministers, officers of the Army in Ireland, were asked whether they would in certain circumstances, which had not then arisen, undertake certain duties or whether they would resign.

The choice having been given to them they tendered their resignations, which as the choice was given them they had the right to do. But, as stated by the Prime Minister in Parliament the night before last 'it is not right to ask an officer (and the same applied to every soldier) in advance what he may do or may not do in a contingency which has not arisen'. To be brought into conflict with our countrymen in any circumstances whatever is hateful to every one of us and any person who states the contrary is as every soldier knows either grossly ignorant or grossly dishonest. We are soldiers not police.

But by the common law of our country we can be called upon to aid the civil power. If, then, His Majesty acting through his Ministers requires us to perform this duty, His Commands should be conveyed to us as ORDERS and in no other way. Such orders, so long as they be lawful, it is our duty implicitly and without question to obey. That is the foundation of all military discipline and if that foundation is disturbed an army ceases to be an army and becomes a mob.

It may happen to any of us to find ourselves in circumstances of very great difficulty. In circumstances where what we believe to be our duty to ourselves, to our country, to our King or to God seems to conflict with our duty as soldiers — That is the greatest misfortune that can happen to us. The greatest of the world's tragedies is the clash of right with right. That battle each one of us must fight out for himself alone, and if so be that our consciences bid us disregard our military duty and compel us to refuse to obey an order given to us, we must be prepared like good soldiers cheerfully and bravely to pay the penalty. That penalty is death. As that most distinguished soldier, General Gallifet,[37] said to the French Army in circumstances somewhat similar to those in which we now stand — 'It is a hard law but it is the law. Of that there can be no question and there must be no doubt.'

H. P. Gough Mss

158
Major-General T. Capper to
Brigadier-General H. P. Gough

[Typescript Copy]

War Office
28 March 1914

Many congratulations on your bold stand in this horrible business, and in the masterly way in which you carried all your points.

I have a very mean feeling of having not been with my late Brigade during this sad crisis, but I must say I could never have carried it through as you did, and so I was better out of it.

Once more the words of Pericles come true: 'It is ever from the greatest hazards that the greatest honours are gained.'

But what a Government to bring things to such a pass, and then to wriggle and squirm and prevaricate. What is wanted now is for the damned Politicians of either side to let the Army alone, but I am sore afraid that the 'Army v the people' is too good an election lie for the Winston Churchill—Lloyd George crew to drop. I hope the Senior Officers of the Army are not going to give in now, for the sake of good faith with one another that could never be.

I am sure your action has stopped what must have been Civil War in Ireland, or, if not that, a much worse situation from the point of view of discipline when the troops were actually face to face with the Ulster forces.

Now the Government are plotting all they know how on earth to keep their miserable seats and salaries, and to hide the issue sufficiently to come in again at an election.

How on earth that poor creature Asquith stays where he is, beats me. A Cabinet repudiating its own action, and keeping in, is about the limit even for a democratic government.

You must be sick of the whole business, and I do wish the politicians and papers would let it alone.

Anyway, I cannot refrain from writing to you all I think. My wife sends her love too.

H. P. Gough Mss

159
Major-General F. S. Robb to
Major-General H. H. Wilson

Mychett Place,
Farnborough.
29 March 1914

[Holograph]

Late last night one of my acting subordinates, a regimental officer doing temporary duty in the H.Q. Office, whom I deputed to try and find out for me the regimental view of the situation, called on me to state what he had gleaned.

He summed up the views as follows:

(1) That the only really *satisfactory* solution to the Army would be the reinstatement of Sir J.F. and Sir S.E. (or rather the withdrawal of their resignations) under another S of S and that the fear was expressed that, unless this were possible, they could not be induced to remain but

(2) That in view of the serious catastrophe to the Army, which the loss of these two would be at such a time, it was universally hoped that they would be all able to make some declaration of personal feeling rather than leave their posts at such a crisis.

(3) That, rather than lose them, the bulk of the Army would put up with the taunts which would be certain to be hurled at it provided that it could be understood that the reason for the change was due to the unwillingness of these two distinguished officers to leave the Army in the lurch at the present moment.

There seems to be a sort of feeling that *we should all make any sacrifice in this crisis to hang together* and the regimental idea, as far as I have been able to gauge it is to implore nobody whom authority [illegible] weight to leave their posts.

The view I first told you of was what I had gleaned with conversations with some of my staff.

You are of course at liberty to show this to Sir J.F. or to Sir S.E. otherwise keep it to yourself and [illegible]

P.S. I am told that there is rather a feeling of pity for J.S. working up. At one time the feeling was very bitter against him.

IWM, 73/1/18, Wilson Mss

160
General Sir Ian Hamilton to
J. E. B. Seely

Sydney,
Australia.
[Typescript copy]
29 March 1914

I have not the heart to launch out into long descriptions of my own more or less humdrum doings whilst you are at home going through this time of terrible strain and anxiety. Still, although that is my feeling, commonsense shows me that this letter will take six weeks getting to you, and by that time, D.V., your Barque of State may have sailed into smoother waters. So I just dictate one line to enclose a cutting or two, and to tell you that I believe I am fulfilling, so far, what is one of the main essentials of these overseas inspections. I mean to say that I have managed to get into touch with the people and with the officers of the army, and, as the weeks pass, they are more and more kind to me, and more and more demonstrative on my public appearances, etc., etc. All this must be to the good whatever my mere recommendations (regarding which I cabled you) may be worth.

In some ways I wish very much I was at home just now so as to be able to hold out a helping hand to you, for whatever it might be worth. On the other—and this from the personal or selfish point of view—I take it for God's mercy that I am as remote from the scene of internecine strife as it is possible for any man still alive on this earth to be.

Goodbye for the present, and may the very best of luck attend you.

P.S. Since I have written this letter the, to me, exceedingly painful and distressing news of your resignation has come to hand. I am dreadfully sorry for I never in my life worked with anyone with whom it was so easy and straightforward a business to serve. There is no use my writing about the actual upset, as we out here can make neither head nor tail of it from the meagre telegrams we receive. But I know you acted with courage, and for what you thought to be the best for the army, and that is the main thing. I am sending you a little cable today. Goodbye for the meantime. I will write again.

King's College, Liddell Hart Centre for Military Archives, Hamilton Mss, 7/8/4j

161

Lieutenant Colonel R. J. Bridgfold to Brigadier-General H. P. Gough[38]

S.S. Mantua,
Aden.

[Typescript Copy]   29 March 1914

I suppose General is still the way to address you. I must write to congratulate you on your latest achievement. We got the telegrams at Port Said a few days ago and are anxious to hear some more news.

It would have been damnable if they had used the Army in the way they evidently intended to and we are all delighted that it has refused to be used against Loyalists. It is excellent that they should have got someone to stand up in plenty of time. I am just on my way out to command my Battalion in India. I wish I had got the Battalion in Ireland. I hate India.

Very best of luck. There is not a soldier here that is not thankful to you.

H. P. Gough Mss

162

W. S. Churchill to First Sea Lord and Secretary of the Admiralty[39]

Admiralty

[Holograph]   31 March 1914

Please call upon the Captain of the Pathfinder[40] for his explanation in writing of the signals which passed between him and the shore during his stay at Carrickfergus, which were published in yesterday's newspapers. He should be asked whether he had received any instructions from General Macready to make such communications.

Instructions should also be given to the commanding officers of the two Scouts now on duty in Belfast Lough that they are not to hold unnecessary communication with the shore, nor to accept from or to offer hospitality to civilians; nor to allow their men to go into Belfast unless there is special reason for it. The discussion of political questions is not to be allowed on board the ships, nor are the officers to enter into the discussion of such questions with civilians.

PRO, Adm 116/1326

163
Julia Alexander Sinclair to
Rear-Admiral R.E. Wemyss[41]

Dunbeath Castle,
Caithness.
3 April 1914

[Holograph]

Our letters crossed. Funnily enough I thought of you both in the bath last week & simply felt I *must* write. I knew you would be feeling the same as we were, & I must risk boring you by writing again today. I thought your letter of y'day very *fine*. I also agree with all you say, and I simply can't believe it all either.

I know you are both interested in everything however small to do with it so I shall risk being a bore & tell you any little things I've heard. I wont say much about Jack,[42] as he said he was going to write to you! And so I thought he'd tell you—but as he hasn't I will just tell you all he told me. They went as you know on 5 days manoeuvres last Monday week—the month of the plot—and Jack had Ad. Colville on board him for the manoeuvres. Jack says on the Sunday before Ad.C. joined, Capt. Bruce[43] came to him

(Jack) & said he had resigned & that he wished Jack to hand his resignation in when Sir S.C. came on board. Jack persuaded him to wait, as he said they hadn't yet been ordered to do anything & he might find himself left in the lurch, but to see Ad C next day with him. So on Monday a.m. Capts. Bruce & Hope[44] came on board Temeraire & they with Jack went to Ad. Colville & told him that they felt he ought to know that if they were ordered to Belfast for blockading purposes or civil war they would not be able to go—and that they would at once resign. Sir S. Colville was very much surprised—'quite taken aback'—And said had they thought of the effect it wd. have on the King. So Jack said he thought if the King knew he had the Army & Navy behind him it wd. immensely strengthen his position. Anyway Sir S.C. said he wd. see the C in C on the Friday. So on Friday morning Jack saw Sir S.C. again & he told him that as things were bubbling up again he hoped Sir S.C. would 'rub it in' to Sir George Callaghan. Sir S.C. said he might have to mention names so Jack said he cd. say his but not the others without asking them first (This was in the train as Jack was going to Exeter to fetch his mother). The sequel so far was a letter to me from Jack saying he had been dining with the Mundys and seen Sir S.C. who told him he'd told Sir G. Callaghan but mentioned no names. Jack says that Sir S.C. said he had much more to say but at a dinner party couldn't! so Jack will tell me when I see him next Tuesday & I will write & tell you 'the more'.—I have heard from lots of people the same story & Jack says the feeling is 'pretty general'. Evidently—Captain Dumaresq[45] I heard from another he went to Ad. Madden & said that he wished to resign & if he wanted to get a new Flag Captain *before* those same manoeuvres he wd. go at once. So Ad. Madden said 'If you do this you will find youself on the beach' so Captain Dumaresq said 'I have well considered that and wish to go'. So Ad. Madden tore up his resignation & said 'It's enough that you tell me'. Jack says he met Capt. Algernon Boyle[46] *bubbling* over with fury with his resignation in his pocket. Capt. Raikes[47] told me Ad. de Robeck was the same 'so I'm in good company as he's a straight one if ever there was one'. I'm telling you all this as I know the *names* will go no further than the Villa Montbrillant![48] but I know you wd. like to hear them. They might not be very interesting people but they show the *spirit*. Ive had several letters from other people saying the same. Capt. Farie[49] etc. I do think the whole things too contemptible & I just wonder what you think of the latest development of Asquith as War M. etc. To me it seems a slim trick to preserve office—nothing else—but I'm glad to see H. Samuel says that they will not go to the country on the Army v People cry. I'm enclosing you a letter of L. Galloways about Haldane—that great fraud—altering Hansard—which I thought hit the mark. A cousin of mine in the K O S Borderers at the Curragh says the whole regt. wd. have struck—all the officers did—& the men were ready to follow them & he says 'the whole thing's ridiculous—the Cavalry were not the only ones by any means—all the Infantry, gunners & sappers wd. have gone too'. Jack says wherever he goes he hears praise of General Gough. So you see your opinion of him is well shared. I'm so glad Genls. French & Ewart struck out in facing their resigs. to teach Seely what *honour* meant. But you see Honest John didn't go! Not he. Oh they are a pitiable crew. The whole thing makes one's blood boil. I am so interested in you telephoning Mr. & Mrs. Chamberlain. How they *must* be feeling it. I wish you had said yr. views on foreign criticism. What they must think of us & what the effect must be—even to the ignorant mind—must be colossal. I had a neighbour here today whose brother is in the Black Watch & he's on the staff at Aldershot. She read me a letter from him today & he says that it isn't only the Curragh but all the Aldershot Command as well & that the feeling there was 'terrific'. I'm so thankful it's all over the place. What about Sir A. Paget? I see the Morning Post is calling on him to resign & say the truth, but it all seems such a muddle & I don't think he is showing up well at *present. But* as you say there's evidence of a lot more to come out. It's all so incredible but for one I think the Unsts. have shown up well. I thought Lords Lansdowne, Salisbury & Methuen were excellent. The latter's speech touched me, when one remembers Lloyd George throwing up his cap & shouting Hurrah with the Nat. Members when Ld. M. was captured. Jack took his motor to Edin. on Friday to Sun. & went back to Devonport Sunday night

& he's coming up next Mon. to Edin. where I join him & we motor there on Tues. & Wed. he goes back Friday. So I shall hear lots more & will — again — to repeat myself — risk boring you by telling you more. As he says there 'is much he can't write'. Oh dear it does appal one. The one thing that cheers me is the crofters here have been swarming down to ask me if they may sign the Covenant. I've sent in 100 names & have had to write for more helpers! But of course it mightn't mean much except if the Election is fought on Home Rule — then it would. Can you read this. I know I write so indistinctly and I got a good snub tonight. I wrote to my sister's gardener for some *anchusa* plants & he sent me a box of chrysanthemum cuttings tonight as he concluded that was what I wrote for!!! So forgive this but if I miss the post I shan't send this! I forgot to say Jack says Captain Hope spoke up so well to Sir S. Colville 'most earnestly & Colville told me after he's been much impressed'. My love to Mrs. Wemyss & forgive me if I've bored you.

Churchill College, WMYS 2/5, Wemyss Mss

164
Captain E. S. Alexander-Sinclair to
Mrs R. Wemyss

H.M.S. Temeraire,
Devonport.
[Holograph]   5 April 1914

*   *   *

There is plenty of excitement about but the way serious matters are juggled with for personal interest & advancement makes one so sick that one scarcely likes writing or even talking about them. The resignation of the Curragh people made us think considerably what our position was — I mean the Captains — there were only 3 ships of this Squadron together when it happened & without any collusion or canvassing we found out directly we were of one opinion & that we wd. have nothing to do with coercing Ulster & we came to the conclusion that we ought to tell our immediate Chief our views privately which we did. I purposely haven't spoken to other Captains, unless they have started it but I think from what I hear most are of the same opinion, only two have I heard in any way disagree. One said he couldn't afford it & the other said he wd. look the other way if given blockade duty. I don't know the opinion of Bayly's Captains but he himself was quite ready to act & besides asking for the field guns gives out that he wd. have no compunction about using them.

* * *

Churchill College, WMYS, 2/5, Wemyss Mss

165
Field Marshal Lord Roberts to Captain A. E. Gilmore[50]

Englemere,
Ascot.
[Carbon]   22 April 1914

I am sorry to have been so long in answering your letter of the 21 March, but the fact is the position of Territorials is very ill defined, and I have been endeavouring to arrive at a clear understanding of their status, with the result that I do not think you have done wrong in signing a form—promising to go to the assistance of Ulster—while still holding the King's commission.

It is true that the Territorial officer appears to be always under military law, but it cannot be the same law as applied to the regular Officer, for the Territorial officer cannot be ordered to go out against strikers, nor can he be prevented from going into the House of Commons, making speeches, writing to the Press, and so forth. If the, as I said in the House of Lords, English law does not presuppose the possibility of civil war, and if the onus of judging when civil disturbances end and civil war begins rests with the conscience of the individual, I think that no fault can be found with your action in promising, in the event of force being used in Ulster, to go to her assistance.

NAM, 7101-12-125-3. Roberts Mss

166

Lieutenant Colonel G. de S. Barrow to Brigadier-General H. P. Gough

Cavalry Club
8 June 1914

[Typescript copy]

Thanks so much for your letter, forwarded me from India. I am just home for the summer. I really did not expect an answer to my wire[51] at all, as I knew how rushed you must be. I sent it because I wanted you to know how appreciated your action was, as I know it has been by all honourable soldiers. It was grand, the way you showed the world that the Army was something more than a wretched tool in the hands of a lot of dirty politicians. You must have had a most trying time but great is your reward.

I should love to hear all about it. I shall try to get to the Cavalry Manoeuvres this autumn as a spectator or in any way I can make myself useful and perhaps we shall meet then.

H. P. Gough Mss

167

[Lieutenant Colonel] A. G[rubb] to Field Marshal Lord Roberts[52]

Elsfield House,
Hollingbourne,
Kent.
No date

[Holograph]

One of my soldier sons[53] is Staff Officer to Gen. Young[54] Commanding the Home Counties Territorials. He told me that 75% of their officers would have declined to go to Aldershot if mobilised to relieve a force from there to go to Ulster—as was (it is stated) contemplated. But your Lordship knows more about this 'plot' than I do.

NAM, 7101-23-202, Roberts Mss

168

Account by Second Lieutenant E. H. L. Beddington, 16th Lancers[55]

[Typescript]   [Circa 1960]

Early in March I received a letter from Colonel Bromley Davenport,[56] Commanding the Staffordshire Yeomanry, whom I had met when I was Staff Captain to the Yeomanry Brigade the previous year, inviting me to come and take a Tactical Course for the officers of his Regiment at Capesthorne, his home. We were to assemble on Friday, March 20th, and thus have the whole of the 21st and 22nd for work, and I could catch the Irish Mail back on Monday the 24th. Both Charles Campbell and McEwan (the Colonel) agreed to my going, so I accepted the invitation.

It so happened that on the evening of the 19th March, your Mother and I dined with the Brigadier (Hubert Gough), a very cheerful party, and the conversation was the usual, hunting, polo, point-to-points, and not a word of politics was discussed.

I got up early next day and caught the Mailboat for England and got to Crewe where Colonel Bromley Davenport came to meet me in a car. We settled our plans for the week end during the drive to Capesthorne, a magnificent house and park amply big enough for all I wanted, and then went up to dress for dinner. As we were nearing the end of dinner the butler brought me a telegram from the Regiment reading much as follows: 'All officers of regiment have resigned rather than take part in operations against Ulster stop we were given our choice—wire your decision'. I asked if I might write a reply and wrote 'Will do the same as the others stop what is it all about'. The question had never been talked about at all in the Regiment, so I was completely in the dark.

When we were going to bed I took Bromley Davenport aside and showed him the telegram and told him of my answer, both in strict confidence. He was an M.P. and had been Under Secretary for War in the previous Government. He told me that I could not have acted differently but was distressed that I should have resigned whilst staying in his house. I soon cheered him up on that point for, as I said, that was entirely fortuitous and as soon as I had sent the reply I went back to my port and two hours had elapsed before I showed him the telegram.

There was nothing in the papers on Saturday about it, and the Sunday papers did not ever reach Capesthorne, and so I went on happily with my Tactical Course which went very well for I kept things simple, on a troop leader and squadron commander level, and when I finished a short summing up of the proceedings after tea on Sunday evening everybody was very nice and grateful to me and hoped I would come again.

The next morning I had to motor to Crewe to catch the Irish Mail before the papers reached Capesthorne, and the first I knew about matters was what I read in the papers of it on the train to Holyhead, though the porters at Crewe having noticed my regiment's name on my suitcase gave me three hearty cheers to my surprise, and when I asked what it was all about they said: 'Your regiment refused to go and fight Ulster; here's luck to you all.'

I called at Barracks on my way home and found that on the Friday, General Paget, G.O.C. Irish Command, had sent for Goughy and others and told them that they and their officers had the choice of resigning their Commissions (in fact being dismissed) or of most probably engaging in active operations against Ulster. Any officers with an Ulster domicile would be allowed to 'disappear'. Paget required an answer that evening. Goughy saw the 5th Lancers in Dublin that morning, and the other officers of the Brigade in our mess that afternoon, and the vast majority (all in 16th Lancers) decided for resignation or dismissal, and reported to Dublin that evening that of the officers on duty 59 out of 71 preferred dismissal. The next day General Paget went to The Curragh to see the officers of the Brigade stationed there, and endeavoured to get them to reconsider their decision: there was some weakening but only very little. Gough and the Colonels of 5th and 16th Lancers were ordered to report to the War Office the next day, Sunday, and left for London by the night mail.

That was all the information available, so I went home and told your Mother that it looked as if very soon I should be out of a job. On the following Wednesday, the Brigadier and the two Colonels arrived back at The Curragh with a written assurance from the Army Council that they would not be ordered to undertake active operations against Ulster, and that they were reinstated in their Commands. Our resignations were of course cancelled.

The affair was a political sensation of the first rank and caused great but very frequently ill-informed controversy both in the Press and Parliament. I don't propose to go into that controversy but it is quite certain that General Paget was entirely wrong in putting a hypothetical question to the officers. Once he had posed that illegal question we could not but win, but very firm handling of the matter was needed by Goughy. Had we been given an order to invade Ulster before Paget's question, we should have had to obey it. At any rate the result of this mishandling of the matter was that the Secretary of State for War, the C.I.G.S., and the Adjutant General all resigned their appointments; General Paget retired shortly afterwards, and the Prime Minister took over the

War Office till the outbreak of war, when Lord Kitchener was appointed Secretary of State.

I should mention that Gough, in asking officers to make their decision, never attempted in any way to influence them either one way or the other.

King's College, Liddell Hart Centre for Military Archives, 'My Life' by Edward Beddington, pp. 54–55

169

Account by Lieutenant H. T. Baillie-Grohman, HMS *Lively*, 7th Destroyer Flotilla

[Typescript]   [Circa 1969]

This idea [Ulster coercion] infuriated many of us junior officers in Devonport. What our seniors thought, we never found out. My personal reaction, and that of many others, was that I joined the Royal Navy to defend my country, and the people in it. I had NOT joined to help force a most loyal part of our people out of the United Kingdom, to come under rule and religion which they utterly detested and whose conduct was so often disloyal to King and Country. To do this was entirely against my conscience, and everything I stood for.

On the other hand, of course, one had, or ought, to obey orders received from a higher authority. Here was a crisis of conscience. We younger C.O.'s argued the matter out time and again. I cannot at this date remember when we first heard of the so called mutiny at the Curragh where many Army officers resigned (including General Gough) rather than take part in forcing Ulster. But I do not believe we were influenced by outside sources of this type. Anyhow, the junior CO's (about half a dozen of us) agreed that if we were not allowed to resign, or otherwise unable to avoid this service, we would steam our ships into Belfast or Londonderry and place ourselves under the orders of Sir Edward Carson. Highly mutinous, no doubt. From our very close contact with our small ship's companies, it was clear that the great majority at any rate would not have objected, for the Liberal Government had split the country over this question to a quite exceptional degree, and unless the 1914 war had intervened, there would in every probability have been civil war in England and Ireland if Asquith had persisted with this Home Rule plan. It was incredible to us then, and still is, how any Government could be so out of touch with the terribly violent feelings aroused by this proposal.

As it happened, the 7th Destroyer Flotilla was not required for the Ulster blockade. We were thankful.

Talking many years later to Admiral Sir William Whitworth[57] who was then a Lieutenant Commander and CO of one of the destroyers employed in this blockade, I asked him what his reactions were at the time. He replied that he and other C.O.'s just did not play. If they saw any ships they turned the blind eye! That certainly was one way of dealing with the situation!

On looking back on our feelings about Ulster, it seems curious we did not ask our Captain[58] for advice: but we never thought of this, although he was a very approachable man.

IWM, P.366. Autobiography of Vice-Admiral H. T. Baillie-Grohman, pp. 116–118

PART 2
THE 'PLOT' AND THE KING'S NAME
MARCH TO JULY 1914

170
Lieutenant-General Sir Arthur Paget
to W. S. Churchill

Royal Hospital,
Dublin.

[Holograph]

28 March 1914

I return herewith the memorandum, representing certain points in the speech which you propose to make in next Monday's debate, forwarded to me by Colonel Seely.[59] I also enclose a memorandum of my own, in which I have pointed out in what respects your memorandum does not entirely represent my opinion of the facts, as I believe them to be.

For the sake of reference, I have marked the passages referred to in your memorandum.

In one respect, and so far as I know, in one respect only, has there been misunderstanding between myself and my officers, and that is upon the subject alluded to in the second paragraph of your memorandum. I did not intend to put the two principles mentioned, as a test or trial to the whole body of officers in the Irish Command. I did intend to find out then and there, whether the Senior Officers present at my conference were of my way of thinking, viz, that duty came before all other considerations. To that extent, and no more, these two principles were used by me as a test or trial.

I had no intention, however, of these principles being submitted as a test to any other officers, and my intention was that the Senior Officers present should simply inform those officers subordinate to them of the exemption granted, and of the result of refusal to obey orders in the case of officers not affected by the exemption clause. I wished particularly to make it perfectly clear

313

to officers that they could not simply resign their commissions, and retire from the service, in possession of pensions, and without penalty.

No notes were taken at the conference. Some of the officers present understood me to say: 'any officer who is not prepared from conscientious or other motives to carry out his duty, should say so'. My intention, as explained above, was perfectly clear in my mind, but the expression which I am informed that I used undoubtedly might convey the impression that I was putting a pistol to their heads, for in answer to a question I did say 'such officers (i.e. officers who are not prepared to carry out their duty) will at once be dismissed from the service'.

I need hardly say that I accept the fullest responsibility for the expressions quoted, and for the wrong impression thereby engendered in the minds of some, but not all, of the officers whom I addressed.

I would be very obliged if you could find occasion in your speech to testify to the sense of duty, and loyalty to myself, of my Divisional Commanders and their Brigadiers during the past week.

I think that I have made matters now so plain that there can be no difference between us as to my own opinion, and as to my own recollection of the facts involved. Such being, as I hope, the case, I do not see that any useful object can be served by a personal interview, such as you suggest might be possibly desirable.[60]

Nuffield College, Ms Mottistone 22, f 268–270, Bodleian, Ms Asquith 40, f 85–86

171
Lieutenant-General Sir Arthur Paget
to J. E. B. Seely

Royal Hospital,
Dublin.
[Holograph]   30 March 1914

I am sending you enclosed the two papers[61] promised in the cypher telegram sent you this afternoon.

As you are already aware there was a misunderstanding. Sir Charles Fergusson realises this, & thinks he may be to some extent to blame. I cannot admit this, so I have cut out any reference to it from his statement which was written out *before* & not after the receipt of your wire.

However, I am sure you will be pleased to know his remarks on the present state of his troops which are as follows. 'I can only point out the fact that as a result the Division remained loyal & that the discipline is absolutely intact, strengthened rather than weakened by what has passed.'

Bodleian, Ms Asquith 40 f 101; Nuffield College, Ms Mottistone 22, f 316

172
Major-General Sir Charles Fergusson to
Lieutenant-General Sir Arthur Paget

Ballyfair,
Curragh.
[Holograph]   3 April 1914

I saw Walker today and he showed me your statement.[62]

Please let me say that I thoroughly understand, and that it was quite unnecessary for you to explain, though very kind and considerate of you to do so. I am only more sorry than I can say that stupidity on my part should have added to your difficulties, and I would gladly have taken the blame instead of letting it fall on you.

I am perfectly certain that all my officers thoroughly understood long ago that there had been an honest misunderstanding, and they are quite sensible enough to appreciate that it is the sort of mistake that is difficult if not impossible to correct. I will stake my reputation that none of them have the slightest feeling towards you but of loyalty and sympathy. So pray do not think more of it.

I am entirely of opinion that the sooner the matter is allowed to drop, the better. Indeed it is pretty well forgotten already.

PRO, WO 35/209 (m)

173
Lord Esher to H. A. Gwynne

Windsor Castle

[Holograph]   9 April 1914

I read your article on the Army & Ulster in the M. P. of April 7 with deep interest.

It is full of information which everyone believes to be perfectly accurate.

However, I am asked to tell you for your private information, that Sir Arthur Paget had no authority to use the King's name, or refer to His Majesty's 'wishes'.

The King, between ourselves, never saw Sir Arthur Paget, and had no communication with him directly or *indirectly* until after the whole affair was over; nor had the King any knowledge of what was going on prior to the public announcement of the resignation of General Gough and his officers.

I hope you will get on holiday at Easter, but I imagine you will *not*!

IWM, Gwynne Mss

174

C. Wigram to Lord Stamfordham

Brookville House,
Raheny,
Dublin.
11 April 1914

[Holograph]

Many thanks for your letter. I put all letters you gave me from Fergusson in the file, and clipped all the Fergusson correspondence together, so it should be among the letters in this clip.

I played golf with A.P. this morning—he was a shaken man, and no gaiety about him. I asked him why he had allowed W and S to shield themselves behind him, and he said he felt he could not give Cabinet minutes away, and practically admitted he could if he liked. I said the Opposition are after a letter S wrote you, and he did not deny the existence of this letter. He said he thought those around the King did not realise how loyal the Army was to the King, and how imperative it was to keep the King's name before the Army in every possible way, that the day might be near at hand when H.M. would have to rely on the support of the Army and Navy to maintain his place in the constitution. I told him he was mistaken, and that we all realised the importance of having the King recognised as Head of the Army, but that it was not fair to take the King's name in vain, and to say that H.M. had issued and approved of orders and instructions to the Army, which had never been submitted to H.M., and of which H.M. was quite ignorant. I asked him if he thought S had submitted these late instructions as regards movements of the Army, and he said he imagined at the time when he addressed the officers that these orders had been laid before H.M., but knew now they had not been. He said he had wished to resign but that French had urged him to keep quiet.

He was very angry with Gough, who, he said, had acted very stupidly, and if Gough had trusted A.P. all would have been well!

I met at lunch today one of the mobilised Second Army Staff, who had been attached to A.P. and he told me that the officers were now being sent back to England. I hope during this next week to go for a tour in a motor, & to visit some of the interesting places in Ulster. I am also trying to fix up a quiet meeting with Richardson.

I am to meet Gough tomorrow, who will probably be highly amusing.

RA GV F.674/72

175
L. S. Amery to Major P. Howell

Eaton Square,
SW1
26 April 1914

[Holograph]

I quite agree about it being unfair to Hogg to drag him into this sorry business in order to make him out a partisan or favourite of Churchill's, & I'll use any influence I can. Meanwhile, ... looking now at ... the telegram of 21st which I think only does credit to Hogg.[63] Somebody probably will ask if Hogg lunched with Churchill on the 22nd—not as a point against Hogg, but to show the insincerity of Churchill's dramatic remark, 'Of course I never answered the telegram', but it is a minor point & if I learn of his question beforehand I'll discourage the question.

You certainly are to be congratulated in your drafting of the letter of March 20 to Paget:[64] it was an essential step to keep your people in the right & its non-acknowledgement of course is a gap in the revised version of Paget's first [?harangue] which cannot be bridged. Could you let me know precisely when this letter reached Paget? I assume it must have been after 7 p.m. when he wired to the W.O. about the 5th Lancers & before 11 p.m. when he wired the details contained in the letter.

Is there any foundation at all for Paget's version of April 1st that the interrogating was only for the Generals, & that subordinate officers were not to be questioned at all but only informed of this domicile exemption & threatened as to the penalties of reluctance outside that exception? The actual orders issued by Fergusson (published in Thursday's *Times*) puts the role they had too definitely to make such a misunderstanding as Paget suggests a possibility. I should be greatly interested in any criticism you can give of Paget's April 1st memo. I imagine Paget's muddled speech of the 21st was a reflection of telegrams received on that morning from Seely & Co to try & make out that it was a misunderstanding kindred with the recollection of his original instructions.

Had Paget any written instructions? Do you know if either at the first interview on the 20th, or on the 21st, he read from any WO document, or from any notes of his own, or just gassed away? Did Gough bring any document down to the Brigade on the 20th or only a recollection of what Paget had said?

You refer to Hogg's wire as of the 20th. Churchill says he received it on Sunday 22nd, but I imagine 20th must be the real date.

Do you understand now whether there was an idea on the 20th of moving the Cavalry as far as the Boyne in any case, so as to be ready to push on to Newry & Armagh at the first trouble, or were they only to move after the first shot? And was Paget talking (on the 20th again) pure hypothetics or did he treat it as practically a certainty that war would be declared on the Saturday?

Is there any foundation for the Ulster Council's statement that he said the police would search for arms or seize the Ulster Headquarters?

What I should really be interested to see would be a history of the whole business reconstructed as you understand the Bulgarian advance into Thrace![65]

Ulster's counterstroke[66] seems to have been devilishly efficient.

King's College, Liddell Hart Centre for Military Archives, IV/C/2/54, Howell Mss

176

Incomplete letter from Charles à C. Repington to Geoffrey Robinson

Maryon Hall,
Hampstead.

[Holograph]
10 June 1914

* * *

Paget's interest is now directed to the South & West, especially Sligo & Limerick. He is not bothering about Ulster, intending to leave the rival factions to fight it out. But he is going to ask the PM tomorrow, in case the Army is called on to keep the peace between contending UVF & INV, how he is to act. It will take a better man than the PM to answer that question!

Paget told me that at the time of the 'Plot' he could only place 4,800 men on the Boyne; that he refused point blank to undertake offensive operations with such a force against the UVF, & that it was as a result of this refusal that he was promised by Seely, French & Ewart, the 1st Division & 1st Cavalry Brigade from Aldershot, the 18th Brigade, & 3 battalions from Scotland. He would then have had 22,000 men to attack with, & he thought this enough. The PM knew nothing of this till weeks later when Kincaid Smith showed him Paget's orders given out at the second conference with the Irish generals. Seely & French curse Paget for letting his officers into the secret of the reinforcement, but Paget naturally replies that arrangements had to be made for the transport, supply & housing of the troops from England, & that it was impossible to keep the thing dark, even had he been told to do so, which he says was not the case.

The troops from Scotland were to come to Larne. All those from England to Dublin. Paget offers to show me the INV, but from what his staff tell me of them I don't think it worthwhile.

I am amused about Macready. Paget got a private letter to say that M would not go back. He refused to accept the private letter, & asked for an official letter. The WO appear to be puzzled over it, and can't fix it up, for when M was first sent over he was made to supercede Gleichen, & the question now is whether Gleichen should not supercede him. But evidently Paget is quite off private letters & conversations, which is a mercy any way.

As the result of an inquiry which has extended to all the brigadiers in Ireland Paget is sure that he still possesses the confidence of his command. He assures me that though he may retire he will not resign.

I don't think French can afford the command. The man who holds it has to spend from £2000 to £5000 a year beyond what he gets out of it.

The Times, Dawson/Repington Mss

177
Lieutenant-General Sir Arthur Paget to Lord Stamfordham

[Holograph]

Royal Hospital,
Dublin.
19 June 1914

I was surprised & distressed to hear that the King had been informed that I had made use of his name in a personal sense at my conference with the officers of the 3rd Cavalry Bde. at the Curragh in March & that they had taken notes to this effect. I have been at great pains to find out if there was any foundation for this rumour, with the result that General Gough informed my Military Secretary that no officer had taken notes or had publicly stated that I had used the King's name. I enclose the statements of the only officers present who were not in the Cav. Bde., Colonel Wolley Dod, Ch. Staff Off. to the 5th Div., who was the second senior officer present in the room and Lt. Mackintosh.[67] Since this rumour has reached the King I shall be glad if you will see that my emphatic denial also reaches His Majesty.

RA GV F.674/86

178

Statement by Colonel O. C. Wolley-Dod[68]

[Holograph]   12 June 1914

I was present at the interview between General Sir Arthur Paget and the Officers of the Cavalry Brigade.

Sir Arthur, having made some statements as to his plan of operations that he proposed should troops be called out in aid of the civil power to overcome an armed rising in Ulster, went on to say that he understood that many officers objected to taking action because they distrusted the Ministry.

Sir Arthur pointed out that the Ministers were the advisers of the King, and that any instructions issued by them were practically instructions from the King, in the same way that orders issued by his (Sir Arthur's) Staff Officer were orders issued by Sir Arthur himself.

I am quite sure that Sir Arthur neither said, nor implied, that he had any mission direct from the King.

RA GV F.674/88; BL, Add Mss 51250, Paget Mss

179

Statement by Lieutenant A. A. Mackintosh[69]

                                                              Mayfair,
                                                              London.
[Holograph]   13 June 1914

I was present at the meeting between General Sir Arthur Paget and the officers of the Cavalry Brigade.

I am quite certain that Sir Arthur Paget neither said, nor implied, that he had any mission direct from the King nor did he at any time refer to the King in any personal sense.

RA GV F.674/87; BL, Add Mss 51250, Paget Mss

180

Lord Stamfordham to
Lieutenant-General Sir Arthur Paget

Buckingham Palace
20 June 1914

Your letter of yesterday and its enclosures,[70] which latter I now return, have been laid before the King.

I do not understand that His Majesty was ever informed that you made use of his name at your conference with the officers of the 3rd Cavalry Brigade at the Curragh, but at the Conference which was attended by the GOC's of the 5th Division, the Brigadier-General of the Cavalry Brigade and the 14th and 15th Infantry Brigades on the morning of the 20th March, when you stated that the orders given by you to them were with the knowledge and had the authority of the King.

I enclose a copy of a letter which Sir John French himself handed to His Majesty telling His Majesty that he had received it from you.[71] This practically states that at all events Sir Charles Fergusson understood that the orders were the King's orders and had received His Majesty's full approval.

When the King saw you at Buckingham Palace on the 23rd March he understood from you that you had told your Generals that your orders were the King's orders. His Majesty expressed surprise at this as he was not aware of anything that had been ordered by the Government except the movement of Troops to Armagh, Omar [sic], Carrickfergus etc., and he was in ignorance as to your interview with your Generals and still more as to anything that you intended to say to them.

I cannot disguise from you the fact that from numerous communications which have reached me there was an unmistakable impression among the Troops at the Curragh that the instructions given to them had been approved of by the King.

RA GV F.674/89; BL. Add Mss 51250, Paget Mss

181

Memorandum by
Major-General L. B. Friend

Parkgate,
Dublin.
24 June 1914

[Holograph]

Friday 20th March 1914. At the morning conference of General Sir Arthur Paget with Maj. Genl. Sir C. Fergusson, B. Gen. Rolt, Cuthbert, H. Gough, Forestier-Walker, Col. F. F. Hill & myself no mention was made of the King's name or authority.

At the afternoon conference of General Sir A. Paget with Maj. Genl. Sir C. Fergusson, W. P. Pulteney, Br. Gen. W. Doran, Ingouville-Williams, Forestier-Walker, Col. de Gex & myself. Just as this conference was about to break up Genl. Sir C. Fergusson asked the GOC in C. if we might take it that the orders were the King's: and the GOC in C. replied to the effect that of course all Army orders were the King's—as were the King's Regulations; & that he—the GOC in C.—could not give orders to us without the technical authority of His Majesty.

I was just starting for Belfast to take temporary command there & wanted to hear what was said: but it did not impress me with any particular consequence.

There was no trouble with the officers & men of the two Battalions at Holywood (Belfast) so I had no occasion to think of using the King's name. All I said to the officers there—was that the GOC in C. had no intention of taking active measures against the Ulster malcontents; but that we were to uphold law & order & aid the Civil Authority in doing so to the best of our powers. If it came to the point of acting against organised armed forces of the Ulstermen, it must be left to the discretion of the Senior Officer at the place (myself in this case) as to what further action should take place.

BL, Add Mss 51250, Paget Mss

182

Major-General W. P. Pulteney to Lieutenant-General Sir Arthur Paget

Government House,
Cork.

[Holograph]   29 June 1914

General Friend has told me about Lord Stamfordham's letter to you with reference to your using the King's name at the conferences on the 20th March.

What happened at the conference either in the morning before luncheon or the one after either General Fergusson or Genl. Doran asked you if they were the King's orders, you replied all orders are from the King, the manner in which you said it left me perfectly certain that you personally had had no instructions from the King himself about the scheme or possible action, so much was this conveyed to my mind that I never used the King's name in the conference with my Brigadiers, nor do I believe for one second that if any of us had thought you had had personal instructions on the matter from the King that any officer or man would have failed to answer the call whatever they were bidden to do.

You will find this borne out by my letter to General Forestier-Walker[72] when asked my views of the feelings of the troops in the matter after the crisis when I said I did not think the officers would go unless it was the King's personal wish.

BL, Add Mss 51250, Paget Mss

183

Statement by
Major-General Sir Charles Fergusson

Ballyfair,
Curragh.

[Holograph]   29 June 1914

On Friday March 20, I asked the GOC-in-Chief whether certain orders were the King's, or had His Majesty's sanction (I am not sure of the exact words used). He replied in the affirmative.

At the time I had in my mind the idea of ascertaining whether the orders actually had His Majesty's sanction and approval, and it was in that sense that I put the question. I interpreted the answer in the same sense.

Consequently, when next morning I was questioned by officers, I first replied (speaking in the technical sense) that of course the orders were from the King. This, however, did not satisfy them; and on being pressed by them as to whether the orders actually had His Majesty's sanction, I answered that I had put the same question to the GOC-in-Chief, and that he had replied 'yes'.

On consideration, I admit freely that my question might easily have been misunderstood, and that the answer of the GOC-in-Chief would apply equally to the question in its technical meaning. No doubt our minds at the moment were running in different grooves.

The Commander-in-Chief never mentioned the King's name at all, except in answering the specific question I put to him. Nor did I use it, until cornered by the questioning of officers, when I thought that under the circumstances there was no alternative if a catastrophe was to be avoided.

I am entirely to blame for the introduction of His Majesty's name. It was I who first introduced it, and I am responsible for the use made of it.

RA GV F.674/93; Fergusson Mss; BL Add Mss 51250, Paget Mss

184
Lieutenant-General Sir Arthur Paget to Lord Stamfordham

[Holograph]

Royal Hospital,
Dublin.
1 July 1914

As I explained to you in my letter of last week, I have been obliged to delay my full reply to your letter of 20 June until I had an opportunity of seeing Sir Charles Fergusson.

I have since seen that officer and am now in a position to reply to the points raised in your letter.

No mention was made, in any connection whatever, of the King's name at the conference held on the morning of the 20th March, which was attended by the officers enumerated by you. About this point there is no possibility of error.

A second conference was held on that day, which was attended by some of the officers who were present at the first conference and in addition by GOC's VI Division, & 16th & 17th Inf. Bdes.

At, or immediately after, this conference General Fergusson did ask me, whether the orders I had given were the King's orders. I answered that all orders were the King's orders, but in so replying did not mean to convey H.M.'s authority otherwise than in a technical sense, and I had no intention of invoking the personal authority of the King or even of inferring that H.M. was personally cognizant of the orders which I had received. I enclose, in this connection three papers from Generals Fergusson, Pulteney & Friend respectively, which give their personal impressions of what passed. I may add that B. Generals Cuthbert & Walker who were present, agree absolutely with the account of General Friend. It was not until the evening of the 21st March when Sir C. Fergusson came to report to me, that I was made aware of the use which had been made of the King's name by him, acting under a misapprehension from the paper bearing his signature.

The letter from Lt. Col. Brett,[73] which was handed to H.M. by Sir John French, was forwarded by me to Sir John, with a request that it should be placed before the King solely in order that H.M. should learn without delay that His troops were absolutely loyal to Him.

I did not therefore think it necessary, in forwarding this letter, to explain the misapprehension into which General Fergusson had fallen.

I greatly regret that, at the interview which the King graciously afforded me on 23rd March, I did not make it clear that I had never used H.M.'s name in the sense understood by him.

I would ask you to give His Majesty my assurance that under no circumstances whatever did I make, or would I have made, use of the King's name without the direct authority of my Sovereign.

Sir Charles Fergusson desires to assume full responsibility for the use which he made of the King's name, and has in consequence tendered his resignation to me. I have refused to forward it because I feel strongly that the responsibility for this grave breach of discipline must be borne by myself. I therefore feel it incumbent on me to tender my own resignation on the same grounds.

The question, however, is one which H.M. may consider affects Him personally. Before, therefore, sending in an application through the official channels to be permitted to retire from the service, I should wish the King to be informed unofficially of the action which I contemplate, since I hesitate to take this step without His Majesty's approval.

RA GV F.674/92; BL, Add Mss 51250, Paget Mss

185
Lord Stamfordham to
Lieutenant-General Sir Arthur Paget

Buckingham Palace
4 July 1914

[Typescript]

Your letter of the 1st inst,[74] with its enclosures, which I now return, have been laid before the King.

From the statements which it contains and from Sir Charles Fergusson's memorandum of June 29th, it appears to His Majesty that considerable misunderstanding occurred both regarding the actual use of the King's name on the 20th March and as to the sense in which it was quoted.

The King appreciates the spirit which prompted you to inform him unofficially that you are disposed to resign your command and retire from the service.

At the same time His Majesty does not feel that the question personally affects him and he regrets that it is not possible for him to express an opinion upon your contemplated action.

P.S. I have taken a copy of Sir C. Fergusson's memo of 29th June.[75] I assume you will have no objection to my doing so.

RA GV F.674/94; BL. Add Mss 51250, Paget Mss

186

Field Marshal Lord Methuen to Lieutenant-General Sir Arthur Paget

Corsham Court,
Wilts.
[Holograph]   14 July 1914

On receipt of your note I arranged to see Stamfordham and just came back from a long interview.

It does not appear that the King doubts your words, but there seems to have been a misunderstanding as to the manner of speech in which you introduced the King's name.

All this seems to have been gone into in March, and you have again brought it forward in June.

The position, in other words, has not changed, and the King will not again rake up the Curragh incident, no more will the P.M.

I cannot go back from what I have said i.e. I should not care for what others may say, but if you feel you have acted as you think right, yet through a misunderstanding have made the King regret

329

the manner in which you introduced his name when speaking to the officers at the Curragh, then I should act as you propose and retire.

That you endeavoured to act loyally to the Government no one doubts; it is on account of your action that you have been placed in so thankless a position.

Knowing as much as I now do I almost wish you had retired in March.

I tried to put myself in your position when speaking to Stamfordham, and whilst writing this letter.

RA GV F.674/97; BL. Add Mss 51250, Paget Mss

187

Memorandum by
Brigadier-General G. T. Forestier-Walker

Dublin
[Holograph]   23 July 1914

I was present at all conferences, presided over by the Commander of the Forces, which were held on the 20th March 1914, and at which Sir Charles Fergusson was present. I was also present on the evening of the 21st March, when Sir Charles Fergusson arrived from the Curragh to interview Sir Arthur Paget at the Royal Hospital.

My recollection of what occurred on these occasions, in connection with the mention of the use of the King's name, is absolutely clear.

At the close of the afternoon conference on the 20th March, the officers present were getting up to leave, when Sir Charles Fergusson asked Sir Arthur Paget whether he (Sir Charles) had authority to say to officers that the instructions, which had been given at the conference, had been issued with the sanction of the King. Sir Arthur Paget replied that of course all orders were issued with the King's sanction, and either Sir Arthur or another officer present said that all orders coming through the Secretary of State had His Majesty's sanction. I myself made a remark to the effect that the authority of the King was expressly laid down in the Preface to the King's Regulations.

From first to last it was perfectly clear to me that Sir Charles Fergusson received no authority from Sir Arthur Paget, at this interview, to use the King's name in any personal sense, or in any other way than as that of the Head of the Army acting through his Ministers. It never occurred to me that Sir Charles Fergusson could place any other construction on the conversation, or I should have asked to have the point made clear before he left.

On the evening of 21st March, Sir Charles Fergusson arrived at the Royal Hospital, in order to report on the situation. I was present at that interview. He told Sir Arthur Paget that he felt that he had gone greatly beyond his instructions. Officers had asked him whether the instructions, which he had given them, had His Majesty's personal authority, and he had given them that assurance. Sir Charles explained that his reason for so doing was that he found that nothing less would induce them to obey.

I do not pretend to be able to quote Sir Charles Fergusson's remarks literally—but he left me under the clearest impression that he at that time realised that he had made, on his own authority, an unauthorised use of His Majesty's name, and that he was anxious to explain to Sir Arthur how strong the reasons were which had led him to do so.

It was not until early in April that I discovered, in conversation with Sir Charles Fergusson, that he was under the impression that he had had Sir Arthur's authority for the action which he had taken.

BL, Add Mss 51250, Paget Mss; PRO, WO35/209 (f)

PART 3
THE LEGACY IN THE ARMY
MARCH TO JULY 1914

188
Major-General L. B. Friend to
Brigadier-General G. T. Forestier-Walker

Holywood,
Belfast.

[Holograph]

22 March 1914

I write to you as I have been told the Chief is travelling about, possibly on his way here, so I may not catch him at once with this letter: but will you please give him the information as soon as possible.

All is very quiet & normal in Belfast and District—and all our information shows the determination of the Ulster Protestant party to keep cool & quiet & prevent any disturbance of the peace.

We have here ready to turn out at short notice:

1 Norfolks—400 trained men
1 Dorsets—300 trained men
1 Section Signal Co   ⎫
1 Section R.E. Field Co   ⎭ from the Curragh
1 Coy ASC from Belfast

The barracks are crowded but not uncomfortably so—the horses, 43, are picketed in the open. The Reserve Arms and Ammunition are stored at the Guard House and in one Barrack Block.

At Belfast 1 off. & 50 men 1 Dorsets, the depot of the RI Rifles and details.

At Carrickfergus 1 company of 2 KOYLI half in the castle & half in the Antrim RGA Bks.

I have been *unable* to get in the following arms & ammunition.

NI Horse in Belfast 100 rifles 13000 rounds SAA
Newtownards   75 rifles a few rounds SAA

333

and I consider it very inadvisable to make any further attempt to do so at present.

I have published an order describing the Belfast District which comprises Bangor, Newtownards, Comber, Lisburn, Antrim, Larne. Commander—Myself. SNO Capt. C. D. Johnson HMS Attentive, Bangor. OC Troops Br. Genl. Count Gleichen.

The communication between Holywood Barracks & the 'Attentive' is difficult at present—owing to want of facilities to connect the warship to the shore but the SNO & the Signal Coy Officer are now arranging a better plan. The wireless messages to & from the Attentive are picked up by several private wireless apparatus on the surrounding properties, but I cannot say if they are *properly* received. Cipher messages are therefore necessary for wireless communication. The instructions for communicating by way of Port Patrick & Holyhead are understood.

The RIC Commissioner in Belfast is in constant communication with me but there is nothing to report as yet.

There has been very little question among the troops here of any officer wishing to resign: and I *most strongly* urge that if the option be given to them it may be given to CO's only—for them to use or not (at their discretion) to their officers. I am confident that no resignations will then take place. The discretion will admit of any officer who feels strongly on the political question being left in charge of Bks, etc. should the troops have to move out in support of the C.P. There are only 1 or 2 at the outside in each Bttn.

I am afraid you have all had a baddish time at Dublin. I expect to be back tomorrow or Tuesday but have no definite news of Macready.

All the troops here are on friendly terms with the people around: the Dorsets are very popular in Belfast. PS. We hear nothing here of any further moves.

PRO, WO 35/209 (k)

189
Lieutenant-General Sir Arthur Paget to
J. E. B. Seely

Parkgate,
Dublin.

[Draft Holograph]

[23] March 1914

I have the honour to report that the situation at Belfast and elsewhere in this country remains peaceful.

A Section of a Field Coy and a Detachment ASC, sent to reinforce the troops at Holywood, Belfast, have arrived without incident.

On the subject of Intelligence, one of my Staff Officers interviewed Sir Neville Chamberlain yesterday with a view to collecting such intelligence as had been already gained by the civil police.

He ascertained that practically no information of any value had been obtained, and formed the opinion that little of value was to be expected from that source.

Although, as my Assistant Military Secretary will have informed the Chief of the Imperial General Staff verbally, I am now assured that the officers of the 5th Division will carry out such orders as they may receive with regard to active operations in Ulster, I am still to some extent in the dark as to the possible attitude of the rank and file. It is generally expected, and in this view I concur, that the men will follow their officers, but feeling on the subject is undoubtedly very bitter, and it is possible that the opinion which I hold may be even largely falsified by events. In this connection one of my officers overheard last night, in a street in Dublin, a civilian, wearing medals, say to another that he had just left the Sergeants' Mess of his old Regiment, and that the Sergeants had declared that neither they nor their men intended to move against Ulster, whatever might be the attitude adopted by the officers. The officer subsequently engaged the speaker in conversation, and was informed by him that he was an ex-sergeant of the Royal West Kent Regt. The discipline of the Battalion alluded to is in my opinion very high, and the story as related by this ex-NCO is almost certainly absolutely untrue. I think it advisable, however, to report it.

The Officer Commanding the Depot at Omagh reports that, though he has no proof, he is of opinion that some 10 per cent of the permanent staff of the Royal Inniskilling Fusiliers, chiefly N.C. officers, cannot be relied on.[76]

Should it be found necessary to establish martial law in Ireland, the Royal Irish Constabulary will presumably, come under my control. I have for some time been of opinion that the Inspector General of that Force is a man lacking in character and initiative, and, in the event alluded to, I consider that it would be advisable to replace Sir Neville Chamberlain by an officer in whom I could repose greater confidence.

PRO, WO 35/209 (i)

190

Captain F. A. Forster to his family

1st Royal Fusiliers,
Spike Island,
Queenstown.
24 March 1914

[Holograph]

Alright m'dear. You may be quite sure none of us are going to fight the U.V.F. Police duty one must do if required, as we've often had to before, much as we hate it.

My mind was made up some time ago—the only question that troubled us was—whether it was 'playing the game' to hang on until the last moment and then chuck one's hand in, and so let in the regiment, & give a direct example of mutiny. Should one not have resigned when the thing was coming on?

Now however the Govt: have prevented that by telling us as they did on Sat: that if you resign you'll be courtmartialled & forfeit everything, & by refusing to allow us to use our consciences at all. So now I'd have not the least compunction in putting my hands in my pockets & walking off directly police duty *in my own* opinion turns into civil strife. We know where we are now.

'Goffy' is splendid & I'm so glad I know him. Everybody loves him, & will now more than ever.

Everybody thinks as above—we don't need any Irishmen in the regt: to make us do that. Hely[77] lives just out of Ulster & feels very strongly of course, & like Bald[78] & so many others has a family dependent on his profession, & he's within 2 or 3 years of getting command, but that wouldn't influence him in the slightest. A lot has been said about the Cavalry B'de. but the Infantry are just as determined. It was brought to a head by the Cavalry being ordered to go & being told it was expected Ulster would be in a blaze by Sat: last.

The officers of an Inf: regt: in Dublin also refused to go and personally I can't conceive that *any* regiment out here will act except as police—as we've had to do in Belfast several times already.

If there's any fighting now it will be Army & U.V.F. against Nationalists.

All my friends in Ireland whose houses I've ever stayed in are registered to go & support Ulster.

IWM, P. 473 (4), Forster Mss

191

Major-General Sir Charles Fergusson to Lieutenant Colonel I. G. Hogg

Ballyfair,
Curragh.
[Typescript Copy]   25 March 1914

On thinking it over, I feel just at present you and I had better not discuss this business at all together.

I should be very sorry to say anything against your Brigadier or the line which he took up, and it would not be fair for me to do any such thing in conversation with you—And it is almost inevitable that something of the sort might occur.

I have assured him and the officers who sided with him that none of us will do anything that could create feeling; that I respect his feelings as I expect him to respect mine, and that on no account must we allow ourselves to drift into two separate parties in camp.

That being so, the less we discuss the thing the better.

I have heard his story of what passed in London, and that of C-in-C so I am more or less acquainted with the situation.

I am sure you wont think me rude, and if I can help at any time or in any way with advice or talk in a non-contentious way, you know that I will gladly do so—But I feel that just at present we had better do nothing that might lead to discussion of our superiors.

Pragnell Mss

192
Lieutenant Colonel de la Panouse to the French Minister of War, Joseph Noulens

25 March 1914

Les Incidents d'Irlande et les démissions des officiers

... J'ai appris d'une manière tout-à-fait confidentielle que si les officiers démissionnaires n'étaient pas ré-integrés dans leur commandement, avec promesse que des opérations actives ne seraient pas entreprises avec le concours de l'armée Régulière, des démissions entre grand nombre se produiraient à l'Etat-Major Général et aussi dans beaucoup de garnisons.

C'est la crainte de ces démissions en masse qui a obligé le Gouvt. à remplacer les officiers démissionnaires ...

... La question de l'intervention de l'armée dans les conflits sociaux sera sans doute agitée; d'autre part le caractère aristocratique du corps d'officiers sera violemment attaqué par les partis radicaux. A ce point de vue, les incidents de Curragh sont malheureux pour l'unité de l'Armée. Un Gouvt. avisé eut dû les prévoir et les éviter . . .

Pour un observateur impartial, il semble que les éxigences de l'Ulster sont inacceptables. L'Ulster a toujours été le maître de l'Irlande. Il se résigne mal à se voir en minorité dans le futur Parlement de Dublin. En somme il combat pour ne pas être gouverné par ceux qu'il a dominés de tout temps. Pour maintenir ses hommes, il a soulevé les passions religieuses, et a ainsi transporté la lutte sur un autre terrain. Celà n'est pas pour rendre sa cause sympathique . . .

Vincennes, Etat-Major de l'Armée de Terre, Box No. 7 N 1228, 279

193
Major-General Sir Charles Fergusson to his brother, Captain J. Fergusson, RN[79]

[Holograph]

Ballyfair,
Curragh.
25 March 1914

It is not difficult to see from the tone of relations' letters that I am a fallen idol! That does not worry me, but to one or two I want to put the considerations which led me to take my stand on what I call the side of discipline, and to which, having made up my mind, I shall stick.

People who are not in the position of having personal responsibility for masses of men hardly realise one's feelings when there is a risk of these men getting out of hand, nor of the danger if they are not held together by their commander.

Needless to say what my inclinations were. All personal considerations invited me to do what Gough did; and if anything could strengthen those feelings it was the 'ultimatum' put to me on Friday last.

But

1st. A soldier must stick to the first principle, obedience to the King and constituted authority. If one lets go of that principle, one is all at sea, and can argue oneself into anything. So long as the King sticks to his Ministers and sanctions the orders to the troops I hold that a soldier has no option but to obey. 2nd *Responsibility*. We officers have all the responsibility of being able to influence, in a greater or less degree according to rank and position, those serving under us. One cannot consider only one's *personal* state and feelings, one must look beyond and see what would be the effect of our decisions on those under us. I may be willing to accept dismissal from the Service myself, but I am not prepared to draw others into the risk of losing everything because of their loyalty to me. Nor should regimental officers forget that their example may bring their men into a position which entails court martial and degradation on them because they follow their officers. 3rd *Logically*, if we officers refuse to fight against our friends, are we prepared to accept the same argument from our men when they are called on to fight their friends in labour disputes etc! 4th The far reaching consequences of our action. If the Army breaks up, and discipline is allowed to become dependent on personal considerations, what is there between the country and revolution? Look at the position in S. Africa the other day.[80] Is it not probable that the same may arise here anyday? In such an event, Ulster and Home Rule become a mere side show. Without a united Army with strong discipline, nothing can save King and Country when the crisis comes. Therefore I will do nothing that will in any way weaken the discipline of the Army, which I hold to be the paramount consideration.

If anything were needed to confirm me in what I've said, look at John Ward's speech last night. Can anyone doubt that it is now going to be a General Election, not on the question of Ulster and Home Rule, but on the cry of 'People versus King and Army'? What will be the result, goodness only knows. But I believe that a revolution is the danger, not Ulster and Home Rule.

It seems to me that those who applaud Gough and his officers are unable to look beyond their noses and see the awful consequences that may come of their action. It is a fine thing, no doubt, to have dished the Govt. by combined action, but the first people to use the same weapon against ourselves will be our troops to whom we have set an example. I don't blame Gough & Co. They acted up to their opinions, but I hold them to be absolutely deluded and wrong. They don't see that they are being used as a tool by the politicians against the Government, and that the weapon will recoil against themselves (a mixed metaphor, but no matter). No doubt it is equally true that the other side proposed to use the Army as their tool. But my answer to that is simply to come back to my original argument: *a soldier's duty is to obey his King and constituted authority*. Lose sight of that, and you can argue into believing that wrong can be right.

The papers are full of the magnificent and heroic action of Gough and his officers, I fully admit them to all credit. But I claim that those who have stood for the other side have had just as hard a struggle and deserve equal praise. They had nothing to fear; in combined action, there is safety. They could not all be court martialled and dismissed. To resist was a course of action that appeals to sentiment and the public; they took the dull and humdrum way of duty, as taught from time immemorial. Dozens of them are being reviled and misunderstood by their friends and relations and they knew this would be the case. But I believe that in keeping the principle of discipline intact, and remaining loyal to authority in the face of awful temptation, they have done right; and society before long will recognise it.

Gough and his officers may have saved Ulster from Home Rule and dished the Government. But they have dealt a blow to discipline from which we shan't recover for a generation, and have started a cry in the country of which no one can foresee the consequences.

I know the argument that civil war cancels all obligations, and of course it is incontestable. But the split must not come till the last moment. The Army must not take the extreme step of taking sides to influence one party or the other in advance.

Can anyone after this have the slightest confidence in such an Army? As the Germans I see are putting it, we have shown what they always said, that as an Army we are not worth consideration. 'The British Army does not enjoy the same respect in the country as ours does; they have now shown they do not deserve it.'

I do not care how soon I leave the Service. But I shall always be proud that my Division stuck to me in the face of the Cavalry's example and public abuse, and showed that duty and discipline and loyalty were not only catchwords. The whole thing is breaking my heart but I know it is right.

You might send this on to S.G.[81] I haven't time to write fully to her. You two are the only ones whose opinion matters twopence to me, and at least I should like you both to know my point of view.

Fergusson Mss

194

Lieutenant Colonel I. G. Hogg to General Sir Alexander Montgomery Moore[82]

[Typescript]

4th Hussars
25 March 1914

I must ask your forgiveness for not having written to you before but, as you will understand, my time has been very fully occupied and I only returned from London last night.

It is true that all the officers of this regiment, including myself, felt compelled at one time to threaten to tender our resignations. Later it appeared that the reasons on which we have done so were based on complete misunderstanding of a verbal message from the Commander of the Forces in Ireland, and the incident is now satisfactorily closed. No officer in the brigade, so far as I am aware, denies his duty to carry out all orders issued by our superiors for the maintenance of law and order in any part of the King's Dominions.

I sincerely trust that the Press will allow the subject to drop and not attempt to drag the arguing into the political arena.

PS. Most of what appears in the press is fabrication. No orders were issued at any time for any unit of this brigade to mass anywhere and therefore none were disobeyed.

Pragnell Mss

195
General Sir Alexander Montgomery Moore
to Lieutenant Colonel I. G. Hogg

Hastings

[Typescript Copy]   26 March 1914

Thanks for your letter. I sent a message through you which no doubt you gave to the officers of my Regiment that I was proud of belonging to the Regiment—for resigning rather than serve against their own countrymen in Ulster, who had made no disturbance.

I fail to see where the misunderstanding comes in—I judge not from the stories in the papers but from the statements in the House of Commons.

The incident does not seem to me to be closed.

I think the country owes a debt of gratitude to General Gough, and the officers of two of the Cavalry Regiments (I regret not to see the 4th mentioned) who have not allowed themselves to be deflected by any political theories of misunderstanding from the time [sic] they at first took up.

It is impossible not to believe, whatever Mr. Winston Churchill may say, that active operations to enforce Home Rule were not intended in Ulster.

PS. Though this letter is private I have no objection to your showing it to any officers in the Regiment.

Pragnell Mss

343

196

Brigadier-General Count A. E. W. Gleichen to Brigadier-General G. T. Forestier-Walker

Belfast
[Holograph]   27 March 1914

I don't know who is responsible—I'm sure it's not you personally, & it smells strongly of Williams[83]—but I really must protest strongly at being woken up at 5 a.m. to receive & *decipher* (some of it wrong) a long message 'In view of the present situation necessary to act with special discretion in order to avoid giving any impression etc.' (for three more lines). *Surely*, if it was necessary to send this at all, it could have been sent by ordinary post en clair. And I think that I might be trusted, being on the spot & in command, not to be such a b. .y fool as to make a splash of any military action I chose to take: considering that our *one* object here is to keep things as quiet as possible.

I had already given Williams a rap over the knuckles about another long & futile message in cypher that he sent us, but he seems incapable of taking a hint.

I'm sorry to hear that you are likely to have trouble, in the South: but if so, you won't have any trouble about officers' resignations! What a glorious bungle it all is! The profoundest peace reigns here.

PRO, WO 35/209 (n)

197

New Army Order issued on 27 March 1914

1. No officer or soldier shall in future be questioned by his superior officer as to the attitude he will adopt, or as to his action, in the event of his being required to obey orders dependent upon future or hypothetical contingencies.

344

2. An officer or soldier is forbidden in future to ask for assurances as to the orders which he may be required to carry out.

3. In particular, it is the duty of every officer and soldier to obey all lawful commands given to them through the proper channel, either for the safe-guarding of public property or the support of the civil power in the ordinary execution of its duty, or for the protection of the lives and property of the inhabitants in the case of the disturbance of the peace.

Hansard 5 s, H. of C., LX 785; RA GV F.674/43; PRO, WO 163/20; H. of Lords RO, Bonar Law Mss 39/2/21; Nuffield College, Ms Mottistone 22, f 263

198
General Sir Alexander Montgomery Moore to Lieutenant Colonel I. G. Hogg

Hastings

[Typescript]   30 March 1914

I was very glad to get your letter of 28th. Please understand that I neither approved or disapproved of your 'subsequent action', being so utterly in the dark as to what took place. I wired at once when I heard the first reports to ask if they were true and received answer that they were not at present—I then saw in the papers that you were lunching with Mr. Churchill and from what I gathered from other reports you had disassociated yourselves from the other two Regiments and the 4th seemed studiously to be kept out of the official and private statements of the occurrence.

I could only attribute this to the influence that had been brought upon you especially as I was still without a reply to my letter. In such a position I think most people would have come to the conclusion that I did. Your letter today of course has put a different complexion on the matter, and I must say General Paget's strong guarantee left you full discretion either to accept it or to act on your former decision. I quite agree with what you say that each man must be guided by his own conscience in advising those under him, and I am far from saying, not having been placed in your position, that I disapprove of the conclusion you came to.

I am sorry if the tone of my second letter has given a sore feeling—It was written without knowing what the reasons were for the 4th being so suddenly separated from the position the rest of the Brigade had taken up and the silence tended to create the position more unintelligible.

All this is made clear by your letter. I am sure you and the officers did what seemed to you to be straight forward and right under the circumstances.

I may add of course in confidence that had your resignations been adopted I should at once have asked to be allowed to send in mine—of the Colonelcy of the Regiment.

P.S. You can let the officers know the contents of this.

Pragnell Mss

199
Brigadier-General H. P. Gough to Major-General H. H. Wilson

Marlfield,
Clonmel.

[Holograph]   30 March 1914

I enclose letter for Sir J.F.'s eyes,[84] or as much of it as you think wise to tell him. It is a difficult one to write. The idea running in my head is that I don't want to make his position impossible, & *if* he does remain, that he can meet me & other officers without feeling shame so acutely as to undermine all discipline, outwardly and inwardly.

But as regards the Army as a whole, in spite of the further trouble & complications that may arise, I personally cannot see how he can expect to retain his own self-respect, or *keep up the honour of the Army*, except by firmly sticking to his resignation. But that is only my opinion & may be worth little.

IWM, 73/1/18, Wilson Mss

200

Brigadier-General H. P. Gough to Major-General H. H. Wilson

Marlfield,
Clonmel.
[Holograph]   30 March 1914

Many thanks for your letter which I answered by wire as best I could, as requested. I hope it was clear.

I hope you will thank Sir John for his first message saying that he fully trusts me & does not believe the astounding lies (for this they are) of my interviews with correspondents, for I have not accorded them any interviews.

As regards the second part of your letter, I would again ask you to thank him very much for putting the question as he did, & whatever he decides to do, he can rest assured that I will not feel that any disloyalty to his own word to me is intended. At the same time, I must make my own position clear, & that is, that I stand exactly where I did on Friday, the 20th, when the question of taking part in civil war was put to me, and on Monday 23rd inst, when I left the War Office to take up command of the 3rd Cavalry Brigade, of which I had been previously deprived, only on the distinct guarantee of what I took to be the Government, that I should not be called on to enforce the present Home Rule Bill on Ulster. The repudiation by the Government does not alter my position in the slightest, & if the Government likes to deceive me, I on the contrary, have not the slightest intention of deceiving the Government & I remain in command of the 3rd Cavalry Brigade, & in the Army, on that understanding.

IWM, 73/1/18, Wilson Mss

201
Brigadier-General H. P. Gough to Commodore R. J. B. Keyes

Marlfield,
Clonmel.
[Holograph]   31 March 1914

Many thanks for your nice letter. It has been a damnable time, but the original decision was, luckily, laid before one, so clearly, that one could hardly do anything else. Johnnie was simply splendid, & far more of a 'tiger' in my cause than he would even have been in his own! He, McEwen, & Parker were my supporters & held up my arms during the struggle like Aaron did for Moses[85] — & so I am going to frame my resignation, with their 3 photos round it, & write those verses of Exodus (which I had some difficulty in finding!) underneath!!

I was very interested to hear about Mrs. Spender. Is it possible that people in such positions & calling themselves ladies & gentlemen would deliberately concoct such a hellish plot? There was not one word of truth in it & I have never interviewed the *Daily News* or any other correspondent.

But Seely has gone all the same—thank God! And what with other changes in high places in the War Office, I now hope a straighter & more honourable spirit will pervade all the officers of the army, for like all such things they 'must come from the top'.

I hope we meet again soon, & I can then tell you all about it. Best remembrances to Eva (if I may have the privilege of so addressing her)—& again many thanks.

BL, Keyes Mss, 3/17

202

Memorandum by Brigadier-General G. T. Forestier-Walker on the Distinction between the Use of Troops for the Purpose of Quelling Disorder and the Use of Troops to Coerce Ulster to accept the Home Rule Bill

[Holograph] [March 1914]

1. The assumption is made that a secret or semi-secret promise has been given to the troops, or to a portion of the troops, that in no case will they be asked to take part in the coercion of Ulster by force to the acceptance of Home Rule.

2. It is also assumed that the troops will be ready to obey all orders received for the preservation of order as apart from the coercion of Ulster.

3. It is believed by the troops that an attempt may be made by the Government, either to coerce Ulster directly under the plea of preserving law and order, or indirectly by military occupation of Ulster under the same plea, in such a manner as to prevent or prejudice any subsequent resistance that the organised Anti-Home Rule Force can make either before or after the act actually becomes law.

It is immaterial whether this belief on the part of the troops is justified or not. It is sufficient that it undoubtedly exists, and that nothing but the most explicit public assurance on the part of the Prime Minister, that under no circumstances whatever will the Army be used to force Home Rule on Ulster, will remove it.

4. It is assumed for the purposes of this memorandum that such an assurance will not be forthcoming.

5. On the above assumption, the troops, or that portion of them directly affected by the promise assumed in para: 1, will, in the absence of some definite and easily understandable condition and being imbued with the belief mentioned in para: 3, consider that

349

they must themselves decide when proposed action crosses the borderline between preservation of order and coercion.

6. It is obvious that this question cannot be left to the troops to decide individually, and therefore it appears essential that some definite condition must be found, simple enough to be understood without equivocation, and applicable to all circumstances likely to arise in Ulster.

7. It must I think be taken for granted that the action of any organised bodies of the Ulster Volunteers, working under their responsible leaders in obedience to orders issued by Sir E. Carson or his lieutenants, is action taken against coercion. This must be considered to be the case, however stupid it may appear to be for the purpose intended, and however much it may tend to bring about rioting and bloodshed.

It follows, therefore, that any counter-action taken by the troops in such a case falls under the heading of action against coercion, and not under the heading of quelling disorder.

8. Consequently, the first article of the necessary condition would appear to be that the troops (or the portion of them concerned) must not be asked to take action under any circumstances against Ulster Volunteers acting in obedience to Sir E. Carson's orders given directly, or through his responsible lieutenants.

Of course, it is obvious that such an arrangement means that Sir Edward Carson (and not the Commander of the troops) is the dominating factor. This cannot be helped.

9. It might be argued that such an arrangement would be impracticable in its application.

For instance, let us assume that a body of Ulster Volunteers are engaged in a fight with a body of the Ancient Order of Hibernians. What in this case should be the attitude of the Troops?

The obvious answer can be given at once. The Ancient Order of Hibernians cannot compel Ulster to accept Home Rule, and therefore this is not a case of coercion.

Further it is inconceivable that Ulster Volunteers under Sir E. Carson's control would be engaged in a fight with the Ancient Order of Hibernians except for their own protection.

So this case falls naturally into the law and order clause.

Let us, however, take another case. It has been suggested that the Ulster Volunteers might be fighting with the Royal Irish Constabulary, and that, in such a case, the boundary line between law and order on the one side and compulsion on the other side, might be difficult to define. This case does not appear to me to present any difficulties. The Royal Irish Constabulary will be under the control of the Military Authorities and therefore the case cannot arise.

10. It is clear, however, that no attempt must be made by the authorities to seize the Post Office or Custom House or otherwise prevent the establishment of the Provisional Government, whether carried out by means of the troops or the Royal Irish Constabulary acting under the Military Commander.

11. If the above conclusions are correct, it would seem that no other definition is required than that given in para: 8.

But the further conclusion arising out of a review of these arguments appears to be simple and unanswerable. It is that, if it is clearly laid down that under no circumstances will the Army be required to act against Ulster Volunteers working under Sir E. Carson's orders, then there can be no coercion.

12. The only remaining point is the difficulty of discovering when the Ulster Volunteers are working under Sir E. Carson's orders, and when they are loose on their own. There may be difficulties with regard to this, but as the action of the Military will in any case be deliberate (as it always is in riots), there should usually be plenty of opportunity of interviewing the momentary leaders. Undoubtedly Sir Edward and his chief men will co-operate fully in this.

PRO, WO 35/209 (h)

203
Major-General Sir Henry Rawlinson to
Major-General H. H. Wilson

Cholderton House,
Cholderton,
Salisbury.

[Holograph]   1 April 1914

As an instance of the deep concern which regimental officers
take in politics witness their remarks on the fat man's latest army
order.[86] On reading it in the mess last week they came and all said
'Well thank God that's the end of all staff rides and these damned
Regimental tours'. Read the first para again and you will see how
well it applies to the cunundrums usually set at all tactical
exercises. I see A.C. [Repington] talks of Smith D[orrien] as A.G.
This would never do and S.I. knows it—it would kill Smith D in
the first place and the brain storms would explode the office
though he has been better lately. I could do A.G. better myself.
Let S.D. succeed S.I. [Hamilton] as I.G.H.F. and put Coddy or
Belfield[87] into A.G. See you at the summer races? We are at
Englemere for the weekend.

IWM, 73/1/18, Wilson Mss

204
Major P. Howell to
J. Ramsay Macdonald

4th Hussars,
Stewart Barracks,
Curragh.

[Holograph]   3 April 1914

The more I think over our dinner last Monday the more
convinced I feel that our interests coincide—mine as an officer
anxious for army reform and yours as a labour leader?

You want *impartiality*, an army which will not unduly favour the Tories & distrust radical reform. We want *efficiency*, a good stamp of recruit & plenty of them, i.e. establishments up to strength; and more competition, more professionalism in the officer class or rank.

Neither impartiality nor efficiency can be got by a sweep of the pen & the only immediately practical step is to organise a sound system of promotion from the ranks. A stratum of rankers of the right sort would soon break down prejudices & make itself felt. Seeley [sic] has tackled & more or less solved, perhaps, the question of the ranker's pay. But that's not enough. We must also decide (a) the process of selection, which cannot be left to mere chance (b) the education after selection and (c) the eventual posting after education.

The great initial difficulty, in my opinion, will be the lack of suitable candidates, not the opposition with which the scheme will be received. At present we get in the army little more than the sweepings of the population: & shall continue to do so until the army offers a real career to those who remain in it & civil employment to those who leave.

Opposition there will be, of course, but not nearly as strong as you, probably, suppose. The army officer is always in close contact with men who represent the masses & the more senior officers (those whose opinions carry weight) have always seen a good deal of the world. They may be very narrow minded when they enter the army but the longer they stay in it the less Tory they tend to become.

If Labour leaders & army officers could be persuaded to recognise their mutual interests and pull together how quickly things would move. Rank ignorance of each other's aims & motives, is the bane of both sides but I don't altogether despair about getting that removed. Meanwhile the more often representatives of both parties meet & compare their points of view the better. So I shall send friends to call upon you, if I may; & I trust that you will help me to come in contact with your colleagues, as opportunities occur!

The moment seems to me opportune to start the first step to get

353

the ranker officer firmly on his legs; because the army is now in the lime light & because there's a big man in the WO. Because, also, we officers know, in spite of Seeley's [sic] efforts to conceal the truth, that the present system, regular & territorial, is a sham; we know that the army is unready for war & that things are going from bad to worse; we realise, therefore, that radical changes must be made & are, so to speak, in a receptive frame of mind.

National service or conscription of any sort your party, you say, could never support. Military service, however, is horribly expensive whatever form it takes & becomes more so year by year. For compulsory service you pay in wealth, which might have been in phantom figures which not all of us can count. For voluntary service (professional is a better word) you have to pay in actual cash, sums we can all see & realise. I believe, therefore, that this cash limit must sooner or later be realised and then the majority will say 'Well, as we can't afford the chauffeurs, we must drive the cars ourselves'—irrespective of the time or wealth we thereby lose. However, we are perhaps a long way off from that & the more important problem for the moment is to keep professional service going by widening the recruiting areas for both officers & men. At present we seem to tap too much the two extremes, those sufficiently well off to be able to lend their services to the state for next to nothing; & those who have sunk to the bitter bottom. The former, by settling an unnecessarily high standard of living shut out the 'upper middles'; and the latter in keeping down the social tone shut out the 'lower middles'. But you can't *force* the 'middles' to be soldiers; you can't *make* them be received as welcome guests by either officers or rank & file. You can only smooth the way.

Forgive this rigmarole. I seem to see day light in the distance but find it very difficult to define!

PRO, 30/69/1158, Macdonald Mss

205
Major P. Howell to C. Wigram

4th Hussars,
Stewart Barracks,
Curragh.
[Holograph] 3 April 1914

After all I had to catch the evening mail back here & to cut the Chatham dinner; which I hope was worth attending. Here things are in a turmoil again & I'd like you to know how the land lies. Because unless something is done the whole business may burst into flames once more. First, all the generals are furious with A.P. for allowing a false account of the original interview to be published in the House. It's quite absurd for him to lay all the blame on them & they much resent the imputation though how far their resentment may carry them I do not know. Secondly, Hogg & all we 4th Hussars consider ourselves left in the lurch. A bald statement to the effect that Hogg withdrew his resignation, when the others did not, fully fits in with a widespread theory that the 4th Hussars funked when it came to the point and failed to follow Goughie because they put pensions etc. before loyalty to the Brigade. Taunts to that effect have been received from the colonel (full colonel) of the regiment who wrote Hogg a most objectionable letter.[88]

In reality we know that A.P. knows, and the Government & the W.O. must know too, that that was not the case. We adhered consistently to the terms of the letter sent by Gough to Paget on the evening of the 20th March.[89] When A.P. came to the Curragh on the morning of the 21st; answered, verbally, that letter in satisfactory terms; appealed to us to trust and support him; and brought in the name of the King, *then* & not till then, Hogg withdrew his resignation. We (Hogg & self) consider, & still consider, that we took the most loyal & most sensible course but that of course is a mere matter of opinion. We were quite content to put up with incorrect imputations feeling that either these would be based on mere surmise (because the case would be kept confidential) or that they would be proved to be false (because the whole truth would be published). The publication of a half-truth which happens to fit in with false theories is not fair. They should publish the whole story or nothing. Hogg, whose name has been used so freely, feels so strongly on the matter that he has written to say that his name must be cleared or he will resign in order to be free to clear it himself.

I quite acknowledge that the matter is a small one & that from the big point of view we ought to let it rest. But still we small people live in small circles; & their own reputation & the reputations of their regiments loom very large whenever they are questioned.

There must be some very big reason why the Government go on concealing Paget's instructions & letting him conceal his actions, but it seems to be a dangerous & a losing game!

PS. When this affair is ended I want to go on with *naval* education—Did you ever get hold of that report?

RA GV F.674/59

206

Brigadier-General H. P. Gough to Brigadier-General J. E. Gough

Brownstown House,
Curragh.
[Holograph]   3 April 1914

I have a lot of little things I want to tell you. I sent you some documents yesterday by J, with a very hurried line which only dealt with the subject matter of the papers enclosed.
Re Paget (who has shown himself (1) unscrupulous scoundrel, in selling himself to the Govt. & furthering their plot. (2) a liar— (3)a coward—)—see a good leading article in M. Post of 2nd. inst.—I sincerely trust he goes.

1) About Wed. 25th March. (the day after my return, from W.O. General Friend (M.G.i/cA) motored down to see me

privately. He said, Paget knew he was coming but did not know what he was going to say.

He said Paget felt in a difficult position as I had a guarantee which he had not, & that in case he wanted to move troops, I could go a certain way & then produce the guarantee & say— no further. Could I, as an act of grace & friendly feeling towards Paget, go to Paget and say 'I place myself unreservedly in your hands?'

I said—No—I would obey all military orders of Paget's in a loyal way (the proviso about Ulster being understood) but I saw no necessity for, & I objected to, any personal interviews. I then told Friend why—viz—my objection to the dishonourable & puerile suggestions put before us by Paget, on Sat. 21st March. Friend then asked if he could take away the guarantee!! I said he could have a copy—the original was in safe custody. He did not want the copy & would not take one away!! That interview ended.

2) I now enclose a copy of a private letter from Watson Cheyne to his boy[90] & my comments on the same, which I have asked the boy to show & explain to his Father. The principal point is that again, an attempt is made to get us to give up the guarantee! This time through a woman—(Mrs. A. is Mrs. Asquith)

It seems to me that they want us to give up the guarantee quietly & then turn round & place us in the false position of acquiesing in the Government repudiation, of acknowledging that we originally took up a wrong position, that we are now sorry & acknowledge our fault, that the Govt. will be completely white-washed, & will graciously tell us to be good boys in future & not offend again!

2) [sic] I also enclose a letter from H.W. on French's behalf, & my answer by wire, & by letter[91]—You will recognize the phrase in both my answer, & my comments on the Cheyne letter!

3) Of course you know that Hogg is not trustworthy, but he is not as dangerous, as he has neither courage or nerve. But I want to warn you against Howell. I may be wrong, but it is as well to be careful. He is very deep. He is of course very much influenced

by his excitable & Radical wife.[92] But on another occasion, over buying a horse, he did not behave at all straightly. Over this business, his attitude throughout was entirely that of sitting on the fence. Now that we are (temporarily!) on top he feels his position uncomfortable. He is now in London—I believe seeing people at the W.O. He is sure to see Robertson. He never let me know that he was going over; I only found it out by chance this morning. What does he want to do or say in London?

Hogg is in close correspondence with Winston—through him Howell may be also. Hogg sent secretly to the correspondent of the Irish Times from Dublin the other day, & was closetted with him for an hour. The gist of it all, was to get it published that the whole affair was a stupid misunderstanding. I suppose Winston was the instigator here.

This was discovered by the accident of the correspondent (or editor) concerned travelling back to Dublin in the same carriage as MacEwen, & as they were great friends, the Irish Times man asked M what sort of fellow Hogg was, & told him what had occurred— I doubt whether any official demand will be made for the guarantee, but if it is, shall I come over & see you before dealing with the matter?

I received a private letter from Friend yesterday saying that we could slack off 'gradually' our warlike preparations (such as ball ammunition in barrack rooms etc.), & resume 'normal' conditions—Personally we never made any warlike preparation in this Brigade, but it is one more proof of the deliberate plot that was contemplated which has now fallen through. Why was the situation abnormal on the 18 March & why is it normal now?

3.45 p.m. Since writing the above, several incidents have occurred which might make one modify bits of it.

(1) I received the enclosed letter from Hogg.[93] His weak action, as so often happens,—has placed him in a false light. But I honestly think he is genuine on this point, & that what he says was his genuine attitude, although of course it was undoubtedly sitting on the fence.

Howell, I went down to see him, as an act of peace. I am doing all I can, on principle, not to allow fellows who did not go the whole hog with us, feel that we have no ill feelings towards them, and that we are all still brothers & comrades

Hogg was writing to *McKenna*—& I think! calls him Reggie—anyhow his letter began, My dear Reggie,—I could not help seeing.

Somewhat to my surprise Howell walked in! He had apparently returned this morning. He told me he had spent 2 days with Haig, so perhaps you saw him? Of course, I may be wrong about him, but so many of my suspicions have been aroused, that I begin to suspect all sorts of people.

The second incident I want to tell you of, is that Hookie [Forestier-] Walker has just been in here. He came down to see all the Generals here & to privately show them a letter Paget had written to Asquith, demanding that in order to clear his honour a full statement of the facts of the Friday interview should be made public.

However, A.P.—after consulting French—& seeing Asquith, came to the conclusion that he would withdraw his demand as it would so greatly embarrass the Government.

How much of this was eye-wash & how much real I don't know. I think Hookie is genuine enough. I also gather that, at present, Paget has no idea of resigning!! And is quite prepared to meet us quite bravely, & as if nothing had happened.

I also enclose some letters from Chetwode,[94] out of fairness to him. Of course he is a poor creature, but I don't want to throw our victory & their weakness in these fellows' teeth, & so really break up the Army.

What is the political & military situation?

I am running Greatheart at Fairyhouse & Punchestown. This affords me a pleasant interest from affairs of state and intrigues etc.

Love to D.

J. E. Gough Mss

207
Brigadier-General H. P. Gough to
Major-General H. H. Wilson

Brownstown House,
Curragh.

[Holograph]   7 April 1914

I was away hunting in Carlow yesterday & did not get back until past 7 p.m. when I found your letter. I wired to you & hope that you did manage to catch Johnnie & get the papers you want copied. But, if not, I will send you everything when I get it all back from him. He arrives here this evening about 8 p.m.—too late for me to catch tonight's mail with the papers.

Could you let me know somehow what developments might arise? I always like to see my enemy coming, & not 'bump into him' as A.P. so wisely said!!

Did you see Tuesday's M. Post?—very straight, & unpleasant for some people. They are wrong in a minor point, however, & as facts are important these days, I will explain. I did not have a separate & lone interview with A.P. first. I was wired for on Thursday night, and as were Fergusson & his Generals, & I suppose Hill.

We all met at 10 a.m. on Friday (20th inst.) at the H.Q.'s office. There were 6 Generals & 1 Colonel present at this—the first interview—; Fergusson, Rolt, Cuthbert, Forestier-Walker, Friend, & self—and Col. Hill.

In spite of poor A.P.'s lame explanation all 7 of these officers were quite clear that the full option (not merely to those domiciled in Ulster) was to be put to officers & that we were to get the results & send them in by that evening.

There would be no difficulty of bringing this home to Friend & Cuthbert, if necessary. These two latter now say that they understood P. to mean that the decision was only to be put to officers domiciled in Ulster!

I have seen Gwynne, & he is coming over here again to tea today.

IWM, 73/1/18, Wilson Mss

208

Private C. Smith to his brother,
W. H. Smith and sister-in-law, Mrs A. Smith

16th Lancers,
Curragh Camp.
11 April 1914

[Holograph]

No doubt you have been wondering how things are at present. Well as far as I know, I can't tell you any more than the papers can tell you, except that one of our officers has resigned his commission, and he is the Hon. Lord Holmpatrick.[95] I see that the Government have passed the Home Rule Bill in the commons, and I suppose they will pass it in the Lords. A great number of police have arrived in different parts of Ulster, and they number 1,000. The O.C. of the Cornwalls has had orders, to send back all married women, and children to the Curragh, as they are at present in Ulster. There are rumours going about that we are standing too but I have not heard anything yet definitely. As soon as I get any valuable correspondence or news I will write you at once. I hope you will excuse this horrible scrawl as I am writing this letter in Review Order, and it is none to pleasant. By the way Harry, how is Alma and the baby, I do hope they are quite well as I am in my prime at present. I am not sure Harry but did I thank you for the two books you sent me a little time back, if not, will you except [sic] my thanks now, as I was very pleased with them.

We are going away on the 10th June to where we have to swim our horses, of course thats if nothing else crops up. I suppose it will end in a bust up sooner or later (I am cushy). Well *mate* I cannot think of anything else now so will pack up. Hoping all are well.

PS. I have just received news from good authority, to the effect that the 3rd Cavalry Brigade in Ireland are for India next October. I think it is for punishment owing to the Regiment refusing to march on Ulster a little time back. Of course Harry I have not seen it in print, but I will send it on to you in print as soon as I can. Give my love to Alma and the baby.

Smith Mss

209

Lieutenant Colonel E. P. Serocold
to Lord Stamfordham

2nd Kings Royal Rifle Corps
Blackdown.
12 April 1914

[Holograph]

In reply to the enquiry in your letter of 11th,[96] I certainly think that the question was put to me officially. It was written personally by my superior officer, Brigadier General Bulfin, on a matter which was purely professional—and although his note was marked *Private*, and was not dealt with in my office, it asked me a question which I should not have answered at all unless it was put to me officially.

How far up the scale of commanders the question originated, is beyond my powers to guess; but from conversation that I have had with officers of other regiments I gather that a great number of Commanding Officers were asked the question.

I am much relieved to hear from you that I was right to report the matter.

I have seldom spent such a wretched week as I did during that Crisis.

Each day shook one's confidence more, until I really felt that if the Army was needed the climax must be reached in a few hours; and every individual would literally have to decide for himself whether he would 'get on or get out'. There was no time for deliberation, and the doubtful ones would follow the men in whom they felt most confidence. It was a time when everybody had to keep cool and quiet, but ready to take a sound line of action at any moment.

The Prime Minister's hope that officers will keep clear of politics is all very well in theory, but in practise it is almost impossible. It is of course unnecessary & much to be deprecated for officers to express strong party views & opinions, but, as (I think) Lord Haldane said about 4 years ago, we soldiers are citizens, & have duties to perform as citizens. And, that being so, it would be unnatural for us not to follow politics and to form opinions on the more important matters. Indeed, since we have the franchise, we are bound to consider the political parties & their proposals.

If either party, or any group, wishes to pick a hole in the Army & its relation to politics, the weak spot is that a very large majority of the officers are Tory by birth & upbringing, and, being removed from contact with persons of differing opinions, they do not cast off the tradition in which they were brought up—and do not have the opportunity of getting an all round view of matters on which to form a judgment for themselves.

RA GV F.674/74

210

C. Wigram to Lord Stamfordham

Brockville House,
Raheny,
Dublin.

[Holograph]   12 April 1914

The enclosed cuttings about the new capital at Delhi may interest you. I saw Gough today, and he tells me attempts have been made to get the guarantee out of him. General Friend was sent by A.P. to try to secure it, and told Gough all would be well if he trusted A.P.!

Mr. Asquith also sent a message through Cheyne of the 16th Lancers, son of Sir Watson Cheyne, with whom Mrs. A. had been chatting, that the Government would consider it a very gracious act if Gough surrendered this guarantee to Asquith, as Asquith could then say a healthy tone prevailed in the Army, which trusted Asquith, and so the cry of the Army against the People would be crushed. Mrs. A. added that this was well worth the consideration of Gough in the interests of the Army. G says the 4th Hussars are settling down, and added that the price of Hogg's honour was not very high!

P.S. Among other things G. told me that A.P. at the famous interview on Saty. swaggered up and down the room, and said: 'Don't you think, officers, that I take orders from these swines of politicians. No, I only take orders from the Sovereign.'

This was to endeavour to get the officers to withdraw their resignations. G. & Co. said they had lost confidence in A.P., & were not taking any chances.

RA GV F.674/73

211

Colonel V. J. M. Huguet to Major-General H. H. Wilson[97]

5 Rue Victor-Hugo,
Bourges.

[Holograph]   13 April 1914

I have written to Sir John to tell him how sorry I have been to see the course of the events which have recently taken place in your Country, the result of which has been his determination of vacating his appointment as Chief of the Gnl. Staff.

I need not tell you how deeply we have all been affected by those events—and I more than any other since I know your country better than most of our people here. On one side, I have been able to witness the continuous & remarkable work of military reorganisation which has been done for these last 10 years, and has brought your Army to the high state of efficiency which it has reached nowadays; but on the other side, I know also your Army, your officers, your soldiers, their minds your organization so special & so different from any other. And I cannot understand how your Government knew so little of all that to have brought on your Army such a crisis, d'un coeur aussi léger et avec une telle inconscience.

I very deeply regret for many reasons the resignation of Sir John, but I am still more afraid of what the future may be. Your politicians seem to have also understood that at last, to have been frightened by what they have done, and to want to stop it—But will it be possible?

If there is no compromise, if the Government appeal to the country, if that heinous cry of: Army against Parliament, which has been uttered by certain politicians, is raised again and becomes the platform for the next elections, what may not come out of it? This frightens me more than anything else; I should like to be persuaded that my fears are exaggerated, that nothing bad will result of all this, and that your Army will get out of the present crisis without further damage. But I am nonetheless much afraid, and all this makes me very sad.

I recently saw Gnl. de Castelnau in Paris, who told me that Gnl. Maxse has been with him for a few days to attend a conference, and that he is to call again, with you, in May or June, to see one of our Staff rides. I am leaving Bourges at the beginning of next month with my regiment to go to the Camp de Neuilly for our Artillery practice, and shall not be back in my quarters before the middle of June, but should you cross Paris at any time after the 13th of June, would you kindly let me know. It will be such a pleasure to see you again; I have not met you since the last manoeuvres, that means more than 6 months, & I shall have so many things to talk over with you.

I hope you are all right, mon Général, and Mrs. Wilson also; your time at the W.O. will be up, if I am not mistaken, in 1 or 2 months; very likely you will be then promoted Major General, and take some holiday before you get the Command of a fine Division, and then I do not know when I may meet you again; I should therefore be greatly pleased to have the opportunity of seeing you this summer.

Well, goodbye, mon Général, kindly remember me to Mrs. Wilson, and believe me.

IWM, 73/1/18, Wilson Mss

212
Extracts from the Diary of
Lieutenant-General Sir John Spencer Ewart

[Holograph]   18 April 1914

The papers had a full 'revelation' of the supposed 'plot' to coerce Ulster. If Paget said half he is supposed to have said he must be if not a lunatic at least a tactless idiot unfit to be in command anywhere.

How atrociously Hubert Gough has behaved over the whole business. The last words he said when leaving French's room, with his Colonels and his celebrated treaty, were: 'I shall not show this to any officers; no one will see it but my three Colonels'. Yet, although nobody but Seely, French & I knew its contents— besides Gough and his three C O's—within 48 hours it had been communicated to the Press. It is also quite clear that Paget's officers have given away everything he said to the Ulster Unionist Council who have published their 'revelations' in the newspapers. It is a melancholy story of Army disloyalty to its own Chiefs.[98]

30 April 1914

I am very much puzzled why the Government have stood so nobly by Paget; he caused all the trouble by his insensate folly and want of tact, but for some reason the Liberals wont throw him over. I don't think he had a vestige of excuse for what he did. Why did he ever mention the question of Ulster to Gough or the officers of the 3rd Cavalry Brigade? There was no idea of moving a single cavalry soldier, unless the situation had become much more serious than it was, or unless the precautionary moves for the protection of depots, arms, etc. had been resisted by Carson and Co.

SRO, RH4/84/3, 126, Ewart Mss

213

Report by Major-General W. P. Pulteney

Government House,
Cork.
[Holograph]   19 April 1914

My opinion of the general state of feeling existing in the 6th
Division, as regards Ulster, is as follows:
1. They can be relied on to support law and order.
2. They would not enforce Home Rule on an actively reluctant
    Ulster.
3. There is little chance of this feeling altering unless H.M. the
    King proclaims the Ulster Volunteers as rebels.
4. In fact the Troops would move for the King.

Bodleian, Ms Asquith 40, f 118

214

Report by
Major-General Sir Charles Fergusson

Ballyfair,
Curragh.
[Holograph]   [19] April 1914

For ordinary duties in the defence of law and order there can
be no question; all ranks will do their duty.

Should, however, a situation arise which entails active operations against formed disciplined forces of Ulster, under their
responsible leaders, in other words, should there be a state of civil
war, there will be a large defection of officers. The extent of these
defections will be greater or less according to the circumstances
which lead up to the crisis. Provided that the Ulster Troops do
nothing to alienate sympathy, in the way of rioting or of
unprovoked attack on soldiers or police involving loss of life
among the latter, the great majority of officers will, I think, refuse

to act aggressively against them; and I am convinced that, generally speaking, the men will follow their officers, and that regiments will stick together.

I hear that the feeling among officers has changed considerably since I forwarded my previous report[99] on the events of last month. This I gather has arisen from three causes:

1. The granting of the guarantee to Gen. Gough and the officers who sided with him.

    This was looked on by most officers as being practically a justification by the authorities of Gen. Gough's attitude. Instead of being looked upon as a mutiny, it was decided that there was a misunderstanding. These officers returned covered with glory, while those who had taken the other line have had to put up with misrepresentations and reproach from their relatives and friends. It is not surprising that many of them, especially the younger, are resentful, and inclined to think that they 'backed the wrong horse'.

2. The subsequent repudiation of the above guarantee had the effect of deepening the resentment against the Government, and of creating a feeling of distrust and unrest. Officers have begun to doubt whether it *is* their duty, in the event of civil war, to decide against those whom they look upon as loyalists, in support of a Government whom they suspect of having recently traded on their loyalty to the King, and deceived them.

3. It is commonly reported and believed that the General Staff of the Army will resign when the crisis comes. Moreover that certain officers holding high appointments, in and out of the War Office, are in the confidence of the Ulster party, and are practically working against the Government and the con-stituted authority of the Army.

Such an impression, whether well founded or not, is bound to produce a feeling of unrest and suspicion, for regimental officers will naturally not do violence to their feelings and sympathies and convictions, if they suspect that their superiors will leave them in the lurch when the crisis comes.

All these considerations are tending to influence officers at present, and the conclusion that I have come to is that the troops can only be depended on to do their duty up to a certain point. They will go a long way before they break up, but if the situation develops into civil war they will at the end disintegrate.

This is tantamount to saying that they are not to be depended on to coerce Ulster into accepting the Home Rule Bill.

The only thing that could possibly influence them would be a personal appeal by the King. Loyalty to the sovereign is very strong indeed. As you know, it was that and only that, which kept the Division together during the recent crisis. Unless officers and men are absolutely convinced beyond doubt that they are carrying out His Majesty's orders and wishes they will not, in my opinion, go against their own convictions, if the actual crisis of civil war comes, and their convictions undoubtedly are that the Army ought not to be employed against the Ulster people to enforce the Bill.

Bodleian, Ms Asquith 40, f 119–121

215
Major A. W. F. Baird to
J. Ramsay Macdonald[100]

1st Gordon Highlanders,
Hut Barracks,
Crownhill,
S. Devon.

[Holograph]   25 April 1914

I have just been reading the report of a speech delivered by you at Newcastle on Tyne on Apl. 24th.

I do not know to what extent you have studied the King's Regulations, but judging from the blackguardly assertions made in your speech, it seems safe to assume that you are well aware of the paragraph which protects you from any chance of a public reply by an Army officer.

Nothing, however, prevents my writing to you privately. I

therefore do so to inform you, that I for one, & hundreds of others of *all* ranks in the service, detest *you* & *all* other politicians of all classes & denominations equally.

In our opinion you are all tarred with the same brush. Your personal interests and your party interests, in so far as the latter coincide with the former (& your £400 a year makes the coincidence wonderfully accurate no doubt!) are all that any of you care for. The King, Empire, & the Flag which are everything to us are little or nothing to any of you.

In stating publicly that those of us in the service (& there are many of us), who would sooner sacrifice, than dishonour, our careers, are influenced in our decisions by the views or advice of any political party, you are stating either a deliberate or an unintentional falsehood. Moreover no one but a blackguard or a politician would make such a statement, knowing as you must have done, that there was no chance of any public reply. In case you may contemplate making any further speeches on this subject, perhaps you will be good enough to mention, that you have heard directly from at least one officer on the active list, that he is prepared to sacrifice his career, his prospects, & his pay (small as it is compared to your own!) rather than take up arms against Ulster & that the motive of his action has nothing whatsoever to do with Tory politicians, but is based on his conscientious belief that the leaders of the Nationalists of Ireland are at heart just as much rebels to our King & our Country today as they have openly & repeatedly proclaimed themselves to be until quite recently.

I must add, that not being a trade unionist, I should not consider it right, in the event of my resigning my commission, to adopt any system of 'peaceful picketing' with regard to those who might differ from me, as I have never seen any justification for bullying the wives & families of those who may desire to continue in their employment.

PRO, 30/69/1423, Macdonald Mss

216

Extracts from Diary of
Captain L. A. E. Price-Davies

[Holograph]   27 April 1914

Talk of moves of troops which turn out to be rumours. Fellows beginning to be restless again wondering what will happen. Hope officers will not resign prematurely as I don't think this Army Council will let them in.

Army Museums Ogilby Trust, Price-Davies Mss

217

Brigadier-General H. P. Gough to
C. Wigram

Brownstown House,
Curragh.
[Holograph]   28 April 1914

Here are various notes of our four days battle, which I promised you.[101] You can keep them. You can show Friday & Saturday accounts to anyone you like (short of the Press!) but Sundays & Mondays events are so purely personal to myself, & have no bearing on the general situation that I would like to keep them private.

I am anxious. Situation looks grave. Are we going to be forced into civil war? Our attitude here is to sit tight, quietly obey all lawful commands, & if ordered to Ulster we will preserve property, & maintain the *peace*. If the action of the police, should be likely to cause bloodshed in the opinion of any officer on the spot, he will ask the police to desist, & report the matter, saying that he could not make himself responsible for the certain bloodshed that would ensue. I think this is a good attitude. It keeps us right in the eyes of the public, & will tend to keep Ulster quiet. It *may* help to avert civil war.

But God only knows. I tell you this, as it may tend to releive [sic] minds in high places. But under no circumstances will we shoot down Ulstermen, or take any part in *attacking* their organised forces.

RA GV F.674/82

218
Brigadier-General H. P. Gough to Major-General H. H. Wilson

Brownstown House,
Curragh.

[Holograph]   28 April 1914

I don't know how much Ulster's last move[102] may obliterate the past, & if it does, A.P. may survive, for I do not think anything will penetrate his own skin. But it is to be sincerely trusted that he will go soon. His presence here is very bad for discipline, for there is not an officer in his command, unless it is the members of his own staff, who, I suppose have their reasons, who does not look at him as a traitor to his subordinates, a liar, & a coward. But what applies to him, applies with equal force to French, & if you can use any influence in this matter, *do* stop French coming here instead of Paget.

We want someone here we can trust & respect. There is no one who would fulfil these conditions to anything like the same degree as Plumer. We feel we want someone here, who will not betray us again, & who will stand up to the Cabinet and protect us from its machinations.

All quiet here; long may it remain so,—but I still feel very anxious. What is the news from your part of the world?

IWM, 73/1/18, Wilson Mss

219

Brigadier-General H. P. Gough to
Major-General H. H. Wilson

Grealey's Hotel,
Roscommon.

[Holograph]
5 May 1914

Many thanks for yours. It will be a dreadful thing for the Army if J.F. gets this command, but particularly so for soldiers here. We feel he sold us once, just as much as A.P. did, & he may easily do it again! So keep him out of this, if you can! Why not send him out as Governor to New South Wales, or some other Colony? He would love it.

I am here with 14 of my 'boys' doing a Staff Ride, or rather a Tactical Exercise, which I believe is the new name! The inhabitants are quite friendly & no one has thrown a brick at us yet!

I am crossing over to my mother's on Saturday night, for Allenby's 'Staff Ride' the following Monday (11–14th inst). I will look you up—not at the W.O. however!

Till then, good fortune.

IWM, 73/1/18, Wilson Mss

220

Major W. Gillman to his mother

Norfolk Lodge,
The Terrace,
Richmond.

[Holograph]
10 May 1914

We soldiers will probably have more trouble over Ulster. The so-called conferences[103] have come to nothing & Carson has gone to Wiesbaden. The Home Rule Bill will therefore be passed and it may take a long time before an amending act is passed which will give Ulster some relief.

I expect that the moment the Bill is passed, Carson will proclaim his provisional Government in Ulster, and it will no doubt sit in some Council Hall in Belfast. The trouble may come if the present Government order soldiers to seize this Council Hall.

As I read the law, we soldiers are bound to suppress disorder, riot, etc, and we have done so in the past and will do so in the future. But where such suppression of disorder will *in our opinion* lead to civil strife, then I think we are acting within the law if we refuse.

If therefore I am ordered to Ulster in case of trouble, I shall of course go. But if I am ordered to seize the Belfast Council Hall by force when it is surrounded by Covenanters bent on defending it, then I shall refuse to do so as in my opinion such action wd stir up civil war.

The sooner some amended Act comes in after the Bill is passed, the better: delays are provocative of trouble. Once Ulster is safe I think the general healing will begin.

With fondest love from us both.

RA Institution, 1161/29/6, Gillman Mss

221
Major-General Sir Charles Fergusson to his solicitor, J. R. Anderson

Ballyfair,
Curragh.

[Holograph]
7 May 1914

I wonder if you can help me in the following matter, as a friend.

In the last issue of Blackwood's Magazine (for May) on page 715, there is a certain reference to me which is most annoying.[104] It begins on the 10th line, with the words 'It is clear also that the Government, etc'.

There is no truth whatever in this story—I have never written

374

any letter at all, & it is the first time I have seen such a thing stated. I am not in the habit of writing to young officers, & obviously would not do so on so delicate a subject as that of the recent Ulster crisis.

Nor have I ever made the statement alleged. It is a distortion of something I did say officially to some of my officers, in addressing them on Saturday 20th March.

I was asked if we were about to take aggressive action against the Ulster people. I explained, in accordance with my instructions, that so far from there being any intuition of this, every possible precaution had been taken to avoid any possibility of the troops coming into conflict with them and I enumerated certain steps that had been taken to that end. For instance, all troops had been withdrawn from Belfast, and the strictest orders had been given that should troops find their way opposed, even by passive crowds, they were at once to withdraw to Barracks. On no account were we to let ourselves be put into any position which would entail our taking any provocative or aggressive action. So that unless the Ulster people attacked troops, there could not possibly be any collision.

As I was trying with all my might and main to persuade my officers that they must stick to their duty, and that nothing had as yet arisen which could justify them in refusing to obey orders, it is obvious that to use such an argument as is alleged in this article would have been absurd, and the very last thing to say to effect my object.

Some account of what I was supposed to have said got into the papers a few days later, and a very distorted account it was; obviously twisted for party purposes into a meaning which my words did not bear.

A question was asked in the House of Lords as to whether I had said something much to the same effect as that alleged in Blackwoods. But it was postponed, and finally never put, and so it was never contradicted. I asked officially that a contradiction might be given, but was told that it was unnecessary, and that it was better that the whole matter should be allowed to drop as soon as possible.

I am of course absolutely precluded by Regulations from contradicting it myself, or from making any communication to the Press; consequently one has to submit to much misrepresentation and misunderstanding.

I do not mind being made to appear a fool, but I object most strongly to be handed down to posterity in Blackwood as a knave; and the inference which anyone would draw from this article is that I lent myself to this 'hellish idea', and tried to persuade my officers to swallow it.

The words in themselves have been twisted into conveying exactly the opposite meaning to what I intended to convey, and to what I actually *did* convey to the officers; for my explanation had the effect of satisfying them, and none of them handed in their resignations.

I want to ask if you could possibly put this right with Blackwood? Possibly you know the present people at the head of the firm, and I cannot believe that they would not contradict this story, in common fairness to me and my family, if they know the facts. I should be the last person to wish to spoil any point they can make against the Government; but their particular point so far as I am concerned (and indeed to the best of my belief), is unfounded, and it does me a cruel injury. I am quite helpless in the matter; for the sake of the Army I would not reopen the discussion, even to right myself. But in any case I am not allowed to speak. I think people hardly realise the difficult position that we soldiers are in, in not being able to explain our position or tell our story.

If you can do anything to help me, will you do so? Of course this letter is private, but you can show it in confidence to Mr Blackwood, and I would be glad if you would take any opportunity you have of contradicting the story if you hear it mentioned. In any case my name must not appear in print as making a statement, or publishing a contradiction.

Fergusson Mss

222

Brigadier-General H. P. Gough to Major-General H. H. Wilson

Brownstown House,
Curragh.

[Holograph]   20 May 1914

I had my interview with Friend this afternoon & I enclose an account of it, which you might return when you have done with it.[105]

The principal point that it brings out about the impossibility, or difficulty, of A.P.'s position here as Chief, is the prospect of another conference, with him, when he proposes to explain to us his use, or misuse, of the King's name.

This means that he is going to try to get us to 'whitewash' him as regards to this, not a very dignified proceeding under any circumstances, but under these, we shall be asked to accept his explanation, which will humiliate us in our own eyes, as we shall know that we are all humbugging & lying—or,—we shall have to let him know that we don't accept his explanation, which we cannot do without telling him in so many words, that he lied in the original instance, & that he is making it worse by lying again!!

This is the prospect that faces us. We are doing all we can possibly do, to maintain discipline & authority, but really his continued presence here, puts all discipline to a very severe strain.

He seems so enraged with me, that if Friend had not been able to pacify him to some extent, after our interview, there was a great risk of some most regrettable scene at our meeting tomorrow. But I hope that has now been obviated.

I will add a line, after our meeting, in case I have anything of importance to tell you.

P.S. Thursday 2 p.m. Our meeting took place this morning without any fracas! A.P. tried at first to take no notice of me, but gave it up after a bit! Officers, S.I.H.[106] quite respectful on parade, but had arranged to lunch elsewhere (in some numbers) in case he stayed to lunch. A.P. held a conference on the Tactical operations in their Mess Tent—a somewhat painful & quite unnecessary affair, but I think he was determined to 'carry it off' with an air.

IWM, 73/1/18, Wilson Mss

223
Brigadier-General H. P. Gough to Major-General H. H. Wilson

Brownstown House,
Curragh.

[Holograph]   5 June 1914

Many thanks for yours. I am sorry there is no news about A.P. but meanwhile you may be sure that I & all of us here, will behave towards him with due decorum & not give him any opening! I will however have a talk with Friend & Kincaid-Smith & ask them to use their influence to stop his (A.P.'s) explanations or discussions with me, which he threatens! It can't do any good & is very stupid of him & is bound to be most difficult, to say the least of it.

I don't like the look of the future at all, & I don't believe the Amending Bill will help matters, or be even intended to help matters—, nor do I think the Government will go to the country. Then Ulster will eventually be forced to set up a Provisional Government. We may then be ordered to support the Police in suppressing this Prl. Govt. If we refuse we shall be in a most difficult position. If we do help to suppress the Govt. of Ulster, we shall be doing the very thing we refused to do in March. But our position & attitude has in no way altered, & we may in consequence be forced to disobey direct orders & not merely decline a hypothetical alternative. I foresee rocks ahead. I am very anxious. I am seriously thinking of chucking the whole show now. These politicians are unscrupulous place-hunters. I hate them.

IWM, 73/1/18, Wilson Mss

224

A Memorandum by the Military Members of the Army Council on the Military Situation in Ireland[107]

[Printed]   4 July 1914

1. At the present time two opposing forces, with approximately a total strength of 200,000 men, are being systematically and deliberately raised, trained and equipped and organised on a military basis in Ireland.

2. In view of this fact we, as the responsible military advisers to His Majesty's Government, deem it to be our duty to point out that if, unfortunately, these two large forces should come into conflict, a situation may arise which may require the whole of our available forces at home to deal with.

3. As we have not been informed what policy the Government proposes to adopt in the event of such a conflict, it is not possible for us to estimate the number of troops which might be required to restore order. No plan of operations of this nature has been prepared or even considered by the War Office, and no plan can, in the circumstances, be prepared.

4. We think it likely, however, that it might be necessary to employ the whole of our Expeditionary Force to restore order, and this would probably involve general mobilisation, placing Special Reserve troops in the ports, and assembling the Local and Central Forces now composed of Territorial troops.

5. So far as numbers alone are concerned there might be no great difficulty in finding garrisons for the ports or in providing a Central Force, but a factor which cannot be overlooked is that, as the Territorial Force cannot be used to maintain order in Great Britain, we should probably be unable to use the whole of our six divisions in Ireland.

6. A still more important factor is that, if the whole of our Expeditionary Force were used in Ireland and to maintain order in Great Britain, we should be quite incapable of meeting our obligations abroad, and in this connection India

and Egypt must be specially borne in mind. It seems to us at least possible that unrest in India and in Egypt may follow the commencement of such operations, whilst certain countries in Europe may take this opportunity of creating trouble.

7. We now summarise the chief points to which we wish to call attention—

   (a) No plan for military operations in Ireland of the nature herein questioned has been prepared or even considered by the War Office.

   (b) No plan can be made until the policy which His Majesty's Government proposes to adopt is given.

   (c) In the event of a conflagration in Ireland, the whole of the Expeditionary Force may be required to restore order, not only in Ireland but in Great Britain as well.

   (d) If the whole of it is required, our Central Force will be inadequate security against invasion; we shall be unable to give any assistance to either Egypt or India; and finally, be unable to meet any of our obligations abroad.

We trust you will not think that in putting this forward we are making any attempt to interfere in a political question which is outside our province; but as the responsible military advisers of His Majesty's Government we feel we should be neglecting our duty if we omitted to draw attention to the serious aspect of the situation which may arise from a military point of view.

PRO, Cab. 37/119/44; Ibid, WO 32/9569; IWM, 73/1/17, Wilson Mss

225

Brigadier-General H. P. Gough to Major-General H. H. Wilson

Brownstown House,
Curragh.
9 July 1914

[Holograph]

I have been away on a Command Signalling Staff Ride, hence the delay in answering your letter.

It looks of course very likely that we shall be faced with the problem of a Provisional Government in Ulster. There were 90 staff officers of sorts on this Signalling Staff Ride, & I sounded a good many on the subject. There is no doubt that the large majority of Regimental & junior Staff officers are firmly opposed to taking any action to coerce Ulster & that there would be resignations on a still larger scale now than was the case last time, but I do not think Senior Staff Officers & Generals are as firm or in as large a proportion. It seems to me that many of them fear the risks & the turmoil which might have to be faced far more than they care for any principles. They want, if they can, to stand with one foot in both camps!! I didn't like Furse's attitude at all for instance.[108] I think he would much rather fight Ulster than face the risks of not doing so, not seeing that in the long run, the risks of fighting Ulster are as great as those created by not doing so.

But if the heads of the Army this time will take up the burden, & act according to their conviction, & not leave it to junior officers to do, I don't think there could or would be any serious row at all. With Douglas & Sclater at the head of affairs, I feel much more confident that no orders to fight Ulster will be given to the Army than I did when French & Paget looked after the interests of the Army & of their juniors.

If *the heads* of the Army will only stand firm against Asquith & the politicians, they will save the Army, & take half, if not all, the sting out of the cry—'Mutinies in the Army', & 'the army v. the People'—But if the action has again to come from the juniors it will not only *look* much worse for the Army, but *be* much worse for the Army. Where French, Paget, Fergusson, Pulteney & others have lost their hold over the Army, & shake its discipline, is in the fact that, now the struggle is over, & the battle won, by junior officers, they say that their opinion is the same, as the juniors' opinion, & that they never had, & never will have any intention of attacking Ulster. But, it is naturally asked by everyone, if that is so, why did not they be firm with the Government & stand fast when the storm burst, instead of merely joining in the general chorus now? Whatever dangers may face us, & whatever difficulties may confront us, I am convinced that we (the Army) will be in a much better posture to meet them if the lead this time came decisively from the head. The tail will rally quick enough to the head, never fear, but there must be a head!

IWM, 73/1/18, Wilson Mss

226

Brigadier-General G. T. Forestier-Walker to Major-General Sir Charles Fergusson

Dublin

[Holograph]   11 July 1914

An incident occurred during the Comd. Exercise, of which I think I ought to inform you. An officer informed me that a paper dealing with political matters was being passed round among the officers assembled for the Exercise. My informant had not himself seen the paper, but I found out who was in possession of it, and I asked that officer for an explanation. He informed me that the paper was intended as a joke and did not bear the significance that I attributed to it. He said that it had been handed to him in joke by an officer whose name he did not wish to disclose since he now realised that he had done a silly thing in showing the paper about, and he did not wish to embroil the officer concerned. I accepted this explanation, and took upon myself to give him a very severe telling off, and pointed out the very serious results which might have accrued to himself and others owing to his peculiar ideas on the subject of humour. He gave me his word of honour that he would destroy immediately the paper (which I did not ask to see), and that he would personally make certain that the two or three officers, to whom it had been shown, understood it to be a joke, and further that any officers, to whom the existence of the paper had thereby become known, also understood it in that sense. Later on, he informed me that he had done this.

I reported the matter to the MG/A yesterday. He considered that the action which I had taken was sufficient from a disciplinary point of view, and that the matter might be considered closed. I think, and Genl. Friend does too, that you should know of the incident, because the officer who was in possession of the paper is one of those under yr command, and it is conceivable, though I hope improbable, that you may hear of it from other sources. In the hope, however, that the matter is finally closed, I have not mentioned his name.[109]

PRO, WO 35/209 (b)

227

Major-General Sir Charles Fergusson to Brigadier-General G. T. Forestier-Walker

Ballyfair,
Curragh.
[Holograph]   14 July 1914

Many thanks. I had not suspected him, but the incident may explain a good deal of leakage that has puzzled me.

Of course the matter is entirely in your own hands, but I must say that in my opinion it ought to have been taken up, and those implicated hunted down to the bitter end.

For months I have been well aware that there was much underhand talk and work going on and I can't tell you how unpleasant it is to live among people and not know who is to be trusted, or who is working behind one's back.

Here was a seditious paper being passed round, and a General Staff officer found circulating it. My own view is that it was an opportunity to be seized of asserting discipline, and personally I would have had no mercy whatever. These fellows think we are afraid to take any action in the interests of discipline, and that the public feeling in favour of Gough and his party prevents anything being said on the other side. They hunt with the hare and run with the hounds, and while holding positions of responsibility on one side are pandering with politics on the other.

They can hold what opinions they like; mine are as strong as any of theirs!; but one has to be loyal and run straight.

A Staff Officer who is untrustworthy in one respect is not to be trusted in another—and is unfit for his position.

Please don't think I am criticising your action. It is entirely a matter of opinion what is best to be done on these occasions. But my own opinion is that an example should have been made, and I have been waiting for such an opportunity.

In his case it is particularly disquieting, for the two Curragh Battalions of his Brigade are the ones which I trust least in the whole Division,[110] and which from the beginning have given me most grounds for anxiety. The demeanour of some of the officers is not altogether satisfactory, and naturally this incident does not make one much happier about them. Of course, this may be fancy. However, there it is and the young gentleman may thank his stars that he didn't fall into my clutches!

PRO, WO 35/209 (b)

228

Lieutenant Colonel de la Panouse to the French Minister of War, Adolphe Messimy

London
18 July 1914

au sujet du recrutement de l'Armée régulière
anglaise

... Divers motifs contribuent à cette crise du recrutement: on observe, en effet, que les unités qui souffrent le plus sont celles qui se recrutent soit dans le nord de l'Angleterre, soit en Ecosse, soit en Irlande ...
... Enfin en Irlande la crise actuelle du 'Home Rule' a pour ainsi dire arrêté les engagements dans l'Armée; les jeunes hommes restent dans les rangs des volontaires ulstériens ou nationalistes*
...

*depuis quelque temps dans certains villages d'Irlande, une campagne est menée contre les engagements dans l'Armée.

Vincennes, Etat-Major de L'Armée de Terre, Box No. 7N1228, 336

229

Poem on Christmas Card sent to All Ranks, 3rd Cavalry Brigade from the People of Ulster

Exchange Publishing Co.,
36Shankhill Road,
Belfast.
[Printed]   December 1914

Saviours of Ulster
(The Immortal One Hundred)

One hundred Noble Officers, of England's pride today,
Have stood upon the Curragh Camp a summons to obey,

Their General said 'I've orders that to Ulster you must go,
And there shoot down their loyal men, as you would a foreign foe.
The Government of England, in the hands of roguish knaves,
Give orders, spite of conscience, you must this Home Rule save,
For we're pledged to John Redmond them to Roman bondage drag,
Their only crime, we must confess, is loyalty to the flag.'

CHORUS—

But it is a famous story, proclaim it far and near,
Of this noble band, *One Hundred*, who stood for honour dear,
And refused to go to Ulster, their rights to take away,
Or be a party to this plan to give John Redmond sway,

General Paget gave the order; cried Gough 'Can it be true?
Are we to shoot down loyal men? Why this we cannot do.
We remember, Sir, when England stood in danger grave,
These very men have shed their blood our noble flag to save.
You may order us to Russia, or to the mouth of hell,
But we'll never go to Ulster and enslave those loyal men.
We're loyal, Sir, to England, until the end of time,
But before we'll coerce Ulster our commands we will resign.'

Written in honour of the One Hundred Officers who have saved Ulster—By T.M.

Pragnell Mss

NOTES

ABBREVIATIONS USED IN THE NOTES

Add Mss: Additional Manuscripts (British Library)
AMOT: Army Museums Ogilby Trust
BL: British Library
H. of Lords RO: House of Lords Record Office
IWM: Imperial War Museum
NAM: National Army Museum
NLS: National Library of Scotland
PRO: Public Record Office
RA: Royal Archives
RA Institution: Royal Artillery Institution
SRO: Scottish Record Office

1. Useful summaries, placing the Curragh in the context of modern British civil-military relations can be found in Adam Roberts, 'The British Armed Forces and Politics: A Historical Perspective', *Armed Forces and Society* 3, 4, 1977, pp. 531–56 and John Sabine, 'Civil-military relations' in John Baylis (ed.), *British Defence Policy in a Changing World* (Croom Helm, London, 1977), pp. 243–50.

2. A. P. Ryan, *Mutiny at the Curragh* (Macmillan, London, 1956); Sir James Fergusson, *The Curragh Incident* (Faber & Faber, London, 1964); A. T. Q. Stewart, *The Ulster Crisis* (Faber & Faber, London, 1967); Patricia Jalland, *The Liberals and Ireland: The Ulster Question and British Politics to 1914* (Harvester, Brighton, 1980); A Farrar-Hockley, *Goughie* (Hart-Davis MacGibbon, London, 1975); Richard Holmes, *The Little Field Marshal: Sir John French* (Cape, London, 1981). Ironically, the only true mutiny at the Curragh occurred in 1923/4 and affected the army of the Irish Free State—see M. M. G. Valiulis, 'The Irish Army Mutiny of 1924', Unpub. Ph.D., Loyola, 1977.

3. Jalland, *Liberals*, pp. 207–47; Holmes, *Little Field Marshal*, pp. 166–94; Elizabeth Muenger, 'The British Army in Ireland, 1886–1914', Unpub. Ph.D., Michigan, 1981, pp. 324–403.

4. *General Annual Returns of the British Army for the year ending 30 September, 1913* (Cmd. 725, 1914); H. A. Hanham, 'Religion and Nationality in the mid-Victorian Army' in M. R. D. Foot (ed.), *War and Society* (Paul Elek, London, 1973), pp. 159–82 has a discussion of the decline of Irish recruitment in the 19th century.

5. G. Fontenot, 'The Modern Major-General: Patterns in the careers of the British Army Major-Generals on active duty at the time of the Sarajevo Assassination', Unpub. M.A., Chapel Hill, 1980, p. 32; Muenger, 'The British Army in Ireland', p. 103.

6. Ann L. Vorce, 'The role of Ireland in British Defence Planning, 1908–1914', Unpub. M.A., London, 1975, pp. 1–4. For a general survey of British strategic re-orientation, see John Gooch, *The Plans of War* (Routledge and Kegan Paul, London, 1974) and the same author's *The Prospect of War* (Frank Cass, London, 1981).

7. Muenger, 'The British Army in Ireland', p. 269.

8. The best guide to RIC and government perceptions is Jalland although Muenger has an informative chapter on the constabulary.

9. A good example is the summary of an official report (not extant) written by the perceptive commander of 15th Infantry Brigade, Count Gleichen in late 1913. See Major-General Lord Edward Gleichen, *A Guardsman's Memories* (Blackwood, Edinburgh and London, 1932), pp. 369–72.

10. Paget's views come from an extraordinary rambling speech to Dublin's Corinthian Club on 24 February 1914. See Fergusson, *Curragh*, p. 66; Ian Colvin, *The Life of Lord Carson* (Gollancz, London, 1934), II, pp. 306–7; D. Gwynn, *The Life of John Redmond* (Harrap, London, 1932), p. 285.

11. The diary of Ewart for 7 January 1913 indicates that he also favoured Home Rule but on the grounds that there were more pressing dangers overseas (SRO, RH4/84/3, 125, Ewart Mss). Similar sentiments with regard to the army's attitude towards the nationalists were expressed by M.P.s such as Arthur Salter and Rowland Hunt (*Hansard* 5s, HofC, LVIII, 87–8 and LX, 1372–3). J. E. Gough's papers include a number of Ulster Loyalist pamphlets recalling the nationalist view of the army during the South African War.

12. See also RA GV F.673/24, Beresford to Stamfordham, 23.3.1914 with enclosure; Churchill College, WMYS 2/5, Beresford to Mrs Wemyss, 7.4.1914; Bodleian, Ms Milner 157, f.76, Unidentified account from 13th Infantry Brigade; H. of Lords RO, Bonar Law Mss, 31/2/65, Carson to Law, 26.3.1914; Ibid, 32/1/84, Currie to Law, 30.3.1914; Ibid, 32/2/9, Midleton to Law, 3.4.1914; Ibid, 39/2/19, Unidentified account from 3rd Cavalry Brigade. Bonar Law also quoted from a letter from the Manchester Regiment in the Commons on 23.3.1914, Fergusson, *Curragh*, p. 83.

13. See, for example, *Hansard* 5s, HofC, LC, 275–7, Thomas, 24.3.1914; Ibid, 906–10, Churchill, 30.3.1914; Ibid, LXI, 1635–8, debate of 28.4.1914.

14. *Hansard* 5s, HofC, LX, 1790, Waring, 7.4.1914; Colvin, *Life of Carson*, pp. 234–45; Gwynn, *Life of Redmond*, p. 281; Stewart, *Ulster Crisis*, p. 78.

15. The best account is that in Robert Blake, *The Unknown Prime Minister* (Eyre & Spottiswoode, London, 1955), pp. 173–82.

16. A. M. Gollin, *Proconsul in Politics* (Anthony Blond, London, 1964), pp. 199–201.

17. H. of Lords RO, Bonar Law Mss, 31/2/48.

18. Further evidence of Roberts' concern can be found in H. of Lords RO, Bonar Law Mss, 30/1/11, Roberts to Law, 14.9.1913; and Bodleian, Ms Milner 16, f.212, Roberts to Milner, 2.11.1913. The views of contemporaries on Roberts' role can be found in W. S. Blunt, *My Diaries* (Martin Secker, London, 1920), p. 440; Lord Riddell, *More Pages from my Diary, 1908–1914* (Country Life, London, 1934), p. 204; IWM, 73/1/18, Wilson Mss, cutting from *Irish Daily Independent*, 27.3.1914; Roy Jenkins, *Asquith* (Collins, London, 1964), p. 310 quoting Asquith's view that 'the main responsibility for all this mutinous talk rested with Lord Roberts, who is in a dangerous condition of senile frenzy.'

19. Blake, *Unknown Prime Minister*, p. 178; H. of Lords RO, Bonar Law Mss, 34/1/21 for the draft letter, which had been suggested to Milner by Ian Malcolm, M.P. as a means of inducing more Unionist M.P.s who were also Territorials to take the lead — see Bodleian, Ms Milner 41, f.16. Incitement of Territorials was also a feature of the press — see Gwynn, *Life of Redmond*, pp. 283–4.

20. E. M. Spiers, *Haldane: An Army Reformer* (Edinburgh University Press, 1980), pp. 161–86; Michael Allison, 'The National Service Issue, 1900–1914', Unpub. Ph.D., London, 1975, pp. 202–6; I. F. W. Beckett, 'The Territorial Force' in Ian F. W. Beckett and Keith Simpson (eds), *A Nation in Arms: A Social Study of the British Army in the First World War* (Manchester University Press, 1985), pp. 128–63.

21. Stewart, *Ulster Crisis*, pp. 83–5. Seely also questioned the advisability of paying pensions to officers assisting the UVF — see PRO, Cab. 37/117/82, Seely Memorandum of 29.11.1913.

22. RA GV K.2553 (II) 26, King George V to Asquith, 22.9.1913 reproduced in Sir Harold Nicolson, *King George V: His Life and Reign* (Constable, London, 1952), pp. 225–9.

23. J. E. B. Seely (as Lord Mottistone), *Adventure* (Heinemann, London, 2nd edit., 1933), p. 165.

24. Nuffield College, Ms Mottistone 22, f.191–194, Trevor to Childs, 14.3.1914, enclosing intelligence notes compiled by Gleichen, which suggest that the North Irish Horse were 'Black Protestants' who would desert to the UVF at the first sign of trouble.

25. Jalland, *Liberals and Ireland*, pp. 56–7.

26. Ibid, pp. 208–9; Charles Townshend, *Political Violence in Ireland* (Oxford University Press, 1983), pp. 267–9.

27. Nuffield College, Ms Mottistone 22, f.147, Paget to French, 19.10.1913; General Sir Nevil Macready, *Annals of an Active Life* (Hutchinson, London, 1925), I, p. 171.

28. Jalland, *Liberals and Ireland*, pp. 216–21; Stewart, *Ulster Crisis*, pp. 126–8; Muenger, 'The British Army in Ireland', pp. 350–1; E. David (ed.), *Inside Asquith's Cabinet* (John Murray, London, 1977), pp. 167–8; Riddell, *More Pages*, p. 210; *The Times* Archive, Ireland Box, Robinson to Repington, 10.3.1914. On the support given by *The Times* to the UVF, see T. C. Kennedy, '*The Times* and the Irish Home Rule Question, 1906–1914', Unpub. M.A., Arizona, 1964, pp. 166–86. For the extant police reports, see B. M. Choille (ed.), *Intelligence Notes, 1913–1916* (Stationery Office, Dublin, 1966).

29. Gleichen, *Guardsman's Memories*, pp. 378–9. Gleichen clearly received the information from Macready.

30. Fergusson, *Curragh*, pp. 47–8.

31. All relevant telegrams are printed in the government's second white paper, *Correspondence relating to Recent Events in the Irish Command* (Cmd. 7329, 1914).

32. It is evident from the surviving references to the attitudes of Paget and French but was also stated by Churchill in the Commons—see Fergusson, *Curragh*, p. 47.

33. Townshend, *Political Violence*, p. 269.

34. Bodleian, Ms Asquith 40, f 13, Simon to Seely, 19.3.1914. Simon's inclusion in the discussions was presumably purely to advise on the legal aspects of Macready's appointment.

35. See Seely to Paget, 20.3.1914; Brade to Paget, 20.3.1914; and two telegrams from Paget to Seely on the same day—all reproduced in Cmd. 7329.

36. Field Marshal Sir William Robertson, *From Private to Field Marshal* (Constable, London, 1921), p. 194.

37. Jalland, *Liberals and Ireland*, p. 218.

38. R. Rhodes-James, *Churchill: A Study in Failure, 1900–1939* (Weidenfeld & Nicolson, London, 1970), pp. 47–8 provides a corrective to R. S. Churchill, *Winston S. Churchill* (Heinemann, London, 1967), II, pp. 492–502. The relevant naval telegrams are printed in Cmd. 7329 and are also available in PRO, Adm 116/1326. IWM, DS/MISC/20, 299, Battenberg Mss, contains two of Churchill's early directives on the naval movements.

39. Townshend, *Political Violence*, p. 269.

40. Fergusson has carefully reconstructed the precise timings of many events during the affair, ascertaining Paget's return time from contemporary train timetables—see *Curragh*, p. 57. Fergusson's orders from Friend are reproduced in *Curragh*, pp. 219–21.

41. H. of Lords RO, Bonar Law Mss, 32/2/53, Campbell to Law, 24.4.1914 gives an account of artillery movements at Kildare on 21 March from the perspective of the Lady Superintendent of the Soldier's Home.

42. Fergusson, *Curragh*, pp. 71–2. See also note 1, Section 2 in this volume.

43. Gleichen, *Guardsman's Memories*, p. 383.

44. See also H. F. Stoneham, 'Forty Years in Africa' (typescript 1956), p. 16 and R. Macleod, 'An Artillery Officer in the First World War', p. 17. Both are to be found in Sunderland Polytechnic, 1914–1918 Archives. Macleod's manuscript is also at the Royal Artillery Institution (Mss MD 1150) and the Liddell Hart Centre for Military Archives at King's College, London. At the latter, Macleod Mss 1/2 is the same as that at Sunderland and Woolwich but 1/1 is typed on a different machine and with different pagination.

45. See Philip Howell to the editor of *The Times*, 26.3.1914 reproduced in R. U. Howell, *Philip Howell: A Memoir by his Wife* (Allen & Unwin, London, 1942), pp. 50–2.

46. Macready, *Annals*, I, pp. 176–7; Major-General Sir Wyndham Childs, *Episodes and Reflections* (Cassell, London, 1930), p. 103.

47. Paget's telegram to Ewart was received in London at 11.35 p.m. See Cmd. 7329 for all relevant telegrams.

48. Telegram of Hubert Gough to Johnnie Gough, 20.3.1914 (Received 8.56 p.m.): 'Situation unchanged. My paper held over by HQ but can't see how this alters eventual result. Practically all officers Cavalry Brigade resigning and about five from each battalion. Don't do anything at present.' (J. E. Gough Mss).

49. Surviving documents relating to the Manchester Regiment give no firm figures but Bonar Law did so—*Hansard* 5s, HofC, LX, 73, Law, 23.3.1914. No trace of this letter has survived among the papers of Bonar Law.

50. Figures for the VIII Brigade are derived from an unidentified account in Bonar Law's papers—H. of Lords RO, 39/2/19. Other unidentified accounts not here reproduced are H. of Lords RO, Bonar Law Mss, 32/1/40 (Cavalry), 65, 84 (possibly by Captain R. A. M. Currie, Brigade-Major of 13th Infantry Brigade); Bodleian, Ms Milner 41, f.76–7 (Cavalry) and Ms Milner 157, f.76 (13th Infantry Brigade); RA GV F.674/25 (RHA).

51. Pragnell Mss, Hogg to HQ, 3rd Cavalry Brigade, 21.3.1914.

52. The best account of Headlam's role is in Fergusson, *Curragh*, passim. Fergusson reproduces a number of Headlam's papers but these are not among those preserved in the Royal Artillery Institution (Mss 183) and all trace of them has disappeared.

53. Pragnell Mss. Notes by Colonel T. W. Pragnell, February 1933.

54. RA GV F.674/36. Note by Lord Stamfordham, 25.3.1914 on a statement by Seely three days earlier: 'Colonel Seely said that Col. Parker, 5th Lancers, was in a very undisciplined state and drastic steps might have to be taken with him.'

55. See, for example, *Hansard* 5s, HofC, LX, 119–21, speech by John Ward, 23.3.1914 or the extracts quoted by Ward from the *Daily Herald* on the following day, ibid, LX, 251–3.

56. Pragnell Mss, Note by Pragnell, February 1933; Fergusson Mss, Graham to Fergusson, 25.11.1962; Ibid, Pielow to Fergusson, 19.5.1964; D. S. Daniell, *4th Hussar* (Gale & Polden, Aldershot, 1959), p. 238; Fergusson, *Curragh*, p. 161; David, *Inside Asquith's Cabinet*, p. 165; G. H. Parker to Keith Simpson, 30.9.1976 (I am grateful to my colleague for giving me a copy of the answers to his questionnaire, circulated to British

army officers of the First World War, by Colonel Parker, who was Orderly Room Sergeant of the 16th Lancers in March 1914). Ironically, there was concern in late July 1914 when men of the Irish Guards cheered Nationalist representatives attending the Buckingham Palace conference, *Hansard* 5s, HofC, LXV, 923, King, 27.7.1914.

57. The sequence of events is outlined in Fergusson, *Curragh*, pp. 96–101 while telegrams are in Cmd. 7329, pp. 9–12. Asquith's account can be found in Jenkins, *Asquith*, pp. 309–10.

58. David, *Inside Asquith's Cabinet*, p. 168. Hobhouse's correspondence with Bonar Law (as Postmaster General) can be found in H. of Lords RO, Bonar Law Mss, 32/2/46, 54. Interestingly, Hobhouse's communications with the Unionist leader over the intercepted telegram may indicate a wider 'bugging' operation by the government. On 24 March Austen Chamberlain interrupted a telephone conversation with Johnnie Gough's wife because he detected interference (J. E. Gough Mss, Chamberlain to Mrs D. Gough, 24.3.1914) while Hubert Gough mentioned his suspicions of 'leakage of wires' in Dublin to Henry Wilson on 27 March (IWM, 73/1/18, Gough to Wilson, 27.3.1914). A Unionist supporter also told Bonar Law that government supporters were openly acknowledging that wires were being tapped (H. of Lords RO, Bonar Law Mss, 32/1/81, Moyers to Law, 29.3.1914).

59. Roberts felt it necessary to defend his conduct during the Curragh Incident by privately distributing an account, 'Ulster and the Army'. Copies may be found in NAM, 7101-23-202, Roberts Mss; Bodleian, Ms Milner 158/12; and NLS, Acc 7726/147, Oliver Mss (incomplete).

60. H. of Lords RO, Bonar Law Mss, 32/1/93; Ibid, 32/2/3, 14; RA GV F.674/66, 67, 68 for the correspondence of Lady Lugard and Mrs Louise Bagnall with Bonar Law and Lord Stamfordham.

61. J. E. Gough Mss, Chamberlain to Mrs D. Gough, 24.3.1914; Birmingham University Library, AC 14/3/1, 2, Chamberlain Mss, J. E. Gough to Chamberlain, 25.3.1914 and Mrs D. Gough to Chamberlain of same date. Dorothy Gough was an old school friend of Chamberlain's sister.

62. Fergusson, *Curragh*, p. 134 is at error in suggesting that Haig would not forward Gough's resignation. The resignation was in the hands of the Military Secretary before Haig returned from Littlehampton.

63. RA GV K.2553(4)/41, Note by Lord Stamfordham, 21.3.1914. Fergusson, *Curragh*, pp. 133, 206–7 reproduces the King's letter to Asquith on 21 March and Asquith's reply. The letters are in RA GV K.2553(4)/39, 40. See also Nicolson, *King George V*, p. 238.

64. Childs, *Episodes and Reflections*, pp. 104–5.

65. Morley's lapse was attributed by Margot Asquith to deafness and being

'much too vain' to admit he did not know what was going on—see Jenkins, *Asquith*, p. 312. For the views of other contemporaries on Morley's role, see Blunt, *Diaries*, p. 441; Sir Almeric Fitzroy, *Memoirs of Sir Almeric Fitzroy* (Hutchinson, London, 1926), II, p. 544; Nuffield College, Ms Gainford 39, f.86–7, diary of H. W. Pease. Seely himself absolved Morley from any blame—see Nuffield College, Ms Mottistone 22, f.327–31, Seely to Morley, 31.3.1914.

66. J. E. Gough Mss, Parker to Gough, 25.3.1914 and MacEwen to Gough, 2.4.1914; Hubert Gough, *Soldiering On* (Arthur Barker, London, 1954) pp. 110–11, 171–3.

67. Haldane's statement on 23 March that 'No orders were issued, no orders are likely to be issued and no orders will be issued for the coercing of Ulster' proved embarrassing in view of a previous speech by Sir Edward Grey. Haldane therefore attempted to amend the record of his remarks in *Hansard*, raising a predictable storm, by inserting 'immediate' before 'coercing'. See Sir F. Maurice, *Haldane* (Faber & Faber, London, 1937), pp. 345–6 and S. Koss, *Lord Haldane* (Columbia University Press, 1969), pp. 112–13.

68. Gough, *Soldiering On*, p. 110. A receipt for the document signed by Gough's solicitor, D. F. Moore of Whitney and Moore of Dublin on 26.3.1914 is in H. P. Gough Mss.

69. Fitz Watt's role is outlined in Holmes, *Little Field Marshal*, p. 192 while Holmes, pp. 189–92 provides the best account of French's dilemma. For Gwynne, see K. M. Wilson, 'Sir John French's resignation over the Curragh affair: the role of the editor of the *Morning Post*', *English Historical Review*, XCIX, 1984, pp. 807–12. See also Lionel Brett (ed.), *The Journals and Letters of Reginald, Viscount Esher* (Nicholson & Watson, London, 1938), III, pp. 159–60; Churchill College, ESHR 4/5, Esher Mss, Esher to Stamfordham, 30.3.1914; Riddell, *More Pages*, pp. 206–7.

70. Brigadier-General John Charteris, *Field Marshal Earl Haig* (Cassell, London, 1929), pp. 72–3. In October 1916 Haig wrote to Leopold de Rothschild that 'Many of us do not forget . . . how he [French] sacrificed the whole Army during the Irish crisis before the war'—NLS, Haig Mss, Acc 3155/214(a), Haig to Rothschild, 13 October 1916—quoted in Gerry de Groot, 'The Pre-war Life and Military Career of Douglas Haig', Unpub. Ph.D., Edinburgh, 1983, p. 348.

71. The suggestion that John Burns should go to the War Office had some support according to Burns' own diary—BL, Add Mss 46336, f.67, entry for 26.3.1914. For Hankey's abortive attempt to use the CID to mediate, see Churchill College, HNKY 4/6, Hankey Mss, Hankey to Balfour, 27.3.1914 (also BL, Add Mss 49693, f.159–60), reproduced in S. Roskill, *Hankey: Man of Secrets* (Collins, London, 1970) pp. 132–3.

72. Riddell, *More Pages*, p. 206.

73. Fergusson, *Curragh*, p. 147.

74. Robertson, *From Private to Field Marshal*, p. 193.

75. Macready, *Annals*, p. 177; Childs, *Episodes*, pp. 105–6; Sir George MacMunn, *Behind the Scenes in Many Wars* (John Murray, London, 1930), pp. 105–7. MacMunn, who was DAD of Remounts under the Quartermaster General, names two Ulstermen as part of the 'cabal' at the War Office—Major A. G. Stewart, 40th Pathans, who was GSO2 in Wilson's directorate, and Captain R. Ommanney, RE, GSO3 on Wilson's staff. One of the few on Wilson's staff who did not go along with the majority was Colonel G. M. W. Macdonogh, leading to an uneasy relationship thereafter between the two—see Keith Jeffery (ed.), *The Military Correspondence of Field Marshal Sir Henry Wilson 1918–1922* (The Bodley Head for the Army Records Society, 1985), p. 347, n. 27 (based on IWM, Kirke Mss). See also Appendix 2 of this volume.

76. D. S. Macdiarmid, *The Life of General Grierson* (Constable & Co, London, 1923), pp. 252–3 reproduces parts of Grierson's diary (later destroyed). These indicate the views of both Grierson as GOC, Eastern Command and Sir Francis Lloyd as GOC, London District. Ironically, in view of their own activities, Wilson and Sackville-West [Document 139] believed Lloyd to be playing politics by refusing all resignations. Lloyd's speeches were twice mentioned in the House of Commons during the crisis—see *Hansard* 5s, HofC, LX, 566–7, Amery and Seely, 26.3.1914, and LXI, 584, Hall, 28.4.1914. Sadly, Lloyd's papers have not been deposited in the Essex Record Office as once thought and seem to have disappeared.

77. General Sir A. P. Wavell, *Allenby* (Harrap, London, 1940), p. 123. Allenby's papers include the notes Wavell made for the biography but these have no mention of the Curragh beyond Lady Allenby's declaration that her husband had no part in it—King's College, Liddell Hart Centre for Military Archives, Allenby Mss 6/V, Lady Allenby to Wavell, 19.12.1936. Other contemporary letters of Wavell (other than that reproduced in this volume) can be found in J. Connell, *Wavell: Scholar and Soldier* (Collins, London, 1964), pp. 82–9.

78. See also Churchill College, WMYS 2/5, Wemyss Mss, Bevan to Wemyss, 26.3.1914 (15th Hussars); Nuffield College, Ms Mottistone 22, f.121, Tennyson to Seely, 21.3.1914 (Rifle Brigade); House of Lords RO, Bonar Law Mss, 32/1/41, Tullibardine to Law, 21.3.1914 (Highland regiments); IWM, 73/1/18, Wilson Mss, R. G(rant) to 'Alan', 21.3.1914 (Rifle Brigade); Fergusson Mss, Dugdale to Fergusson, 31.3.1964; Fergusson, *Curragh*, p. 202. The latter two references give an

indication of support for the Goughs at RMA, Woolwich. See also Appendix 2.

79. See *Hansard* 5s, H. of C., LX, 1366–7, Ponsonby, 2.4.1914 and 1948, Cowan, 8.4.1914 for suggestions that officers of the National Reserve and Territorials attended or were invited to attend the Unionist rally in Hyde Park on 4.4.1914 in uniform. Fourteen retired or reserve officers had indicated their determination not to assist in the coercion of Ulster by 25.3.1914—see Nuffield College, Ms Mottistone 22, f.250. Other reservists corresponded with Bonar Law (H. of Lords RO, Bonar Law Mss, 32/1/61, 86; 39/2/22) or sent congratulations to Hubert Gough (H. P. Gough Mss). Both Johnnie Gough and Captain Price-Davies attended the Hyde Park demonstration (AMOT, Price-Davies, Diary for 4.4.1914).

80. H. P. Gough Mss, Evelyn Byng to Hubert Gough, 1.4.1914 (Cairo); R. Meinertzhagen, *Army Diary, 1899–1926* (Oliver & Boyd, London & Edinburgh, 1960), pp. 70–4, reproducing a lengthy entry for 31.3.1914 written from the Staff College, Quetta; King's College, Liddell Hart Centre for Military Archives, Isacke Mss, Diary entry for 29.3.1914, indicating the support of Major H. Isacke, GSO2 at the Staff College, Quetta, for the Goughs. See Appendix 2.

81. Jalland, *Liberals and Ireland*, pp. 234–67; Blake, *Unknown Prime Minister*, pp. 198–209; Jenkins, *Asquith*, pp. 312–15; Fergusson, *Curragh*, pp. 159–69, 182–93.

82. NAM, 8001-6-10, MacEwen Mss, Frewen-Laton to MacEwen, 3.4.1914; 8001-6-11, Gray to MacEwen, 4.4.1914; 8001-6-12, Gray to MacEwen, 7.4.1914; 8001-6-17, Frewen-Laton to MacEwen, 2.5.1914; IWM, 73/1/18, Wilson Mss, Milner to Wilson, 24.3.1914; H. of Lords RO, Bonar Law Mss, 32/2/9, Midleton to Law, 3.4.1914; J. E. Gough Mss, Repington to Gough, 25.3.1914 and Oliver to Gough, 26.3.1914; Ibid, Mrs D. Gough to Oliver, 17.4.1914; NLS, Acc 7726/96, f.109, Amery to Oliver, 26.3.1914; Churchill College, ESHR 4/5, Esher Mss, Esher to Balfour, 26.4.1914.

83. RA GV F.674/37, 41, 51 (a) and (b), 64, 69, 91 for other correspondence on the King's name. Much of this is reproduced in Fergusson, *Curragh*, pp. 170–81. See also Repington to Robinson, 9.6.1914 in *The Times* Archive, Repington Mss and, for Paget's only supporter other than Methuen, see PRO, WO35/209(m), Stuart-Wortley to Forestier-Walker, 1.4.1914.

84. IWM, DS/MISC/80, HHW 23, Wilson Diary, 16.4.1914; BL, Add Mss 51250, Methuen to Paget, 12.7.1914; RA GV F.674/99, Methuen to Paget, 18.7.1914 and /100, Methuen to Stamfordham, 18.7.1914.

85. On Asquith's absences from the War Office, see IWM, DS/MISC/

80, HHW 23, Wilson Diary, 22.4.1914 and *The Times* Archive, Repington Mss, Repington to Robinson, 18.6.1914.

86. See also BL, Add Mss 51250, Macready to Paget, 26.3.1914; Sunderland Polytechnic, 1914–1918 Archives, Macleod Mss, Macleod's father to his mother, 27.3.1914.

87. Gooch, *Plans of War*, p. 125. Douglas was the choice of both French and Ewart—see SRO, RH4/84/3, 126, Ewart Diary, 1.4.1914. There had been some horror at the prospect of Hamilton securing the appointment. Macready hoped to become Adjutant General but this was blocked by Douglas (Ewart Diary, 2.4.1914) and Sclater was appointed Ewart's successor.

88. PRO, WO 32/5319, Sclater to Paget, 27.4.1914; Ibid, Friend to Sclater, 28.4.1914; Ibid, Paget to Brade, 30.4.1914; Ibid, note by K. Lyon, 30.4.1914; Bodleian, Ms Asquith 7, f.117–20, Asquith to the King, 2.5.1914 quoting the advice of Macready, who had gone to Belfast.

89. Macdiarmid, *Grierson*, p. 253 quotes Grierson's diary for 27.4.1914: 'To WO and saw Douglas as to whether my troops would fight Ulster, to which I said I didn't think so if it came to coercion, but that they would maintain law and order.' See also C. E. Callwell, *Field Marshal Sir Henry Wilson* (Cassell, London, 1927), I, p. 146; Bodleian, Ms Asquith 41, f.18–24, Aberdeen to Birrell, 26.4.1914 in which Aberdeen states, 'No troops can be fully relied upon to move when ordered.'

90. IWM, DS/MISC/80, HHW 23, Wilson Diary entries for 30.6.1914, 1.7.1914 and 4.7.1914. On 10 July Douglas told Wilson that Asquith 'is furious with the Mil: Members for sending him in a paper drawing attention to the military aspect of civil war.'

91. PRO, WO35/60/3 contains the official enquiry file. The report of the Royal Commission is available in Bodleian, Ms Asquith 41, f.111–18. The 5th Lancers were ordered to prepare a detachment for possible use on 27 July but were not required. The subsequent enquiry disrupted mobilisation in Ireland by drawing out key personnel while the compensation was not finally settled until January 1915.

92. Churchill College, ESHR, 4/4, Esher Mss, Esher to Balfour, 26.4.1914 reproduced in Brett, *Journals and Letters*, III, pp. 163–5; *Hansard* 5s, H.ofC., LXII, 1272, Currie, 18.6.1914.

93. IWM, 73/1/18, Wilson Mss, Rawlinson to Wilson, 23.3.1914 and Gough to Wilson of 29.3.1914 and 3.6.1914; Countess of Fingall, *Seventy Years Young* (Collins, London, 1937), p. 172.

94. Fergusson Mss, Fergusson to Lady Fergusson, 23.3.1916 reproduced in Fergusson, *Curragh*, p. 198; BL Add Mss 51250, Lady Paget to French, August 1914 and French to Lady Paget, 9.8.1914; John Gooch, 'The War Office and the Curragh Incident', *Bulletin of the Institute of Historical*

Research XLVI, 1973, pp. 202–7. Tim Travers claims, on the evidence of a conversation between Basil Liddell Hart and the official historian, Edmonds, in 1937 that Paget failed to secure command of III Corps because of a disagreement with French at the 1913 manoeuvres but the Curragh, which Travers does not mention in his otherwise interesting examination of rivalries in the army, was a rather more significant factor in the relationship of French and Paget—see T. H. E. Travers, 'The Hidden Army: Structural Problems in the British Officer Corps, 1900–1918', *Journal of Contemporary History* 17, 1982, pp. 523–44.

95. Ewart believed that French's influence in the army was strengthened by the Curragh (SRO, RH4/84/3, 126, Diary for 1.4.1914) but this seems unlikely. For French's mood in July see W. S. Churchill, *Great Contemporaries* (Thornton Lutterworth, London, 1937), p. 83. On Rolt, see Fergusson Mss, Fergusson to Lady Fergusson of 18.10.1917, and 29.8.1927.

96. IWM, 73/1/18, Wilson Mss, Gough to Wilson, 26.3.1914; and J. E. Gough Mss, Hubert Gough to Johnnie Gough, 26.3.1914 are almost identical telegrams containing the phrase, 'Don't let us become tools of either Political Party.' See also B.L. Keyes Mss 3/17, Hubert Gough to Lady Keyes, 5.4.1914, in which Gough indicates that the army has been saved by the Curragh 'from becoming a political plaything'.

97. H. P. Gough Mss, Rawlinson to Gough, 25.3.1914: 'I have just heard on the telephone that the "White Paper" is out and that it will probably break the Government! Hurrah!'

98. Jalland, *Liberals and Ireland*, p. 247. See also Townshend, *Political Violence*, pp. 273–6.

99. See Johnnie Gough's letter to *The Times* using the pseudonym of 'Soldier', 25.3.1914 (J. E. Gough Mss).

100. MacMunn, *Behind the Scenes*, p. 107.

NOTES TO SECTION I

1. Robinson refers to the meeting of the sub-committee of the Committee of Imperial Defence conducting the so-called third 'invasion enquiry'. See H. R. Moon, 'The Invasion of the United Kingdom: Public Controversy and Official Planning 1888–1918', Unpub. Ph.D., London, 1968, II, pp. 429–82.

2. The article appeared in *The Times* on 14 July 1913 drawing attention to the 'spirit of anxious restlessness' in the Army. See T. C. Kennedy, '*The Times* and the Irish Home Rule Question, 1906–1914', Unpub. M.A., Arizona, 1964, pp. 166–86.

3. The annual manoeuvres were conducted in Buckinghamshire and Northamptonshire from 15 to 26 September 1913, one 'army' being commanded by Lieutenant-General Sir Douglas Haig and the other by Lieutenant-General Sir Arthur Paget.

4. Princess Alexander of Teck, later Princess Alice, Countess of Athlone (1883–1981), was the daughter of Leopold, Duke of Albany, the eighth child of Queen Victoria and Prince Albert.

5. Prince Alexander of Teck, later Earl of Athlone (1874–1957). Service in Matabeleland, 1896; South African War; European War, 1914–18; Governor-General of South Africa, 1923–31.

6. See Document 5, Wilson diary for 26 December 1913, which indicates that the discussion between Wilson, Rawlinson and J. E. Gough took place on that day and not 'a few days previously'. This account by Gough appears to date from late March or early April 1914.

7. Cecil was Henry Wilson's wife.

8. Sir Charles Hunter (1858–1924), Unionist M.P. for Bath, 1910–18.

9. Major-General Sir Henry Rawlinson.

10. Wilson was staying at Englemere, the Ascot home of Field Marshal Lord Roberts.

11. Roberts.

12. Major (later Major-General) L. H. R. Pope-Hennessy (1875–1942), OBLI, was Brigade-Major of 1st West Riding Infantry Brigade (TF). Service in West Africa, 1897–8; East Africa, 1901, 1903 and 1905; Nandi, 1905–6; Somaliland, 1908–10; European War, 1914–16; Mesopotamia, 1916–17; BGGS to 1st Indian Corps, 1917–19.

Confusion surrounds the date of this conversation since Roberts subsequently related to Bonar Law that it took place on 28 December (H. of Lords RO, Bonar Law Mss, 31/2/16, Roberts to Law, 4 January 1914) while Wilson records it two days earlier in his diary (Document 5). Arthur Elliot (1846–1923) was Unionist M.P. for Roxburgh, 1886–92 and Durham City, 1898–1906.

13. Major-General F. J. Davies.

14. Paget's divisional commanders were Major-General Sir Charles Fergusson commanding 5th Division and Major-General W. P. Pulteney, commanding 6th Division.

15. Field Marshal Lord Wolseley had warned of the dangers of coercing Ulster in 1893, his warnings being liberally repeated in 1913 and 1914: See Walter Long's speech in the Commons, 10 February 1914 (*Hansard* 5s, LVIII, 69–70).

16. Document No. 10.

17. F. S. Oliver, *The Alternatives to Civil War* (John Murray, London, 1913).

18. The memorandum here reproduced is Seely's Cabinet paper of 9

December 1913. Subsequently, Seely spoke to GOCs on 16 December in very similar terms, the latter memorandum being reproduced in the White Paper.

19. Captain W. B. Spender had been allowed to retire from the Army on 7 August 1913 following a protracted dispute with the War Office after subscribing to the Covenant. See A. T. Q. Stewart, *The Ulster Crisis* (Faber & Faber, London, 1967), pp. 83–5.

20. The copy of the letter was enclosed in a communication from Roberts to Bonar Law dated 4 January 1914 (H. of Lords RO, Bonar Law Mss, 31/2/16).

21. January is the wrong date. See Note 12 above.

22. Another name for Roberts.

23. George (later Sir George) Cave (1856–1928), Unionist M.P. for Kingston, 1906–18.

24. Commissioner of the Royal Irish Constabulary.

25. Dr (later Sir Leander) L. Starr Jameson (1853–1917), best known for the Jameson Raid and subsequently Prime Minister of Cape Colony, 1904–8.

26. Wilson visited Ulster in early March to lecture on the Balkans.

27. Lieutenant Colonel (later Major-General Sir Hugh) H. B. Williams (1865–1942) was appointed GSO2 in the Irish Command for the forthcoming operations (See French to Paget, 19 March 1914 in IWM, 75/46/8, French Mss). Service in South African War; European War, 1914–18; Colonel Commandant of Royal Engineers, 1930–5.

28. Colonel (later Major-General Sir William) W. B. Hickie (1865–1950), Royal Fusiliers, was AQMG in the Irish Command. Service in South African War; European War, 1914–18, becoming GOC 16th Division; Senator in Irish Free State, 1925–36.

29. Colonel F. J. de Gex (1861–1917), West Riding Regiment, was AAG in the Irish Command. Service in South African War; European War, 1914–15, died on active service, 2.4.1917.

30. This document is undated but clearly refers to the discussions between French, Wilson and Robertson, under whose authority as DMT the Ulster operations were to be conducted. See Document 24, Wilson diary for 19 March, and Sir William Robertson, *From Private to Field-Marshal* (Constable, London, 1921), pp. 193–5.

NOTES TO SECTION 2

1. The order was issued verbally to infantry units but was recorded in identical terms by Lieutenant A. N. Acland, 1st DCLI (diary fragment

in Fergusson Mss) and in the 'Record of Services' of the 2nd Manchesters (Manchester Central Library, M25/2/16). Brigadier-General S. P. Rolt had the same recollection of the ultimatum—see Sir James Fergusson, *The Curragh Incident* (Faber & Faber, London, 1964), p. 82 and Document 62.

2. Lieutenant Colonel H. L. James (1863–1946), 2nd Manchesters. Service in South African War; European War, 1914–18.

3. Lieutenant J. B. Gough, D. Battery, III Brigade, RHA was the cousin of Hubert and J. E. Gough. Commissioned in 1907, he was killed in action, 9 September 1914.

4. Major (later Brigadier-General) G. Gillson (1867–1937), D Battery, III Brigade, RHA. Service on North-West Frontier, 1897–8; Nile, 1899; European War, 1914–18.

5. Second Lieutenant (later Lieutenant Colonel) W. Scott-Watson, 80th Battery, XV Brigade, RFA. Service in European War, 1914–18.

6. Those Majors serving with 16th Lancers were R. L. Macalpine-Leny; C. J. Eccles; C. L. K. Campbell; and C. E. St. J. Harris-St. John. See notes 63 and 84 below.

7. Major (later Lieutenant Colonel) A. E. Haig, 2nd KOSB. Service in Sudan, 1885; Nile, 1889; Chitral, 1895; Tirah, 1897–8; South African War; captured at Le Cateau, 26 August 1914. Haig also commanded the detachment of the KOSB who fired on crowds at Bachelors' Walk in Dublin on 26 July 1914 following the Howth gun running.
   Captain (later Major) C. F. Kennedy, 2nd KOSB. Service in South African War; European War, 1914–18 being wounded at Mons, 23 August 1914.

8. Although referring to the events of Friday, 20 March, the telegram was not actually sent until 8 a.m. on Saturday 21 March. Hogg had served in the 4th Hussars with Churchill and regarded him as 'an old brother officer'—see Document 56.

9. Lieutenant (later Captain) H. F. Stoneham, 1st East Surreys. Service in European War, 1914–18.

10. There was no secret letter—see Document 61.

11. Major-General Sir Charles Fergusson and Brigadier-General J. E. W. Headlam respectively.

12. Lieutenant Colonel C. M. Stephenson, 2nd KOSB. Service in Chin Lushai, 1889–90; South African War; European War, 1914 being severely wounded at Le Cateau, 26 August 1914.

13. Major M. P. Buckle, Royal West Kents. Service in South African War; killed in action, 27 October 1914.

14. Major (later Colonel) M. Earle (1871–1953), Grenadier Guards, was the second of three intelligence officers attached to the Irish Command in

March 1914. Service in Matabeleland, 1893; South African War; European War, 1914; Deputy DSD, 1921; Lees Knowles Lecturer, 1921-3.

Captain (later Lieutenant Colonel) B. Walcot (1880-1918), RE, was the third intelligence officer attached to Irish Command with Williams and Earle. Service in South African War; European War, 1914-18 dying on active service, 14 September 1918.

15. Colonel M. W. J. Edye, Retired List. Service in Egypt, 1882; Sudan, 1884-5; re-employed on LOC, 1914-18.

16. Brevet Lieutenant Colonel (later Major General) C. F. Romer (1869-1962), Royal Dublin Fusiliers, was DAQMG in the Irish Command. Service in South African War; European War, 1914-18, DSD, 1922-5; AG, 1933-5.

17. Fergusson did not forward this communication until 25 March—Document 59.

18. I.e. Document 33 of which Rolt had a verbal rather than a written version—see Note 1 above.

19. Captain F. A. Forster, 1st Royal Fusiliers, was shortly to leave the 1st Battalion to become Adjutant of the Leeds, Nottingham, Manchester and Sheffield OTCs. Recalled to the 4th Battalion, he died of wounds at Mons, 23 August 1914. Service in West Africa, 1906.

20. Document 31.

21. Anglo-Indian slang for 'browbeat' or 'threaten'.

22. Second Lieutenant (later Major) J. B. Oakes, 1st Norfolks. Service in European War, 1914-18, being wounded at Mons, 23 August 1914.

23. Lieutenant Colonel (later Brigadier-General) C. R. Ballard (1868-1941), 1st Norfolks. Service in Burma, 1891; Chitral, 1895; Tirah, 1897; South African War; Somaliland, 1903-4; European War, 1914-16 commanding 7th, 95th and 57th Brigades; Military Attaché in Roumania, 1917-18.

24. Captain J. B. Orr, 1st Norfolks. Service in South African War; died of wounds, 24 August 1914.

25. Captain (later Brigadier-General) H. R. Done (1876-1950), 1st Norfolks. Service in European War, 1914-18 commanding 145th Brigade.

26. Wife of Captain R. H. Brudenell-Bruce, 1st Norfolks.

27. Strickland had been offered command of the 1st Manchesters on 14 March 1914, the appointment being due to be gazetted on 1 June.

28. Document 34.

29. Major R. A. Birley, 80th Battery, XV Brigade, RFA. Severely wounded at Le Cateau, 26 August 1914.

30. Lieutenant (later Brigadier-General) A. G. Hewson, 80th Battery, XV Brigade, RFA. Service in European War, 1914-18.

31. Captain (later Lieutenant Colonel) J. V. Ramsden (1876–1952) was Adjutant of XXVII Brigade, RFA at Newbridge. Service in European War, 1914–18.

32. Lieutenant Colonel (later Major-General Sir William) W. H. Onslow (1863–1929). Service in South African War; European War, 1914–15; Balkans, 1916–9.

33. Private Charles Smith (1892–1914), enlisted in 16th Lancers 1911. Killed in action, 29 August 1914. See *OFH, France and Belgium, 1914* (HMSO, London, 1932), I. p. 226 for an account of Smith's death.

34. W. H. Smith was Art editor of the *Illustrated London News*.

35. Lieutenant (later Captain) Lord H. W. Holmpatrick (1886–1942), was a Special Reserve officer acting as Adjutant of 16th Lancers. Service in European War, 1914–18. Holmpatrick resigned his commission on 19 May 1914 but returned in August.

36. Major (later Brigadier-General Sir Robert) R. H. Kearsley (1888–1956), 5th Dragoon Guards, was Brigade-Major of 3rd Cavalry Brigade. Service in South African War; European war, 1914–18.

37. Captain A. V. W. Stokes, Adjutant 4th Hussars. Service in South African War; incapacitated by wounds, 23 February 1915.

38. Document 31.

39. Document 39.

40. The Ancient Order of Hibernians, an illegal Catholic and Republican Society.

41. Hogg refers to a letter of 21 March 1914 in which he lists the choices made by his officers after hearing Paget's address: 10 for duty, 1 claiming the domicile exemption, and 6 undecided (Pragnell Mss).

42. Document 100.

43. Brigadier-Generals G. J. Cuthbert and S. P. Rolt respectively.

44. A brief note of the interview survives in RA GV F.674/22—see Fergusson, *Curragh Incident*, p. 170.

45. During industrial troubles in Belfast, notably the shipyards, men of the 2nd KOSB together with elements of 1st Cheshire and HLI were deployed from 23 July to 14 August 1912 (PRO, WO 35/60/1).

46. Lieutenant Colonel C. M. Stephenson—see Note 12 above.

47. Captain J. B. Hartley, 2nd KOSB. Killed in action while serving with 1st KOSB at Gallipoli, 4 June 1915.

48. Lieutenant (later Captain) R. Joynson, 2nd KOSB. Captured at Le Cateau, 26 August 1914.

49. Captain H. Cobden, 2nd KOSB. Service in South African War; missing at Le Cateau, 26 August 1914.

    Second Lieutenant G. P. Hammond, 2nd KOSB. Killed in action, 10 September 1914.

50. Captain R. C. Y. Dering, Adjutant of 2nd KOSB. Died of wounds, 19 April 1915.
51. Lieutenant (later Major) J. B. W. Pennyman, 2nd KOSB. Service in European War, 1914–18.
52. Major C. Leigh (1873–1914), 2nd KOSB. Service in South African War; Sudan, 1905; died of wounds, 29 August 1914.
53. Document 46.
54. Stamfordham had sent a copy of Brett's letter to Fergusson on 26 March asking for an explanation of the use of the King's name and the 'secret' War Office letter to which Brett referred (RA GV F.674/37).
55. Document 33.
56. The account may have been written for Major-General L. B. Friend— see Fergusson, *Curragh Incident*, p. 176.
57. Lieutenant (later Brigadier-General) Lord D. Malise Graham (1883– 1974), RA, was ADC to Fergusson. Service in European War, 1914– 18; Commandant of School of Artillery at Larkhill, 1934–6.
58. See Note 1 above.
59. Brigadier-General W. R. B. Doran (1861–1945), Royal Irish Regiment, commanded 17th Brigade in 6th Division. Service in Egypt, 1882; Nile, 1884; Hazara, 1888; Sudan, 1897–8; South African War; European War, 1914–15; BGGS at Aldershot, 1915–19.
    Brigadier-General (later Major-General) E. C. Ingouville-Williams (1861–1916), The Buffs, commanded 16th Brigade of 6th Division. Service in Sudan, 1884–5; Nile, 1898; South African War; European War, 1914–16; killed in action 22 July 1916.
60. Paget's speech to the Corinthian Club is recounted in Fergusson, *Curragh Incident*, p. 66.
61. Document 59, which is in fact dated 25th March 1914.
62. Lieutenant (later Captain) A. A. Mackintosh, RHG, was Paget's ADC. Died of wounds, 14 October 1918.
63. Major (later Lieutenant Colonel) C. L. K. Campbell (1873–1918), 16th Lancers. Service on North-West Frontier, 1897–8; South African War; died on active service, 31 March 1918.
64. A note by Stamfordham on 11 April 1914 records the officer as Captain P. Hunloke (RA GV F.674/71). This seems problematical since the only Hunloke in the Army List is Captain (later Major Sir Philip) Hunloke (1868–1947), Bucks Imperial Yeomanry. Service South African War; European War, 1914–18. The letter was forwarded to Gretton not by the officer but by the officer's father. John (later Lord) Gretton (1867–1947) was Unionist M.P. for South Derbyshire, 1895–1906; Rutland, 1907–18; Burton, 1918–43.
65. Lieutenant Colonel (later Brigadier-General) M. N. Turner (1865–

1944), 1st DCLI. Service Burma, 1892–3 and 1895–6; European War, 1914–18; North Russia, 1919.

66. No memorandum is extant.

67. See Document 62 where Fergusson indicates that he has written to all units. None is extant—see Fergusson, *Curragh Incident*, p. 120.

68. The copy of the letter was forwarded to Bonar Law by J. H. Howell, the writer being the daughter of one of Howell's workmen at Clifton, Bristol.

69. Captain W. Barber-Starkey, 52nd Battery, XV Brigade, RFA. Mortally wounded at Le Cateau, 26 August 1914.

70. This was an exaggeration as only the move of the 1st Division plus two infantry and one cavalry brigade was contemplated.

71. Major (later Brigadier-General) J. B. Jardine (1870–1955), 5th Lancers, wrote this account in March but it was only forwarded by his wife to the King on 7 April (RA GV F.674/60, 71). Jardine's service was in South African War; Russo-Japanese War as military attaché; European War, 1914–18.

72. Lieutenant Colonel Arthur Parker.

73. This 'further note' is, in fact, Gough's only full account of the events of Friday 20 March, his original written recollection (Document 64) being an account of Saturday 21 March. However, he had written a brief statement of events which he handed to Ewart in London on 22 March (Document 96).

74. Gough makes exactly the same point in his account of 21 March (Document 64) and it is conceivable that he confused the two although, equally, Paget may have repeated himself.

75. Document 31.

76. This may not be correct as A. Farrar-Hockley states in *Goughie* (Hart-Davis, London, 1975), pp. 104–5 that the letter was handed in error to J. E. Gough. The story is repeated by Richard Holmes, *The Little Field Marshal* (Cape, London, 1981), pp. 182–3, presumably based on Farrar-Hockley but no source is given in the former. J. E. Gough's own account (Document 122) makes no mention of the incident. Fergusson, *Curragh Incident*, p. 131 is at error in suggesting Gough did not receive the letter.

77. Documents 63 and 65.

78. Presumably Lieutenant C. G. Robinson of HMS *Pathfinder*.

79. Colonel Sir Neville Chamberlain (1856–1944), Inspector-General of the Royal Irish Constabulary, 1900–16. Service in Afghanistan, 1878–80; Burma, 1886–7; South African War, where he had been private secretary to Roberts.

80. Major (later Lieutenant Colonel) M. F. McTaggert (1874–1936), 5th Lancers. Service on North-West Frontier, 1897–8; Tirah, 1898; South African War; European War, 1914–18 commanding 1/5th Gordon Highlanders from 1915.

Captain (later Major) A. Neave, 16th Lancers. Service in South African War; died of wounds, 21 February 1915.

Lieutenant (later Captain) E. R. Nash, 16th Lancers. Killed in action, 21 February 1915.

81. Lieutenant J. Penrose, 3 Signal Troop, RE. Service European War, 1914–18 transferring to Machine Gun Corps.

82. Document 31.

83. Document 65.

84. Major (later Lieutenant Colonel) R. L. Macalpine-Leny (1870–1941), 16th Lancers. Service in South African War; European War, 1914–18.

85. Major-General (later Lieutenant-General Sir James) J. M. Babington (1854–1936) was Honorary Colonel of the 16th Lancers. Service in Bechuanaland, 1884–5; South African War; European War, 1914–18 commanding 23rd Division, 1914–15 and XIV Corps, 1918–19.

86. Brigadier-General J. E. Gough, V.C.

87. Document 99.

88. Second Lieutenant (later Brigadier-General) W. H. Brooke (1887–1975), 2nd KOYLI. Service in European War, 1914–18.

89. Second Lieutenant (later Captain) J. B. Noel, 2nd KOYLI. Wounded and captured at Le Cateau, 26 August 1914. Later service in North Russia, 1919.

90. Second Lieutenant (later Captain) G. C. Wynne. Captured at Le Cateau, 26 August 1914. Employed in CID Historical Section from 1922 working on the Official History. Author of *If Germany Attacks* (London, 1940).

91. Lieutenant Colonel H. Wells-Cole (1864–1914), commanding 2nd KOYLI. Service on North-West Frontier, 1897–8; South African War. Died 30 April 1914.

92. Major (later Lieutenant Colonel) R. C. Bond (1866–1936), 2nd KOYLI. Service in Zhob, 1890; North-West Frontier, 1897–1898; South African War; succeeded Wells-Cole as CO but captured at Le Cateau, 26 August 1914.

93. Second Lieutenant (later Major) T. E. F. Penny, 2nd KOYLI. Service in European War, 1914–18 acting as Adjutant to 6th KOYLI, 1914–17.

94. Brigadier-General G. J. Cuthbert.

95. Bandsman F. C. Wynne enlisted in the 1st East Surreys as a boy aged $15\frac{1}{2}$ in April 1913. Service in European War, 1914–18.

96. Austen Chamberlain, M.P.

97. Document 99.

98. Document 100.

99. A. H. (later Lord) Lee (1868–1947), Unionist M.P. for South Hampshire, 1900–18.

100. Major (later Brigadier-General) A. H. Ollivant (1871–1919), RA, was GSO2 attached to the Admiralty. Service in East Africa, 1903–4; European War, 1914–18, at Antwerp and Dardanelles with RN Division, with BEF, 1916–17 and as GSO1 to the Supreme War Council.

101. Sir Arthur Nicholson (later Lord Carnock) (1849–1928), was Permanent Under-Secretary at the Foreign Office, 1910–16.

102. Major-General Sir Charles Knowles (1835–1924), Retired List. Service in Crimea 1855; Afghanistan, 1878–80.

 Major A. J. B. Percival (1870–1914), Northumberland Fusiliers, was GSO2 at Staff College. Service on the Nile, 1898; South African War; Sudan, 1905–6; killed in action, 31 November 1914.

 Major (later Field Marshal Sir Archibald Montgomery-Massingberd), A. A. Montgomery (1871–1947), RA, was GSO2 at Staff College. Service in South African War; European War, 1914–18; A.G. 1931–3; CIGS, 1931–6.

 Major (later Major-General) H. M. de F. Montgomery (1870–1954), RA, was GSO2 at Staff College. Service in South African War; European War, 1914–18; becoming AQMG of V Corps.

 Colonel (later Major-General) G. M. Harper (1865–1922) was GSO1 in the Directorate of Military Operations. Service in South African War; European War, 1914–18 commanding 51st Division; GOC, Southern Command, 1919–22.

 Major (later Major-General Sir Warren) W. H. Anderson (1872–1930) was GSO2 at Staff College. Service in South African War; European War, 1914–18; Commandant of Staff College, 1919–22; QMG, 1927–31.

 Lieutenant Colonel (later Major-General Sir Arnold) A. F. Sillem (1865–1949), Queens Royal Regiment, was Assistant Commandant at RMC, Sandhurst. Service in South African War; European War, 1915–19; MGA of Eastern Command, 1920–4.

 Colonel (later Major-General Sir Victor) V. A. Couper (1859–1938), Rifle Brigade, was Inspector of Gymnasia at Aldershot. Service in Burma, 1888–9; European War, 1914–18.

103. Document 162.
104. Document 117.
105. Document 95.
106. Document 99.
107. Maurice (later Sir Maurice) Bonham-Carter (1880–1960) was private secretary to Asquith, 1910–16.
108. The statement by Major (later Brigadier-General) K. J. Kincaid-Smith, RA, can be found in Nuffield College, Ms Mottistone 22, f.221–3 and Bodleian, Ms Asquith 40, f. 40, 68. Kincaid-Smith (1871–1949) was

Paget's Assistant Military Secretary. Service in South African War; European War, 1914–18.

109. Document 108.

110. General Sir William Mackinnon (1852–1929), Grenadier Guards, was GOC, Western Command. Service in South African War commanding City Imperial Volunteers; DGTF, 1908–10; Director of Recruiting, 1916.

Major-General (later Lieutenant-General Sir Thomas) T. D'O. Snow (1858–1940), SLI, was GOC of 4th Division in Eastern Command. Service in South Africa, 1879; Sudan, 1884–5; Nile, 1898; European War, 1914–18, commanding 4th Division, 1914, 27th Division, 1915 and VII Corps, 1915–18.

Major-General S. H. Lomax (1855–1915), Scottish Rifles, commanding 1st Division at Aldershot. Service in South Africa, 1877–8; badly wounded by shell fire at 1st Ypres, 31 October 1914; dying of his injuries, 10 April 1915.

Major-General (later General) Sir Archibald Murray (1860–1945) was GOC of 2nd Division at Aldershot. Service in South Africa, 1888 and 1899–1902. CGS to BEF, 1914; CIGS 1915.

111. General Georges Boulanger (1837–91) was French Minister of War, 1886–7 and would-be Bonapartist.

112. Document 197.

113. Document 117.

114. In an album containing the telegram, J. E. Gough wrote: 'This telegram was received by me at 2 p.m. on Friday (20 March) on my returning to my home—it had been lying on the hall table for two hours! I wired Hubert saying "I will not fight against Ulster & will resign if any action taken against you." I then motored up to London (with my Wolseley valise & war kit on the back of the car). Saw Dorothy & mother & went to H. Wilson's house. H.W. was at the War Office but we got him over. I told him the story & he got on the telephone with Seely & Sir J. French. This was the first those plotters knew about the failure of their precious plot.' (J. E. Gough Mss.)

115. Noted on the copy received by Haig is 'Received about lunch time Sat. 21st at Littlehampton, DH.' (NLS, Acc 3155, 91h). See Document 84 for Haig's reply.

116. Lady Haig.

117. Mrs Bischoffesheim, widow of H. L. Bischoffesheim, FRGS.

F. E. Smith (later Lord Birkenhead) (1872–1930) was Unionist M.P. for Liverpool Walton, 1906–18 and for Liverpool West Derby, 1918–19.

Sir Ernest Cassell (1852–1921). Banker.

Sir Matthew Wilson (1875–1958) was Unionist M.P. for Bethnal Green, 1914–22.

Lady Edith Helen Londonderry (1879–1959) was wife of the 7th
Marquess of Londonderry. DG of the Women's Legion, 1915–19.

Walter Long (1854–1924) was Unionist M.P., 1880–92, 1893–1921.
First Lord of Admiralty, 1919–21.

118. Noted on Haig's copy: 'Sent in receipt of Gough's letter about noon,
21st.' See Document 81.

119. Noted in J. E. Gough's album: 'This letter I handed personally to the
Military Secretary at the War Office on Saturday (21st). The Military
Secretary asked me whether I wd like to keep the letter until I had been
able to verify the news from Ireland. I said "yes", but told the M.S. that I
did not wish him to make any secret of my intention to resign & I wd be
glad if he cd tell both Seely & French.' (J. E. Gough Mss.)

120. Lady Wantage, widow of Robert Loyd-Lindsay, Lord Wantage.

121. Document 10.

122. Document 39.

123. Document 86.

124. W. W. Ashley (later Lord Mount Temple) (1867–1939) was Unionist
M.P. for Blackpool, 1906–18; Fylde, 1918–22; New Forest, 1922–30.

125. Leo Maxse (1864–1932), editor of *National Review*.

126. Document 85.

127. Noted in J. E. Gough's album: 'On seeing Hubert on Sunday (22nd), I
wrote this letter and sent it to the Military Secretary with the covering
letter. I have never received any reply to this epistle! Sir Douglas Haig
told me that he saw my letter lying on the Adjutant General's table (on
Monday 23rd)—Sir J. French told D.H. that "Your Gough is as bad as
any of them, what business is it of his that he should interfere."' Franklyn
did as Gough requested (Document 92) and sent the new letter to Ewart
after destroying the original (Document 85). This second resignation
letter is among Seely's papers (Nuffield College, Ms Mottistone, 22,
f.217–219) with a note by Franklyn to Ewart, 'This does not seem a
resignation but an invitation to discipline which is dealt with by
you.'

128. Document 89.

129. French replied on 24 March regretting that he had 'misunderstood'
Roberts (NAM, 7101-23-202 and IWM, 75/46/8).

130. The questions asked by Ewart exist in draft form in the Monro of
Williamwood Mss with an additional statement to be made by Ewart:
'Having carefully considered your answers it will be my duty as Adjutant
General to recommend to the Secretary of State for submission to the
King the action which I consider appropriate to your case.'

131. Captain (later Sir Henry) H. Greer (1855–1934), late HLI, was a
leading member of the Irish racing fraternity with a horse-breeding

establishment at the Curragh. He was later Director of the National Stud. See Document 134.

132. Frank Dugdale is presumably Lieutenant Colonel F. Dugdale (1857–1925), Warwickshire Yeomanry, who was an equerry to the King. Gibbon may be Colonel J. A. Gibbon, RE, but neither this nor the identity of Godfrey is certain. Neither a Gibbon nor a Godfrey are included among the collection of letters received and retained by Hubert Gough.

133. Colonel Sir Philip Chetwode.

134. Roberts had telephoned to Austen Chamberlain on the previous day after hearing an account of events from J. E. Gough. Over the telephone Roberts stated that the terms offered to Hubert Gough and his officers were 'outrageous and insulting' (NAM, 7101-12-125-3, Roberts Mss).

135. Major H. W. Viscount Crichton, RHG. Service in South African War; killed in action, 31 October 1914. Crichton had inspected the 'Enniskillen Horse' of the UVF in October 1913 but had done so in mufti (PRO, CO 904/27/1.

136. Document 100.

137. As indicated in the letter this refers to *Exodus* 17, verses 11–12: 'And it came to pass, when Moses held up his hand, that Israel prevailed: and when he let down his hand, Amalek prevailed. But Moses' hands *were* heavy; and they took a stone, and put *it* under him, and he sat thereon; and Aaron and Hur stayed up his hands, the one on the one side, and the other on the other side; and his hands were steady until the going down of the sun.' Gough again alluded to it in a letter to Roger Keyes (Document 201) while MacEwen mentioned to J. E. Gough on 2 April 1914 that he was about to be photographed for the framed display Hubert Gough wanted (J. E. Gough Mss).

138. General Sir Charles Gough, VC (1832–1912). Service in Punjab, 1848–9; Indian Mutiny; Bhootan, 1864–5; Afghanistan, 1878–80.

139. The full telegram read 'Officers in Mess 2nd Worcesters regiment drank your health tonight. Mess President, Aldershot.' 24 March 1914, 8 41 p.m. (H. P. Gough Mss). Gough received a similar telegram from the 21st Lancers on 24 March while J. E. Gough received a similar one from the 16th Lancers on 6 April (H. P. and J. E. Gough Mss).

140. J. E. Gough had been invited to dine with Seely on 27 March 1914 at the United Services Club but Seely cancelled the arrangement on 26 March to the great relief of both Hubert Gough and Haig (Haig to J. E. Gough, 26 March 1914 in J. E. Gough Mss.)

141. Dorothy Gough was J. E. Gough's wife.

142. In a letter of the same date, Roberts, in suggesting to Wilson a series of newspaper articles on army discipline to be penned by a pliant civilian,

similarly accused French of conniving in the coercion of Ulster and being a 'tool' of ministers (IWM, 73/1/18).

143. Documents 89 and 90.
144. See Ewart Diary for 25 March 1914 (Document 78).
145. Document 41.
146. Document 78 and Document 82, Ewart and Haig diaries for 26 March.
147. Document 197.
148. Field Marshal Lord Grenfell (1841–1925). Service in South Africa 1879–81; Egypt, 1882, Sudan, 1884–5 and 1885–9; C. in C. Ireland, 1904–8.
149. In the two existing drafts, the last two paragraphs are reversed.
150. Document 117.
151. Lieutenant-General Sir James Wolfe Murray (1853–1919) was GOC, South Africa. Service in Ashanti, 1895–6; South African War; MGO, 1904–7; CIGS, 1914–15.

General Sir Reginald Hart (1848–1931). Service in Afghanistan, 1879; Egypt, 1882; Tirah, 1897–8; North-West Frontier, 1901–2.
152. Document 111.
153. Document 117.
154. *The Morning Post.*
155. Document 71.
156. Documents 63, 64 and 65.
157. Document 99.
158. Haig met Stamfordham and the King at the Army Football Cup at Aldershot. Haig's recollection was that 'HM spoke to me all the match of his action in the recent crisis.' (NLS, Acc 3155, 2m).
159. The details of Adam's case are unknown. It can be noted that Macready was only present at this first interview on 22 March at which he took notes (Document 95) but it is sometimes suggested that he also attended in Seely's office on 23 March. The error originates with Hubert Gough's own memoirs, *Soldiering On* (Arthur Barker, London, 1954), pp. 107–8. Knowing that Macready had by then departed for Belfast, Fergusson suggests that it may have been Cowans who was present (*Curragh Incident*, p. 148) but, in fact, it is clear from this contemporary account by Gough that only French, Paget and Ewart were present and that there was no mystery officer. It can further be noted that Gough unaccountably mixes up Ewart and Macready in his memoirs (p. 106 and footnote).
160. Document 96.
161. Document 99.
162. The evidence suggests that this was written in early April 1914.
163. i.e. Nicholson himself.
164. Document 99.
165. Document 100.

NOTES TO SECTION 3

1. 3rd Division in Southern Command.
2. Vice-Admiral Sir John Jellicoe.
3. Two days later, Allenby sent a telegram to Hubert Gough: 'I congratulate you heartily, and I am delighted at the result of the enquiry.' (H. P. Gough Mss.)
4. 'Reconstructed as far as possible from illegible entries in my little pocket book.' This will explain the *post-facto* reference to 'the First War'. (Amery Mss).
5. Mary Arnold-Forster, widow of H. O. Arnold-Forster (1855–1909), late Secretary of State for War, 1903–1905.
6. In his reconstructed diary, Amery refers to three Brigade-Majors but in his later memoirs, *My Political Life* (Hutchinson, London, 1953), I, p. 448 he refers to three Adjutants. Presumably he means the following:

    Lieutenant (later Captain Sir Ulick) J. U. F. C. Alexander (1889–1973), Adjutant of the 1st Coldstream Guards. Service in European War, 1914–15; Egypt and Palestine, 1916–21.

    Captain A. A. L. Stephen, Adjutant of the 1st Scots Guards at Aldershot. Service in South African War; died of wounds, 31 October 1914.

    Major (later Major-General Sir Charles) C. E. Corkran (1872–1939), Grenadier Guards, Brigade-Major of 1st Infantry Brigade. Service on the Nile, 1898; South African War; European War, 1914–18.

    Conceivably, in referring to the two officers with Alexander as both being killed in the Great War, Amery may have confused Corkran with Second Lieutenant R. S. Corkran, Grenadier Guards, who died of wounds, 15 June 1915.
7. On 10 January 1914 Price-Davies had recorded in his diary, 'I think we must not fight Ulster, if we feel we ought not to do, though we must face the consequences of our actions.' (AMOT.)
8. Frank Butler is possibly Lieutenant Colonel F. N. Butler, 5th Beds (TF) but 'Raymond' is a Christian name and is not positively identifiable. Lady Alice is Fergusson's wife.
9. The Hon. (later Sir) Arthur Stanley (1869–1947) was Unionist M.P. for Ormskirk, 1898–1918.
10. Derby was Chairman of the West Lancashire Territorial Association.
11. Harry Lawson (later Lord Burnham) (1862– 1933) was proprietor of the *Daily Telegraph* and Unionist M.P. for Mile End, 1905–6 and 1910–16.

    J. L. Baird (later Lord Stonehaven) (1874–1941), Unionist M.P. for

Rugby, 1910–22 and for Ayr Burghs, 1922–5, was Bonar Law's Parliamentary private secretary.

12. Possibly the Hon. A. G. Brodrick (1868–1934), commanding the 5th Queens Royal West Surreys (TF), 1912–19, and Major H. Munro-Fergusson, commanding the Lovat Scouts Yeomanry.

13. Captain (later Major-General Sir Hereward) H. Wake (1876–1963), KRRC, had been Roberts' ADC. Service in South African War; European War, 1914–18; GOC, 162nd Brigade, 1928–9; GOC, 12th Brigade, 1929–32; GOC, 46th Division, 1934–7.

14. Lieutenant-General Sir Horace Smith-Dorrien, GOC, Southern Command.

15. Wife of Lieutenant-General Sir Edward Bethune, the DGTF.

16. Bridges had been military attaché at Brussels, the Hague, Copenhagen and Christiania, 1910–14.

17. T. Riversdale Walrond remains a mystery figure, appearing in no standard reference book.

18. Lieutenant Colonel the Hon. G. H. Morris (1872–1914) commanded the Irish Guards. Service on North-West Frontier, 1897; South African War; killed in action, 1 September 1914.

19. Jackson had asked Kiggell, Commandant at the Staff College, if he could rejoin his battalion—the 1st Beds—in Ireland to persuade officers to return to duty. Jackson was almost alone at Staff College in taking this line (Jackson to Fergusson, 27 March 1964, Fergusson Mss) but, in the event, Kiggell refused him leave. Neither Jackson's original letter to Kiggell or Kiggell's reply is extant.

20. The report in *The Weekly Dispatch* that the 1st Dorsets had mutinied was strenuously denied by their CO, Lieutenant Colonel L. J. Bols who requested that the Honorary Colonel, Major-General H. Cook, should deny the rumours (Bols to Cook, 22 March 1914 in Bodleian, Ms Asquith 40, f.42).

21. Major (later Brigadier-General) O. K. Chance (1880–1935), 5th Lancers. Service in South African War; European War 1914–18 on the staff, ending as DAAG in Eastern Command.

22. Captain (later Brigadier-General) C. N. French (1875–1959), Royal Hampshires, was a Company Commander at RMC, Sandhurst. Service in South African War; European War, 1914–18. He was a cousin of the Goughs.

23. Gillman repeated the story of only one officer being prepared to move from Aldershot in a letter to his mother on 23 March 1914 (RA Institution, 1161/29/4, Gillman Mss) while also commenting that the Unionists were 'just as vile politically' as the Liberals. For another version of the officer at Aldershot story see T. Riversdale Walrond to Milner, 24 March 1914 (Bodleian, Ms Milner 41, f.66–69).

24. Sister of Commodore R. J. B. Keyes. Roger Keyes telegraphed himself to J. E. Gough on 23 March: 'Hurrah, hurrah. Well done Goughs. Heartiest congratulations. Result will give enormous satisfaction to the Navy.' (J. E. Gough Mss).

25. Captain (later Admiral) R. G. A. W. Stapleton-Cotton (1873–1953) was Flag Captain to the C.-in-C. Portsmouth, 1914–16.

26. Stapleton-Cotton's brother-in-law was Colonel Sir Philip Chetwode. Mrs Wemyss repeated much of the story about Chetwode to Sir Albert Gray's wife, Gray then communicating it to MacEwen of the 16th Lancers—see Gray to MacEwen, 4.4.1914 in NAM, 8001-6-11, MacEwen Mss.

27. Captain (later Admiral Sir Henry) Pelly (1867–1942) was commanding officer of HMS *Invincible* at the time of the Curragh.

    Admiral (later Admiral of the Fleet) Sir Henry Jackson (1855–1929) was Chief of the Naval War Staff, 1912–14; First Sea Lord 1915–16.

    Captain (later Admiral Sir Archibald) A. G. H. W. Moore (1887–1934) was a Lord Commissioner of the Admiralty, 1912–14.

    Captain G. W. Vivian (1869–1921) commanded HMS *Sirius*.

28. Major G. S. Tweedie, 2nd Royal Scots. Service in European War, 1914–18.

29. Engineer Lieutenant Francis Ranken was serving in HMS *Lurcher*, 4th Destroyer Flotilla.

30. Captain of HMS *Firedrake* was Lieutenant-Commander B. W. Barrow.

31. Brevet-Colonel A. L. Caldwell, Reserve of Officers (late ASC). Service in Zululand, 1888; South African War; European War in home staff appointments ending as District Barrack Officer in Northern Command.

32. General Sir Neville Lyttelton (1845–1931). Service in Fenian Raid, 1866; Jowaki, 1877; Egypt, 1882; Nile, 1898; South African War; CIGS, 1904–8.

33. Cherry Emmett was the brother-in-law of Louis Botha and was himself captured by forces under Sir Ian Hamilton in April 1902.

34. Haig is at error as he spoke to his commanders on 25 March (see Document 82).

35. For Howell's interests in military education, see R. U. Howell, *Philip Howell: A Memoir by his Wife* (Allen & Unwin, London, 1942).

36. Lieutenant (later Major) G. W. Nightingale, 1st Royal Munster Fusiliers. Service at Gallipoli; North Russia, 1919; West Africa, 1925–6.

37. General Gaston de Gallifet (1830–1909) was French Minister of War, June 1899 to May 1900, being recalled from retirement at the age of seventy to restore discipline in the French Army during the Dreyfus case.

38. Lieutenant Colonel (later Brigadier-General) R. J. Bridgfold (1869–1954) was gazetted to command 2nd KSLI in Rangoon on 11 February

1914. Service in South African War; European War, 1914–18, commanding 31st and 32nd Divisions in 1918.

39. Admiral HSH Prince Louis of Battenberg and Sir Graham Greene were First Sea Lord and Secretary of the Admiralty respectively.

40. Captain Leake had allowed his men to visit Carson and to practise signalling with the local UVF. See PRO, Adm 116/1326, Leake to Admiralty, 30.3.1914; Churchill College, DRBK 3/33, Leake to Robeck, 5.4.1914.

41. The wife of Captain E. S. Alexander Sinclair.

42. Captain (later Admiral Sir Edwyn) E. S. Alexander Sinclair (1865–1945) commanded HMS *Temeraire* in the 1st Battle Squadron. Commanded 3rd Light Cruiser Squadron, 1917–20; 1st Battle Squadron, 1922–4.

43. Captain (later Admiral Sir Henry) H. H. Bruce (1862–1948) commanded HMS *Hercules* in the 1st Battle Squadron. Commanded Rosyth Dockyard, 1915–20.

44. Captain (later Admiral Sir George) G. P. W. Hope (1869–1959) commanded HMS *Superb* in the 1st Battle Squadron. Deputy First Sea Lord, 1918–19; Commandant of RNC, 1923–6.

45. Captain (later Rear-Admiral) J. S. Dumaresq (1873–1922) commanded HMS *Shannon* in 2nd Cruiser Squadron. Commanded Australian Fleet, 1919–22.

46. Captain (later Admiral Sir Algernon) the Hon. A. Boyle (1871–1949) was attached to HMS *Vivid*, the gunnery school at Devonport. Fourth Sea Lord, 1920–4.

47. Captain (late Vice-Admiral) C. D. S. Raikes (1874–1947) commanded HMS *St George*. SNO in East Africa, 1916–19.

48. Wemyss' home at Cannes.

49. Captain (later Rear-Admiral) J. U. Farie (died 1957) commanded HMS *Adventure*, 2nd Destroyer Flotilla.

50. Captain (later Major) A. E. Gilmore, 1st Kent Battery, 3rd Home Counties (Cinque Ports) Brigade, RFA (TF). Service in South African War with Imperial Yeomanry; European War, 1914–18.

Roberts wrote in similar terms on the same day to Second Lieutenant J. T. Waite, 5th (Weald of Kent) Battalion, The Buffs (TF), who was killed in action, 21 January 1916; and Major (later Lieutenant Colonel) A. G. R. Syms, 12th County of London Battalion, London Regiment (TF). Syms served in South African War; Aden, 1903–4; Sudan, 1908; died on active service, 22 January 1918.

51. Barrow's telegram from Dera Ismail Khan on 27 March 1914 had read simply 'Well done.' (H. P. Gough Mss.)

52. Lieutenant Colonel Alexander Grubb had served in the New Zealand War, 1863–4.

53. Captain H. W. Grubb (1875–1934), Border Regiment, was DAA & QMG to the Home Counties Division (TF). Service in South African War; European War 1914–18 in staff appointments.
54. Major-General J. C. Young (1858–1926), Royal Sussex Regiment, commanded the Home Counties Division. Service in Egypt, 1882; Sudan, 1884–95; European War, 1914–17 commanding division on home service.
55. Lieutenant (later Brigadier Sir Edward) E. H. L. Beddington (1884–1966), 16th Lancers. Service in European War, 1914–18; 1940–5. High Sheriff of Hertfordshire, 1948–9.
56. Colonel (later Brigadier-General Sir William) W. Bromley-Davenport (1862–1949) was Unionist M.P. for Macclesfield, 1886–1906. Service in Egypt, 1916 and Italy, 1917–18 including command of 22nd Mounted Brigade, 1916.
57. Commodore (later Admiral Sir William) W. J. Whitworth (1884–1973) commanded HMS *Cockatrice*. Second Sea Lord, 1941–4.
58. Captain (later Vice-Admiral) F. Clifton-Brown (1874–1963) commanded HMS *Skirmisher* and 7th Destroyer Flotilla.
59. Churchill had first asked Seely for Paget's comments on a draft memorandum on 27 March (BL, Add Mss 51250), a request sent on by Seely to Paget on the same day (ibid). The memorandum was carried over to Ireland by Lieutenant O. E. Wynne, RE, ironically borrowed from Henry Wilson's department of the War Office (Brade to Wilson, 28 March in IWM, 73/1/18). Seely then reported Wynne's departure to Churchill (Nuffield College, Ms Mottistone 22, f.265). Churchill's memorandum is printed in full in R. S. Churchill, *Winston S. Churchill* (Heinemann, London, 1969), II, Companion Part 3, pp. 1411–13, the original being in Bodleian, Ms Asquith 40, f.88–94.
60. Churchill had suggested that Paget be brought over for an interview (BL, Add Mss, 51250, Churchill to Seely, 27 March 1914).
61. Documents 33 and 62.
62. Document 68.
63. Document 39.
64. Document 31.
65. Howell had been *Times* special correspondent during the Balkan Wars and published *The Campaign in Thrace* (Hugh Rees, London, 1913).
66. The landing of the arms consignment for the UVF at Larne on 24 April 1914. See Stewart, *Ulster Crisis*, pp. 196–212.
67. Documents 178 and 179.
68. Colonel (later Brigadier-General) O. C. Wolley-Dod (1863–1942), was GSO1 of 5th Division. Service on the Nile, 1898; South African War; European War, 1914–15 commanding 86th Brigade; Inspector of

Infantry, 1915; commanding Lucknow and Bangalore Brigades, 1917–18.

69. See note 62 in Section 2.

70. Documents 177, 178 and 179.

71. Document 41.

72. Probably Document 213.

73. Document 41.

74. Document 184.

75. Document 183.

76. Major R. F. Uniacke, Royal Inniskilling Fusiliers, had telegraphed to HQ Irish Command on 22 March: 'Although I have no proof for saying so, I estimate that about ten per cent of Fusiliers, chiefly NCO's, are disaffected.' (PRO, WO35/209n.) Uniacke was killed in action, 28 May 1915.

77. Major (later Colonel) R. Hely-Hutchinson, 1st Royal Fusiliers. Commanded 16th Royal Fusiliers then 4th Royal Fusiliers during European War, 1914–18.

78. Captain (later Major) E. A. Bald, 2nd Duke of Wellington's Regiment. Service with Indian Army, 1915–18.

79. Captain (later Admiral Sir James) J. Fergusson (1871–1942) commanded HMS *Benbow* from May 1914. Commanded 2nd Light Cruiser Squadron during the war.

80. Troops had been employed during railway strikes in South Africa in January 1914.

81. Fergusson's sister, Mrs George Baird.

82. General Sir Alexander Mongomery Moore (1833–1919). Honorary Colonel of the 4th Hussars. He only ever served in staff appointments. He sent a telegram of congratulation to Hubert Gough on 23 March (H. P. Gough Mss).

83. See Section 1, Note 27.

84. Document 200.

85. Document 106. See also Section 2, Note 137.

86. Document 197. The 'fat man' is Asquith.

87. Lieutenant-General Sir Alfred Codrington (1854–1945). Service in Egypt, 1882; South African War; Military Secretary to the Secretary of State for War, 1914; GOC, Central Force in Britain, 1914–16.
    Lieutenant-General Sir Herbert Belfield (1857–1934). Service in Ashanti, 1895–6; South African War; Director of Prisoners of War, 1914–20.

88. Documents 194, 195 and 198.

89. Document 31.

90. Lieutenant (later Colonel Sir Joseph) J. L. Cheyne (1888–1957), 16th

Lancers. Service in European War; CO of 16/5th Lancers, 1929–33. See also Document 210.

91. Document 200.
92. Rosalind Upcher Howell.
93. No enclosure extant.
94. No enclosure extant.
95. See Section 2, Note 35.
96. Letter not extant.

Brigadier-General (later General Sir Edward) E. S. Bulfin (1862–1939) commanded 2nd Infantry Brigade. Service in Burma, 1892–3; South African War; European War, 1914–17; GOC, 28th Division, 1914–15; 60th Division 1915–17; XXI Corps in Palestine, 1917–19.

97. Colonel V. J. M. Huguet (later Général de Brigade) had been an influential French military attaché in London during the Anglo-French staff conversations in 1905/6. A close friend of Wilson, he was later a liaison officer at British Headquarters in 1914. His reference to Wilson's rank is puzzling as Wilson was gazetted Major-General in November 1913.

General Noel Marie Joseph Edouard de Curières de Castelnau (1851–1944) was a member of the French *Conseil Supérieur de la Guerre*. Commanded French 2nd and 7th Armies, 1914; French Chief of Staff, 1915–16.

Brigadier-General F. I. (later General Sir Ivor) Maxse (1862–1958) commanded 1st Infantry Brigade at Aldershot. Service on the Nile, 1897–9; South African War; European War, 1914–18 commanding 18th Division, 1914–17, 18th Corps, 1917–18; IG of Training, 1918–19.

98. Ewart modified this view in 1928 when visited by Brigadier-General J. Charteris, Haig's former Chief of Intelligence, who was writing the latter's biography. From Charteris, Ewart learned that Wilson, not Gough, had given Haig a copy of the document the same evening (SRO, RH4/84/3, 128 Ewart Diary, 30 September 1928).

99. Presumably Document 59.
100. Major (later Brigadier-General) A. W. F. Baird (1876–1931), 1st Gordon Highlanders. Service in South African War; North-West Frontier, 1908; European War, 1914–18; Military Attaché at Constantinople, 1920–4.
101. Documents 64, 71 and 124.
102. See Note 66 above.
103. Consultations between party leaders resumed in early May.
104. *Blackwoods* in an article entitled 'A Page of History' (May 1914), pp. 713–22 suggested that Fergusson had claimed that the object of troop movements was to provoke Ulster into undertaking aggression. To

Fergusson's grief, the theme was taken up by a number of writers including a former fellow Guardsman, Lord Percy—see Fergusson, *Curragh Incident*, pp. 190–1. Friend had suggested that Fergusson write to *Blackwoods* (Friend to Fergusson, 3 May 1914) and Fergusson's letter to Anderson bore fruit with a retraction printed in the June issue of the magazine.

105. Not extant.

106. South Irish Horse.

107. The members of the Army Council were the CIGS, General Sir Charles Douglas; the Adjutant General, Lieutenant-General Sir Henry Sclater; the QMG, Major-General Sir John Cowans; and the MGO, Colonel (temporary Major-General) Sir Stanley von Donop. In effect the Army Council paper, which was drafted by Wilson, ruled out any attempt to return to a policy of coercion. See Introduction, and Note 90 to the Introduction.

108. See Document 9 for Furse's view in 1913.

109. Fergusson wrote back to Forestier-Walker on 12 July, requesting the name of the officer concerned. Forestier-Walker's reply on 13 July gave the name of Captain J. R. Wethered, Gloucestershire Regiment, who was Brigade-Major of 14th Infantry Brigade (PRO, WO35/209b). Captain (later Colonel) Wethered (1873–1942) saw service in the European War, 1914–18 and was AAG at the War Office, 1925–6.

110. The Curragh battalions of 14th Infantry Brigade were the 2nd Suffolks and the 2nd Manchesters, the 1st DCLI having been deployed to Ulster in March.

APPENDIX I

BIOGRAPHICAL NOTES

Allenby, Edmund Henry Hynman (1861–1936). Major-General and Inspector of Cavalry in March 1914. Inniskilling Dragoons. Service in Bechuanaland, 1884–5; Zululand, 1888; South Africa, 1899–1902; 1st Cavalry Division, 1914; Cavalry Corps, 1914–15; 5th Army Corps, 1915; knighted, 1915; 3rd Army, 1915–17; CinC, Egyptian Expeditionary Force, 1917–19; Viscount, 1919; High Commissioner for Egypt and the Sudan, 1919–25; Field Marshal, 1919.

Amery, Leopold Charles Maurice Stennett (1873–1955). Con. M.P. for Birmingham South, 1911–18; Birmingham Sparkbrook, 1918–45. Parl. Under. Sec. for the Colonies, 1919–21; Parl. and Fin. Sec., Admiralty, 1921–2; First Lord of Admiralty, 1922–4; Sec. of State for Dominions, 1925–9; Sec. of State for India, 1940–45.

Asquith, Herbert Henry (1852–1928). Prime Minister in March 1914. Lib. M.P. for Fife East, 1886–1918; Paisley, 1920–24. Home Sec., 1892–95; Chancellor of Exchequer, 1905–8; Prime Minister, 1908–16; Sec. of State for War, 1914; Leader of Lib. Party, 1908–26; Earl of Oxford and Asquith, 1925.

Baillie-Grohman, Harold Tom (1888–1978). Lieutenant commanding HMS *Lively*, 7th Destroyer Flotilla, in March 1914. Service in European War, 1914–18. Head of British Naval Mission to China, 1931–3; 1st Destroyer Flotilla, 1934–6; HMS *Ramillies*, 1939–40; Rear-Admiral, Combined Operations, 1942; Vice-Admiral, 1943.

Balfour, Arthur James (1848–1930). Conservative M.P. in March 1914. Con. M.P. for Hertford, 1874–85; Manchester East, 1885–1906; City of London, 1906–22. Pres. Local Govt. Board 1885–6; Sec. for Scotland, 1886–7; Chief Sec. for Ireland, 1887–91; First Lord of Treasury, 1891–2 and 1895–1905; Prime Minister, 1902–5; First Lord of Admiralty, 1915–16; Foreign Sec., 1916–19; Lord Pres. Council, 1919–22 and 1925–9; Earl, 1922.

Barrow, George de Symons (1864–1959). Lieutenant Colonel, 35th Scinde Horse in March 1914. Service in Waziristan, 1894–5; China, 1900; European War and Palestine, 1914–18; Afghanistan, 1919. DAQMG, India, 1903; DAAG, Staff College, 1908; knighted 1918; GOC, Peshawar; 1919–23; AG, India, 1923; General, 1925; GOC, Eastern Command (India), 1923–8.

Battenberg, Louis Alexander Mountbatten (1854–1921). Admiral and First Sea Lord in March 1914. Prince Louis of Battenberg and First Marquis of Milford Haven. DNI, 1902–5; Rear-Admiral, 1904; 2nd Cruiser Squad., 1905–7; CinC, Atlantic Fleet, 1908–10; 3rd and 4th Divs., Home Fleet, 1911; Second Sea Lord, 1911–12; First Sea Lord, 1912–14; Admiral of the Fleet, 1921.

Bayly, Lewis (1857–1938). Vice-Admiral and Commanding 3rd Battle Squadron in March 1914. Service in Ashanti, 1874; Congo, 1875; Egypt, 1882. Pres. Naval War College, 1908–11; 1st Battle Cruiser Squad., 1911–12; 3rd Battle Squad., 1913–14; 1st Battle Squad., 1914; knighted, 1914; CinC, Western Approaches, 1915–19; Admiral, 1917.

Bethune, Edward Cecil (1855–1930). Lieutenant-General and Director-General of the Territorial Force in March 1914. Service in Afghan War, 1878–80; Boer War, 1881; South Africa, 1899–1900 commanding Bethune's Horse. Commanded 16th Lancers, 1900–4; West Lancashire Division (TF), 1909–12; DGTF, 1912–17; Lieutenant-General, 1913; knighted, 1915.

Birrell, Augustine (1850–1933). Irish Secretary in March 1914. Lib. M.P. for Fife West, 1889–1900; Bristol North, 1906–18. Pres. Board of Educ., 1905–7; Chief Sec. for Ireland, 1907–16.

Bonar Law, Andrew (1858–1923). Leader of Conservative Party in March 1914. Con. M.P. for Glasgow Blackfriars, 1900–6; Dulwich, 1906–10; Bootle, 1911–18; Glasgow Central, 1918–23. Parl. Sec. Board of Trade, 1902–5; Colonial Sec., 1915–16; Chancellor of Exchequer, 1916–19; member of War Cabinet, 1916–19; Lord Privy Seal, 1919–21; Prime Minister, 1922–3; Leader of Con. Party, 1911–21, 1922–3.

Brade, Reginald Herbert (1864–1933). War Office Secretary in March 1914. Sec. War Office Council, 1901–4; Assistant Sec. War Office, 1904–14; Sec. War Office 1914–20; knighted, 1914.

Breeks, Richard William (1863–1920). Lieutenant Colonel, III Brigade, RHA in March 1914. Service in South Africa, 1899–1900; European War, 1914–15; Gallipoli as BGGS, 1915. Brigadier-General, 1915; DOAGC, 1916–18; Commandant of Woolwich, 1918–19.

Brett, Charles Arthur Hugh (1865–1914). Lieutenant Colonel, 2nd Suffolks in March 1914. Service in Hazara, 1888; South Africa, 1899–1900; killed in action, 3.9.1914.

Bridges, George Tom Molesworth (1871–1939). Major in 4th Dragoon Guards in March 1914. Service in South Africa, 1899–1901; Somaliland, 1902–4. Commanded 4th Hussars, 1914; Head of British Military Mission with Belgian Army, 1914–16; Major-General, 19th Division, 1916–17; Head of British War Mission to USA, 1918; Head of British Mission, Allied Armies of the Orient, 1918–20; knighted, 1919. Gov. South Australia, 1922–7.

Callaghan, George Astley (1852–1920). Admiral and CinC Home Fleet in March 1914. Service at Relief of Peking, 1900. Rear-Admiral, Channel Fleet, 1906; 5th Cruiser Squad., 1907–8; 2nd Division, Home Fleet, 1910–11; CinC, Home Fleet, 1911–14; knighted, 1910; CinC, Nore, 1915–18; Admiral of the Fleet.

Capper, Thompson (1863–1915). Major-General and Inspector of Infantry in March 1914. Service in Chitral, 1895; Nile, 1898–99; South Africa, 1899–1902. Commandant, Quetta Staff College, 1906–11; 13th Infantry Brigade, 1911–14; knighted, 1915; Inspector of Infantry, 1914; 7th Division, 1914–15; died of wounds, 26.9.1915.

Carson, Edward Henry (1854–1935). Leader of Ulster Unionists in March 1914. Unionist M.P. for Dublin University, 1892–1918; Belfast Duncairn, 1918–21. Knighted, 1900; Solicitor-General 1900–6; Attorney-General, 1915; First Lord of Admiralty, 1917; member of War Cabinet, 1917–18; Lord of Appeal in Ordinary, 1921–29.

Chamberlain, Joseph Austen (1863–1937). Conservative M.P. in March 1914. Con. M.P. for Worcester East, 1892–1914; Birmingham West, 1914–37. Civil Lord of Admiralty, 1895–1900; Fin. Sec., Treasury, 1900–2; Postmaster General, 1902–3; Chancellor of Exchequer, 1903–5 and 1919–21; Sec. of State for India, 1915–17; member of War Cabinet, 1918–19; Lord Privy Seal and Leader of Con. Party, 1921–2; Foreign Sec., 1924–9; knighted, 1925; First Lord of Admiralty, 1931.

Chetwode, Philip Walhouse (1869–1950). Colonel in March 1914 selected to replace Hubert Gough. 19th Hussars. Service in Burma, 1892–3; South Africa, 1899–1902; European War and Egypt, 1914–19. Succeeded as 7th Baronet, 1905; Desert Corps, 1916–17; 20th Corps, 1917–18; Military Sec. at War Office, 1919–20; Deputy CIGS, 1920–22; GOC, Aldershot, 1923–7; CinC, India, 1930–5; Field Marshal, 1933; Baron, 1945.

Childs, Borlace Elward Wyndham (1876–1946). Brevet Major and DAAG to the Director of Personal Services in the War Office in March 1914. Royal Irish Regt. European War, 1914–18; DAG to BEF, 1914–16; AAG in War Office, 1916; Director of Personal Services, 1916–19; Major-General 1917; DAAG to Forces, 1919–21; knighted, 1919.

Churchill, Winston Leonard Spencer (1874–1965). First Lord of the Admiralty in March 1914. Con. M.P. for Oldham, 1900–04; Lib. M.P. for Oldham, 1904–6; Manchester North West, 1906–8; Dundee, 1908–22; Con. M.P. for Epping, 1924–45; Woodford, 1945–64. Service in 4th Hussars; Malakand, 1897; Tirah, 1898; Sudan, 1898; South Africa with South African Light Horse, 1900; European War with 6th Royal Scots Fusiliers, 1915–16. War correspondent, South Africa, 1899–1900. Under Sec. for Colonies, 1905–8; Pres. Board of Trade, 1908–10; Home Sec., 1910–11; First Lord of Admiralty, 1911–15 and 1939–40; Chancellor of Duchy of Lancaster, 1915;

Minister of Munitions, 1917–19; Sec. for War and Air, 1919–21; Colonial Sec., 1921–2; Chancellor of Exchequer, 1924–9; Prime Minister, 1940–5 and 1951–5; knighted, 1953.

Colville, Stanley Cecil James (1861–1939). Vice-Admiral and commanding 1st Battle Squadron in March 1914. Service in Zululand, 1879; Egypt, 1882; Nile, 1884; Sudan, 1896. Knighted, 1912; Admiral, 1914. 1st Battle Squad., 1912–14; Special Service, 1914–16; CinC, Portsmouth, 1916–19; Rear-Admiral of the UK, 1927–9.

Congreve, Walter Norris (1862–1927). Brigadier-General, 18th Infantry Brigade in March 1914. Rifle Brigade. Service in South Africa, 1899–1902 winning V.C. 18th Infantry Brigade, 1911–15; 6th Division, 1915; XIII Corps, 1915–17; VII Corps, 1918; knighted, 1917; GOC, Egypt and Palestine, 1919–23; GOC, Southern Command, 1923–4; CinC, Malta, 1924–7.

Cory, George Norton (1874–1968). Major and GSO3 in DMT in March 1914. Royal Dublin Fusiliers. Service in South Africa, 1899–1902; Aden, 1903; European War, 1914–18; Major-General G. S. at Salonika, 1917–19; Caucasus, 1919; Mesopotamia, 1920–1; Deputy CGS, India, 1922–6; knighted, 1925; GOC 50th Division (TA), 1927–8.

Cowans, John Steven (1862–1921). QMG at the War Office in March 1914. Rifle Brigade. Service with Indian Army, 1906–7; DSD, India, 1907–10; DGTF, 1910–12; Major-General, 1910; QMG, 1912–19; knighted, 1913.

Craig, James (1871–1940). Ulster Unionist M.P. in March 1914. Service in South Africa, 1899–1902; Captain, Royal Irish Rifles; South West Africa, 1914–15. Unionist M.P. for Down East, 1906–18; Mid Down, 1918–21. Baronet, 1918; Parl. Sec., Ministry of Pensions, 1919–20; Fin. Sec., Admiralty, 1920–21; Prime Minister of Northern Ireland, 1921–40; Viscount Craigavon, 1927.

Crewe, 1st Marquis of, Robert Offley Ashburton Crewe-Milnes, 2nd Baron Houghton (1858–1945). Lord Privy Seal in March 1914. Baron, 1863, Earl of Crewe, 1895; Marquis, 1911. Lord President, 1905–8 and 1915–16; Sec. of State for Colonies, 1908–10; Lord Privy Seal, 1908–11 and 1912–15; Pres. Board of Educ., 1916; Ambassador to France, 1922–8; Sec. of State for War, 1931.

Cuthbert, Gerald James (1861–1931). Brigadier-General, 13th Infantry Brigade in March 1914. Scots Guards. Service in Sudan, 1885; South Africa, 1899–1902. 1st Scots Guards, 1904–6; 4th London Infantry Brigade (TF), 1909–13; 13th Infantry Brigade, 1914; 140th Infantry Brigade, 1915–16; 39th Division, 1916–17; Major-General; 72nd Division, 1918–19.

Davies, Francis John (1864–1948). Major-General and DSD in March 1914. Grenadier Guards. Service at Suakin, 1885; Jebu, 1892; South Africa 1899–

1901; Major-General, 1913; European War, 1914–16; knighted, 1915; Military Sec. to Sec. of State for War and Sec. to Selection Board, 1916–19; GOC, Scotland, 1919–23; Lieutenant of the Tower, 1923–6.

de Chair, Dudley Rawson Stratford (1864–1958). Rear-Admiral and Naval Secretary in March 1914. Naval Sec. to First Lord of Admiralty, 1910–12; Naval Adviser to Foreign Office, 1916–17; Pres. Inter-Allied Comm. on Enemy Warships, 1921–3; Governor of New South Wales, 1923–30; Admiral.

Derby, 17th Earl of, Edward George Villiers Stanley (1865–1948). Conservative peer in March 1914. Grenadier Guards, 1885–95. Con. M.P. for Westhoughton, 1892–1906; succeeded father, 1908. Postmaster-General, 1903–5; Director-General of Recruiting, 1915–16; Under Sec. for War, 1916; Sec. of State for War, 1916–18; Ambassador to France, 1918–20; Sec. for War, 1922–4.

de Robeck, John Michael (1862–1928). Rear-Admiral and Admiral of Patrols in March 1914. Commanded Eastern Mediterranean Squad. at Gallipoli, 1915–16; knighted, 1916; CinC, Mediterranean, 1919–22; High Commissioner for Constantinople, 1919–20; CinC, Atlantic, 1922–4; Admiral of the Fleet, 1925.

Donop, Stanley Brenton von (1860–1941). Colonel (temporary Major-General) and MGO at the War Office in March 1914. Royal Artillery. Service in South Africa, 1900–2. Director of Artillery, 1911–13; knighted 1914; MGO, 1913–16; Comm. Humber Garrison, 1917–20.

Douglas, Charles Whittingham Horsley (1850–1914). Replaced French as CIGS in March 1914. Gordon Highlanders. Service in Afghanistan, 1879–80; Suakin, 1884; South Africa, 1880–1 and 1899–1901. AG, 1904–9; GOC, Southern Command, 1909–12; knighted, IG of Home Forces, 1912–14; CIGS, 1914 collapsing from over-work, 25.10.1914. General.

Esher, Reginald Baliol Brett (1852–1930). Lib. M.P. for Penryn and Falmouth, 1880–5. Sec. Office of Works, 1895–1902; succeeded as 2nd Viscount Esher, 1899; permanent member of Committee of Imperial Defence, 1905–18; Pres. County of London Territorial Assoc., 1912–21; Chm., Army in India Committee, 1919.

Ewart, John Spencer (1861–1930). Lieutenant-General and AG in March 1914. Cameron Highlanders. Service in Egypt, 1882; Nile, 1884–5; Sudan, 1885–6 and 1898; South Africa, 1899–1901. Military Sec. at War Office, 1904–6; DMO, 1906–10; knighted, 1911; AG, 1910–14; GOC, Scotland, 1914–18.

Fergusson, Charles (1865–1951). Major-General, 5th Division in March 1914. Grenadier Guards. Service in Sudan, 1896–8; AG of Egyptian Army, 1901–

425

3; succeeded as 7th Baronet, 1907; Inspector of Infantry, 1909–13; 5th Division, 1913–14; 2nd Corps and 17th Corps in European War; General; Military Gov. of Occupied German Territory, 1918–19; Governor Gen. of New Zealand, 1924–30.

Forestier-Walker, George Townshend (1866–1939). Brigadier-General, GS to the Irish Command, March 1914. Royal Artillery. Service in South Africa, 1899–1900; East Africa, 1902–4; European War, 1914–18 and Salonika. BGGS in Ireland, 1912–14; knighted, 1919; Major-General; Col. Commandant, RA, 1931–6.

Franklyn, William Edmund (1856–1914). Lieutenant-General and Military Sec. at War Office in March 1914. Yorkshire Regiment. Service on North-West Frontier, 1897–8. Assistant Military Sec., War. Office, 1899–1902; 10th Infantry Brigade, 1902–4; Director of Personal Services, 1904–6; 3rd Division, 1906–10; Military Sec. at War Office, 1911–14; knighted, 1912.

French, John Denton Pinkstone (1852–1925). Field Marshal and CIGS in March 1914. 19th Hussars. Service in Sudan, 1884–5; South Africa, 1899–1902. 1st Cavalry Brigade, 1899; knighted, 1900; GOC, Aldershot, 1902–7; CIGS, 1911–14; Field Marshal, 1913; CinC, BEF, 1914–15; CinC, Home Forces, 1916–18; Lord Lieutenant of Ireland, 1918–21; Viscount, 1915; Earl of Ypres, 1921.

Friend, Lovick Bransby (1856–1944). Major-General in charge of Administration, Irish Command in March 1914. Royal Engineers. Service in Sudan, 1898. Director of Works to Egyptian Army, 1900–4; Assistant D of Fortification, 1906; Major-General in Irish Command, 1912–14; GOC, Ireland, 1914–16; President, Claims Commission of British Armies in France, 1916–18; knighted, 1919.

Furse, William Thomas (1865–1953). Colonel and GSO1 to 6th Division in March 1914. Service in South Africa, 1899–1900. GSO2 at Staff College, 1908–11; GSO1 in Ireland to 6th Division, 1913–14; BGGS to II Corps, 1915; GOC, 9th Division, 1915–16; MGO, 1916; knighted, 1917; Lieutenant-General; Director of Imperial Institute, 1925–34.

Gillman, Webb (1870–1933). Major and GSo2 in DMO in March 1914. Royal Artillery. Service in South Africa, 1899–1900; Nigeria, 1902; European War, 1914–18; knighted, 1919; Commandant of Woolwich, 1920–4; Inspector of Artillery, 1924–7; MGO, 1927–31; General, 1931.

Gleichen, Lord Albert Edward Wilfred, Count (1863–1937). Brigadier-General, 15th Infantry Brigade in March 1914. Grenadier Guards. Service on the Nile, 1884–5; Sudan, 1896; South Africa, 1899–1900. Military Attaché in Berlin, 1903–6 and in Washington, 1906; Assistant DMO, 1907–11; 15th Infantry Brigade, 1911–15; 37th Division, 1915–16; Major-General, 1915.

Gough, Hubert de la Poer (1870–1963). Brigadier-General, 3rd Cavalry Brigade, March 1914. 16th Lancers. Service in Tirah, 1897–8; South Africa, 1899–1902. Commanding 16th Lancers, 1907–11; 3rd Cavalry Brigade, 1914; 2nd Cavalry Division and 7th Cavalry Division, 1915; I Corps, 1916, 5th Army, 1916–18; Chief, Allied Mission to the Baltic, 1919; General, 1922. Exonerated for collapse of 5th Army (March 1918) in 1936.

Gough, John Edmund (1871–1915). Brigadier-General, GS at Aldershot, March 1914. Rifle Brigade. Service in British Central Africa, 1896–7; Nile, 1898; South Africa, 1899–1902; Somaliland, 1902–3 winning V.C.; IG of Kings African Rifles, 1908–9; GSO1 at Staff College, 1909–13; BGGS, Aldershot, 1913–14; Chief of Staff to Haig, 1914–15. Died of wounds, 21.2.1915; posthumously knighted.

Grant-Duff, Adrian (1869–1914). Major in Black Watch, March 1914. Assistant Sec. Committee of Imperial Defence, 1910–13; Lieutenant Colonel, 1st Black Watch, 1914. Service on North-West Frontier, 1897–98; South Africa, 1902; European War, 1914; killed in action, 21.9.1914.

Grey, Edward (1862–1933). Foreign Secretary in March 1914. Succeeded as 3rd Baronet, 1882. Lib. M.P. for Berwick, 1885–1916. Under Sec. Foreign Affairs, 1892–5; Foreign Sec., 1905–16; Viscount, 1916; temporary Ambassador to USA, 1919.

Grierson, James Moncrieff (1859–1914). Lieutenant-General and GOC, Eastern Command in March 1914. Royal Artillery. Service in Egypt, 1882; South Africa, 1900; China, 1900–1. Military attaché in Berlin, 1896–1900; DMO, 1904–6; 1st Division, 1906–10; Eastern Command, 1912–14; II Corps, 1914; died on active service, 17.8.1914. Knighted.

Gwynne, H. A. (1865–1950). Editor of *Morning Post* in March 1914. Reuter correspondent in Roumania, 1893; and on Dongola expedition, 1896 and in Turkish-Greek War, 1897; Sudan, 1897; Peking, 1898–9; South Africa, 1899–1902. Foreign Director of Reuters, 1904; editor, *Standard*, 1904–11; *Morning Post*, 1911–37.

Haig, Douglas (1861–1928). Lieutenant-General and GOC, Aldershot in March 1914. 7th Hussars. Service in Sudan, 1898; South Africa, 1899–1902. Chief of Staff, India, 1909–12; GOC, Aldershot, 1912–14; knighted, 1913; 1st Army, 1914–15; CinC, BEF, 1915–19; Forces in Great Britain, 1919–20; Earl, 1919; Field Marshal, 1917.

Haldane, Richard Burdon (1856–1928). Lord Chancellor in March 1914. Lib. M.P. for Haddingtonshire, 1885–1911. Sec. of State for War, 1905–12; Viscount, 1911; Lord Chancellor, 1912–15 and 1924.

Hamilton, Ian Standish Monteith (1853–1947). General and IG of Overseas Forces in March 1914. Gordon Highlanders. Service in South Africa, 1881 and 1899–1901; Egypt and Sudan, 1884–5; Burma, 1886–7; Tirah, 1897–8.

Chief of Staff to Kitchener in South Africa, 1901–2; Military representative of India with the Japanese Army, 1904–5; GOC, Southern Command, 1905–9; AG, 1909–10; GOC in the Mediterranean and IG of Overseas Forces, 1910–14; CinC, Mediterranean Expeditionary Force, 1915. Knighted, 1900; General, 1914.

Hankey, Maurice Pascal Alers (1877–1963). Secretary to Committee of Imperial Defence in March 1914. Royal Marine Artillery, 1895–1912 retiring with rank of Captain. Sec. to Committe of Imperial Defence, 1912–38; Sec. to War Council, 1914–15; to Dardanelles Committee, 1915; to Cabinet War Committee, 1915–16; to War Cabinet and Cabinet, 1916–38; knighted, 1916; Baron, 1939; Minister without Portfolio, 1939–40; Chancellor of Duchy of Lancaster, 1940–1; Paymaster-General, 1941–2.

Headlam, John Emerson Wharton (1864–1946). Brigadier-General commanding RA, 5th Division, March 1914. Service in South Africa, 1900–2; European War, 1914–18. Major-General, 1915; knighted, 1919; Colonel Commandant, RA, 1928–34.

Hill, Felix Frederic (1860–1940). Commanding No. 11 District as Colonel, March 1914. Royal Irish Fusiliers. Service in Sudan, 1884; South Africa, 1899–1902. No. 11 District, 1910–14; Brigadier-General, 31st Brigade, 1915; 186th Brigade, 1916.

Hogg, Ian Graham (1875–1914). Lieutenant Colonel, 4th Hussars, March 1914. Service in South Africa, 1901; West Africa, 1901–4; European War, 1914; killed in action, 2.9.1914.

Hopwood, Francis Stephens (1860–1947). Additional Civil Lord of Admiralty on March 1914. Perm. Sec., Board of Trade, 1901–7; knighted, 1901; Perm. under Sec., Colonies, 1907–11; Vice Chmn. Development Commission, 1911–12; Additional Civil Lord of Admiralty, 1912–17; Baron Southborough, 1917.

Howard, Henry Cecil Lloyd (1881–1950). Lieutenant and GSO3 in DSD in March 1914. 16th Lancers. Service in South Africa, 1899–1902; European War, 1914–18; Commanding 16th/5th Lancers, 1921–5; 6th Cavalry Brigade, 1929–31. Colonel.

Howell, Philip (1877–1916). Major in 4th Hussars, March 1914. Service on North-West Frontier, 1908; European War, 1914–16. Brigade-Major to IG Cavalry, 1908; GSO3 in War Office, 1909–11; GSO2 at Staff College, 1912–13; Lieutenant Colonel, 4th Hussars, 1914; BGGS on staff, 1915; killed in action, 10.10.1916.

Hunt, Rowland (1858–1943). Con. M.P. for Ludlow, 1903–18. Service in South Africa with Lovat Scouts.

Jackson, Henry Cholmondeley (1879–1972). Captain in 1st Beds attending Staff College in March 1914. Service in European War, 1914–18; Commandant, MG School, 1924–6; DMT in India, 1926–30; Major-General, 1930; GOC, 2 Division, 1931–5; knighted, 1936; GOC, Western Command, 1936–9 and 1940; General, 1939.

Jellicoe, John Rushworth (1859–1935). Vice-Admiral and Second Sea Lord in March 1914. Director of Naval Ordnance, 1905–7; Controller of Navy, 1908–10; Atlantic Fleet, 1910–11; 2nd Division, Home Fleet, 1911–12; Second Sea Lord, 1912–14; CinC, Grand Fleet, 1914–16; First Sea Lord, 1916; Chief of Naval Staff, 1917; Governor-General of New Zealand, 1920–4. Knighted; Earl, 1925; Admiral of the Fleet.

Keyes, Roger John Brownlow (1872–1945). Commodore of Submarines in March 1914. Service in China, 1900. Commodore of Submarines, 1910–14; Chief of Staff to Eastern Mediterranean Squad., 1915; Director of Plans, 1917; Vice-Admiral, Dover Patrol, 1918; Knighted; CinC, Mediterranean, 1925–38; CinC, Portsmouth, 1929–31; Special Liaison Officer to King of the Belgians, 1940; Director of Combined Ops., 1940–1; Con. M.P. for Portsmouth North, 1934–43. Baron, 1943; Admiral of the Fleet, 1930.

Kiggell, Launcelot Edward (1862–1954). Brigadier-General and Commandant of the Staff College, March 1914. Royal Warwickshire Regt. Service in South Africa, 1899–1902. DSD, 1909–13; Commandant, Staff College, 1913–14; Director of Home Defence, 1914–15; Chief of Staff to Haig, 1915–18; knighted, 1916; Lieutenant-General; GOC, Guernsey, 1918–20.

Lambton, William (1863–1936). Colonel and AAQMG to London District in March 1914. Coldstream Guards. Service in Sudan, 1898; South Africa, 1899–1902. Military Sec. to Lord Milner, 1900–4; AAQMG, London District, 1913–14; Military Sec. to CinC, BEF, 1914; Major-General, 4th Division, 1915–19; knighted, 1919.

Lansdowne, 5th Marquis of, Henry Charles Keith Petty-Fitzmaurice, Viscount Clanmaurice, Earl of Kerry (1845–1927). Conservative peer in March 1914. Succeeded as 5th Marquis, 1866. Parl. Under-Sec. War Office, 1872–4 and India Office, 1880; Governor-General of Canada, 1883–8; Viceroy of India, 1888–94; Sec. of State for War, 1895–1900; Sec. of State, Foreign Affairs, 1900–5; Minister Without Portfolio, 1915–16.

Leake, Francis Martin (1869–1928). Captain, HMS *Pathfinder* in March 1914. HMS *Achilles*, 1915–17; Chief of Staff to Admiral, Queenstown, 1918–19; Vice-Admiral, 1926.

Leveson, Arthur Cavenagh (1868–1929). Rear-Admiral and Director of Operations Division at the Admiralty in March 1914. Commanded 2nd Battle Squad, 1919–20; CinC, China, 1922–4; knighted, 1919; Admiral, 1922.

Lloyd, Francis (1853–1926). Major-General and GOC, London District in

March 1914. Grenadier Guards. Service at Suakin, 1885; Nile, 1898; South Africa, 1900–2; 1st Guards Brigade, 1904–8; Welsh Division (TF), 1909–13; knighted, 1911; GOC, London District, 1913–19; Lieutenant-General.

Lloyd George, David (1863–1945). Chancellor of the Exchequer in March 1914. Lib. M.P. for Caernarvon Boroughs, 1890–1945. Pres. Board of Trade, 1905–8; Chancellor of Exchequer, 1908–15; Minister of Munitions, 1915–16; Sec. for War, 1916; Prime Minister, 1916–22; Earl, 1945.

Lugard, Lady Flora (died 1929). Née Shaw, married Sir Frederick Lugard, 1902. Head of Colonial Division of *The Times*; Joint Founder of the War Refugees Committee.

Macdonald, James Ramsay (1866–1937). Lab. M.P. for Leicester, 1906–18; Aberavon, 1922–9; Seaham, 1929–31; Nat. Lab. M.P. for Seaham, 1931–5; Scottish Universities, 1936–7. Prime Minister and Sec. for Foreign Affairs, 1924; Prime Minister, 1929–35; Lord President of Council, 1935–7.

Macdonogh, George Mark Watson (1865–1942). Colonel and GSO1 in DMO, March 1914. Royal Engineers. Service in European War, 1914–18; DMI, 1916–18; knighted, 1917; AG, 1918–22; Lieutenant-General, 1919; member of RC on Local Government, 1923–9; President of Federation of British Industries, 1933–4.

MacEwen, Maurice Lilburn (1869–1943). Lieutenant Colonel, 16th Lancers in March 1914. Service in South Africa, 1900–3 with IY; European War, 1914–16; Brigadier-General.

Macleod, Roderick (1892/3–1984). Second Lieutenant, 80th Battery, XV Brigade, RFA in March 1914. Royal Artillery, 1910–19; in European War; served with Ironside as GSO2, 1920–30; GSO1 at Meerut, 1939; Colonel; Military Assistant to Ironside, 1939–40; responsible for D-Day deception planning, 1944.

MacMunn, George Fletcher (1869–1952). Brevet Lieutenant Colonel and DAD of Remounts in March 1914. Royal Artillery. Service in Burma, 1892; Kohat, 1897; Tirah, 1897–8; South Africa, 1899–1902; Gallipoli, 1915; Mesopotamia, 1917–18; knighted, 1917; GOC, Mesopotamia, 1919–20; QMG, India, 1920–4; Lieutenant-General.

Macready, Cecil Frederick Nevil (1862–1946). Major-General and Director of Personal Services at the War Office in March 1914. Gordon Highlanders. Service in Egypt, 1882; South Africa, 1899–1902; knighted, 1912; GOC in Belfast, 1914; AG to BEF, 1914–16; AG to the Forces, 1916–18; Lieutenant-General; Commissioner of the Metropolitan Police, 1918–20; GOC in Ireland, 1920–3; Baronet, 1923.

Madden, Charles Edward (1862–1935). Rear-Admiral and commanding 2nd Cruiser Squadron in March 1914. Fourth Sea Lord, 1910–11; 3rd and 2nd

Cruiser Squads. 1912–14; Chief of Staff to CinC, Grand Fleet, 1914–16; 2ic, Grand Fleet, 1917–19; Baronet, 1919; CinC, Atlantic, 1921–22; First Sea Lord and Chief of Naval Staff, 1927–30; Admiral of the Fleet.

Malcolm, Neill (1869–1953). Major in 2nd Argylls in March 1914. Service on North-West Frontier, 1897–8; Uganda, 1898–9; South Africa, 1899–1900; Somaliland, 1903–4; European War, 1914–18; Major-General, 1918; Chief of British Military Mission to Berlin, 1919–21; GOC, Malaya, 1921–4; knighted, 1922.

Maude, Frederick Stanley (1864–1917). Colonel and GSOI in DMT in March 1914. Service in Sudan, 1885; South Africa, 1899–1901. Private Sec. to Sec. of State for War, 1905; GSOI at War Office, 1914; 14th Infantry Brigade, 1914; 33rd Division, 1915; 13th Division on the Tigris, 1916; CinC, Mesopotamia, 1916; Lieutenant-General, 1916; knighted, 1916; died on active service, 18.11.1917.

McKenna, Reginald (1863–1943). Home Secretary in March 1914. Lib. M.P. for Monmouth North, 1895–1918. Fin. Sec. at Treasury, 1905–7; Pres. Board of Educ., 1907–8; First Lord of Admiralty, 1908–11; Home Sec., 1911–15; Chancellor of the Exchequer, 1915–16.

Meinertzhagen, Richard (1878–1967). Captain in Royal Fusiliers and student at the Staff College, Quetta in March 1914. Service in East Africa, 1904; Nandi, 1905–6; European War 1914–18 in East Africa, Palestine and France. Chief Political Officer in Palestine and Syria, 1919–20; Military Adviser to Colonial Office, 1921–4; War Office, 1939–40; Colonel.

Methuen, Paul Sanford (1845–1932). Scots Guards. Service in Ashanti, 1874; Egypt, 1882; Bechuanaland, 1884–5 commanding Methuen's Horse; 1st Division in South Africa, 1899–1902. CinC, Eastern Command, 1903–8; GOC, South Africa, 1908–9; Governor of Natal, 1909; GOC, Malta, 1915–19. Succeeded as 3rd Lord Methuen, 1891; Field Marshal.

Miles, Eric Grant (1891–1977). Second Lieutenant in KOSB, 1914. European War, 1914–18; GSo3 in War Office, 1923; Brigade-Major to Shanghai Defence Force, 1927–8; GSo2 in War Office, 1930–3; GSOI in Malaya, 1938–9; Major-General, 1940; 126th Brigade, 1940; 42nd Division, 1941; 56th Division, 1941–3; GOC of SE District, 1943–6.

Milner, Alfred (1854–1925). Conservative peer in March 1914. Under Sec. for Finance in Egypt, 1889–92; Chm. Board of Inland Revenue, 1892–5; knighted, 1895; High Commissioner for South Africa, 1897–1905; Baron, 1901; Viscount, 1902; member of War Cabinet, 1916–18; Sec. for War, 1918–19; Colonial Sec., 1919–21.

Morley, John (1838–1923). Lord President of the Council in March 1914. Lib. M.P. for Newcastle, 1883–95; Montrose Burghs, 1896–1908. Chief Sec. for Ireland, 1886 and 1892–95; Sec. of State for India, 1905–10 and 1911; Lord President of Council, 1910–14; Viscount, 1908.

Nicholson, George Crosfield Norris (1884–1915). Private secretary to Sec. of State for War, 1912–14. European War, 1914–15 as Captain, RFC. Killed in flying accident, 11.3.1915.

Oliver, Frederick Scott (1864–1934). Barrister, 1889. Political journalist.

Paget, Arthur Henry Fitzroy (1851–1928). Lieutenant-General and GOC, Ireland in March 1914. Scots Guards. Service in Ashanti, 1873; Sudan, 1885; Burma, 1887–8; Sudan, 1888–9; South Africa, 1899–1900. 1st Division, 1902–6; Eastern Command, 1908–1911; GOC, Ireland, 1911–14; knighted, 1906.

Parker, Arthur (1867–1941). Lieutenant Colonel in 5th Lancers in March 1914. Service in South Africa, 1899–1902; European War, 1914–18; Brigadier-General.

Plumer, Herbert Charles Onslow (1857–1932). Lieutenant-General and GOC, Northern Command in March 1914. York and Lancaster Regt. Service in Sudan, 1884; South Africa, 1899–1902. QMG, 1904–5; knighted, 1906; GOC, Northern Command, 1911–14; 5th Corps, 1915 and 2nd Army, 1915–17 and 1918; GOC, Italy, 1917–18; Army of the Rhine, 1918–19; Malta, 1919–24; High Commissioner, Palestine, 1925–28; Viscount, 1929; Field Marshal, 1919.

Price-Davies, Llewellyn Alberic Emilius (1878–1965). Captain and GSO3 in DMO in March 1914. KRRC. Service in South Africa, 1899–1902 winning V.C.; European War, 1914–18; liaison officer at Italian GHQ, 1918; Pres. Standing Committee of Enquiry regarding POWs, 1918–19; AAG at Aldershot, 1920–4; 145th Infantry Brigade, 1924–27; AA and QMG, Gibraltar, 1927–30; Major-General, 1930.

Pulteney, William Pulteney (1861–1941). Major-General, 6th Division in March 1914. Scots Guards. Service in Egypt, 1882; Unyoro, 1895; Nandi, 1895–6; South Africa, 1899–1902. 16th Infantry Brigade, 1908–9; 6th Division, 1910–14; III Corps, 1914–18; knighted, 1915; Lieutenant-General.

Rawlinson, Henry Seymour (1864–1925). Major-General, 3rd Division in March 1914. KRRC. Service in Burma, 1887–8; Sudan, 1898; South Africa, 1899–1902. Commanded 4th Division, 1914; 7th Division and 3rd Cavalry Division, 1914; IV Corps, 1914–15; knighted, 1914; 1st and 4th Armies, 1915–18; General, 1917; British Representative at Supreme War Council, 1918; 4th Army, 1918–19; GOC, North Russia, 1919; Baron, 1919; GOC at Aldershot, 1919–20; CinC, India, 1920–5.

Redmond, John Edward (1851–1918). Nationalist M.P. for New Ross, 1881–5; Waterford, 1891–1918; Chairman of Irish Parliamentary Party, 1900–18.

Repington, Charles à Court (1858–1925). Military correspondent of *The Times* in March 1914. Rifle Brigade. Service in Afghanistan, 1878–9; Burma, 1888–9; Sudan, 1898; South Africa, 1899–1900. Military Attaché at Brussels and the Hague, 1899–1902; resigned over indiscretion with another officer's wife; military correspondent of *The Times*, 1904–18 and *The Daily Telegraph*, 1918–25.

Richardson, George Lloyd Reily (1847–1931). Commander of UVF in March 1914. Service in Hazara, 1868; Afghanistan, 1879–80; Waziristan, 1881; Zhob, 1890; Tirah, 1897–8; China, 1900–1. Commanded Hyderabad Contingent, 1902; Agra Brigade, 1903; Poona Division, 1904–8; knighted, 1909; Lieutenant-General. Commanded UVF.

Robb, Frederick Spencer (1858–1948). Major-General in charge of Administration at Aldershot in March 1914. 68th Foot. Service on the Nile, 1898, European War, 1914–15. 11th Infantry Brigade, 1905–9; Major-General at Aldershot, 1910–14; Assistant CIGS, 1914; Military Sec. to Sec. of State of War, 1914–16; Major-General at Eastern Command, 1916–19; knighted, 1915.

Roberts, Frederick Sleigh (1832–1914). Retired Field Marshal in March 1914. Bengal Artillery. Service in Indian Mutiny winning V.C.; Abyssinia, 1867–8; Lushai, 1871–2; Afghanistan, 1879–80; Burma, 1886; South Africa, 1900–1. QMG in India, 1875–8; Kuram, Kabul and Kandahar Field Forces, 1878–80; CinC, Madras, 1881–5; CinC, India, 1885–93; GOC, Ireland, 1895–9; CinC, South Africa, 1899–1900; CinC, 1901–4. Baron, 1892; Field Marshal, 1895; Earl, 1901.

Robertson, William Robert (1860–1933). Major-General and DMT in March 1914. 16th Lancers as private, 1877; 3rd Dragoon Guards, 1887. Service in Chitral, 1895; South Africa, 1900. Commandant, Staff College, 1910–13; DMT, 1913–14; knighted, 1913; QMG to BEF, 1914–15; Chief of Staff, BEF, 1915; CIGS, 1915–18; GOC, Eastern Command, 1918; CinC, Home Forces, 1918–19; British Army of Rhine, 1919–20; Baronet, 1919; Field Marshal, 1920.

Robinson, Geoffrey (1874–1944). Editor of *The Times* in March 1914. Assumed surname of Dawson, 1917. Private sec. to Milner, 1901–5; editor of *Johannesburg Star*, 1905–10; editor, *The Times*, 1912–19 and 1923–41.

Rolt, Stuart Peter (1862–1933). Brigadier-General, 14th Infantry Brigade, March 1914. York and Lancaster Regt. Service in South Africa, 1899–1900. Inspector of Gymnasia, 1905–10; 14th Infantry Brigade, 1912–14; Commandant at Sandhurst, 1914–16.

Sackville-West, Charles John (1870–1962). Lieutenant Colonel, 4th KRRC in 1914. Service in Manipur, 1891; Burma, 1891–2; South Africa, 1899–1900; European War, 1914–16, Major-General, 1917; British Military Representative on Allied Military Committee, 1918–19; knighted, 1919; Military Attaché in Paris, 1920–4; Lieutenant-Governor of Guernsey, 1925–9; succeeded brother as 4th Baron Sackville, 1928.

Salisbury, 4th Marquis of, James Edward Herbert Gascoyne, Cecil, Viscount Cranborne (1861–1947). Conservative peer in March 1914. Succeeded as 4th Marquis, 1903. Con. M.P. for Darwen, 1885–92; Rochester, 1893–1903. Parl. Under-Sec., Foreign Affairs, 1900–3; Lord Privy Seal, 1903–5 and 1924–9; Pres. Board of Trade, 1905; Chancellor of Duchy of Lancaster, 1922–3; Lord President of Council, 1922–4.

Sclater, Henry Crichton (1855–1923). Succeeded Ewart as AG in 1914. Royal Artillery. Service on Nile, 1884–5; South Africa, 1899–1902. Director of Artillery, 1903–4; QMG in India, 1904–8; Quetta Division, 1908–12; AG, 1914–16; GOC, Southern Command, 1916–19, knighted, 1913; General.

Seely, John Edward Bernard (1868–1947). Secretary of State for War in March 1914. Con. M.P. for Isle of Wight, 1900–4; Lib. M.P. for IOW, 1904–6 and 1923–4; Lib. M.P. for Liverpool Abercromby, 1906–10; Ilkeston, 1910–22. Parl. Under-Sec. Colonial Off., 1908–11; Parl. Under-Sec. War Office, 1911–12; Sec. of State for War, 1912–14; Parl. Under-Sec. Ministry of Munitions, 1918–19; Parl. Under-Sec. Air Ministry, 1919. Service in South Africa with Imperial Yeomanry, 1900–1; European War, 1914–18 commanding Canadian Cavalry Corps; Baron Mottistone, 1933.

Serocold, Eric Pearce (1870–1926). Lieutenant Colonel, 2 KRRC in March 1914. Service in South Africa, 1899–1900; European War, 1914–18; Brigadier-General.

Simon, John Allsebrook (1873–1954). Attorney-General in March 1914. Lib. M.P. for Walthamstow, 1906–18; Spen Valley, 1922–31; Lib. Nat. M.P. for Spen Valley, 1931–40. Solicitor-Gen., 1910–13; Attorney-Gen., 1913–16; Sec. of State for Home Affairs, 1915–16 and 1935–7; Foreign Sec., 1931–5; Chancellor of the Exchequer, 1937–40; Viscount, 1940; Lord Chancellor, 1940–5.

Smith, Frederick Edwin (1872–1930). Con. M.P. for Liverpool Walton, 1906–18; Liverpool West Derby, 1918–19. Solicitor-Gen., 1915; Attorney Gen., 1915–19; Lord Chancellor, 1919–22; Viscount, 1921; Earl of Birkenhead, 1922; Sec. of State for India, 1924–8.

Smith-Dorrien, Horace Lockwood (1858–1930). Lieutenant-General and GOC, Southern Command in March 1914. Sherwood Foresters. Service in Zululand, 1879; Egypt and Sudan, 1882 and 1884–6; Chitral, 1895; Tirah, 1897–8; Sudan, 1898; South Africa, 1900 commanding brigade and division; knighted, 1904. GOC at Aldershot, 1907–12; Southern Command, 1912–14; II Corps and 2nd Army, 1914–15; East Africa, 1915–16; Governor of Gibraltar, 1918–23; General.

Spender, John Alfred (1862–1942). Editor of *Eastern Morning News*, 1886–96; *Westminster Gazette*, 1896–1922.

Spender, Wilfrid Bliss (1876–1960). Royal Artillery, 1897–1913 when resigned to join UVF. Service in European War with 36th and 31st Divisions; Lieutenant Colonel. Re-raised UVF (later Special Constabulary), 1920; Sec. to Cabinet of Northern Ireland, 1921–5; head of Northern Ireland Civil Service, 1925–44; knighted, 1929.

Stamfordham, Lord, Arthur John Bigge (1849–1943). Private Secretary to the King in March 1914. Service in Zululand, 1878–9 with Royal Artillery. Private sec. to Queen Victoria, 1895–1901; to Prince of Wales, 1901–10; to King George V, 1910–31; Baron, 1911.

Strickland, Edward Peter (1869–1951). Major in Norfolk Regt in March 1914. Service in Burma, 1887–9; Sudan, 1896–8; Nigeria, 1906; European War, 1914–18. Major-General, 1916; 6th Division, 1919–22; knighted, 1919; 2nd Division, 1923–6; GOC, Egypt, 1927–31; General, 1931.

Ward, John (1866–1934). Labour M.P. in March 1914. Lab., later Constitutional Lib. and Constitutionalist M.P. for Stoke, 1906–29. Founder of the Navvy's Union.

Warrender, George John Scott (1860–1917). Vice-Admiral and commanding 2nd Battle Squadron in March 1914. Service in Zululand, 1879; CinC, East Indian Station, 1907–9; 2nd Cruiser Squad, 1910–12; 2nd Battle Squad., 1912–16; Baronet, 1913; Vice-Admiral, 1913; CinC, Plymouth, 1916–17.

Wavell, Archibald Percival (1883–1950). Captain and GSO3 in DMO in March 1914. Black Watch. Service in South Africa, 1901–2; North-West Frontier, 1908; European War, 1914–18 including France, Caucasus and Egypt. 6th Infantry Brigade, 1930–4; 2nd Division in Palestine, 1935–7; GOC, Southern Command, 1938–9; CinC, Middle East, 1939–41; knighted, 1939; CinC, India, 1941–3; Field Marshal, 1943; Supreme Commander in South-West Pacific, 1942; Viceroy of India, 1943–7; Earl, 1947.

Wemyss, Rosslyn Erskine (1864–1933). Rear-Admiral on half-pay in March 1914. Rear-Admiral, 2nd Battle Squad., 1912–13; 12th Cruiser Squad., 1914; commanding Squad. at Gallipoli, 1915; knighted, 1916; CinC, East Indies and Egypt, 1916–17; First Sea Lord, 1918–19; Baron Wester-Wemyss, 1919; Admiral of the Fleet, 1919.

Wigram, Clive (1873–1960). Assistant Private Secretary to the King in March 1914. Service on North-West Frontier, 1897–8 with 18th KGO Lancers. ADC to Lord Curzon, 1899–1904; Military sec. to GOC at Aldershot, 1908–10; Assistant Private Sec. to the King, 1910–31; Private Secretary to King George V, 1931–6; knighted, 1931; Baron, 1935.

Wilson, Henry Hughes (1864–1922). Major-General and DMO in March

1914. Rifle Brigade. Service in Burma, 1886–7; South Africa, 1899–1901. Commandant of Staff College, 1907–10; DMO, 1910–14; Assistant CGS to BEF, 1914–15; Liaison Officer with French Army, 1915; knighted, 1915; IV Corps, 1916; British Military Representative, Supreme War Council, 1917–18, CIGS, 1918–22; Ulster Unionist M.P., 1922; assassinated, 1922.

Wolseley, Garnet Joseph (1833–1913). 90th Foot. Service in Burma, 1852–3; Crimea; Red River, 1870; Ashanti, 1873–4; Egypt, 1882 and 1884–5. Governor of Natal, 1875; AG, 1882–90; GOC, Ireland, 1890–5; CinC, 1895–1900; Viscount, 1885; Field Marshal, 1894.

APPENDIX II

Lieutenant Colonel H. R. Adair, RGA. Military Assistant to the Chief Superintendent of Ordnance Factories.

Major B. Atkinson, RA. GSO2 to the Home Counties Division (TF).

Captain H. Boyd-Rochfort, 21st Lancers.

Major R. E. Cecil, 21st Lancers. Brigade-Major, South-East Mounted Brigade (TF).

Honorary Major G. J. Chapman. Inspector of Works, Hounslow.

Colonel A. G. Dallas. GSO1 in the Directorate of Military Operations, War Office.

Major A. C. Daly, 1st West Yorkshire Regiment.

Captain J. C. Darling, 20th Hussars.

Major the Hon. Hugh Dawnay, 2nd Life Guards.

Major H. de Pree, RA. GSO2 at the Staff College, Quetta.

Major-General A. J. Godley, GOC, Military Forces, New Zealand.

Captain Francis Grenfell, 9th Lancers.

Major R. J. F. Hayter, Cheshire Regiment. GSO2, Canadian Militia.

Major A. B. R. Hildebrand, RE. Stationed at Limerick.

Major G. H. Lawrence, East Lancashire Regiment, OC, Preston depot.

Brigadier-General H. P. Leader. GOC, Sialkott Brigade.

Major K. J. W. Leather, 4th Durham Light Infantry (Special Reserve).

Major R. L. Ricketts, 10th Duke of Cambridge's Own Lancers (Hodson's Horse). Attached Imperial Cadet Corps, Delhi.

Major E. S. Sandys, RE. Stationed at the Curragh.

Lieutenant Colonel G. H. Thesiger, 2nd Rifle Brigade.

Sources: H. P. Gough Mss; J. E. Gough Mss

APPENDIX III

Major-General in charge of Administration   Major-General L. B. Friend

GOC, Parkgate, Dublin
Lieutenant-General Sir Arthur Paget

General Staff
BGGS Brigadier-General G. T. Forestier-Walker
Administrative, Technical and Departmental Staff
Major-General in charge of Administration   Major-General L. B. Friend

3rd Cavalry Brigade, Curragh
Brigadier-General H. P. Gough
    4th Hussars, Curragh   III Brigade, RHA, Newbridge
    5th Lancers, Dublin   4 Fd Troop, RE, Curragh
    16th Lancers, Curragh   3 Signal Troop, RE, Curragh

5th Division, Curragh
Major-General Sir Charles Fergusson

    13th Infantry Brigade, Dublin
    Brigadier-General G. J. Cuthbert
    2 KOSB   1 RWK
    2 West Riding 2 KOYLI

    14th Infantry Brigade, Curragh
    Brigadier-General S. P. Rolt
    2 Suffolks
    1 East Surreys (Dublin)
    1 DCLI
    2 Manchesters

    15th Infantry Brigade, Belfast
    Brigadier-General Count Gleichen
    1 Norfolks (Holywood)
    1 Beds (Mullingar)
    1 Cheshire (Londonderry)
    1 Dorsets (Belfast)

    Divisional Artillery
    Brigadier-General J. E. W. Headlam

439

VIII (Howitzer) Brigade, RFA	Kildare	37, 61, 65 Batteries
XV Brigade, RFA	Kildare	11, 52, 80 Batteries
XXVII Brigade, RFA	Newbridge	119, 120, 121 Batteries
XXVIII Brigade, RFA	Dundalk	122, 123, 124 Batteries

Divisional Engineers
7 Fd Co, RE   Curragh
59 Fd Co, RE   Curragh
5 Signal Co, RE   Carlow

6th Division, Cork
Major-General W. P. Pulteney

16th Infantry Brigade, Fermoy
Brigadier-General E. C. Ingouville-Williams
1 East Kent (Fermoy)
1 Leicesters (Fermoy)
1 SLI (Tipperary)
2 York and Lancaster (Limerick)

17th Infantry Brigade, Cork
Brigadier-General W. R. B. Doran
1 Royal Fusiliers (Kinsale)
1 North Staffs (Buttevant)
2 Leinsters (Cork)
3 Rifle Brigade (Cork)

Divisional Artillery, Mallow
Brigadier-General W. L. H. Paget

XII (Howitzer) Brigade, RFA	Fethard, Clonmel, Kilkenny	
		43, 86, 87 Batteries
II Brigade, RFA	Cahir	21, 42, 53 Batteries
XXIV Brigade, RFA	Ballincollig	110, 111, 112 Batteries
XXXVIII Brigade, RFA	Fermoy,	
Divisional Engineers	Waterford	24, 34, 72 Batteries
12 Fd Co, RE	Moore Park	
38 Fd Co, RE	Cork	
6 Signal Co, RE	Limerick	

Defended Ports

North Irish Coastal Defences—Lough Swilly and Belfast
South Irish Coastal Defences—Queenstown Harbour and Berehaven
No. 11 District   No. 12 District
Colonel F. F. Hill   Colonel S. W. Scrace-Dickins

BIBLIOGRAPHY

1 **Manuscript Sources**
Official Papers
Public Record Office: Adm. 116/1326, 1327, 1328.
                       Cab. 37/117, 119, 120.
                       CO. 904/27.
                       WO. 32/9353, 9569; 35/60, 209; 163/20.
Vincennes: État-Major de L'Armée de Terre: Service Historique, Box No 7N1228 (Military Attaché to Great Britain, 1913–14)

Private Papers
Allenby Mss (Liddell Hart Centre for Military Archives, King's College, London)
Amery diaries (Rt. Hon. Julian Amery, M.P.)
Asquith Mss (Bodleian Library)
Aston Mss (Liddell Hart Centre for Military Archives, King's College, London—Now transferred to Royal Marines Museum, Eastney)
Baillie-Grohman Mss (Imperial War Museum)
Balfour Mss (British Library)
Battenberg Mss (Imperial War Museum)
Beddington Mss (Liddell Hart Centre for Military Archives, King's College, London)
Bonar Law Mss (House of Lords Record Office)
Brooke Mss (Lieutenant Colonel M. P. Brooke)
Burns Mss (British Library)
Carson Mss (PRO of Northern Ireland)
Chamberlain Mss (Birmingham University Library)
Dawson/Repington Mss (*The Times* Archive)
Dawson (Robinson) Mss (Bodleian Library)
De Broke Mss (House of Lords Record Office)
De Chair Mss (Imperial War Museum)
De Robeck Mss (Churchill College)
Esher Mss (Churchill College)
Ewart Mss (Scottish Record Office; Sir Hector Monro, M.P.)
Fergusson Mss (Sir Charles Fergusson)
Floyer-Acland Mss (Sunderland Polytechnic, 1914–18 Archives)

Forster Mss (Imperial War Museum)
French Mss (Imperial War Museum)
Gainsford Mss (Nuffield College)
Gillman Mss (Royal Artillery Institution)
Gladstone Mss (British Library)
Glenesk-Bathurst Mss (Brotherton Library)
Gough (H.P.) Mss (Mrs Denise Boyes)
Gough (J.E.) Mss (Mrs Diana Pym)
Grant-Duff Mss (Imperial War Museum)
Gwynne Mss (Imperial War Museum; Bodleian Library)
Haig Mss (National Library of Scotland)
Haldane Mss (National Library of Scotland)
Hamilton Mss (Liddell Hart Centre for Military Archives, King's College, London)
Hankey Mss (Churchill College)
Howell Mss (Liddell Hart Centre for Military Archives, King's College, London)
Hutton Mss (British Library)
Isacke Mss (Liddell Hart Centre for Military Archives, King's College, London)
James Mss (Manchester Central Library)
Jellicoe Mss (British Library)
Keyes Mss (British Library)
Kirke Mss (Imperial War Museum)
KOYLI Mss (Regimental Museum of KOYLI)
Lloyd George Mss (House of Lords Record Office)
Macdonald Mss (Public Record Office)
MacEwen Mss (National Army Museum)
Macleod Mss (Sunderland Polytechnic, 1914–18 Archives; Liddell Hart Centre for Military Archives, King's College, London; Royal Artillery Institution)
Manchester Regiment Mss (Manchester Central Library)
Midleton Mss (British Library; Public Record Office)
Miles Mss (Mrs Jean Morris-Eyton)
Milner Mss (Bodleian Library)
Mottistone (Seely) Mss (Nuffield College)
Nightingale Mss (Public Record Office)
Northcliffe Mss (*The Times* Archive)
Oliver Mss (National Library of Scotland)
Paget Mss (British Library)
Pragnell Mss (The Queens Royal Irish Hussars)
Price-Davies Mss (Army Museums Ogilby Trust)

Rawlinson Mss (National Army Museum; Churchill College)
Richardson Mss (National Army Museum)
Roberts Mss (National Army Museum)
Royal Archives (Windsor Castle)
Scott Mss (British Library)
Selborne Mss (Imperial War Museum; Bodleian Library)
Simon Mss (Bodleian Library)
Smith Mss (R. H. Smith Esq.)
Stoneham Mss (Sunderland Polytechnic, 1914–18 Archives)
Strachey Mss (House of Lords Record Office)
Strickland Mss (Imperial War Museum)
Wavell Mss (Lady Pamela Humphreys)
Wester-Wemyss Mss (Churchill College)
Wilson Mss (Imperial War Museum)
Wood Mss (Bedfordshire Record Office)
Wynne Mss (Imperial War Museum)
Note: A number of collections utilised by previous authors in studies of the
    Curragh could no longer be traced: Headlam Mss (other than those in the
    Royal Artillery Institution); Hewson Mss; Cheyne Mss; and Younger Mss.
    The Rt. Hon. Julian Amery, M.P. kindly allowed access to the diaries of
    Leo Amery but the remaining papers are still closed to scholars.

2 **Parliamentary Papers**
Correspondence relating to Recent Events in the Irish Command (Cmd. 7318,
    1914)
Correspondence relating to Recent Events in the Irish Command (Cmd. 7329,
    1914)

3 **Memoirs and Biographies**
Amery, L. S., *My Political Life* (Hutchinson, London, 1953) Volume 1
Bayly, Admiral Sir Lewis, *Pull Together* (Harrap, London, 1939)
Blake, Robert, *The Unknown Prime Minister* (Eyre and Spottiswoode,
    London, 1955)
Blunt, W. S., *My Diaries* (Martin Secker, London, 1920)
Brett, L. V. (ed.), *Journals and Letters of Reginald, Viscount Esher* (Nicholson
    and Watson, London, 1938) Volume 3
Brooke, Major-General G., *Good Company* (Constable, London, 1954)
Callwell, Major-General Sir Charles, *Field Marshal Sir Henry Wilson: His Life
    and Diaries* (Cassell, London, 1927) Volume 1
Charteris, Brigadier-General John, *Field Marshal Earl Haig* (Cassell,
    London, 1929)

Childs, Major-General Sir Wyndham, *Episodes and Reflections* (Cassell, London, 1930)

Churchill, Randolph S., *Winston S. Churchill* (Heinemann, London, 1967) Volume 2

Colvin, Ian, *The Life of Lord Carson* (Gollancz, London, 1934) Volume 2

Connell, John, *Wavell: Scholar and Soldier* (Collins, London, 1964)

David, E. (ed.), *Inside Asquith's Cabinet* (Murray, London, 1977)

Farrar-Hockley, Anthony, *Goughie* (Hart-Davis MacGibbon, London, 1975)

Fingall, Countess of, *Seventy Years Young* (Collins, London, 1937)

Fitzroy, Sir Almeric, *Memoirs of Sir Almeric Fitzroy* (Hutchinson, London, 1926) Volume 2

Gleichen, Major-General Lord Edward, *A Guardsman's Memories* (Blackwood, London and Edinburgh, 1932)

Gollin, A. M., *Proconsul in Politics* (Anthony Blond, London, 1964)

Gough, General Sir Hubert, *Soldiering On* (Arthur Barker, London, 1954)

Gwynn, D., *The Life of John Redmond* (Harrap, London, 1932)

Havinghurst, A. F., *Radical Journalist: H. W. Massingham* (Cambridge University Press, 1974)

Holmes, Richard, *The Little Field Marshal: Sir John French* (Cape, London, 1981)

Howell, Rosalind, *Philip Howell: A Memoir by his Wife* (Allen and Unwin, London, 1942)

James, David, *Lord Roberts* (Hollis and Carter, London, 1954)

Jeffery, Keith (ed.), *The Military Correspondence of Field Marshal Sir Henry Wilson, 1918–1922* (The Bodley Head for the Army Records Society, London, 1985)

Jenkins, Roy, *Asquith* (Collins, London, 1964)

Koss, S., *Lord Haldane* (Columbia University Press, New York, 1969)

Koss, S., *Fleet Street Radical* (Allen Lane, London, 1973)

Macdiarmid, D. S., *The Life of General Grierson* (Constable, London, 1923)

MacMunn, Sir George, *Behind the Scenes in Many Wars* (Murray, London, 1930)

Macready, General Sir Nevil, *Annals of an Active Life* (Hutchinson, London, 1925) Volume 1

Maurice, Sir Frederick, *Haldane* (Faber and Faber, London, 1937)

Meinertzhagen, Richard, *Army Diary, 1899–1926* (Oliver and Boyd, London and Edinburgh, 1960)

Mottistone, Lord (J. E. B. Seely), *Adventure* (Heinemann, London, 1930)

Nicolson, Sir Harold, *King George V: His Life and Reign* (Constable, London, 1952)

Rhodes-James, Robert, *Churchill: A Study in Failure* (Weidenfeld and Nicolson, London, 1970)

Riddell, Lord, *More Pages from My Diary* (Country Life, London, 1934)
Robertson, Field Marshal Sir William, *From Private to Field Marshal* (Constable, London, 1921)
Roskill, *Hankey: Man of Secrets* (Collins, London, 1970) Volume 1
Spiers, E. M., *Haldane: An Army Reformer* (Edinburgh University Press, 1980)
Wavell, General Sir Archibald, *Allenby* (Harrap, London, 1940)

4 Secondary Works

Beckett, Ian F. W. and Simpson, Keith, (eds), *A Nation in Arms: A Social Study of the British Army in the First World War* (Manchester University Press, 1985)
Choille, B. M. (ed.), *Intelligence Notes, 1913–16* (Stationery Office, Dublin, 1966)
Dangerfield, G., *The Damnable Question* (Constable, London, 1977)
Daniell, D. S., *4th Hussar* (Gale and Polden, Aldershot, 1959)
Fergusson, Sir James, *The Curragh Incident* (Faber and Faber, London, 1964)
Gooch, John, *The Plans of War* (Routledge and Kegan Paul, London, 1974)
Gooch, John, *The Prospect of War* (Frank Cass, London, 1981)
Graham, Colonel H., *History of the 16th the Queens Light Dragoons (Lancers), 1912–25* (Privately published, 1926)
Harvey, Colonel J.R., *History of the 5th Royal Irish Lancers* (Privately published, 1923)
Jalland, Patricia, *The Liberals and Ireland: The Ulster Question and British Politics to 1914* (Harvester, Brighton, 1980)
Morris, A. J. A., *The Scaremongers* (Routledge, London, 1984)
Murphy, C. C. R., *The History of the Suffolk Regiment, 1914–27* (Hutchinson, London, 1928)
Ryan, A. P., *Mutiny at the Curragh* (Macmillan, London, 1956)
Spiers, E. M., *The Army and Society, 1815–1914* (Longman, London, 1980)
Stewart, A. T. Q., *The Ulster Crisis* (Faber and Faber, London, 1967)
Townshend, Charles, *Political Violence in Ireland* (Oxford University Press, 1983)

5 Articles

Curragh Commemorative Issue, *An Cosantoir* XXXII, 5 (1972)
Crosbie, G., 'Behind the Curragh', *Army Quarterly* 103, 4, 1973, pp. 490–7
Gooch, John, 'The War Office and the Curragh Incident', *Bulletin of the Institute for Historical Research* XLVI, 1973, pp. 202–7
Roberts, Adam, 'The British Armed Forces and Politics: A Historical Perspective', *Armed Forces and Society*, 3, 4, 1977, pp. 531–56
Sabine, John, 'Civil-military Relations' in Baylis, John (ed.), *British Defence Policy in a Changing World* (Croom Helm, London, 1977), pp. 243–50

Travers, T. H. E., 'The Hidden Army: Structural Problems in the British Officer Corps, 1900–1918', *Journal of Contemporary History* 17, 1982, pp. 523–44

Wilson, K. M., 'Sir John French's resignation over the Curragh Affair: the role of the editor of the *Morning Post*', *English Historical Review* XCIX, 1984, pp. 807–12

6 Theses

Allison, M., 'The National Service Issue, 1900–1914', Unpub. Ph.D., London, 1975

de Groot, G., 'The Pre-War Life and Military Career of Douglas Haig', Unpub. Ph.D., Edinburgh, 1983

Fontenot, G., 'The Modern Major-General: Patterns in the Careers of the British Army Major-Generals on active duty at the time of the Sarajevo Assassination', Unpub. M.A., Chapel Hill, 1980

Kennedy, T. C., '*The Times* and the Irish Home Rule Question, 1906–14', Unpub. M.A., Arizona, 1964

Muenger, Elizabeth A., 'The British Army in Ireland, 1886–1914', Unpub. Ph.D., Michigan, 1981

Valiulis, M. M. G., 'The Irish Army Mutiny of 1924', Unpub. Ph.D., Loyola, 1977

Vorce, Anne L., 'The Role of Ireland in British Defence Planning, 1908–1914', Unpub. M.A., London, 1975

INDEX

447

ARMY RECORDS SOCIETY
(FOUNDED 1984)

The Army Records Society was launched with the assistance of an appeal supported by the institutions and individuals listed in the first volume issued by the Society. The following have also contributed towards the costs of our publications:

The British Academy
15th/19th King's Royal Hussars

Members of the Society are entitled to purchase back volumes at reduced prices.
Orders should be sent to the Hon. Treasurer, Army Records Society, c/o Barclays Bank, 54 Lombard Street, London EC3P 3AH.

The Society has already issued:

Vol. I:
*The Military Correspondence of
Field Marshal Sir Henry Wilson 1918–1922*
Edited by Dr Keith Jeffery.